THE
PORTABLE MBA

Available in Spring 1992

THE PORTABLE MBA IN FINANCE AND ACCOUNTING
  John Leslie Livingstone

THE PORTABLE MBA IN MARKETING
  Alexander Hiam and Charles Schewe

THE
PORTABLE MBA

Eliza G.C. Collins
Mary Anne Devanna

John Wiley & Sons, Inc.

New York • Chichester • Brisbane • Toronto • Singapore

Library of Congress Cataloging-in-Publication Data
Collins, Eliza G. C.
    The portable MBA / Eliza G. C. Collins, Mary Anne Devanna.
        p.   cm.
    Includes bibliographical references (p.).
    ISBN 0-471-61997-3
    ISBN 0-471-54895-2 (pbk.)
    1. Industrial management.   2. Marketing.   3. Accounting.
4. Personnel management.   I. Devanna, Mary Anne.   II. Title.
III. Title: Portable MBA
HD31.C6134   1990
658-dc20   89-27382
                                                          CIP

Printed in the United States of America.

10 9 8

CONTENTS

Introduction

The MBA has been described as the ultimate business credential: an academic version of a passport to the executive suite. But what if the time (up to two full years of study), money ($25,000 to $30,000 tuition at a top school), or lost time and opportunity at your current company give you pause before making the MBA commitment? Is it possible to get many of the benefits of an MBA without the time and costs involved? We believe so and that's the reasoning for *The Portable MBA*. While there is no substitute for actually completing a full MBA program, we think that you'll receive a number of significant benefits from *The Portable MBA*, including:

- **An opportunity to learn the language of business.** If you want to participate in the life and culture of another country, you need to know its language and customs. Business is no different. It has a language all its own and *The Portable MBA* will provide you with a basic understanding of important business functions: accounting, finance, marketing, strategy, and more, giving you a common business vocabulary and the means with which to develop managerial literacy, regardless of your professional background or function.

- **A framework for making reasoned business decisions and judgments.** You won't, for example, be an expert in accounting after reading this book, but you will understand the role cash flow statements and balance sheets play in a business. Nor will you be a strategy guru, but you will understand the importance that developing and implementing a strategy has for an organization. *The Portable MBA* offers you the opportunity to understand how a business fits together: why a decision in marketing may have serious impact on a company's strategy; or why your human resource practices may affect your company's competitive position in its industry.

- **The opportunity to learn from faculty members in a broad range of leading MBA programs.** All of the chapters in this book were written by experts from leading business schools: Columbia, Harvard, Stanford, Wharton, MIT, George Washington, Babson, University of New Hampshire. *The Portable MBA* is a unique opportunity to get the thinking of an exceptional group of people.

Before previewing the chapters of this book, it would be useful to ask a seemingly self-evident question: What is a manager's job? The answers to this question are as varied as the chapters in this book. Some say that a manager doesn't have a single job, but a series of jobs or roles. Others assert that the manager is like an orchestra conductor relying on the talents of many players for performance while giving directions from an elevated podium. Still others maintain that managers, as distinct from leaders who do the right things, simply do things right.

All of these views have merit. Managers do play roles. At times they are spokespeople for their organizations; at other times they are communicators, letting their employees know how the company is doing or making sure that all players have the same goals or priorities. They are also conductors; in the same way that an orchestra leader calls on each player to do his part, managers need to know how to draw on the expertise of a number of people to perform toward a common end. Managers do the right things; if they didn't, they wouldn't be managers for very long.

These descriptions, as true as they may be, don't tell much about what managers think their job is, about what they think about when driving to work in the morning, and about their concrete thoughts about getting things done that day. Most likely it's not about playing a role, or leading various efforts, or doing the right thing, although what they do can be described in these terms. More likely, it's about how to satisfy those hot heads in manufacturing without offending the creative types in marketing. Or, it's about how to give a raise to a certain vice president without dampening peer motivation; or thinking about how to introduce the new information technology system that will ultimately increase communication and production without upsetting the daily routine so that work continues to get done.

What the manager is thinking about is how to balance the conflicting demands and needs of the many constituencies to which he or she is answerable. The manager's job is daily, weekly, and yearly, to make as many fair allotments of resources of all possible kinds, to various stakeholders within and without the business, in order to further the growth of the business while taking care of its employees and customers.

In performing their balancing acts, managers play roles, lead, and do the right things. But the one thing they must do before they can do any of these, is understand the different functions of the business and what role each plays and what each contributes. In this book, our aim is to give both managers and aspiring managers the essentials of the functions they will have to balance and a grasp of the tools at their disposal to do the balancing.

Many competent people already in organizations may have found they don't understand fully how the different functions further the organization's goals. These bright, motivated people are hired for their technical expertise. As engineers, computer scientists, personnel specialists, accountants, or market researchers, they bring a depth of expertise to the organization that would astound those hired even two decades ago. But the depth of their knowledge has been bought at the expense of a breadth of understanding of how organizations work. This book is for these people as well.

Organizations that work well require integration as well as specialization, synthesis as well as analysis. Previously, in a machine age with relatively slow change in the environment, this integration could be accomplished at the top of bureaucracies where the collected wisdom of marketing, finance, engineering, and other contributors could be brought to bear on the decisions that the organization needed to make. With the advent of the information age, the need for speed in adapting to the marketplace increased dramatically. The organizations that are flourishing are those that learn more rapidly than their competitors. And, as a consequence, new standards for productivity result in moving from a world in which decisions were made at the top of the organization. These new organizations have self-directed workforces.

The ability to make decisions at all levels of the organization enables the organization to respond far more rapidly to the marketplace. But the success of these new organizational processes depends on the ability of employees at all levels to understand the impact of their actions on the organization's goals. To accomplish this objective, employees must understand how the pieces fit together and how their actions affect other employees at all levels of the organization.

This book starts with a description of the manager's job that elaborates on the sketch we've already drawn. Leonard Schlesinger sets out the six tasks of the manager who is interested in long-term effectiveness.

These tasks are building a positive work environment, generating competitive edges in strategy, allocating resources strategically, upgrading the quality of top management, organizing the effort of the organization, and creating excellence in operations and execution.

The basic tools available to the manager are the building blocks of the behavioral sciences, quantitative analysis, and economics. In his chapter on managerial behavior, Allan Cohen focuses on an issue that has preoccupied both organizational theorists and practitioners for the past 10 years—how to motivate employees to deliver their best. Current thinking has moved away from the notion that the art of "Japanese" management had its roots in an essentially collaborative culture and would be difficult to replicate in the West. Indeed, the productivity and quality of Japanese-managed plants in the United States that are staffed by American workers equals or exceeds that of comparable plants in Japan. Excellence is not culture bound but it does require a deep-seated understanding of human behavior and the way the organization encourages or discourages people from doing their best.

In the chapter on quantitative methods, Brian Forst explains various ways that numbers are useful for improving the performance of the business. While revenues, costs, and operating budgets have long been in the domain of the "number crunchers," much of the current emphasis on quality control, accurate forecasting, and efficient resource allocation requires a basic understanding of statistics and quantitative techniques to support production management, marketing, finance, R&D, and corporate planning.

Managerial economics provides guidelines for choices and decisions the organization makes in the marketplace. It provides the basis for the environmental scanning that has become a large part of the strategic planning process in many organizations. In this chapter, Frank Lichtenberg examines the impact that government interventions on behalf of the public good as well as the impact of different market structures—monopoly vs. many competitors—have on the organization's field of choices.

In Part Two of the book, we show how these building blocks are utilized by functional specialists. John Leslie Livingstone provides insight into the role that accounting plays in management control, planning, and financing a business, for tests of short-term and long-term solvency as well as current profitability.

In addition to a crash course on the terminology that sets the financial wizards apart from the rest of the organization, James Walters helps us understand the rationale behind the financial headlines that result from the interaction between organizations and the financial community. These include the equity and bond markets that provide cash for expansion and merger and acquisition activity.

Robert Davis makes an important distinction in his chapter on marketing management—he points to the difference between a market-driven company that tries to provide what the buyer wants and a marketing company that prefers to sell what it already makes. In a globally competitive world, successful companies are increasingly market driven which means that everyone in the organization needs to understand how to determine customer needs and how to fill them both in terms of the products it makes and the service it provides.

Mary Anne Devanna provides us with a look at the role a sophisticated human resource function plays in leveraging organizational performance in the way it attracts and retains, evaluates, rewards, and develops its human resources. This function, which started as recordkeeping, is now at the heart of developing the new self-directed workforce.

While the dramatic changes the human resource management system has undergone in the past two decades are documented in Chapter 8, Chapter 9 would not have existed if this book had been written two decades ago. Yet, it is the development of information technology that has catapulted organizations from the machine age to the information age. N. Venkatraman documents the impact and challenges that emerge as information technology is linked to strategic management. They include its impact on changing industry boundaries, on business definitions, on sources of competitive advantage, and on the creation of new business opportunities.

Linda Sprague looks at the operations function where the responsibility for output and, therefore, for productivity and quality as well as cost and delivery performance rests. In a globally competitive world, an effective operations function is an essential part of the competitive arsenal. Superior R&D capability can never be fully realized if an organization cannot produce goods and services faster and with fewer quality problems than its competitors.

The functions are managerial tools to be used to formulate and implement the organization's strategy. In his chapter, Richard Hamermesh brings us full circle. In formulating strategy, Hamermesh points out, the manager is asked to create a fit among opportunities in the external industry environment, the strengths and weaknesses of the company, the personal values of its key implementers, and the expectations society has for the company. Here, where the company meets the marketplace is where we are able to judge just how well the manager has balanced the conflicting demands for resources. If the manager has done it well, the company should flourish.

Organizations do not exist in a vacuum. They are part of a larger society and Russell Ackoff in our concluding chapter looks at the role of business in a democratic society. Managers and professionals today, more than ever, need to think about this issue. Are organizations mere profit maximizers and creators of wealth? Or does business have a role to play in the actual distribution of wealth? Ackoff also looks at how more democratic organizations can be designed and looks at the rewards and pitfalls in so doing.

It is our hope that this book will provide readers with the tools, and more important, the desire to do the tough balancing act a management job requires.

September, 1989   Eliza G. C. Collins
                                                           Mary Anne Devanna

HOW TO THINK LIKE A MANAGER: THE ART OF MANAGING FOR THE LONG RUN

1

Leonard A. Schlesinger

Effective management is much more than the production of immediate results. Effective management includes creating the potential for achieving good results over the long run. The manager who as president of a company produces spectacular results for a 3- to 10-year period can hardly be considered effective if, concurrently, he or she allows plant and equipment to deteriorate, creates an alienated or militant workforce, lets the company develop a bad name in the marketplace, and ignores new product development.

Dealing with current or impending problems is a key reality of managerial behavior in almost all modern organizations. Coping with complexities associated with today and the immediate future absorbs the vast majority of time and energy for most managers. This chapter sets the stage for the rest of the book by placing management in a longer time frame. How do managers develop their organizations to assure the potential for facilitating organizational effectiveness in the long run?

THE LONG RUN

Most managers will readily admit that their ability to predict their company's future is limited. Indeed, with the possible exceptions of death and taxes, the only thing entirely predictable is that things will change. Even for the most bureaucratic company in the most mature and stable environment, change is inevitable.

Over a period of 20 years, it is possible for a company, even one that is not growing, to experience numerous changes—in its business, product markets, competition, government regulations, available technologies, labor markets—and its own business strategy. These changes are the inevitable products of its interaction with a world that is not static.

Growing organizations tend to experience even more business-related changes over a long period of time. Studies have shown that growing businesses not only increase the volume of the products or services they provide but also tend to increase the complexity of their products or services, their forward or backward integration, their rate of product innovation, the geographic scope of their operations, the number and character of their distribution channels, and the number and diversity of their customer groups. While all of this growth-driven change is occurring, competitive and other external pressures also increase. The more rapid the growth, the more extensive the changes that are experienced.

These types of business changes generally require organizational adjustments. For example, if a company's labor markets change over time, it must alter its selection criteria and make other adjustments to fit the new type of employee. New competitors might emerge with new products, thus requiring renewed product development efforts and a new organizational design to support that effort. In a growing company, business changes tend to require major shifts periodically in all aspects of its organization (see Figures 1.1 and 1.2).

The inability of an organization to anticipate the need for change and to adjust effectively to changes in its business or in its organization causes problems. These problems sometimes take the form of poor collaboration and coordination; they may involve high turnover or low morale. Always, however, such problems affect the organization's performance—goals are not achieved and/or resources are wasted.

Because change is inevitable and because it can so easily produce problems for companies, the key characteristic of an effective organization from a long-run viewpoint is its ability to anticipate needed organizational changes and to adapt as business conditions change. Anticipatory skills can help prevent the resource drain caused by organizational problems, while adaptability helps an organization avoid the problems that change can produce. Over long periods of time, this ability to avoid an important and recurring resource drain can mark the difference between success and failure for an organization.

FIGURE 1.1. Greiner's summary of required changes in organization practices during evolution in the five phases of growth.

Category	Phase 1	Phase 2	Phase 3	Phase 4	Phase 5
Management focus	Make and sell	Efficiency of operations	Expansion of market	Consolidation of organization	Problem solving and innovation
Organization structure	Informal	Centralized and functional	Decentralized and geographic	Line-staff and product groups	Matrix of teams
Top management style	Individualistic and entrepreneurial	Directive	Delegative	Watchdog	Participative
Control system	Market results	Standards and cost centers	Reports and profit centers	Plans and investment centers	Mutual goal setting
Management reward emphasis	Ownership	Salary and merit increases	Individual bonus	Profit sharing and stock options	Team bonus

Source: Larry E. Greiner, "Evolution and Revolution as Organizations Grow," *Harvard Business Review*, July-August 1972, p. 45.

3

FIGURE 1.2. Summary of changes during three stages of organizational development.

Company Characteristics	Stage I	Stage II	Stage III
The Business:			
1. Product	Single product or single line	Single product line	Multiple product lines
2. Distribution	One channel or set of channels	One set of channels	Multiple channels
3. R&D	Not institutionalized—oriented by owner-manager	Increasingly institutionalized search for product or process developments	Institutionalized search for *new* products as well as for improvements
4. Strategic choices	Needs of owner vs. needs of firm	Degree of integration. Market share objective. Breadth of product line.	Entry and exit from industries. Allocation of resources by industry. Rate of growth
The Organization:			
1. Organization structure	Little or no formal structure—"one man show"	Specialization based on function	Specialization based on product/market relationship
2. Product/service transactions	Not available	Integrated pattern of transactions: A→B→C→Market	Not integrated: A B C ↓ ↓ ↓ Market
3. Performance measurement	By personal contact and subjective criteria	Increasingly impersonal, using technical and/or cost criteria	Increasingly impersonal, using *market* criteria (return on investment and market share)
4. Rewards	Unsystematic and often paternalistic	Increasingly systematic with emphasis on stability and service	Increasingly systematic, with variability related to performance
5. Control system	Personal control of both strategic and operating decisions	Personal control of strategic decisions, with increasing delegation of operating decisions based on control by policies	Delegation of product/market decisions within existing businesses, with indirect control based on analysis of "results"

Source: Adapted from Bruce Scott, "Stages of Corporate Development," Boston: *HBS Case Services*, 1971.

A CASE OF ORGANIZATIONAL DECLINE

To fully appreciate the importance of anticipatory skills and adaptability in the long run, consider this somewhat extreme case. The company involved was founded in the late 1920s, primarily through acquisitions. It was created as the response of an entrepreneur to a variety of changing market conditions. Over a 5- to 10-year period, he established an enormously successful venture. In its market, it became the largest and most profitable organization of its kind.

Historical records do not reveal how much, if anything, the entrepreneur did to develop the company's long-run organizational adaptability. Two facts, however, are known. First, the ongoing operations were so profitable that he submitted to the demands of the national union just to avoid a disruption of operations. This resulted in the establishment of innumerable "work rules" and the entry of first-line supervisors into the union. Second, he did almost nothing to bring in or develop mid- or top-level managers. As an extremely talented person capable of making a large number of effective business decisions himself, he saw no need for assistance from others.

In the mid-1940s, the entrepreneur died. His brother took over as president and tried to maintain the company's existing policies and profitability. For the first few years of his tenure, everything seemed to work well.

After World War II, the company's industry, like many others, began to undergo significant changes. These changes occurred gradually but continuously over at least a 10-year period. During this time, the company made very few organizational adjustments to adapt to these changes, for a number of reasons. First, the few people who had any real decision-making authority in the company did not seem to see a need for many changes. They simply did not have the information that would have shown them what was happening in their industry and in their market area. Second, when they did have information on the changes that were occurring, they had difficulty deciding how to adjust to them. They were, for example, completely unaware of the typical development sequences shown in Figures 1.1 and 1.2. The intuitively brilliant leadership supplied by the original entrepreneur was gone, and nothing had taken its place. Finally, when they did identify a change and saw what response was needed, the managers were generally unable to implement it. For one thing, union rules prohibited a great deal of change; for another, there was no middle management to help them implement it. The firm was not at all flexible.

Some of the company's competitors were successful in identifying and reacting to the industry and market changes. As a result, the rate of increase of this company's sales and profits began to decrease. At the same time, problems with employees and the union began to surface.

The company's president initially focused his efforts on trying to stop the profit decline. In this endeavor, he was somewhat successful, yet in slowing the profit decline, he was forced to hold salaries and maintenance budgets down, thereby adding to the problems with his employees and the union. A climate of antagonism and distrust developed.

Between 1956 and 1965, the company's real (noninflated) annual growth in sales declined from 5 to 0 percent. Its profits leveled out and then fell to a net loss in 1965. By that time, the company's stock price was so low that a larger corporation successfully acquired a controlling interest. This corporation brought in its own top management group (which included a number of extremely successful managers) and predicted a quick turnaround.

The company resumed profitable operations in 1969 and, with the exception of 1973, has remained profitable to this time. Nevertheless, its profitability levels remain below the industry average, and its 1975 sales were, in real dollars, about the same as in 1965. It has gone through two more presidents since 1965, and the current one has been quoted in the business press as saying that the job of organizational "renewal" that is ahead of them remains extensive.

CHARACTERISTICS OF AN EFFECTIVE ORGANIZATION— FROM A LONG-RUN POINT OF VIEW

It is possible to infer the characteristics that contribute to long-run effectiveness by looking for what was missing in the previous example. The picture that emerges is one of an organization where (1) changes in its business are anticipated or quickly identified, (2) appropriate responses are quickly designed, and (3) the responses are implemented at a minimum cost. This behavior would be possible because the company is staffed with talented managers who are skilled at organizational analysis, as well as having relatively adaptable employees. Informal relations among these people would be characterized by trust, open communications, and respect for others' opinions. The formal design would include effective integrating devices, sensitive and well-designed measurement systems, reward systems that encourage adaptability, and selection

FIGURE 1.3.   Characteristics of a highly effective organization: A long-run point of view.

Employees:

1. The company is staffed with more than enough managerial talent.
2. Managers are skilled at organizational analysis and understand typical stages of organizational development.
3. A large number of employees are relatively adaptive and have skills beyond a narrow specialty.
4. Employees have realistic expectations about what they will get from, and have to give to, the company in the foreseeable future.

Informal Relations:

1. There is a high level of trust between employees and management.
2. Information flows freely, with a minimum of distortion within and across groups.
3. People in all positions of responsibility are willing to listen to, and be influenced by, others who might have relevant information.

Formal Design:

1. The organizational structure includes more than enough effective integrating mechanisms for the current situation and relies minimally on rules and procedures.
2. Measurement systems thoroughly collect and distribute all relevant data on the organization's environment, its actions, its performance, and changes in any of these factors.
3. Reward systems encourage people to identify needed changes and help implement them.
4. Selection and development systems are designed to create highly skilled managerial and employee groups and to encourage the kinds of informal relations described above.

and development systems that help support all other characteristics (see Fig. 1.3).

Unlike the declining company described earlier, an organization with the characteristics listed in Figure 1.3, as well as other characteristics that specifically fit its current business, could successfully respond to growth, industry changes, top management turnover, and virtually anything else that came its way. Its adaptability would allow it to continue changing the organization to fit its changing business, and it would survive and even prosper over long periods of time.

BUREAUCRATIC DRY ROT

Very few companies or nonprofit businesses have organizations with characteristics even close to those described in Figure 1.3. This fact has been emphasized by a number of social scientists who, in the past decade, have expressed serious concern over what they call *bureaucratic dry rot.* We all pay a heavy price, they note, for the large, bureaucratic, nonadaptive organizations that are insensitive to employees' needs, ignore consumers' desires, and refuse to accept their social responsibilities.

Existing evidence suggests that although most contemporary organizations cannot be described as adaptive, many managers nevertheless appreciate the benefits of adaptability. When polled, managers often respond that "ideally" they would like to have the kind of organization suggested by Figure 1.3, but they also admit that their current organization does not have all or even some of these characteristics.

At least five reasons account for the inflexibility and shortsightedness of most contemporary organizations. The first and most significant is related to resources. Creating a highly adaptive organization requires time, energy, and money. In the case of the company that went into decline, creating an adaptive organization early in its history might have required:

- Hiring, assimilating, and training a management team, both at the top and in mid-level ranks
- Selecting and training all other personnel
- Concentrating efforts from the managers to develop integrative devices, measurement systems, and the like
- Developing and maintaining good, informal relationships among managers and their employees

The organization may not have had the resources to invest in these systems. Had it tried, the company might have been compelled to divert resources from some of its current operations. If its competitors did not choose to follow its lead but continued to invest as heavily as possible in current operations, perhaps the company would have lost market share and income and even gone out of business long before it could enjoy the benefits of its long-term investment in adaptability.

A second reason for the nonadaptive and bureaucratic behavior of modern organizations is that their managers are not very skilled at producing the characteristics of an effective organization in the long run. Organizations generally invest resources in current operations and not in producing adaptive human systems. The on-the-job education of managers is usually focused on current operations, not on producing adaptability. Generating the characteristics shown in Figure 1.3 requires skills that have to be developed and nurtured.

Still a third reason for the inflexibility of many contemporary organizations is that some people clearly benefit from a static situation. The entrepreneur who established the nonadaptive organization described earlier thoroughly enjoyed the way he ran the company. It is doubtful that he would have invested resources in developing a management team, or developed one even had it cost him nothing. Furthermore, financial backers approved of how he ran the business, which included passing on a large share of the firm's earnings in dividends. Had he tried to cut the dividends to invest more in something as intangible as adaptability, they undoubtedly would have protested.

A fourth reason for nonadaptive behavior also is evident in the case of decline. Once an organization reaches a certain size, if it has not developed a certain minimally adaptive human organization, it becomes very difficult to turn things around without a gigantic infusion of resources. Considerable effort is required simply to overcome the "organizational entropy" that makes the organization even more non-adaptive and rigid.

A fifth reason more companies do not have organizational characteristics like those in Figure 1.3 is their management's decision that such characteristics are unnecessary. Based on their projection of what the future has in store for their company, management estimates how much adaptability they will need and then invests their resources to produce only that level of adaptability. If the company is growing very quickly or if it is in a volatile market and management expects rapid changes to continue in their business, they would invest considerable resources in creating an adaptive human organization. However, if the company is not growing, if it is in a stable market, and if management feels the future will not demand many changes of them, they generally invest relatively few resources.

In short, the forces that prevent organizations from developing a high level of adaptability are strong. The forces that can push successful organizations into decline are numerous as well. As a result, one of the most difficult of all management tasks involves developing an organization that has *enough* adaptability to promote effectiveness in the long run.

SIX TASKS OF THE MANAGER WHO MANAGES FOR THE LONG RUN

If a manager's goal is to create a lasting, high-performance company, focusing on the six key tasks that constitute the "basics" of the manager's job in any company is one way to achieve that elusive goal. These six basic tasks cut across the issues raised in all of the chapters in this book and include: (1) building a positive work environment, (2) establishing strategic direction, (3) allocating and marshalling resources, (4) upgrading the quality of management, (5) organizing effort, and (6) creating excellence in operations and execution.

Nothing should be surprising about this list; the fundamentals of the job should sound familiar. What makes it important is that it cuts the job down to size. The vast majority of the activities that managers perform in any situation can be grouped into these headings. The tasks help a manager define the scope of the job, set priorities, and see important interrelationships among the six areas.

Task 1: Building a Positive Work Environment

Every company has a particular work environment that dictates to a considerable degree how its managers respond to problems and opportunities.

A company's work environment is partly a heritage of its past leaders. However, shaping that environment is a critically important part of every incumbent manager's job, regardless of what he or she inherits from the past. This includes small companies, medium-sized ones, and giants like General Motors and General Electric. Over time, most managers exert influence on their work environment by three types of actions: (1) the goals and performance standards they establish, (2) the values they establish for the organization, and (3) establishing business and people concepts that are consistent with their goals and values.

The basic goals of the company provide a unifying force to channel efforts in chosen directions and to elevate performance standards. Individually, they provide direction in selected areas. Collectively, they influence the way people act in a company. Specific, action-oriented goals describe an aggressive and demanding work environment and influence the way people respond to strategic opportunities and business problems within the company. Conversely, a company with no specific goals or vague or undemanding ones is much more likely to drift, be bureaucratic, or tolerate unexciting results.

Successful managers typically set high standards across the whole business. High standards are reflected in many ways, including: (1) the relative quality of the company's functional strategies and its market leadership; (2) the detailed end results that are sought and achieved, as compared to relevant competitors; (3) the quality of written plans and oral presentations that people make, both in terms of substance and style; (4) the relative quality of managers at all levels; (5) rising productivity in all functions of the business, particularly as compared with major competitors; and (6) consistent product quality and reliability.

Values reflect the relative concern that an organization has for its employees, customers, investors, suppliers, and other stakeholders. Values help define not only the manner in which business will be conducted (how these stakeholders will be treated), but the types of business in which an organization will engage. The "fit" between an individual and an organization is often determined by these values.

Business concepts reflect an organization's values, for example: (1) the kinds of products or services the business will offer, (2) the company's position or role in its industry, and (3) structural devices, such as levels of organization, methods of communication, and planning processes to be employed in conducting business.

Policies that support such values include, for example: (2) the stress on internal growth from operations, (2) emphasis on hiring from within, (3) the way performance is judged and rewarded, (4) emphasis on fairness in dealing with people, and (5) the importance of candor, integrity, and high ethical standards in relationships.

In any organization, the manager's personal style influences associates for better or worse. If the manager insists on long memos or frequent meetings, these usually will be the order of the day throughout the organization. A "hands-on" style will be widely copied. The cost-conscious manager results in cost consciousness throughout much of the organization. If the manager favors complex systems, this too will usually have a "ripple" effect throughout the company. Other managers take their cues from the manner in which their manager responds to others' successes or failures.

The manager's style influences the ethical tone of the business. The manager's actions tell associates far more than words. A manager who lacks integrity, fairness, or a sense of commitment quickly creates confusion and cynicism in the organization. Conversely, managers who set high standards in these areas usually find their associates following their lead. The importance of consistency between what general managers say and how they act in creating a sound working environment hardly can be overstated.

Managers can be most effective if they have an all-encompassing theme for the working environment. The theme can range from converting a slow moving company into a dynamic business to becoming our industry's innovative merchandising leader to becoming a blue chip company. Successful leaders frequently use such broad themes to help focus the working environment on one overriding purpose.

Task 2: Establishing Strategic Direction

Whether the manager is the main architect of the company's strategy, he or she is responsible for ensuring that a process is in place for strategic planning. There is no universally accepted definition of what constitutes a good strategy. Some companies make elaborate efforts to spell out what they mean by a strategy; in others, the strategy consists largely of ideas contained in the manager's head. In any case, the manager is the executive who must decide whether or not the business will be run on the basis of an explicit, formalized strategy and, if so, the process to be employed in developing, reviewing, and implementing it.

A commonly accepted framework for strategy formulation and appraisal highlights the following elements: (1) the task, including the environment and concept of the business, its definition, mission, competitive position, and functional goals and efforts; (2) available resources including leadership, human, financial, technological, customer franchise, stakeholder relationships, and working environment; and (3) structure including organization, controls, systems, standards, rewards, policies, processes, and values.

A starting point in the process of strategy formulation and appraisal is an understanding of the task facing the business. Devices such as Michael Porter's "five forces analysis" can be useful here. Just as important is an understanding on the part of the manager of the way a business runs and the important factors in its success or failure. An *operational* understanding of the business is critical.

Managers typically face several issues in organizing people's efforts to develop and review strategy including: (1) those who will be directly involved and in what role; (2) the format of the plans; (3) the mechanisms needed to gain input, understanding, and commitment of key managers as plans evolve; (4) the nature of the review and approval process; and (5) the manager's individual role in the process.

During the process of strategy formulation and review, the manager is faced with a sequence of important decisions that determine the effectiveness of the strategy. Successful strategies usually start with good ideas and evolve over time as they are exposed to the realities of the market place.

The scarce resource in strategy development often is bold, innovative ideas, those that provide a new vision for the business rather than a slight alteration of existing strategy. Hence, managers must stimulate everyone, including themselves, to think creatively and to be willing to consider fresh approaches. This is true whether the manager does most of the thinking personally or serves more as the prime mover for the process.

Task 3: Allocating and Marshalling Resources

Successful strategies require resources to convert them into reality (including both "hard" resources like cash, plant and equipment, and offices, and "soft" resources such as people and technology).

The manager's unique role in resource allocation stems from three distinctive features of the job. First, the manager is the only person who can commit resources across the entire business. Since nearly every major strategy entails cross-functional commitments, the manager is normally the only executive empowered to make these commitments.

Second, the manager must be the chief decision maker of trade-offs among key projects and functions competing for limited resources. Since most businesses lack the resources to do everything that is proposed, this is usually a major responsibility.

Third, once a decision is made to pursue a strategy, the manager assumes the responsibility for marshalling the resources needed to ensure success.

Marshalling resources often involves the manager in a series of negotiations with external entities, (i.e., financial institutions, major investors, government agencies, and labor unions) as well as internal constituents.

While strategy decisions have an important influence on resource allocations, managers, of course, also routinely allocate resources to operate the business. It is important for a manager to be sure that both kinds of resources—strategic and operational—are productively employed.

Task 4: Upgrading the Quality of Management

Many managers contend that the selection, development, and deployment of people are the most important responsibilities. They also feel it is a satisfying part of the job to see managers grow and the organization strengthen as a result of their efforts. Managers who attach a high priority to this activity usually find their associates do also.

In addition, most skillful managers personally involve themselves in: (1) defining and supervising the process for selecting and developing the company's senior and upper-middle management (such as stressing individual evaluations and development assignments), (2) seeing that each function periodically analyzes its skill requirements and people needs and has a strategy to fill those needs, (3) setting job requirement standards (at least at top levels), (4) making sure that outstanding managers have challenging, timely development assignments that effectively utilize their talents, (5) ensuring that compensation programs are both competitive and rewarding for managers who meet assigned goals, and (6) making sure that entry-level management jobs are sufficiently challenging to attract the best people.

Task 5: Organizing Effort

Because of their cross-functional responsibilities, managers normally play a dominant role in designing the company's organization. This function usually includes three important activities:

1. *Defining the organizational concepts for the company.* This means deciding (in light of the company's competitive and general environment) the appropriate level in the organization at which important business decisions should be made, how tightly or loosely controlled the business will be operated, and the role that measurements, controls, and policies play in running the business.

2. *Deciding on the organization structure at the top.* Important questions to be addressed here include: What is expected of each key functional area? Where does it report? What subunits will it contain? How will each function work together? What are the necessary line and staff relationships? What role will the general manager play?

3. *Defining interfunctional relationships.* In most organizations, the manager is the only executive who can be held responsible for coordinating major functional relationships. Moreover, how the manager defines and supervises these important relationships usually determines how smoothly functional groups work together.

Organizations are naturally dynamic. They change with shifts in competitive conditions, strategic thrust, or the talent available to the general manager. Therefore, the process of organization design, staffing, and coordination is nearly always an ongoing, high-priority concern of the manager.

Task 6: Creating Excellence in Operations and Execution

Typically, the manager influences day-to-day operations in three major ways: (1) by his or her style, (2) by the management processes used (consistent with that style), and (3) by the way time is allocated. If the manager is a direct, personal leader, things will usually be done in a direct, personal way. Less direct leaders may rely on a consensus-driven approach. Whatever the style, the manager is responsible for understanding day-to-day operations and for establishing the processes that govern them. The manager will typically be involved in: (1) operational planning, including the development of annual plans and efforts to see that they are met; (2) coordination among the direct-report functions, with special concern that functional units work together so that proper trade-offs are made, parochial departmental interests do not dominate, and inevitable interfunctional conflicts are resolved; (3) decision making, with primary emphasis on cross-functional matters and major commitments; and (4) problem identification and solution, whether through direct involvement or setting in motion a process for the purpose.

The manager's responsibilities cover a wide range of activities. Individually, they may not be as important or as interesting as the development of a business strategy. Taken together, however, they keep the business going effectively, meeting its short-term sales and profit goals. Without an understanding of day-to-day operations, a manager will have difficulty identifying important elements of the strategic task facing the firm.

CONCLUDING COMMENTS

These six basic tasks of the manager represent an arbitrary selection. However, they do represent discrete and broad responsibilities important to the successful performance of the manager's job in most companies.

A primary skill of the manager is to pick the specific areas where his or her involvement will have the greatest impact on business results. The scope of the job is such that a manager nearly always faces many more problems and opportunities thanhe or she can possibly deal with personally. The manager may decide to put greater emphasis on strategy formulation; at another time, the focus will be on the development of people or the working environment. Knowing what to emphasize, when to emphasize it, what and when to delegate, and to whom to delegate are crucial decisions.

Success as a manager isn't solely a function of focusing on these key tasks. Some managers are simply better leaders than others. Some bring a personal package of experience or style that is especially suited to a particular situation.

However, whatever leadership skills or personal package a manager brings to the job, he or she still must decide specifically how to focus efforts in order to fundamentally improve the business. Therefore, the key tasks come into play in nearly every situation.

A skillful manager usually is the most important contributor to an organization's success over time. Those contributions are most effective when efforts are concentrated in the six areas described within this chapter.

FOR FURTHER READING

Bennis, Warren, and Burt Nanus, *Leaders: The Strategies for Taking Charge* (New York: Harper & Row, 1985).

Harvard Business Review, *Strategic Management* (New York: John Wiley, 1983).

Itami, Hiroyuki, *Mobilizing Invisible Assets* (Cambridge: Harvard University Press, 1987).

Kimberly, John C., and Robert E. Quinn, *Managing Organizational Transitions* (Homewood, IL: Richard D. Irwin, 1984).

Kotter, John P., *The Leadership Factor* (New York, Free Press, 1988).

PART ONE

THE FOUNDATIONS OF MANAGEMENT

MANAGING PEOPLE: THE R FACTOR

2

Allan R. Cohen

All of the skills covered by a good MBA program are important for effective management, but the key ones relate to managing people. The sad truth is that within an organization, some people will not view problems as you do, will not always want or be able to do what you believe they should and, indeed, may overtly oppose your (undoubtedly) flawless plans. Even direct subordinates will resist your orders when they are convinced you are wrong, or worse, will appear to comply while subtly dragging their heels. Others whom you don't supervise, including your boss and colleagues, can be downright ornery, if not hostile. Yet your effectiveness depends on others; few decisions can be made or implemented in splendid isolation.

Being part of an organization inherently means being interconnected with many others—for worse *and* better. Sometimes those who refuse to cooperate actually have valuable knowledge or abilities; they may even be indispensable to your success. "Managing others" is not only about gaining their compliance, but also about learning from and accommodating them, when appropriate.

We will approach the enhancement of managerial capacity in these areas by focusing first on *diagnosis*—understanding what causes people in organizations to behave as they do. Then we will consider how to alter this behavior. Taking appropriate action is easier, although seldom

Thanks to my colleagues J.B. Kassarjian, Les Livingstone, Lynne Rosansky, Phyllis Schlesinger, and Robin Willits for their comments on an earlier draft of this chapter.

automatic, when the diagnosis is solid; at the least, careful diagnosis prevents foolish errors. In any organization, there are daily occurrences of managers leaping before looking, causing unforeseen consequences they later regret. Even worse, managers can cultivate a mountainous problem where a mere molehill previously existed.

A manager chews out a subordinate who arrives late for the third time, without realizing that the subordinate had worked several nights on a big project. Another manager demands a faster pace from a work team without anticipating the effect on their concern for quality. A third manager, who in the past has accomplished great results through kindness, falls behind schedule because a subordinate needed constant reminders and close monitoring. All of these managers share the problem of taking action without understanding the particular circumstances. We begin by offering a way of sorting through the complexities of ongoing organizational life to understand the forces causing behavior.

PERSONALITY AND SITUATION

A preliminary cut at explaining behavior in organizations is to differentiate between forces within the behaver's *personality* and "everything else," that is, the forces in the *situation* surrounding the person. Most Americans are psychologically oriented, so the natural tendency is to resort to explanations of behavior that are within the person. "He needs to be in control." "She is a perfectionist." "They are a bunch of mavericks." Even when such observations may be correct in some way, they are usually incomplete, therefore misleading, and not easily amenable to managerial action. Even extended psychotherapy has a poor record of changing personality, and managers are not trained therapists. While it is helpful to understand something about the forces inside people, usually more leverage results from special attention to diagnosing the external forces.

If an employee's manager criticizes every action, the equipment is designed wrong for the work, the organization pays the lowest possible wages, and fellow workers refuse to talk to anyone who produces at a high rate, we will be helped very little by diagnosing a poor performer as "lazy" or "stupid." Although that could also be true, a valid conclusion is unlikely when so many organizational conditions are stacked against conscientious performance. The person may well be clever in figuring out "how the game is played" in this organization; in another more favorable setting, that cleverness might lead instead to greater investment and higher performance.

The individual's personality and internal motivation do come into play but seldom are sufficient to explain observed behavior. Therefore, we will examine external forces extensively and look for ways in which they inter- act with personality. Indeed, an important working assumption is that all significant behavior has *multiple causes* which reinforce each other. In that sense, most behavior is overdetermined, with several causes. If you can sort the causes out, then you will be in the best position to determine where to intervene and what the likely consequences of that intervention will be.

THE NEED FOR A CONCEPTUAL MODEL

Because the realities of individuals and organizations are so complex, a conceptual scheme for simplifying and ordering is desirable. Using *any* model provokes the dangerous temptation to treat the model's abstrac- tions as if they were the whirling reality—or alternatively, the temptation to dismiss the model as mere jargon. We will treat the model as a tool, a walking stick to help us navigate difficult terrain, rather than as an end in itself. It should be relied on only insofar as it is useful in guiding attention and uniting many factors that together cause behavior.

With only a bit of stretching and poetic license, we can fit an abun- dance of social science research and theory into a conceptual scheme where all key words begin with "R."

R FACTORS: THE SITUATION

Although we will discuss one factor at a time, note that all situational R factors interact with each other (and with individual factors) to shape behavior. Together they send powerful messages to individuals about what is expected, right, good—even possible. Although different individ- uals may vary their responses according to their personalities, a consistent set of situational R factors will often produce similar results among a wide range of individuals.

The situational R factors we will examine are *roles, relationships, rewards*, and *rites*. (See Figure 2.1.)

Roles

Roles are positions in an organization defined by a set of expectations about behavior of any incumbent. Organizational roles have attached to

FIGURE 2.1. R factors affecting behavior in the *situation*.

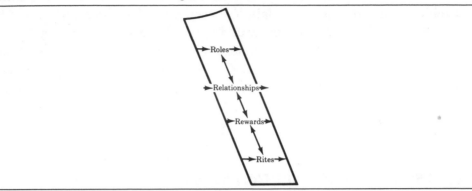

them a required set of tasks and responsibilities (often, but not always, spelled out in a job description). The *formal* role tells its occupant what activities are expected, and often what results are desired. Since salaries are paid in return for performance of the role, roles have a powerful effect on behavior. Roles can also evolve *informally,* creating expectations that are not official, but that strongly influence behavior. Both formal and informal roles can have "requirements" about both tasks and interactions. The role tells the person who holds it not only what tasks to carry out but also with whom to interact in carrying out the tasks. Though the requirements of the role may never be written, they will be conveyed to the occupant and more or less enforced; in any event, they strongly influence behavior. The following example illustrates these ideas.

Formal Role

Dan Alighieri is a quality control manager in a large plant. He is responsible for seeing that the products leaving the plant are produced to customer specifications within certain tolerances. His job requires that he apply statistical sampling techniques and high standards to insure that work at every stage of manufacture is done appropriately. His colleagues at the plant have divergent roles; they want to manufacture quickly with minimal rework, and ship everything that has been completed. Dan feels obligated by role to be critical and suspicious; if he were not, substandard parts might be shipped by his people.

Dan's colleagues, the managers of manufacturing, engineering, and sales, consider him a royal pain since his stance at meetings is perpetually negative. Even on subjects unrelated to quality control, he usually focuses on limitations, weaknesses, and dangers. They joke (behind his back) about his being a "sadistic s.o.b." and a "black cloud." Yet when Dan coaches his son's Little League team, he is warm, patient, and supportive. The issue at work is not his personality, but his role, which signals him about expected behavior. In fact, Dan sometimes carries over the critical set appropriate to his job into problem-solving sessions where it interferes, but not because he is inherently negative.

The Evolution of an Informal Role

Compounding the problem is the emergence in Dan's peer group of an informal role—group skeptic—that has evolved for Dan. As the group began to notice Dan's critical approach, they came to expect that on any issue he would point out the pitfalls. In turn, they stressed the positive. Dan interpreted their consistent stance as a sign that if he did not exercise extra caution, they would go off half-cocked. Soon, everyone left to Dan the job of looking for negative possibilities, and the role of group skeptic became his. This item did not appear on his job description, but the expectations were no less powerful. Although the group complained about Dan's negativity, he often prevented their leaping before thoroughly looking and occasionally rescued them from impending disaster.

The Impact of Tasks on Roles

Whether a role is formal and written, or emerges from informal interaction with others, expectations draw behavior from the person who holds the role. However, roles also shape behavior in other, less direct ways.

The nature of the tasks assigned to a role have an impact on the feelings of the occupant about how hard to work, depending upon whether the tasks are simple or complex, repetitive or varied, stationary or mobile, concentration-intense or not, equipment/technology-oriented or not, and so on. In general, researchers have found that increasing numbers of individuals respond with greater commitment and effort when the tasks of their job provide stimulation and challenge. The exceptions are those individuals whose skills and aspirations are so low that they do not respond to challenge—a declining breed in developed economies.

The Connection Between Roles and Relationships

A Role's Required Interactions Impact Relationships

Tasks assigned to roles impact behavior because they determine with whom the occupant will have contact. Some organizational tasks are performed alone, but most are carried out in *relationship* to others. With whom a role-holder is required to interact, how often, and toward what end, all have important consequences. One of the basic laws of behavior is that, in general, greater interaction (especially among relative equals) will lead to greater liking; in turn, greater liking usually leads to more frequent interaction. It is hard to develop liking for those with whom we have no contact, and we tend to seek out those we like. As a result, people in organizations develop connections—friendships or "acquaintance-ships"—with those to whom their job leads them. (Sometimes no interaction is *required,* but geographical proximity promotes it, with similar results.)

The relationships resulting from interaction can impact behavior. When the relationships are with single individuals, the pair will develop ideas about what is expected from one another, how to view the company, how much effort to put into work, and so forth. Strongly developed friendships may become more important in shaping behavior at work than the formal tasks or the individual's personal inclinations.

Relationships That Become Self-Sealing

When relationships with colleagues are positive, work is more enjoyable, information flows more freely, disagreements are more readily resolved, and greater trust evolves. On the other hand, negative relationships among peers can result in great unhappiness and poor ability to accomplish work requiring cooperation or collaboration.

When two individuals develop a negative working relationship, they often do so because the actions of each causes the other to produce more of the behavior irritating to the other, which in turn provokes the first person, and so on. This self-sealing reciprocity can be extremely frustrating to the parties caught in it, as well as to those working around them.

For example, Joan Jeffries and Kirk Rulon were colleagues in a professional services firm. Joan recruited Kirk to head a newly established research unit; within a year she was at war with Kirk. Joan was a creative, enterprising wheeler-dealer who had an excellent reputation with clients. Her motto was, "It's easier to beg forgiveness than to obtain advance permission," and she constantly bent rules to accomplish her goals. Kirk, on the other hand, was careful, systematic, and a bit plodding. A skilled bureaucratic infighter, he was a master of budget procedures and organizational rules as a means of achieving his projects.

When Joan and Kirk had to deal with one another, each drove the other wild. Joan would be too busy to answer memos or attend planning meetings; at the last minute, she would have a brainstorm and want to have input. Kirk would say, "Gee, you had a chance but didn't say anything, so now it's too late." Joan would hit the roof, railing about Kirk's rigidities; in turn, Kirk would point out reporting lines, published deadlines, and so on. Kirk's repeated inflexibility provoked Joan to avoid him, prompting her to miss more meetings and deadlines. Around they went, until Joan resolved to eliminate Kirk—who was working on transferring to another unit where Joan could not hamper him. Their battles frustrated their colleagues and boss, who liked both of them, but could not determine how to motivate them to pool their talents.

Relationships Develop Informal Norms

Even more powerful influences can be the groups that form at work. Whether a formally designated work team or an informal group that develops out of casual interaction, mutual interests, or outside connections, groups develop *norms*—ideas about how members are supposed to behave. In a well-developed group, the norms will be extensive and well-enforced. Norms about how much to produce, how hard to work, how to treat other members, how to talk to managers, how to relate to nongroup members, even how to dress, are common features of groups at work.

For the individual member, these norms can feel like powerful "requirements" of the job and constitute price of admission to membership. Following the group's norms is necessary to be a member in good standing, and groups enforce the norms in a variety of ways. In a classic study of a workgroup, the punishment for breaking a norm was "binging," a sharp rap on the arm. In higher-level work teams, norms may be enforced by kidding remarks ("Nice jacket, Kim; was there a polyester glut at your tailor's?"), by direct disapproval ("That's not what we expect from design engineers, Chris") or by subtle hints ("I didn't see you at the office when I was here on Saturday, Sandy; is everything okay?").

When a member does not conform to a group's norms, increased interaction is addressed to that person in an attempt to bring him or her into line; if that fails, the group gradually ignores the person. Only a very determined individual, or one with one or more satisfactory memberships in outside groups, can long resist a group working to enforce its norms. The signals sent by work teams to its members can strongly influence behavior; if the team's norms are different from the person's task requirements, as often happens, the team may well be the greater influence.

One exception to the tendency of greater interaction leading to greater liking is when the interaction required is between people of acutely opposing values or status. Those with differing values (e.g., "I live to work" versus "I work to be able to live well") may find that more contact only clarifies their differences and drives them to reduce contact, even if the job requires it.

People of highly unequal status also may wish to avoid one another to minimize potential discomfort arising from the inequality. Although North Americans tend to downplay status differences, it is still likely that the president of a large company will not seek out his or her driver beyond those times when work requires it. The president may be overtly friendly, but probably not engage in personal conversation or revelations. The driver is likely to be polite and, if highly confident, may exchange a bit of banter, without presuming friendship. This reticence in no way suggests that one is a better, more worthwhile person than the other; the differences in organizational power usually work to create barriers and distance, however politely each pretends none exists.

These same impulses push some managers to avoid social contact with subordinates, even when previously they have been friendly as peers. North Americans are so uncomfortable with the idea of status creating distance that they work to deny status differences. For example, when the oldest member of a team of MBA whiz kids is perceived by his peers as aspiring to become the group's liaison with management, they deny there is any need for the role, despite the company president's interest. A manager seeking openness or closeness with subordinates will have to work hard to overcome this universal recognition of the impact of unequal status.

Relationships Upward; The Impact of Leadership

We have already begun to discuss the ways relationships affect behavior; one of the key relationships is with the person's direct supervisor. A few extremely independent people behave the same no matter what their bosses do, but most people are affected by the relationship the boss creates (or allows to be created).

Does the subordinate want personal closeness, and will the boss give it? Does the subordinate know the work so well that it can best be done without close supervision, and will the boss allow that? Or, is the work so complicated that more attention is needed (or so boring that constant watching is required), and will the boss provide that? Does the subordinate have valuable contributions toward setting methods or solving problems, and does the boss listen?

A number of conditions yield high performance and commitment when the boss manages tightly; other conditions require greater latitude and participation by subordinates. Performance can be harmed by a bad fit between the complexity of the tasks, the manner in which the employee desires to be supervised, and the leadership style. In general, when inexperienced, dependent subordinates are engaged in simple, routine tasks, tighter supervision produces better performance; with complex, changing tasks, knowledgeable, mature subordinates perform best when leadership style is participative and warm. Some dilemmas complicate these issues:

1. A style that fits may yield performance in the short run, but how can subordinates and tasks be developed to make new styles appropriate. As we head into the 1990s, fewer organizational tasks are simple and unchanging, fewer subordinates are uneducated and submissive. Can directive styles continue to achieve high performance? Can managers afford to be heroic, to disseminate all the answers, to keep total control and responsibility? Where will talented people come from if current members are not developed?

2. Individual and collective satisfaction may not match performance. There is no necessary correlation between satisfaction and performance; happy employees can be productive or unproductive, as can unhappy ones. Does employee satisfaction matter then? Does it matter only when unemployment is low, allowing dissatisfied people to easily leave and obtain other jobs? Or in the long run, is a satisfied workforce needed to retain good people and keep them growing as the environment changes?

3. How will employees learn if managers fail to provide challenge and autonomy? How can the managers be sure the employees will do the right things well?

The way in which an individual's manager resolves these relationship issues has profound effects on the person's behavior. Managers are also someone else's subordinates, so their relationships with their bosses are likely to affect the way they deal with their subordinates!

Rewards

Discussing leadership must include the subject of *rewards,* both formal and informal. It is not exactly startling news that people tend to do what they are rewarded for, although organizations sometimes have difficulty implementing that truth. Identifying the desired tasks or behaviors is challenging, as is measuring their accomplishments and attaching appropriate rewards. Furthermore, individuals may find very different things to be rewarding, so a uniform system may not touch everyone as intended.

Whatever the difficulties of establishing a reward system that performs as planned, all organizations have them. The particular nature of the system contributes to individual behavior. Is salary fixed, no matter what the performance? Is it partly or totally contingent on performance, as with commissioned salespeople? Are there performance bonuses; are some or all levels eligible for them; are bonuses individual, group, departmental, or total-organization based? How easily can good performance be measured? Are decisions about who to reward perceived as fair, objective, or subjective? Do actual rewards match what top management says is important?

No one reward system works for every situation, but whatever is in place will affect individual behavior. Consider the impact on behavior of a plant that produces hazardous chemical gases, claims to be safety conscious, yet posts the volume per minute produced by each shift. Although operators are paid a fixed wage, the competition engendered by the charting of volume produced (combined with lax supervision) is one factor that led to sloppy performance and contamination of the plant on the third shift one night. Other organizations have found that rhetoric about quality, excellence, or innovation fall on deaf (or cynical) ears unless accompanied by concrete rewards for those who contribute to those goals.

In addition to the impact of formal reward systems, it is useful to identify the rewards that have evolved informally within the organization. What behaviors help people get ahead (or get along)? Many of these are products of the group or team to which a person belongs (as discussed above), but some reflect the morés of the wider organization.

These methods can vary widely; in some fast-growing high-tech firms (like Digital Equipment Corp.), the aggressive, innovative person receives rapid promotions and recognition; in some more traditional firms (like Royal Bank of Canada), hard work, sincerity, and "fitting in" lead to advancement. In fact, at Royal Bank it was believed that "the tallest weed is cut down first," so no one wanted to take big risks; at Digital Equipment, anyone who saw a problem or opportunity and avoided taking initiative was frowned on. These informal rewards lead to quite different behavior.

Rites

As suggested by the discussions of informal rewards, organizations can differ dramatically in their cultures—the unspoken assumptions about proper behavior. The culture usually reflects a combination of the organization's founders(s), current leadership, key crises and events in the history, size, and particular industry of the organization. The organization's resulting *rites* —its routines, rituals, and general "way we do things"— also impact individual behavior.

Just as a small group's norms "direct" members about what it takes to be in good standing, an organization's culture directs appropriate behavior, and its rites reinforce ideas about how to behave in many circumstances. For example, are people expected to follow orders, or challenge anything illogical? Is hierarchy rigidly respected or played down? Do new members receive formal training in the organization's practices (as at Hewlett Packard), or are they left to fend for themselves? Do Friday afternoon beer-busts reinforce informal connections (as at many Silicon Valley companies), or do members rarely socialize? Does customer satisfaction really matter? Are divisions or units autonomous or centrally controlled? Do long-run considerations take precedence over short-term gain (increasingly rare in American industry) or vice versa?

The nature of the industry contributes to the answers to these questions. All siding salesmen may not behave as unethically as those depicted in the movie *Tin Men*, but because of industry practices, most are probably closer to that image in reality than are IBM salespeople or trust officers at traditional banks.

Reinforcement

Although it is necessary for clarity to discuss factors one at a time, in reality, the factors interact and reinforce one another (or conflict with each other, sending confusing signals to organizational members). The pressures from the tasks in a role may be formally rewarded while the relationships that arise create a different set of informal rewards. The organization's rites may encourage a different kind of behavior or align with the other factors. The interaction of these factors allows a total situation to emerge, with its resultant impact on the individual.

R FACTORS: THE INDIVIDUAL

Most behavior is shaped by factors outside the individual. However, personality does matter, and it shapes responses to the various factors in the situation. Thus, the next part of the scheme deals with individual internal factors brought to any organizational situation. The factors relate to each other, organizing the person's self-view. We will discuss each of the factors in turn: *recall, reach, reasoning, repetition* and their overall configuration, *reconciliation of self.* (See Figure 2.2.)

Recall

One of the key influences on how we see ourselves and our organizational situation is *recall* of our past experience. Experiences provide the skills and competencies that shape what people are willing to tackle or like to do (and may over-rely on). Experiences also shape attitudes about work, people, and organizations.

How does the person feel about his or her skills? What are a person's experiences with those in positions of authority? They may explain current reactions to his or her boss. Has work usually been enjoyable or a burden? Has the person been supported by peers or found them to be nasty competitors? Has the person learned that new skills are readily mastered or cause fumbling and confusion?

Not only does recall of general experiences impact how a person behaves, but recall of key incidents in the particular organization often determines one's attitude toward current issues. Both kinds of experiences help shape how open a person is, how trusting, how willing to be a committed organizational member. Often, when someone is reacting oddly, it is worth exploring what related experiences the person recalls since the behavior may be logical when the source is revealed.

FIGURE 2.2.   R factors affecting behavior within the *individual*.

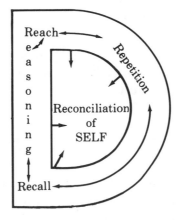

Reach

Another powerful determinant of behavior is the person's *reach*, his or her goals or values. Goals are the objects or events for which a person strives to fulfill needs. Goals may be realistic or unrealistic, depending on the person's talents and the opportunity inherent in the organization; in either case, most of the interesting behavior in organizations is goal-driven.

Values are more fundamental than goals; they are beliefs about what is important in life, conceived as ultimately unobtainable ideals. Examples of values include:

1. Always do one's best.
2. Never put work above friendship.
3. Always be honest with others.
4. Never deliberately hurt anyone's feelings .
5. Win at all costs.

Notice that it is unlikely anyone could perfectly live up to each of his or her values, and that an individual may well hold contradictory values for some situations. For example, the person who holds values 3 and 4 could easily come into conflict when faced with a nice but weak colleague who fears he has insufficient skills for a job and requests "an honest opinion."

Because values are global, they can easily conflict with one's specific goals. This clash creates tensions within the person; how the tensions are resolved helps to shape the person and may result in alteration of either the goals or values. For example, Bill Flynn took a job as a systems analysis trainee, determined to enhance his computer skills. Shocked by the rigorous, competitive program and the management's strictness, he gradually broke the program's rules to succeed. Although he thought of himself as honest, eventually he shuffled through his boss' desk late one night to read the trainee evaluations that were unavailable to the trainees. Afterward, he could barely justify his action to himself or his friends, and he struggled to reconcile his values with his goal of successfully completing the program. In such experiences, identity and self-image are formed.

Reasoning

In addition to goals and values, people *reason*—develop beliefs—about the world, other people, organizations, and more. These beliefs form a cognitive pattern that also shapes behavior. If a manager (we'll call her Kim) believes, for example, that all managers in the division would walk over their parents to get ahead, Kim is likely to be on guard when dealing with them. Indeed, Kim may take any opportunity to disparage them as a defensive tactic against their "aggressiveness." Is it a surprise, then, that Kim's colleagues become increasingly nasty due to their beliefs that Kim is a vicious competitor, thus "confirming" to Kim the validity of the original views?

Beliefs make it possible to function since they provide guides for unforeseen situations (imagine trying to act if you lacked beliefs about how people react, organizations work, bosses behave, and so on!), but beliefs can become self-fulfilling prophecies, as they did for Kim.

This cycle complicates diagnosis. Organizational members act on beliefs they do not always articulate and often are certain their beliefs are correct because others behave accordingly—even though the causes of others' behavior are actually contrary to what is assumed.

Because human beings prefer to have explanations for what they see around them, they are prone to "explain" the behavior of others by attributing motives. When Mark Bennett, president of a high-tech company, failed to inform Jacque Laroux, the chairman and founder, about several important issues, Jacque was upset. He felt increasingly excluded from daily operations and unappreciated for his many technical contributions. Puzzled that "any reasonable president would cut me out," he attributed to Mark unpleasant motives: jealousy, ambition, and fear. In fact, Mark believed that Jacque's loose style of interacting with technicians and scientists at all levels of the organization was disruptive, and Mark wanted to keep him from "messing up the organization." But Jacque was so sure of his attributions that he was convinced of the futility of asking Mark why he was holding Jacque off, so he never asked. Instead he convinced the board to fire Mark.

In general, people act on their beliefs as if they were true; it is therefore useful to explore what another's beliefs are when trying to understand his or her behavior.

Repetition

Many aspects of behavior are no longer consciously intended, but are rote *repetition*. Habits form (often based on what worked to solve a problem at some earlier time) and persist independent of their appropriateness to current situations. Some habits are harmless, amusing, or only mildly annoying—for example Michael Jordan, a great basketball player, sticks out his tongue when going up for a shot—and are not especially significant in understanding behavior. (Imagine, however, someone unfamiliar with basketball asking Michael Jordan a tough question and facing what looks like an impertinent stuck-out tongue!).

Other habits can be equally automatic but more significant in consequence. Based on early experiences, managers develop favored ways of dealing with sticky situations which they automatically repeat in vaguely similar situations, even when the behavior is essentially ineffective. *Repetition* of a particular response builds the manager's skill, so that its frequent success reinforces its automatic use. The strength then becomes a weakness because it is overused, even when not appropriate.

Ted Chatham, for example, was trained as an actuary. Brilliant and analytical, he rose through the ranks in his insurance company relatively rapidly. Then he plateaued, much to his consternation. Peers, to whom he felt intellectually superior, were selected for senior vice-presidential posts he coveted. The problem was that he had overdeveloped his analytical skills and used them in situations where compassion or intuition was needed. He could not deal with less brilliant subordinates or peers, especially when they were upset or tackling ambiguous problems. The dispassionate analytical skills that advanced him early in his career had been so often repeated that they were automatically called into play even when totally inappropriate.

When examining puzzling behavior, try the hypothesis that the person is acting out of habit rather than from careful situational diagnosis. The notion that the behavior may be an overused strength can lead to useful understanding.

Reconciliation of Self (Self-Concept)

The individual components, *recall, reach, reasoning,* and *repetition* have been discussed as if they were separate elements, but they interact within the person as well. Together they form the person's self-concept (*reconciliation of self*)—the way the person sees himself or herself. The goals, values, and beliefs arising from experience converge to form a view of self that in turn shapes behavior. Once such a self-concept is formed, people strive to maintain that concept by engaging in behavior consistent with it. Thus, a person who sees herself as ambitious and honest can aggressively confront a boss she believes to be blocking her career advancement, while one who sees herself as ambitious but inexperienced and powerless will tolerate managerial ineptness that the first person would readily tackle.

Perhaps the most useful observation about self-concept is that viewed from within a person, even behavior that an outsider might find strange usually makes sense. Bill Flynn, who bewildered his friends by searching his boss' desk in the middle of the night, did not see himself as dishonest; rather, he saw himself as ambitious and determined in a situation where pertinent information was being unreasonably withheld. He *recalled* earlier experiences in which assertive, harmless actions had helped him. His *reach* for success in becoming a systems analyst and broadening his computer experience was shared by colleagues. His *reasoning* told him bosses and companies inconsiderate of employees did not deserve blind obedience. Finally, the resourcefulness he had used to get through college and find good jobs was *repeated* as, "on impulse, Bill let himself into [his boss'] office and closed the door."

Diagnosing the elements of individual behavior, *recall*, *reach*, *reasoning*, and *repetition*, and their combination to form a *reconciliation of self*, increase your understanding of the behavior of individuals in organizations. When combined with the situational R factors, enough of behavior is understandable to determine possible leverage points for change.

Reinforcement (Again)

Just as the situational R factors reinforce each other, individual R factors overlap and reinforce each other (or send contradictory, mixed messages about behavior). Careful analysis of each particular situation is required to see whether, and how, the factors unite to shape behavior that at first glance may be puzzling if attributed only to personality or a single situational factor. As stated at the beginning of this chapter, most behavior has multiple causes and is not explainable by single factors.

Situation Refracts Through Self-Concept

All of the situational R factors are interpreted through the individual's self-concept, as if they were light waves *refracted* through water to shine on the pond's interior. The same set of factors may have differential impacts on individuals with different views of themselves, although, as noted earlier, perhaps less often than is usually assumed.

The following example illustrates the interconnections among R factors. The sales manager at Healthco, Inc. had a problem. The turnover rate in his salesforce was too high, and far too many of those who left were women. Knowing his own good intentions about employing women, he assumed that selling to male-dominated groups of physicians and hospitals was probably difficult for women and that they needed more sales-skill training.

This preliminary diagnosis leapt from a problem (turnover) to the conclusion that one situational factor (poor sales skills) was the cause. The sales manager was thus ready to begin a training program.

Fortunately, he was persuaded to allow a more thorough diagnosis. To his surprise, numerous other situational factors were identified:

- Women were assigned easier territories by considerate intention, but as a result they could not prove their worth to their supervisors. If the woman succeeded, the performance was discounted as an easy sale; if she did not do well, no further support was offered.

- From the assumption that women would not want to travel, many territories were not offered to them. Then others believed that the women were inflexible.

- Male salesmen met for drinks and, while together, informally traded information and sales tips. They assumed the women would not want to go drinking, so did not invited them. As a result, women were inadvertently excluded from important learning.

- Secretaries at headquarters flirted and chatted with the unmarried male salesmen, so they knew the men better and readily helped them in preference to the female salespersons.

- The organization had traditionally been male in its orientation, which provoked some supposedly innocent joking and teasing that professional women found insulting.

Indeed, when those women who left were tracked, the survey revealed that many of them had obtained even better sales jobs and were performing successfully. Thus, it was unlikely that chauvinist customers or lack of skills were the causes. The roles, relationships, rewards, and rites were inadvertently stacked against women who wanted to stay.

Not every female salesperson had left, however. A few were challenged by the situation, believed strongly in their ability to overcome the situational obstacles, and did not want to work elsewhere. Despite the general response of women salespeople, one or two had self-concepts that counterbalanced the situational forces.

Results

The reader, like the sales manager at Healthco, is probably interested in *results* of individual behavior to try to produce more successful behavior or alter unsuccessful behavior.

What results are managers interested in? There are at least five important dimensions to pay attention to:

1. *Productivity.* How much does the person produce, for how much input? Does the work get done? Does the right work get done?

2. *Growth/learning.* Is the person learning new skills, developing greater ability to contribute to the organization in the future?

3. *Satisfaction.* Does the person enjoy the work, fellow workers, and the organization?

4. *Commitment.* Does the person genuinely care about the organization and its success? Does he/she want to do what is good for the organization?

5. *Competitive capability.* As a result of the previous four dimensions, does the person's behavior help the company compete better against its rivals, serve customers better, and keep costs down?

Note that any combination of results on these dimensions is possible. Individuals can be ecstatically happy while unproductive; productive at present but learning nothing (and therefore less likely to be productive as tasks, technology, or requirements change); highly committed but frustrated; and so on. Rarely does any set of circumstances produce highly positive results simultaneously in all five dimensions, although that is the goal of many organizations. If trade-offs are necessary, realistic managers try to balance short- and long-term objectives, and realize that over time, attention may have to shift if one dimension falls off too far. (See Figure 2.3 for a summary of all the R factors that affect behavior.)

REVISION/REFORM

What can managers do about results below their standards? Unsatisfactory results usually prompt an attempt to *revise* some or all of the culprit situational and individual factors. A group of workers is choosing to use its technical discovery to finish work early rather than to produce more; a new MBA is productive but her style disturbs her supervisor and co-workers; experienced and new supervisors are at war against each other, affecting productivity; a group of engineers has low morale and slipping productivity; or a newly appointed president of an acquired company finds enormous resistance from his predecessor and the vice-presidents he will have to manage—what can be done? How does the manager who wants to alter current results proceed?

FIGURE 2.3.   All R factors conceptual scheme.

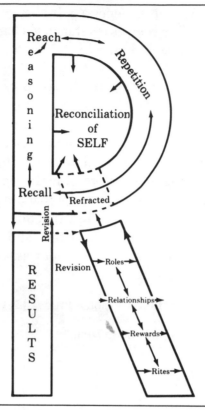

First, it is necessary to do a careful diagnosis, as suggested previously. Since it is easier to change situational R factors than personality R factors, all of the possible causes related to *roles, relationships, rewards,* and *rites* need to be identified. Then those that are most readily in your control can be addressed first. If, for example, tying people's rewards to measures of quality (or other indicators such as safety or customer complaints) will achieve the desired results, much aggravation may be avoided.

Often, however, the situational factors are complex and interwoven, so that one simple change will not achieve the desired results—or worse, it moves performance in the wrong direction. Many grand schemes for change, including the latest and hottest fads, produce unanticipated results because they ignore the interconnected strands that are causing current behavior. Introduction of new technology, for example, does not merely alter a few tasks; it often affects opportunities for interaction, existing social relationships, skills required, status attached to different roles, long-standing rites, and so on.

Care in understanding all the R factors is not just a nuisance dreamed up by behavioral scientists; it is necessary if change is to be successfully accomplished. What is often seen as resistance to change may not be resistance to all change, (unexpected salary bonuses, for example, are seldom resisted). However, expect resistance to appearing unintelligent before peers while learning new skills, to the breakup of established relationships, or to group norms that pressure people not to produce so much that weaker members appear inadequate. Helping those affected by change gain needed competence is beneficial. In general, a close understanding of the web of R factors that are causing behavior and that will be affected by the proposed change, is needed before plunging in; therefore, planning must proceed accordingly. Some ways of approaching the problem follow.

Behavior changes when there is dissatisfaction with the status quo, a vision or model of how things could be better, and a process or pathway for getting to the improved state. This concept was written as a formula by a consultant, David Gleicher, as

$$\text{Change} = (\text{Dissatisfaction} \times \text{Vision} \times \text{Process}) > \text{Cost of change}.$$

We will examine each component in turn.

Managing Dissatisfaction

Dissatisfaction is a motivator for change. This statement not only refers to the manager who wants to change someone else's behavior, but it also applies to those who are the targets of change. People are most responsive to learning when they are moderately dissatisfied; too little, and they don't want to bother; too much is paralyzing. Therefore, if you want to increase a person or group's readiness to change, you need to manage their dissatisfaction. In practice, that often requires finding ways to increase dissatisfaction (suggesting that a happy worker is not always the best worker). This strategy can be accomplished in several ways:

1. Provide data from, or direct contact with, those who use the person's or group's services or products. Whether the "customer" is outside the firm or employees from other departments, they can show how performance needs to be better.
2. Provide other kinds of data on how performance falls short. This can be quantitative and impersonal, or qualitative and personally delivered; however, it should demonstrate important gaps in performance. Effective managers learn to give timely, concrete feedback in a supportive, useful, nonpunitive manner. Most employees want to

please their bosses and co-workers; direct feedback provides the information they need to see what is necessary.

3. Create educational programs that broaden perspectives or teach new skills.

4. Arrange for people to see better ways of doing things in other departments, divisions, or outside companies.

5. Create an exciting vision of some future state in which performance is higher or better quality, satisfaction is greater, and so on.

Creating Vision

The creation of vision can in itself help raise dissatisfaction to increase readiness for change, but vision is also necessary as a natural part of the change process. Without a clear view of the new, desired behavior and conditions, it is hard for even very dissatisfied people to change. The manager needs to create the paradox of a tangible vision, one that is futuristic but vivid enough so the targets of change can understand and be excited about it. The tangible vision needs to be sold to affected members of the organization.

Vision does not simply descend from above. The creation of vision comes from a considerable amount of exploring, analyzing, and rooting around in the territory of the problem. First-hand data, from spending time with the people involved, is almost always needed, along with the more quantitative, impersonal data acquired for analysis. Small experiments or pilots are often helpful, especially if they are genuinely observed for learning and modification, rather than treated as ultimate solutions disguised as "just experiments" so no one will object.

"Getting to know the territory" can provide a clearer picture of what is desired. This knowledge would clarify whether the manager could induce the work group to use its technological discovery to increase productivity; whether the new MBA figured out how to gain the support of old-timers; and not only whether the experienced supervisors taught the new supervisors the ropes, but also if they were stimulated by their own fresh ideas; and so on.

Specifying Procedures/Process

People may be dissatisfied with the present and excited about a future state when all is better, but if they lack the knowledge to get there, frustration increases, and often cynicism sets in. Therefore, it is crucial to create and identify the pathways to achieve the vision. This process entails thinking through a number of issues and acting accordingly.

One place to start is by analyzing (for any particular change) who has an interest in it, who is a stakeholder in some way. For example, if your boss wants you to start using the computer, you are clearly a stakeholder, but so may be your co-workers, the department that receives your work, your boss' boss, the information systems manager, and so forth. Often, the number of stakeholders is far greater than is at first apparent; the manger of a regional office in a federal agency was astounded when, using this tool, she identified 236 stakeholders on a key issue she was trying to resolve. To visualize the concept, place a brief label for the change in the center of a blank page, and draw a circle around it. Then, one at a time add spokes to link it to the name of each possible stakeholder.

Once all the possible stakeholders are identified, then try to determine the following for each:

- What exactly are their stakes in the issue?
- What are their needs/desires in relation to the issue?
- What are their resources in relation to the issue? Information? Allies? Funds or supplies?
- Exactly how will they be affected by the change? Finances? Relationships with others? Status? Influence? Reputation? What might cause them to resist?
- Is their cooperation or goodwill necessary, desirable, or unimportant?

Having done this analysis for each stakeholder, do the same for yourself. What do *you* bring to the issue? Then prioritize those stakeholders most critical to your success. Your attention should first be directed to figuring out what you can offer them from your resources that would fit with their needs or desires, in return for whatever you need from them. Before initiating action, however, try to trace through all the possible implications for all the stakeholders, and plan accordingly. This can be tedious, but it saves aggravation later. Too many good ideas for change have been sunk because the well-intentioned manager did not anticipate who would be affected and how to deal with them.

After the stakeholders have been identified, part of planning is to determine how the resistance of key people (including those directly targeted for changed behavior) can be overcome. For some, clear and accurate information about your plans, progress, and problems will reduce uncertainty. Since no change plan leads to guaranteed results, there is always uncertainty, so anything that can reduce unnecessary uncertainty will be useful.

Another practical way to reduce resistance is to increase the amount of control in the hands of those affected. This end is often best achieved by encouraging their participation in diagnosing the problem(s) and devising solutions. The level of expertise regarding the particular change and the degree to which the change depends upon their cooperation, determine how appropriate will be their participation in shaping it. Occasionally the targets of the change lack relevant expertise and are replaceable if they do not cooperate, but as education levels rise and organizations become more complex, that situation is less often the case. The need is increasing for managers to share responsibility with their subordinates, often as a team. Furthermore, organizational stress occurs when individuals do not have control over much of their life at work. The resulting stress can lead to passivity, overt resistance, or even physical illness and burn out. This negatively affects not only implementation of change, but even everyday work.

As suggested earlier, since almost any change in behavior will require new knowledge or skills, and since most people are embarrassed about appearing awkward while learning, plans need to be made for training and support of learning. Providing training in advance allows time for trial and error, time for peers also to be in the learning situation, and time to identify unanticipated skill gaps that need to be addressed.

If the change involves more than a few people in one area, there may be need for a demonstration project, utilizing participants who are primed for the change, capable of learning what is needed, and eager to cooperate. It is always useful to load early attempts for success (although managers sometimes erroneously begin with their toughest audience, believing that once the change works with them it can work anywhere). Early wins and successes spur future efforts and overcome skepticism.

Another important part of planning is the anticipation of what other changes in related R factors will be necessary to support the change. Given a group of disenchanted engineers, for example, a new committee to allow their input on decisions may require other changes to make it work: new access to information, new tasks, or even altered performance measures. Accurate diagnosis of R factors helps identify the related changes that need to be made.

Again, for complex change projects, creation of a transition management structure addresses all these issues, coordinates this change with others in progress, links to higher management for support or resources, and in general guides the change effort during its introduction while regular work continues. It is difficult to put on new athletic shoes and tie them while running in a marathon, but that feat is analogous to making changes while keeping the work flowing. A special temporary management structure can ease the overload. All of the methods mentioned so far minimize the costs of change.

CONCLUDING REMARKS

Careful diagnosis and planning aid in managing people. Without the understanding of situational forces acting on individuals, the internal factors that determine how the forces are interpreted, or the action steps available to alter behavior causing undesirable results, effective management is only an accident. Yet, managing others requires skill and art as well as careful analysis. Whatever natural talents you have will be enhanced by extensive practice at putting yourself in managerial situations, and a willingness to subsequently reflect on your own behavior to learn from it. Your self-concept, your own attitude and sensitivity toward other people, needs to be open enough to permit constant alterations in your own behavior. You need to view management as an ongoing attempt to find mutual interests and make modifications, not as a test of how much power you have or to what extent you are correct.

No one book can teach you all the skills vital to management, such as to listen carefully to what is important to those with whom you work, to give honest feedback to aid their learning, to judge appropriate times to build concensus from below or to take strong initiatives, to find ways to link your interests to others and the organization, to look carefully before leaping yet be comfortable leaping when an absolute outcome cannot be predicted; and to mix challenge and support. Nevertheless, you need to acquire these skills.

Perhaps a final R factor should be added to the already lengthy list: *reflection*. If you can learn *to learn* from your experience, and practice *revision* on yourself as well as those you want to manage, no single mistake will matter for long. Changing yourself is usually the best way to begin changing others. In your managerial pursuits, my best *regards*.

FOR FURTHER READING

Argyris, Chris, *Interpersonal Competence and Organizational Effectiveness* (Homewood, IL: Irwin & Dorsey Press, 1962).
    One of many books by Argyris that looks closely at interpersonal skills and their impact on ability to manage (or follow).

Bennis, Warren G., and B. Nanus, *Leadership* (New York: Harper & Row, 1985).
A look at diverse leaders and what they have in common, especially emphasizing vision.

Bradford, David L., and Allan R. Cohen, *Managing for Excellence: The Guide to Developing High Performance in Contemporary Organizations* (New York: John Wiley, 1988).
This book presents a new model of leadership, emphasizing the need to go beyond heroic assumptions to create tangible vision, a shared responsibility team and continuous development of subordinates.

Bradford, David L, "Group Dynamics," In *Modules in Management* Series (Chicago: S.R.A., 1984).
Summarizes many important aspects of managing groups at work.

Cohen, Allan R., and David L. Bradford, *Influence Without Authority,* (New York: John Wiley, 1990).
A statement of how exchange and reciprocity can be used to increase influence with peers and superiors.

Combs, A.W., and D. Snygg, *Individual Behavior* (New York: Harper & Row, 1959).
Excellent treatment of the self-concept as an organizing principle shaping individual behavior.

Fiedler, Fred, *A Theory of Leadership Effectiveness* (New York: McGraw-Hill, 1967).
An influential book on the contingencies under which different leadership styles are appropriate.

Herzberg, F., "One More Time: How Do You Motivate Employees?" *Harvard Business Review 46*, 1968, pp. 53–62.
Classic look at factors that work positively to drive behavior versus those that only dissatisfy.

Kanter, Rosabeth M., *The Changemasters: Innovation for Productivity in the American Corporation* (New York: Simon & Schuster, 1983).
A powerful book on how members can achieve change (as well as what organizational conditions increase the likelihood of it).

Kanter, Rosabeth M., *Men and Women of the Corporation,* (New York: Basic Books, 1977).
The best example of how situational factors shape behavior when most people would explain it by personality or gender.

Kotter, John, and Leonard Schlesinger, "Choosing Strategies for Change," *Harvard Business Review,* March–April, 1979.
A good summary of considerations needed for choosing a strategy for managing change.

Mintzberg, Henry, *The Nature of Managerial Work* (New York: Harper & Row, 1973).
A careful look at what managers actually do, and a clear exposition of the interconnection between the relationship requirements of the manager's role and the decision-making roles that are dependent upon relationships.

Trice, H.M., and J.M. Beyer, "Studying Organizational Cultures Through Rites and Ceremonials," *Academy of Management Review,* Oct. 1984, pp. 653–69.
Helps sort out confusions about organizational culture, and shows how rites and ceremonial activities reveal important forces in organizations.

Vroom, V., and P. Yetton, *Leadership and Decision Making* (Pittsburgh: University of Pittsburgh Press, 1973).
An important look at what style of decision making fits which situations.

Whyte, W.F., *Street Corner Society,* (rev. ed), (Chicago: University of Chicago Press, 1955).
A classic study, not inside formal organizations, showing the power of the group on individual behavior.

Zander, A., *Groups at Work* (San Francisco: Jossey-Bass, 1977).
Summarizes much of the small group research as it applies to work groups.

QUANTITATIVE TOOLS: NUMBERS AS THE FUNDAMENTAL LANGUAGE OF BUSINESS

3

Brian Forst

Numbers are the fundamental language of business—the bottom line on the income statement is a number. Efficiency on the production line is expressed numerically; numbers can be improved through statistical analysis and can, in turn, powerfully affect the bottom line. The business plan is expressed specifically as numbers on the operating budget, numbers that may derive largely from statistical projections of revenues and costs. Decisions to invest in assets that can accelerate the growth of the business are usually based on numbers that reflect the expected profits and risks of each alternative use of invested funds. Success and failure of the business or any of its parts typically comes down to numbers.

While it is unnecessary to learn the intricacies of statistics and applied mathematics to gain control of the numbers and improve them, executives and managers stand to gain significantly from knowing that many of their real-world problems can be solved with tools that work with numbers, the tools of quantitative methods. Such knowledge empowers the manager to make the best possible decision of where to turn and what to expect from the computer programs and experts that carry out the detailed problem-solving calculations. This knowledge is bound to improve the business and make the manager more successful.

This chapter provides an overview of these tools and the kinds of problems that they help managers solve. The five sections—statistical estimation and the control of quality, regression analysis as a tool for explaining statistical associations, statistical forecasting, decision analysis, and operations research—use a hypothetical company to illustrate how each tool can improve the bottom line.

STATISTICAL ESTIMATION AND THE CONTROL OF QUALITY

It has been well-established that quality is the key to long-run growth in revenues. A time-tested way to control the *quality of goods* is by inspection as they proceed through the production line, keeping track of the rate at which defects occur. Control of the *quality of service* is achieved by asking customers about the service they have received, keeping track of the proportion who are dissatisfied and why.

However, measuring quality isn't enough. Controlling the quality of production in a manufacturing plant or the quality of customer service by inspecting and measuring goods and customer satisfaction does not eliminate the need for commitment-to-excellence programs, thorough training of production and service personnel, and preventive maintenance of equipment.

If quality begins with a commitment to excellence, it ends with something much more prosaic—measurement. And measurement usually requires sampling. When defective products are capable of imposing grave costs on users, as in the case of faulty automobile brakes, *all* the products must be carefully inspected. Most goods and services, however, do not require 100 percent sampling to ensure that quality is properly controlled. The testing itself may destroy the product, as in the case of foods, disposable goods, and explosives; 100 percent sampling would leave no products for the customer.

For virtually all companies, the problem is this: How can we minimize the total cost of inferior-quality goods and services, taking into account both the cost of inferior quality and the cost of a quality control program?

In a time of intense worldwide competition in the quality of goods and services, this is no academic issue. It is of particular importance to our example company, Power Tools, Inc. You have been appointed to manage this company during the course of this chapter. Power Tools enjoyed industry dominance during the 1950s and 1960s, but has gradually lost business to Asian and European competitors ever since. Your marketing people are sure of the primary cause: The quality of the products made by foreign competitors has surpassed that of your goods, and the customers know it. The marketing vice president supports this claim by a compelling fact: 3 percent of Power Tool's chainsaws and 2 percent of its power drills are returned under the one-year warranty, while the rate of return for your leading competitor is only 1 percent for each of the two products.

To remedy the problem, your engineers disassemble and carefully examine the competitor's chainsaw with a view to understanding and correcting the leading cause of your warranty claims: the central gear assembly. The basic design of the competitor's gear assembly is the same as yours; that finding leaves as a leading candidate for the cause of the problem excessive variability in the dimensions of the gears (length, outside diameter, tooth height, tooth width, etc.) in your products. To validate this suspicion, you compare the variability of a sample of 20 of their gears with 20 of yours. Table 3.1 presents the measurement for the outside diameter of the largest gear in the sample.

Gear variability can be measured in several ways. The simplest measure is the *range*, the difference between the largest and the smallest value in the distribution. For Power Tools, the range is 0.007 (1.158 − 1.151) and for Brand X it is 0.006 (0.976 − 0.970). That seems fairly close, but the Power Tool gear is slightly larger to begin with, and range does not adjust for that. More important, the range is a limited measure in that it considers only two values out of the entire distribution, in this case, ignoring the variability of the other 18 gears in each sample. Other measures of variability (or dispersion) take all 20 observations into account. Three widely used measures that do this are the *standard deviation, variance*, and *coefficient of variation*. The standard deviation is commonly used in quality control problems; the variance, which is the square of the standard deviation, is more commonly used in inquiries into the causes of variability; and coefficient of variation is used to standardize variability by the

TABLE 3.1. Distribution of gear diameters:
Power Tools and leading competitor.

	Power Tools	Brand X		Power Tools	Brand X
1.	1.155	0.976	11.	1.153	0.973
2.	1.157	0.972	12.	1.156	0.973
3.	1.151	0.974	13.	1.156	0.974
4.	1.153	0.974	14.	1.157	0.972
5.	1.158	0.970	15.	1.157	0.973
6.	1.154	0.974	16.	1.152	0.975
7.	1.157	0.973	17.	1.155	0.972
8.	1.151	0.974	18.	1.152	0.972
9.	1.158	0.972	19.	1.158	0.974
10.	1.151	0.971	20.	1.153	0.973

mean value of the distribution. The formulas for calculating these statistics and their values for this example are shown in Table 3.2.

All of the measures of variation other than the range reveal the diameter of the Power Tools' gear to be substantially more variable than that of the competitor's. The standard deviation, as estimated from the sample, is 82 percent larger; the estimated variance is over three times larger; and the sample coefficient of variation is 53 percent larger. The probability that the competitor's gears are in fact as variable as ours—that the observed differences could be due only to randomness for samples of size 20—is virtually zero.

Note also in Table 3.2 the three measures of central tendency or "average" value of the distribution: *mode, median,* and *mean.* the mode is the most commonly observed value in the distribution; the median is the middle value when the observations are sorted; and the mean is the sum of the values divided by the number of values. (The term *average* is perhaps best avoided because it is ambiguous; sometimes it connotes any measure of central tendency, and sometimes it connotes the mean in particular.) The mean is the generally preferred measure of central tendency, although for most applications it doesn't hurt to report all three.

Your primary concern, however, based on analysis of the numbers in Table 3.2, is dispersion around the mean. To improve the quality of your products, you purchase gears from a new vendor with more reliable specifications, modernize the production line, and retrain your production

TABLE 3.2. Basic descriptive statistics and their values for Power Tools and brand X.

Statistic	Definition	Power Tools	Brand X
Fundamental Measures:			
Sum	Σy	23.094	19.461
n	Number of observations	20	20
Measures of Central Tendency:			
Mode	Most common value	1.157	0.974
Median	Middle value	1.155	0.973
Mean	$\bar{y} = \Sigma y \div n$	1.15470	0.97305
Measures of Dispersion:			
Range	Maximum – minimum	0.007	0.006
Standard deviation	$s = \sqrt{\dfrac{\Sigma y^2}{n} - (\bar{y})^2}$	.002472	.001359
Variance	$s^2 = \dfrac{\Sigma y^2}{n} - (\bar{y})^2$	.0000061	.0000018
Coefficient of variation	$s \div \bar{y}$	.002141	.001397

crew. Now you wish to set up a quality control system that will improve your ability to find inferior products before they come into the customer's hands. You set up various quality control tests all along the production line. One is a vibration test of finished goods: The production process should produce chainsaws that operate with about 0.06 millimeter of wobble, with a standard deviation of 0.01 millimeter.

Because this test is more labor intensive than other tests and is one of several, you don't test every unit—only a random sample of five units every two hours, which a quality control expert recommends to you as a sensible balance between the cost of random error associated with small samples and the cost of sampling. Any chainsaw that exceeds 0.10 millimeters of wobble will be disassembled, adjusted, reassembled, and retested. Any sample of five that exceeds the 0.06 production line standard by more than two standard deviations (an arbitrary limit that leads to the rejection of just under 5 percent of all samples) will call for a production process adjustment that will delay production for about an hour.

The standard deviation for the distribution of means for samples of size n is given by the formula $s_n = s \div \sqrt{n}$. Since the standard deviation for a single product is 0.01, for our sample of five, two standard deviations beyond the production line standard of 0.06 will give a boundary of acceptable products of $0.06 + (2)*[(0.01) \div \sqrt{5}]$, or 0.0689.

This result can be displayed on a *quality control chart,* a useful tool to monitor the quality of products by graphing the results of periodic samples of products. If the production line runs from 8:00 A.M. until 6:00 P.M., and five units are sampled during each two-hour period, the quality control chart for Power Tools, Inc., for one week will look like Figure 3.1.

The quality standard of 0.0600 is shown as the horizontal line at the center of the chart, and the lines above and below represent variations of

FIGURE 3.1.   Quality control chart.

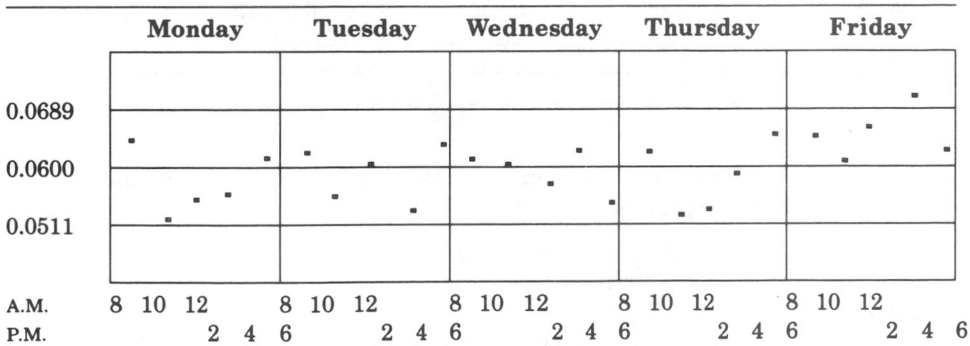

two standard deviations from that level in either direction. In many production processes, parts are rejected if they fall outside of either of the two standard deviation boundaries, since uniformity of part size is usually the primary objective; in this case, we are concerned only if the wobble exceeds the top line, at 0.0689 millimeters.

How likely is it that a sample will exceed that limit? Let's rephrase this question in more specific terms, so that the answer can be more clearly derived: If we take repeated samples of five per sample and measure the mean wobble for each sample, what will the distribution of those mean values look like, and what fraction of the distribution will have mean values that exceed 0.0689?

First, how will the distribution look? Under a basic proposition known as the *central limit theorem,* the distribution of repeated samples will take on the shape of the familiar bell-shaped *normal distribution,*[1] regardless of the shape of the distribution of items taken one at a time (which in this case is also normal). The distribution for this example, with a mean of 0.0600, a standard deviation for the parent distribution of 0.010, and $n = 5$, is shown in Figure 3.2.

The probability that a sample will exceed the 0.06894 boundary is the proportion of the curve that is shaded. To find the area under a normal curve, we can go to a book of standard statistical tables or to a computer

FIGURE 3.2. **Distribution of mean values from repeated samples** ($\bar{y} = 0.060$; $s = 0.01$; $n = 5$).

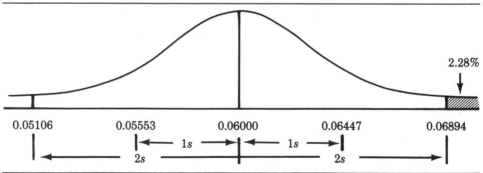

[1] For the reader with a background in mathematics or engineering, the normal distribution is defined by the expression

$$\frac{1}{s_y\sqrt{2\pi}}\, e^{-(y-\bar{y})^2/\, 2s_y^2},$$

where

$$\pi = 3.14159 \text{ and } e = 2.71828.$$

program that gives areas under a special normal curve—one that is standardized with mean = 0 and standard deviation = 1. Doing so yields the following information: 15.87 percent of the curve lies beyond the one standard deviation mark above (or below) the mean, in this case beyond the value 0.06447, and 2.28 percent lies beyond the two standard deviation mark, 0.06894. Therefore, we can expect over 2 percent of all samples of five chainsaws to have a mean wobble of more than the 0.06894.

Should we assume that such occurrences are just due to luck of the draw, or *random error,* with no need to adjust the production process? Absolutely not. When the production process is working properly, it will produce samples with values that *exceed* the acceptable limit 2 percent of the time, but *the production process does not always operate at that standard!* Some errors are *nonrandom.* A common sense look at the data shown in Figure 3.1 suggests that Friday's production process was operating above the 0.060 standard all day, and quite possibly an extension of a trend that started the previous day, not just a stroke of bad luck for the period from 2:00 to 4:00. Five successive samples above the standard for an entire day suggests that something else may be going on. Such patterns are often caused by factors that are well-known to the staff on the production line: excessive pressure to meet accelerated end-of-week production schedules, key people out sick, beer-soaked TGIF lunches, and so on. Regardless of the underlying causes, simple descriptive statistics, properly organized, can be potent tools for ferreting out the patterns that, when known, provide the basis for action.

REGRESSION ANALYSIS AS A TOOL FOR EXPLAINING ASSOCIATIONS

The data graphed in Figure 3.1 reveal some random fluctuations and the prospect of a nonrandom "Friday" effect, but a closer look suggests more: A daily cycle is also evident. The mid-day products tend to be better than those produced at either the start or end of the day. But you are viewing only one week's data. By retrieving data for several weeks, you could establish more conclusively the existence of both a daily cycle and the Friday phenomenon. Such findings could induce you to inquire into the causes of these patterns. In the meantime, you can use the data graphed in Figure 3.1 and reported in Table 3.3 to test both the Friday and mid-day effects.

Here is how: You speculate that the amount of wobble is determined in part by whether the day is Friday, in part by whether it is mid-day

TABLE 3.3. Quality control data for one week of production.

Time	Monday	Tuesday	Wednesday	Thursday	Friday
8–10	.0641	.0618	.0612	.0618	.0641
10–12	.0522	.0552	.0605	.0529	.0612
12–2	.0552	.0604	.0575	.0535	.0659
2–4	.0559	.0545	.0621	.0588	.0699
4–6	.0612	.0629	.0559	.0639	.0621

(between 10:00 A.M. and 4:00 P.M.), and in part by random forces. Then you designate the amount of wobble as the variable y, the day of the week as x_1 ($x_1 = 1$ if Friday, $x_1 = 0$ if any other day), and the time of day as x_2 ($x_2 = 1$ if mid-day, $x_2 = 0$ if either before 10:00 A.M. or after 4:00 P.M.); and you write the linear equation

$$y = a + bx_1 + cx_2 + r.e. \tag{1}$$

where a, b, and c are coefficients you want to estimate with your data, and r.e. represents random error, a factor assumed to be normally distributed with a mean of zero.

This equation is your model of the relationship between vibration and three hypothesized determinants of vibration: the Friday effect (you think it may increase vibration), the mid-day effect (you think it may decrease vibration), and the random effect (all the other factors that affect vibration). The variable being explained or predicted, y, is called the *dependent variable*, and the variables used as explainers or predictors, x_1 and x_2, are the *independent variables*. In this case, the independent variables are *binary* (often called "dummy") *variables*, that is, variables that can assume only the values zero or one. You use a linear equation both because you have no compelling reason to believe the relationship is nonlinear and because a linear equation is simpler to estimate than other equations.

If you can now imagine this equation as a plane in a space containing the 25 dots that represent the observations of one week, any number of planes can "fit" your 25 data points reasonably well; but statisticians have developed the *least squares* criterion, under which you should choose the plane with the coefficients that minimize the sum of the squared vertical deviations from each observation to the plane. Your 25 data points to be used for estimating the equation of this plane are shown in Table 3.4.

To estimate the parameters (i.e., the true coefficients of the relationship, as distinct from the coefficient values obtained from the sample) of Equation 1, you enter the data points into a computer that can perform *regression analysis*.

TABLE 3.4.   Data for regression estimate to explain variation in quality.

	y	x_1	x_2		y	x_1	x_2
1	.0641	0	0	14	.0621	0	1
2	.0522	0	1	15	.0559	0	0
3	.0552	0	1	16	.0618	0	0
4	.0559	0	1	17	.0529	0	1
5	.0612	0	0	18	.0535	0	1
6	.0618	0	0	19	.0588	0	1
7	.0552	0	1	20	.0639	0	0
8	.0604	0	1	21	.0641	1	0
9	.0545	0	1	22	.0612	1	1
10	.0629	0	0	23	.0659	1	1
11	.0612	0	0	24	.0699	1	1
12	.0605	0	1	25	.0621	1	0
13	.0575	0	1				

Regression analysis was once done either on a large mainframe computer or with some effort using a calculator and a pad of paper; today, it can be done easily on a personal computer with any modern spreadsheet program, such as Lotus 1-2-3®, or standard statistical analysis software. For the data in Table 3.4, the linear equation with the least squares property is

$$y = .060681 + .006067*x_1 - .00351*x_2 \quad r^2 = .461$$
$$(.003427)\ (.001713) \quad (.001399) \tag{2}$$

Or using words, you can estimate the amount of wobble by taking the constant .060681, adding .06067 to it if the saw was produced on Friday (don't subtract .06067 if it was produced on another day), and then subtracting from it .00351 if the saw was produced between 10:00 A.M. and 4:00 P.M. The r^2 statistic is the *coefficient of determination;* it can be interpreted as follows: 46.1 percent of the variance in y is accounted for (or explained) by the variables x_1 and x_2. The numbers in parentheses below the estimated regression coefficients are *standard errors of estimates* which are needed for testing whether the coefficients themselves are "statistically significant"—that is, whether they are different enough from zero to allow you to say that it is just too unlikely that such differences are attributable to chance alone. You can determine whether a coefficient is significant by dividing the coefficient by its standard error, thus getting the *t statistic.* Some sample t statistics and their significance levels are shown in Table 3.5. The *degrees of freedom* are the number of observations (n) minus the total number of variables in the regression equation. For your problem, there are 25 observations and 3 variables in the regression equation, yielding 22 degrees of freedom.

TABLE 3.5. t Statistics and corresponding significance levels.

Degrees of Freedom	Significance Levels		
	.10	.05	.01
10	1.81	2.23	3.17
20	1.73	2.09	2.85
30	1.70	2.04	2.75
40	1.68	2.02	2.70
50	1.68	2.01	2.68
100	1.66	1.98	2.63
∞	1.64	1.96	2.58

To establish the effect of time of day and day of week on the quality of your chainsaws, you obtain t statistics of 3.54 for the day-of-week effect (.006067/.001713) and −2.51 for the time-of-day effect (−.00351/.001399). From Table 3.5, with 22 degrees of freedom, we can see that these results are significant at .01 and .05, respectively.

Here is what the figures mean: If there were no day-of-week effect, you would obtain a statistical association between product vibration and day of week as strong as you did less than 1 percent of the time just due to randomness and, if there were no time-of-day effect, you would obtain this same association less than 5 percent of the time just due to randomness. If you are not yet convinced that the patterns are real rather than random and if you perceive that the value of further investigation exceeds the cost, you can retrieve data from additional weeks and analyze them the same way to see whether higher levels of statistical significance result.

How Much Quality?

One of the most basic quality control issues is this: How much quality control is enough? Earlier, it was suggested that the right amount takes into account both the cost of controlling quality and the cost of inferior quality. Specifically, the right amount is the point at which the cost of additional quality control *begins* to exceed the additional benefit of higher quality. To know that level, you must know not only the cost of the quality control program—which includes the labor cost of the program, the cost of destroying materials in sampling, and the cost of production downtime associated with quality control improvements—but also the benefit of higher quality (or the cost of inferior quality) and the relationship between the quality control program and product quality.

The benefit of higher quality should show up in subsequent revenues, as we will see in the next section. Other factors are bound to influence revenues too, factors that may be related to the quality control program, making it more difficult to isolate the effect of the program on revenues. For example, a new manager may introduce a quality control program and a host of other stimulants to revenues at the same time, in which case one could easily make the mistake of attributing higher revenues to the quality control program rather than the new manager or his or her other programs. Alternatively, one could assess the benefit of a quality control program using a measure more directly related to quality than revenue, such as the rate of customer complaints or product returns, and regressing that variable on the cost of the program and its other measurable characteristics in earlier periods.

As a practical matter, the strength of the relationship is more likely to be presumed as an article of faith. Most U.S. companies have begun to see that they have been underspending on quality control programs for years.

STATISTICAL FORECASTING—USING DATA TO ANTICIPATE THE FUTURE

We have seen that regression analysis helps to *explain* relationships among variables. When we can state a plausible theory in terms of an equation with a dependent variable and a set of explanatory independent variables, the least-squares method of regression analysis offers a tried-and-true way to estimate the parameters of the model and draw useful inferences about the factors that cause the dependent variable to take on specific values. Until you examined Figure 3.1 and ran the regression analysis to validate what the graph suggested, it might never have occurred to you that Friday and the start and end of each work day were problems that deserved scrutiny.

We may, after all, have been incorrect about the structure of the model. It may not be linear; it may consist of more than a single equation; and the explanatory variables in the model may be stand-ins for other variables that are not measured. In our example, the variable "Friday" stands in for certain behaviors of the people working on the production line, behaviors that are related to Friday and perhaps to other events. Even with such distorted representations, the regression model may serve as an extremely useful way of explaining relationships among those variables for which we do have data.

Predicting Quality

Regression analysis is useful for more than explaining relationships among variables of interest; it is useful also for *prediction*. If you had no other basis for predicting the result of the quality control test for product vibration by time of day and day of week, the regression result of Equation 2, $y = .060681 + .006067*x_1 - .00351*x_2$, could be used as a basis for predicting next week's test result; that prediction is shown in Figure 3.3.

Of course, more than a week of data would be better. Just as more data improve our ability to explain relationships among variables more reliably, data also improve our ability to predict or forecast values of dependent variables more accurately. Additional data tend to improve the accuracy of predictions by reducing both random and nonrandom errors. The greater the amount of data, the less the random error because the estimate becomes more *precise* —the variance of the distribution of predicted values tends to decline as the number of observations used to produce the regression increases. Additional data can also reduce nonrandom error by producing estimates that are less *biased*. In our example, there may be a quality cycle within the month or year, such as a month-end or a seasonal effect, that we cannot learn about with one week's data. Our regression result, based on one week of data, will produce biased parameter estimates for a week that happens to be in a different phase of a monthly or seasonal cycle.

Forecasting Sales

You have worked hard now to analyze and improve the quality of your products so that your market share could expand, and now you wish to bring the same analytic power to help you forecast revenues, so that you

FIGURE 3.3. Quality control prediction.

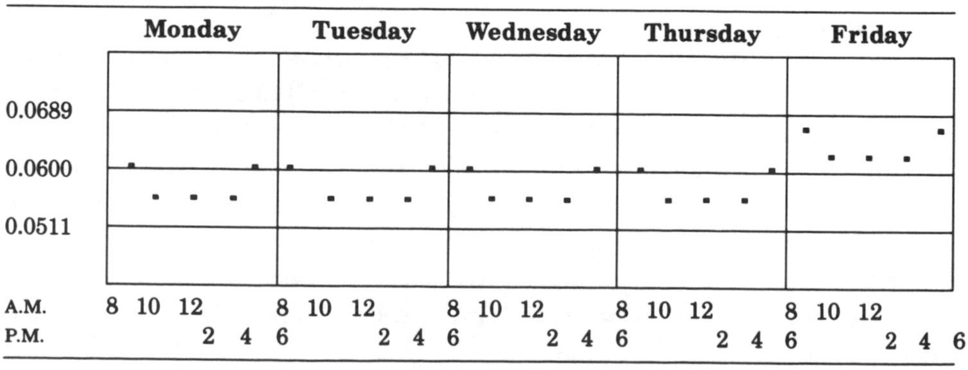

can develop your operating budget for the coming year. Suppose that you have been tracking your sales now for five years, and wish to forecast sales for the next four quarters. Your numbers for the past 20 quarters are shown in Table 3.6.

You can project sales for the next four quarters by estimating the parameters of the regression equation

$$y = a + bx_0 + cx_1 + dx_2 + ex_3 \tag{3}$$

where y is the quarterly sales for Power Tools, x_0 is the year (from 1 to 5, historically), x_1 is a binary variable representing the first quarter (1 if first quarter, 0 otherwise), and x_2 and x_3 are corresponding binary variables for the second and third quarters, respectively. The result is

$$y = -189450 + 769750x_0 - 371600x_1 - 65000x_2 + 109800x_3 \tag{4}$$

with $r^2 = .970$, which means that this model explains all but 3 percent of the variance in quarterly sales. (We don't show the standard errors or t statistics here; those are more useful for models designed to explain relationships than for those designed to predict values of a dependent variable.) From this result, you are able to forecast the sales for the coming year by quarter (in thousands of dollars):

Q_1	Q_2	Q_3	Q_4
4057	4364	4538	4429

You might be able to improve these forecasts and learn something useful along the way with different data. The model we have just estimated is a *naive* model—it ignores all causal factors that may influence your firm's sales. It provides a rough-and-ready basis for projecting sales. In this case, however, explaining sales is also critical, especially to your marketing people.

One factor that you strongly suspect will influence your revenue statistics is the quality of your products, as reflected by the proportion of your products that are returned under the one-year warranty in the previous quarter; let's call this x_4. Another factor you are pretty sure will drive

TABLE 3.6. Power Tools, Inc. revenues by quarter ($000's).

Quarter	19X1	19X2	19X3	19X4	19X5
Q_1	331	802	1827	2685	3096
Q_2	392	1253	2005	3212	3412
Q_3	466	1393	2441	3230	3618
Q_4	468	1485	2258	3118	3270

your sales is the health of the construction industry. Therefore, you find a statistical almanac and obtain the construction industry component of the quarterly data on the gross national product (x_5, in \$billions). Your revenues by quarter are still y. The data are shown in Table 3.7.

Note that the year and quarter variables used in the previous model are excluded here. You exclude them because the construction data already contain both the annual trend and the seasonal variation that influence your sales figures, and because you have only 20 observations and wish to preserve degrees of freedom. You then put these numbers into your electronic spreadsheet and obtain the following regression result:

$$y = 3{,}459{,}989 - 146{,}444{,}000x_4 + 23{,}410.8x_5 \quad r^2 = .987 \qquad (5)$$
$$\quad (138{,}005) \quad (6{,}017{,}816) \quad (4907.0)$$

With this result, you have reduced the unaccounted-for variance in y from 3.0 percent to 1.3 percent; along the way, you learn that product quality and construction industry revenues drive your own revenue numbers, both having t statistics well above 4. Then, by predicting that your product return rate will remain at 0.9 percent all year and plugging trade association forecasts of next year's construction industry component of GNP (48.0, 57.9, 61.5, and 47.9, respectively) into Equation 5, you get a more modest (because you are assuming an end to the improvement in quality) set of sales projections for next year (in thousands of dollars):

Q_1	Q_2	Q_3	Q_4
3267	3497	3581	3262

An important element of this forecast is that it serves to remind you that you have some control over the success of your business. Unlike the naive models of Equations 3 and 4, this result says that you can increase

TABLE 3.7. Data for regression estimate to predict quarterly revenues.

	y	x_4	x_5		y	x_4	x_5
1	331	.027	30.1	11	2441	.015	50.7
2	392	.028	38.5	12	2258	.013	35.8
3	466	.027	41.2	13	2685	.012	39.8
4	468	.025	29.5	14	3212	.010	49.9
5	802	.024	32.2	15	3230	.011	55.0
6	1253	.020	41.7	16	3118	.009	41.1
7	1393	.021	43.0	17	3096	.010	42.6
8	1485	.018	32.3	18	3412	.010	54.4
9	1827	.017	37.3	19	3618	.008	59.2
10	2005	.015	46.6	20	3270	.009	42.4

revenues by \$146,444 per quarter for each 0.001 reduction in the rate at which customers return your product: Improve quality and you will improve sales.

Time Series Forecasts

Even though they offer little by way of explaining causal relationships among variables, naive models can still be extremely useful for forecasting. Models that forecast a variable based strictly on past patterns of movement of the variable over time are naive models known as *time series* models. The central idea of time series forecasting (or time series analysis) is that data ordered over time can be decomposed into three distinct parts: an underlying trend (up, down, or flat); cycles (daily, weekly, seasonal, etc.); and irregular fluctuations. Equations 3 and 4 exemplify how a regression model can decompose the variance: x_0 is the trend variable; x_1, x_2, and x_3 are aspects of a cycle; and the unexplained (or residual) variance is the third part.

Another method of time series analysis is the *moving average* time series method. This approach differs from the regression approach, which is calculated in a single operation, in that it proceeds in stages: First, measure and project the trend, then smooth the data to measure the cycle, and finally adjust the initial projection to account for the average cycle.

Let's see how this works with your last 20 quarters of sales data, shown in Table 3.7. First, the trend is estimated by fitting a regression line to the 20 sales values:

$$y = a + bx \tag{6}$$

where y is your firm's quarterly sales and x is the corresponding quarter number ($x = 1, 2 \ldots 20$). The least squares result is

$$y = 42563 + 190051x \qquad r^2 = .967 \tag{7}$$

By plugging x values from 21 through 24 into Equation 7, you can project sales for the coming year unadjusted for the quarterly cycle:

Q_{21}	Q_{22}	Q_{23}	Q_{24}
4034	4224	4414	4604

Next you isolate the quarterly cycle using a four-period moving average. The moving average technique smooths the data so that an adjustment factor can be calculated for each phase of the cycle. The worksheet for carrying out this exercise is shown in Table 3.8.

TABLE 3.8. Estimating the quarterly adjustment factors using the moving average method.

(1)	(2)	(3) 4 Qtr Moving Sum	(4) 4 Qtr Moving Average	(5) Centered Moving Average	(6) Adjustment Factors (Column 2 / Column 5)	(7)	(8)	(9)
Qtr	Sales				Phase 1	Phase 2	Phase 3	Phase 4
1	331							
2	392							
		1657	414.3					
3	466			473.13	0.98494			
		2128	532.0					
4	468			639.63		0.73168		
		2989	747.3					
5	802			863.13			0.92918	
		3916	979.0					
6	1253			1106.13				1.13278
		4933	1233.3					
7	1393			1361.38	1.02323			
		5958	1489.5					
8	1485			1583.50		0.93780		
		6710	1677.5					
9	1827			1808.50			1.01023	
		7758	1939.5					
10	2005			2036.13				0.98471
		8531	2132.8					
11	2441			2240.00	1.08973			
		9389	2347.3					
12	2258			2498.13		0.90388		
		10596	2649.0					
13	2685			2747.63			0.97721	
		11385	2846.3					
14	3212			2953.75				1.08743
		12245	3061.3					
15	3230			3112.63	1.03771			
		12656	3164.0					
16	3118			3189.00		0.97774		
		12856	3214.0					
17	3096			3262.50			0.94897	
		13244	3311.0					
18	3412			3330.00				1.02462
		13396	3349.0					
19	3618							
20	3270							
				Means:	1.03390	0.88777	0.96640	1.05739

In Columns 3 to 5, we create the smoothed data. Since each number in Column 5 is based on exactly one year's worth of data, the result is purged of the cycle; since each is based on four observations, much of the unaccounted-for variation is dampened as well. In the last four columns, the ratio of the actual to the smoothed number is created for each phase of the cycle; these ratios are then averaged to provide the four adjustment factors at the bottom of the worksheet.[2] The four unadjusted quarterly projections are then divided by these adjustment factors to create the final projections. Here is the end result:

$$\frac{Q_{21}}{3901} \quad \frac{Q_{22}}{4758} \quad \frac{Q_{23}}{4567} \quad \frac{Q_{24}}{4354}$$

OTHER FORECASTING TECHNIQUES AND APPLICATIONS

Regression analysis and moving average method of time series analysis are two of the most commonly applied forecasting tools used in business,[3] largely because they are robust yet easy to use. However, they are not the only ways to forecast the numbers that are critical to the success of the business. Other forecasting techniques range from qualitative approaches, such as juries of expert opinion and subjective estimates of the sales staff, to highly sophisticated statistical methods of time series analysis, such as the Box-Jenkins and spectral analysis methods.

We have seen how such techniques can forecast quality and sales, but they are also useful for estimating future levels of a host of other factors that influence the success of the business. They are important in strategic planning to project consumer demographics that can be critical to your ability to anticipate future consumption patterns. They are useful in marketing—to estimate the effects of changes in pricing policy on sales volume and market share. They can be used in accounting—to provide a basis for estimating reserves for bad debts based on the company's history

---

[2]Some analysts prefer to create the adjustment factors using a measure of central tendency other than the mean, such as the median or the geometric mean (the square root of the product of the column elements), since the column elements are ratios and the arithmetic mean of a series of ratios is subject to distortion when the denominator of one or more of the ratios approaches zero. In most real-world applications, use of the mean is acceptable.

[3]Steven C. Wheelwright and Darral G. Clark, "Corporate Forecasting: Promise and Reality," *Harvard Business Review* (November-December 1976), reprinted in the *HBR* publication no. 17055, *Planning: Part V*, p. 101. Wheelwright and Clarke's results were based on a survey of 127 U.S. companies.

of uncollectables by the characteristics of the products, services, and customers.

Decision Analysis

Your actions to improve the quality of Power Tools products have helped to increase the company's revenues, and your improved projections of future business have strengthened the company's planning and budgeting performance, but you can continue the turnaround of the company in several other areas.

One critical area is the need to expand. Your production facility in Atlanta has started generating profits, but it is now operating at full capacity, unable to satisfy the current demand. Your markets in the West have begun to grow faster than your other markets. With this in mind, you have narrowed the list of candidate sites for building or purchasing a facility in that region to Phoenix and Los Angeles. You have determined that it is much less expensive to purchase and convert an existing facility than to build a new one. The estimated capital and operating costs of the two prospective sites are ready to review—the present values of those costs over a 25-year horizon amount to $15 million for Los Angeles and $12 million for Phoenix. You also estimate the future stream of gross profits for the two facilities under a best case scenario, a most likely case scenario, and a worst case scenario. The present values of gross profits in each case and their accompanying probabilities are shown in Table 3.9.

A sound basis for deciding what to do is provided by a set of techniques known as *decision analysis*. Problems that lend themselves to solution by decision analysis are ones in which a decision maker confronts two or more alternative courses of action, each action having measurable outcomes that are contingent on forces beyond the decision maker's control. When the decision maker can assign probabilities to the contingencies, decision analysis offers a framework for selecting among the options. The problem at hand has all of the ingredients for solution by decision analysis.

TABLE 3.9.   Present values of gross profit streams ($ millions): Two prospective sites and three scenarios.

Scenario	Probability	Los Angeles	Phoenix
Best case	.20	$25	$20
Most likely	.60	20	17
Worst case	.20	9	9

The basic procedure of decision analysis is to lay out the set of available courses of action and contingencies in the form of a *decision tree* (Figure 3.4), calculate the *expected value* of each available option, and then select the option that offers the largest expected return (or smallest expected loss) to the decision maker.

The present value of profit figures in Figure 3.4 result from subtracting the present value of capital and operating costs for Los Angeles ($15 million) or Phoenix ($12 million) from the corresponding present value of gross profit figures shown in the last two columns of Table 3.9. For example, the best case scenario for Los Angeles is $25 million minus $15 million, or $10 million. An *expected value* is defined as an amount times the probability of that amount occurring; the expected value of the best case scenario for Phoenix is the amount $8 million times the probability of obtaining that amount, .2, or $1.6 million. The expected value of any alternative course of action is the sum of the expected values of all possible outcomes; the expected value across all contingencies is $4 million for Phoenix, $3.8 million for Los Angeles, and $0 for the status quo, no expansion. If expected profit were all that mattered and if you were indifferent to incurring risk,[4] your choice would be to set up the facility in Phoenix, since you could "expect" the equivalent of $200,000 more profit in Phoenix than in Los Angeles. If, on the other hand, you were a

FIGURE 3.4.   Decision tree for site selection problem.

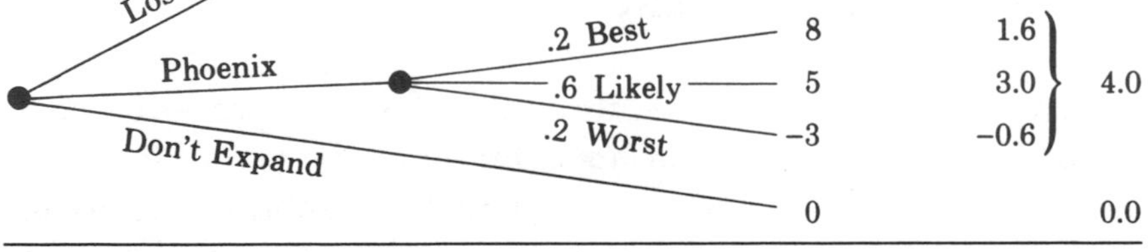

		Present Value of Profit ($ millions)	Expected Value
Los Angeles	.2 Best	10	2.0
	.6 Likely	5	3.0 } 3.8
	.2 Worst	−6	−1.2
Phoenix	.2 Best	8	1.6
	.6 Likely	5	3.0 } 4.0
	.2 Worst	−3	−0.6
Don't Expand		0	0.0

---

[4]Decision analysis can deal with risk explicitly by assessing the decision maker's willingness to incur risk through a series of questions (e.g., what is the most you would pay to obtain a 50–50 chance of winning $100,000?) and then representing the decision maker's risk preference or aversion with a *utility function*. The decision maker then selects the available course of action that maximizes *expected utility*, rather than expected profits.

risk taker drawn to the larger profit for Los Angeles under the best case scenario, or if you had a nonpecuniary attachment to Los Angeles that was worth more than $200,000, you would be inclined to select Los Angeles for your second production facility.

Your ability to make decisions under conditions of uncertainty can be enhanced significantly by making each essential aspect of the decision problem explicit in a decision tree, assigning probabilities to contingencies beyond your control that affect the final result, and calculating the expected value for each available option under your control. If you don't like the result, you can ask yourself why you don't—you may have left out an important factor or factors to which you might assign a dollar value equivalent (e.g., the amount that your firm would be willing to pay for a twofold reduction in pollution or in the risk of labor unrest) and then include that explicitly in the analysis.

Decision analysis becomes increasingly useful as the problem grows more complex. You could, for example, analyze whether to spend $50,000 to conduct surveys in Los Angeles and Phoenix that would improve your estimates of the probabilities and the contingent outcomes by certain amounts; you could consider sites other than Los Angeles and Phoenix; you could explicitly account for a host of intangible factors by assigning equivalent dollar amounts to advantages and disadvantages of each site (weather, access to athletic and cultural activities, etc.); you could build in your aversion to risk; and so on. Decision analysis derives power from its ability to assist you in dealing with such complexity by following an ancient maxim: Divide your problem into manageable parts, thus enhancing your ability to conquer it.

OPERATIONS RESEARCH AND THE IMPROVEMENT OF EFFICIENCY

The quantitative tools we have been using thus far to improve the company's performance are grounded in *statistics;* they have to do with drawing *inferences* from the data to inform and thus enhance decisions. Another set of quantitative tools, belonging to a field commonly known as *operations research*, is grounded in *applied mathematics;* these tools help to solve problems *deductively.* Just as you don't have to be a statistician to know what kinds of problems lend themselves to solutions involving statistical methodology, neither do you have to be a mathematician to know what kinds of problems lend themselves to solutions involving operations research methods.

Inventory Management Models

One widely used class of operations research models aims at more efficient inventory management. For firms that have large amounts of capital tied up in inventory or that frequently lose sales because their inventory keeps running out, more efficient inventory management can result in substantial increases in profit. Inventory includes raw materials, work in process, and finished goods; *inventory management models* deal primarily with the problems of how often to order more raw materials and how much to order, and how many goods to produce during a period to keep the finished goods inventory at the right level.

What levels are the right levels? You should aim for the *economic order quantity,* the level that balances two kinds of inventory costs: *holding (or carrying) costs,* which increase with the amount of inventory ordered, and *order costs,* which decrease with the amount ordered. (See Figure 3.5.)

The largest components of holding costs for most companies are the cost of space to store the inventory and the cost of tying up capital in inventory, capital that could otherwise be used either to obtain assets that increase profits or to pay off debt that imposes interest costs on the firm. Other components of holding costs include the labor costs associated with inventory maintenance, insurance costs, and costs associated with deterioration, spoilage, and obsolescence.

The costs of more frequent orders include lost discounts for larger quantity purchases; labor and supply costs of writing the orders, paying the bills and processing the paperwork; associated telephone and mail costs; and the labor costs of processing and inspecting incoming inventory.

FIGURE 3.5.   The economic order quantity.

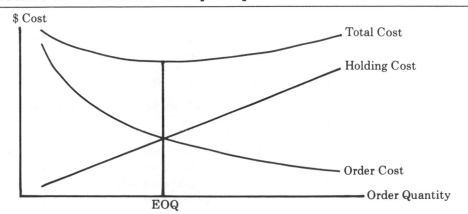

Notice that the economic order quantity—the size of order that minimizes the total of holding and ordering costs—is the amount at which holding costs equal order costs. The economic order quantity (EOQ) can be expressed in more detailed terms:

$$EOQ = \sqrt{\frac{2UO}{H}} \qquad (8)$$

where U is the number of units used annually, O is the order cost per order, and H is the holding cost per unit.[5]

This inventory management model can help you at Power Tools. Your raw materials inventory for chainsaws has averaged $500,000, with a $1 million purchase every six months to satisfy the annual demand for 40,000 saws. You have calculated that it costs a total of $20 to hold the raw materials for one saw per year and $50 to place an order for more material. So your economic order quantity for chainsaws is

$$EOQ = \sqrt{\frac{2 \times 40,000 \times 50}{20}} = \sqrt{200,000} = 447 \qquad (9)$$

How much of an improvement is this amount over your current practice of an order for parts for 20,000 saws every six months? Currently, your costs come to $200,000 of holding costs (10,000 of average inventory times $20 in holding cost per saw) plus $100 of order costs (two orders at $50 per order), or $200,100 of total cost annually for your raw materials inventory. Under the EOQ ordering policy, your costs will come to $4470 of holding costs (223.5 of average inventory times $20 in holding cost per saw) plus $4470 of order costs (89.4 orders—about seven orders every four weeks—at $50 per order), or $8940 of total cost annually—a cost reduction of $191,160. It's not called the economic order quantity for nothing!

---

[5]This formula can be derived by writing the equation

Total costs = Holding costs + Order costs

then expressing holding costs as the product of the average inventory level times the holding cost per unit per year, H; replacing the average inventory level with one half the quantity ordered per order; expressing order costs as the product of the number of orders placed per year times the order cost per order, O; replacing the number of orders per year with the total annual demand divided by the quantity ordered per order; taking the derivative of total costs with respect to the quantity ordered per order and setting it equal to zero; and solving for the quantity ordered per order.

Linear Programming

You can produce further economies by using other operations research models. One widely used class of such models comes under the heading of *linear programming*. Developed around 1950 as a way of maximizing some desirable quantity (or minimizing an undesirable one) that is subject to one or more constraints, linear programming is useful for a variety of problems: allocating scarce resources to jobs, finding the best mix of inputs in accomplishing some objective, routing resources through a complex network, and determining the least cost flow of goods from a set of production facilities to a set of warehouses or retail outlets. When a measurable objective to be maximized or minimized and a set of quantifiable constraints can all be expressed as linear algebraic statements, with at least as many unique statements as variables in the system, we have the fundamental elements of the linear programming problem.

Optimal Mix Problem

Suppose, for example, that the two Power Tools, Inc. production lines at your Atlanta facility can be set up for power saws or power drills; that production line A has 36 hours of time available for saws and drills this week while production line B has 30 hours of available time; a power saw takes 2 hours to go through each production line while each power drill requires 2 hours on production line A and 1 hour on line B; the marginal profit is $50 per saw and $30 per drill; and your company can sell as many of each product as it can produce this week. Your problem is to determine how many of each product to produce. If we let

$$x_1 = \text{the number of saws}$$

and

$$x_2 = \text{the number of drills,}$$

your objective is to maximize profit, $50x_1 + 30x_2$, subject to the constraints:

$$2x_1 + 2x_2 \leq 36 \text{ for production line A}$$
$$2x_1 + x_2 \leq 30 \text{ for production line B}$$

and

$$x_1, x_2 \geq 0$$

The last equation states that you can't produce negative amounts of either saws or drills.

A standard way of solving this problem is by graphing the constraints, shading the resulting polygon that represents the area of all feasible solutions, and then observing the value of the *objective function* (i.e., the expression being maximized or minimized; in this case, the profit line $50x_1 + 30x_2$) as it passes through each corner of the polygon. This process and the optimal solution are shown in Figure 3.6. The objective function passes through the polygon of feasible solutions at an infinite number of points. Figure 3.6 shows the function for the profit levels $200, $400, and $600.) However, the firm's profit is maximized at one point: $x_1 = 12$ and $x_2 = 6$. By producing 12 saws and 6 drills, your firm will satisfy the capacity constraints for both production lines and produce a profit of $780, higher than for any other feasible combination of saws and drills.

Transportation Problem

Another major area of Power Tools, Inc.'s business that has potential for improvement is transportation costs. Your firm's increase in revenues has brought with it a substantial increase in transportation costs. The company has grown to the point where your production facilities in Phoenix and Atlanta are now shipping finished goods to three warehouses—in Los Angeles, Chicago, and New York, and you suspect that your system of routing goods to the warehouses is inefficient.

FIGURE 3.6.   Graphical solution to an optimal mix problem.

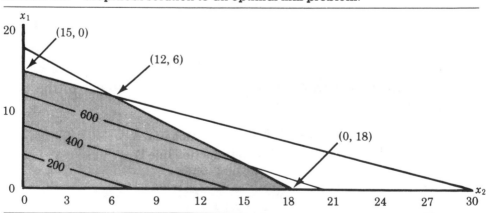

Your sales projections indicate the need for 8000 power drills next year in Los Angeles, 8000 in Chicago, and 10,000 in New York. Your production facility in Phoenix can make and distribute up to 15,000 drills, and your Atlanta facility can produce 13,000 drills per year, assuming last year's mix of drills and saws.[6] The cost of shipping a drill from each production facility to each warehouse is shown in Table 3.10.

If you let

x_{pl} = the number of drills shipped from Phoenix to Los Angeles
x_{pc} = the number shipped from Phoenix to Chicago
x_{pn} = the number shipped from Phoenix to New York
x_{al} = the number shipped from Atlanta to Los Angeles
x_{ac} = the number shipped from Atlanta to Chicago and
x_{an} = the number shipped from Atlanta to New York

your problem is to minimize the total shipping costs:

$$x_{pl} + 4x_{pc} + 5x_{pn} + 5x_{al} + 2x_{ac} + 4x_{an}$$

subject to the demand requirements:

$$x_{pl} + x_{al} = 8000 \quad \text{for Los Angeles}$$
$$x_{pc} + x_{ac} = 8000 \quad \text{for Chicago}$$
$$x_{pn} + x_{an} = 10,000 \quad \text{for New York}$$

the supply constraints for your two production facilities:

$$x_{pl} + x_{pc} + x_{pn} \leq 15,000 \text{ for Phoenix}$$
$$x_{al} + x_{ac} + x_{an} \leq 13,000 \text{ for Atlanta}$$

and the nonnegativity constraints $x \geq 0$ for all routes.

There are a variety of techniques for solving transportation problems of this kind, most of which involve developing an initial *feasible* solution

TABLE 3.10. Shipping costs per drill shipped.

To From	Los Angeles	Chicago	New York
Phoenix	$1	$4	$5
Atlanta	5	2	4

[6]As a practical matter, you should be interested in considering whether to change the mix of saws and drills, given projected shifts in demand and in the profit margins of each. We're keeping the problem simple to facilitate understanding of basic principles.

(i.e., one that satisfies *all* the constraints) and improving on it until an *optimal* solution (i.e., one that cannot be improved upon) is reached. As a practical matter, these problems are most efficiently solved using linear programming software on a computer (including the personal computer, except for extremely large problems). Here is a common method for producing an initial solution manually that is virtually always close to optimal: Allocate as many units as possible to the routes that are the lowest cost for both a source and a destination, and then allocate to the remaining lowest cost alternatives in a common sense manner until the source and destination constraints are satisfied.

For the problem at hand, the routes that have the lowest cost for both a source and a destination are Phoenix to Los Angeles and Atlanta to Chicago—you can satisfy Los Angeles's demand for 8000 drills by sending them all from Phoenix, leaving 7000 in Phoenix to satisfy part of the remaining demands, and you can satisfy Chicago's demand for 8000 drills by sending them all from Atlanta, leaving 5000 in Atlanta to satisfy the New York demand. Then, since the cost of satisfying New York's demand for 10,000 drills is $1 cheaper for each unit sent from Atlanta rather than from Phoenix, you use up Atlanta's remaining inventory of 5000 and fill the remainder with 5000 drills from Phoenix. This solution, displayed in Table 3.11, is optimal; no other routing arrangement produces a lower cost solution. By multiplying each of the six primary cell values shown in this table by the transportation cost per unit for the corresponding cell shown in Table 3.10 and calculating the sum of all the resulting products, you obtain the total transportation cost for this solution: $69,000.[7]

Simulation Models

Many quantifiable business problems are just too complex to lend themselves to solution through a linear programming or other optimization technique. For such problems, it is often more effective and less costly to use a *simulation* model. Simulation models solve complicated problems by allowing the user to characterize a real-world situation as a system of

---

[7]Space limitations and the existence of readily available personal computer software make a more thorough discussion of manual solutions to the transportation problem impractical here. The solution procedure presented here does not always produce the optimal solution to the transportation problem, but it is rarely far from optimal and has the virtue of simplicity. For a treatment of transportation algorithms that always produce optimal solutions, you should refer to Russell L. Ackoff and Maurice W. Sasieni's *Fundamentals of Operations Research* (New York: John Wiley, 1968).

TABLE 3.11.   Solution to transportation problem.

To From	Los Angeles	Chicago	New York	Excess Supply	Total Supply
Phoenix	8,000	0	5,000	2,000	15,000
Atlanta	0	8,000	5,000	0	13,000
Total demand	8,000	8,000	10,000	2,000	28,000

formulas that reflect the relationships among the various components of the situation, including the uncertainties and dynamic interdependencies that make the problem difficult to solve in the first place. The uncertainties are simulated with the use of random numbers, and the dynamic interdependencies are dealt with through the use of explicit formulas stating the relationships. By testing different structures (e.g., what if we reconfigured the production line?) and converging on values of the factors over which you have control (what if we kept production in operation for nine hours rather than eight?) that maximize system performance or minimize system cost, you can solve problems that defy solution using more elegant analytical procedures.

Simulation models have become especially attractive as computers have become so capable and accessible. The marriage of simulation models and computers permits brute force "number crunching" solutions to complex problems that not very long ago could be addressed only by simplifying the problem to the point where it bore little resemblance to reality. For many applications, simulation models today are much more efficient than analytical models and infinitely more efficient than running tests on the system itself.

You begin the simulation process generally by defining the problem, and proceed by identifying the most important variables; constructing the simulation mode; specifying the alternative structures of the system and values of the variables to be tested; running the model and examining the results; modifying the model as appropriate; and, when you are satisfied with the modifications, selecting the course of action that works best.

One common application of simulation modeling in business is that of determining how many servers (e.g., checkout counters, telephone operators, maintenance stations, tollbooths) to use in situations where the demand for service is random. This is called the *queuing problem*. The queuing problem is solved by estimating the demand for service (i.e., the average number of arrivals per unit of time) and the average time required to serve each customer or unit, making assumptions about the distributions of demand and service time, and testing the effects of alternative structures—how many servers and queue discipline (e.g., first-come first-served vs. separate lines for each server)—on system performance and cost. System performance is often measured in terms of the ability to satisfy demand for service, the amount or percent of idle time of servers, and the average waiting time of customers. As a general rule, it doesn't hurt to translate those factors into dollars.

The telephones at Power Tools are often swamped with calls, and you would like to get a better grip on how many operators you should have handling them. Calls arrive at a rate of 120 to 240 per hour, depending on the time of day and day of week. On average, it takes 10 seconds to process a call. You would be willing to pay $5 to prevent each minute of a caller's waiting. Operators cost $10 per hour. How many operators should you have during the peak hours? During the lowest calling rate hours? What should your decision rule be for the other times?

You can begin by thinking of this problem like you did the inventory problem: Having either too many or too few operators is analogous to having too much or too little inventory on hand. In this case, you'd like to know the number of operators that minimizes the total costs of waiting for telephone service, where the two principal components of cost are the cost of operators and the cost of having callers wait. As you add operators, the cost of callers waiting declines and your labor costs increase. Your total costs can be expressed as:

Total costs = Operator costs + Caller waiting costs

This is very much like the model displayed in Figure 3.5 (substituting the number of operators for the order quantity on the x-axis), except that it is a good deal easier to express the inventory order cost component in terms of the number of units ordered than it is to express the waiting cost in terms of the number of operators, a feature that makes the problem of optimization more complex in queuing models than in the standard inventory model. For your problem, the total costs are the sum of your operator costs of $0.167 per operator per minute plus your waiting costs of $5 times the average number of minutes each caller waits for an operator times the number of callers per minute.

To estimate how the average wait per caller declines with the number of operators and the resulting effect on costs, you can either make some simplifying assumptions about the distributions of arrivals and service time and use queuing formulas that apply to your unique situation, or you can use a computer spreadsheet to build a simple simulation model, such as the one displayed in Table 3.12. This table shows the results of selected one-hour simulations on a second-by-second basis, varying the

TABLE 3.12.[8] Simulation of waiting costs and operator costs.

Four Calls Arrive per Minute, One Operator:

Second Number	Random Number	No. of Calls	No. in System	No. on Hold	Costs		
					Waiting	Operator	Total
1	.8081	0	0	0	$0.000	$0.003	$0.003
2	.0650	1	1	0	0.000	0.003	0.003
3	.4598	0	1	0	0.000	0.003	0.003
4	.8836	0	1	0	0.000	0.003	0.003
5	.0301	1	2	1	0.083	0.003	0.086
⋮	⋮	⋮	⋮	⋮	⋮	⋮	⋮
3600	.9447	0	1	0	0.000	0.003	0.003
				Totals:	$49.367	$10.000	$59.367
				Costs per minute:	$ 0.823	0.167	$ 0.989

Four Calls Arrive per Minute, Two Operators:

Second Number	Random Number	No. of Calls	No. in System	No. on Hold	Costs		
					Waiting	Operator	Total
1	.5382	0	0	0	$0.000	$0.006	$0.006
2	.0729	0	0	0	0.000	0.006	0.006
3	.7171	0	0	0	0.000	0.006	0.006
4	.0243	1	1	0	0.000	0.006	0.006
5	.8414	0	1	0	0.000	0.006	0.006
⋮	⋮	⋮	⋮	⋮	⋮	⋮	⋮
3600	.3400	0	0	0	0.000	0.006	0.006
				Totals:	$9.633	$20.000	$29.633
				Costs per minute:	$0.161	$ 0.333	$ 0.494

---

[8]Queuing formulas are specific to the number of servers, the number of lines that feed the servers, and whether the arrivals are from a finite or an infinite population. Arrivals are commonly assumed to follow the Poisson probability law, described by the function

$$\frac{\lambda^n}{n!} e^{-\lambda},$$

where λ is the arrival rate, n is the number of units in the system, e is the constant 2.71828, and the expression $n!$ refers to the product $n(n-1)(n-2) \ldots 1$. Service times are commonly assumed to follow the exponential probability law, described by the function

$$\lambda e^{-\lambda x},$$

where x is the service time.

We use the simulation approach here primarily because it requires less mathematical sophistication and lends itself to a wider variety of queuing problems. For further details about queuing models for specific situations, see Elwood S. Buffa, *Modern Production Management: Managing the Operations Function* (New York: John Wiley, 1977).

FIGURE 3.7.   The effects of arrival rate and number of operators on total costs.

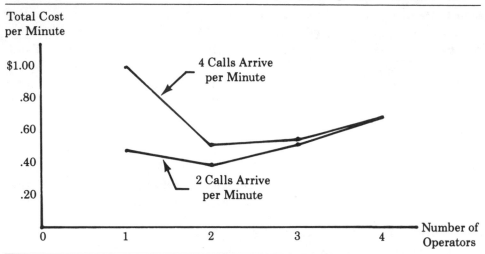

number of operators from one to four and the arrival rate from two calls per minute to four. At an arrival rate of two calls per minute, the model simulates an arriving call when the random number is between 0 and 0.0333; at a rate of four calls per minute, the model simulates an arriving call when the random number is between 0 and 0.0667. Waiting costs show up at a rate of 8.33 cents for each second a caller is put on hold. The model calculates the sum of waiting costs and operator costs in the last column.

You can organize and display the results of these simulations in a graph to see more clearly the effects of variations in arrival rates and the number of operators on total costs. Such a graph is shown in Figure 3.7.

This graph makes it clear that you minimize costs by having two operators, regardless of whether calls arrive at the rate of two or four per minute. Further use of the model indicates that it will be time to use a third operator when the arrival rate goes above 4.5 calls per minute. As your business continues to grow and calls arrive at higher rates, you can simulate further to help decide when to add still more operators.

CONCLUSION

Effective management is much more than just a matter of working with numbers. The successful manager relies on common sense and intuition; sensitivity to human factors that defy quantification; and creativity that transcends the numbers. (It didn't take a quantitative genius to realize that the waiting costs at the Hudson River tollbooths in New York City could be cut in half with virtually no loss in revenues by doubling the fares of the eastbound booths and eliminating the westbound booths altogether.) When the numbers send up a red flag, the successful manager looks beneath them to find out what is going on.

Most successful managers also know that the business cannot thrive without close attention to the numbers, and that tools designed to work with the numbers can be indispensable. Today's successful manager understands that quantitative methods can be powerful agents for solving the problems of human institutions and human beings.

FOR FURTHER READING

General

Gallagher, C. A., and H. J. Watson, *Quantitative Methods for Business Decisions* (New York: McGraw-Hill, 1980).

Markland, Robert E., and James R. Sweigart, *Quantitative Methods: Applications to Managerial Decision Making* (New York: John Wiley, 1987).

Tilanus, C. B., O. B. DeGans, and J. K. Lenstra, *Quantitative Methods in Management: Case Studies of Failures and Successes* (New York: John Wiley, 1986).

Statistics and Quality Control

Deming, W. Edwards, *Quality, Productivity, and Competitive Position* (Cambridge, MA: Center for Advanced Engineering Study, 1982).

Freund, John E., *Modern Elementary Statistics* (Englewood Cliffs, NJ: Prentice-Hall, 1988).

Ishikawa, Kaoru, *Guide to Quality Control* (Tokyo: Asian Productivity Organization, 1976).

Regression Analysis

Draper, Norman, and Harry Smith, *Applied Regression Analysis* (New York: John Wiley, 1981).

Wonnacott, Thomas H., and Ronald J. Wonnacott, *Regression: A Second Course on Statistics* (New York: John Wiley, 1981).

Forecasting

Box, George E. P., and Gwilym M. Jenkins, *Time Series Analysis: Forecasting and Control* (Oakland, CA: Holden-Day, 1976).

Wheelwright, Stephen C., and Spyros Makridakis, *Forecasting Methods for Management* (New York: John Wiley, 1985).

Decision Analysis

Brown, Rex V., A. S. Kahr, and C. R. Peterson, *Decision Analysis: An Overview* (New York: Holt, Rinehart and Winston, 1974).

Raiffa, Howard, *Decision Analysis: Introductory Lectures on Choices Under Uncertainty* (New York: Random House, 1986).

Operations Research

Taha, Hamdy A., *Operations Research: An Introduction* (New York: Macmillan, 1987).

Wagner, Harvey M., *Principles of Operations Research* (Englewood Cliffs, NJ: Prentice-Hall, 1975).

4 MANAGERIAL ECONOMICS: GUIDELINES FOR CHOICES AND DECISIONS

Frank Lichtenberg

In a capitalist economy such as that of the United States, managers of firms are continuously faced with numerous choices. How much output should they produce? What techniques should be employed to produce this output? How many workers should the firm employ, and how much should the firm spend on new plant and equipment in a given year? (In a command economy such as that of the Soviet Union, managers of enterprises do not make these decisions—they are dictated by a central government authority.) One of the central objectives of economic analysis is to provide answers to these questions. Managers of firms are assumed to have certain objectives, such as the maximization of profits or shareholder wealth, or the minimization of the cost of producing a given level of output. Economics provides managers with a set of *decision rules* that tell them what choices they should make (how much output to produce, how many workers to employ) to best achieve these objectives under a given set of conditions (the extent of demand for the firm's product or the level of prevailing wages). These rules also indicate how the manager should *change* the choices he or she makes when economic conditions change, for example, how the rate of investment should respond to interest rate changes.

Because managers (and consumers) are pursuing their own private interests and decisions are made in a decentralized manner (rather than by a central planner), a very important question concerning the *coordination* of economic activities arises. Thousands of firms are autonomously choosing which products to produce, how much they will produce, and how they will produce them. At the same time, millions of consumers are autonomously choosing how much of various products and services they will purchase. Is there any reason to believe that these decisions independently formulated by millions of firms and households will be mutually consistent? Is there any guarantee that firms will decide to produce the goods consumers wish to purchase, and in the appropriate quantities? Will the total number of workers that firms wish to employ equal the number of people willing and able to work, so unemployment will be eradicated?

Until the late eighteenth century, economists saw little reason to believe that the multiplicity of actions and decisions taken in a decentralized, free-market economy would be mutually consistent and harmonious. Indeed, they suspected that only chaos could result from the operation of such an economy. They argued that a detailed system of government regulations was required to ensure the coordination of the diverse activities of producers and consumers. Such regulations might require, for example, that all adult men wear wool caps on Sundays to ensure sufficient demand for wool to maintain the employment of the nation's shepherds. The need for a detailed system of economic regulations was an important part of the doctrine of *mercantilism*.

In 1776, the same year a political revolution occurred in England's American colonies, the Scottish political economist Adam Smith launched an ideological revolution by publishing *The Wealth of Nations*. Smith argued that the coordination and integration of diverse economic activities did not require detailed government regulation, that this function could be performed much more efficiently without human intervention by the operation of a *price system*. Producers would be guided as to which products to produce, in what quantities, and by what techniques of production, by *prices* established in the marketplace. Similarly, decisions by households about how much of various commodities to consume and how much labor to supply would be based on prices (including the wage rate which is the price of labor services). Smith argued that under many circumstances the prices established in competitive markets—markets with a large number of both buyers and sellers—would induce firms to produce, and households to consume, the *socially optimal* quantities of various goods and services. In other words, a system of unregulated markets and prices would, as if guided by an "invisible hand," ensure that society's limited resources yielded the maximum possible satisfaction of wants.

How are prices determined in competitive markets, and how do prices influence firms' decisions about what and how to produce? How do changes in government policies (e.g., taxes), technology, and other market conditions affect price, output, and the number of firms in an industry? What is the theoretical justification for the government's pursuit of antitrust policy, the policy to promote competition and prevent monopolization? One of the two main branches of economics, *microeconomics,* seeks to provide answers to these and related questions. Microeconomics is concerned with the behavior of individual households, firms, and industries. The other branch of economics—*macroeconomics*—focuses on the behavior of the economy as a whole. Some of the questions central to macroeconomic inquiry are: Why do modern capitalist economies often fail to achieve the goals of full employment and price stability? (In other words, what are the causes of unemployment and inflation?) Can the government's monetary and fiscal policies be used to help the economy realize these goals? Is there an inescapable trade-off between unemployment and inflation—to achieve lower inflation, must we accept higher unemployment? Why has the U.S. economy grown more slowly since 1973 than before? Why is it growing more slowly than the Japanese economy?

This chapter provides brief introductions to both branches of economic analysis. Although we discuss the two branches separately, it is important to recognize the important connections and similarities between microeconomics and macroeconomics. Both analyze how prices and quantities of goods and services are determined within the context of supply-and-demand models. In the case of microeconomics, the quantity and price are those of specific commodities (such as bicycles or floppy disks), whereas *aggregate* output (the *sum* of the quantity produced of all commodities) and aggregate price (the average of all prices) are the concerns of macroeconomics.

Both branches of economics have *positive* as well as *normative* objectives. The positive objective is to *explain* what has happened in the past and to *predict* what will happen in the future, without making value judgments about these events. (Why was the unemployment rate so high in 1982? Will interest rates rise after the 1992 national elections?) The normative objective is to evaluate alternative economic decisions and policies in terms of their consequences for economic welfare, and thereby to facilitate rational decision making. (Should the government attempt to prevent hostile takeover of U.S. companies, or do the latter contribute to economic welfare? Should the income tax be replaced by a tax on consumption?)

Despite the connections between microeconomics and macroeconomics, for many years, microeconomists and macroeconomists were happy to conduct research in relative isolation from one another. This is no longer the case. Today, macroeconomists recognize that in order to understand the relationships among key economic aggregates such as income, consumption expenditure, interest rates, and the inflation rate, they must have carefully constructed theories of the behavior of individual households, firms, and markets. One of the most important developments in economic thinking in recent years has been the construction of *microfoundations of macroeconomics*.

MICROECONOMICS

Microeconomics seeks to provide a general theory to explain how the quantities and prices of individual commodities are determined. The development of such a theory will enable us to predict the effects of various events, such as industry deregulation and oil price shocks, on the quantity and price of output. For concreteness, we will consider a hypothetical market for wine, and pose the question "How is the quantity (number of bottles) and price (per bottle) of wine determined?"

We assume the existence of a *market demand curve* (or schedule) for wine, which indicates the total number of bottles consumers are willing to purchase at different possible prices of wine (Figure 4.1). Assumption: Wine is a perfectly homogenous commodity—there is no distinction between Thunderbird and Chateau Lafite Rothschild. For

FIGURE 4.1.   The market demand curve for wine.

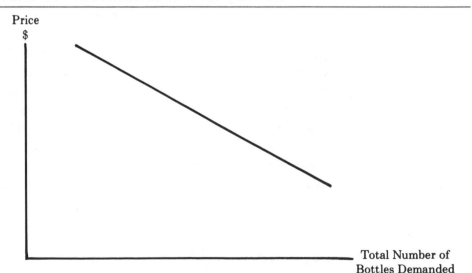

two reasons the demand curve assumes a downward slope—the higher the price, the lower the quantity demanded. First, as the price of wine increases, wine becomes more expensive *relative* to possible *substitutes* for it, such as beer, spirits, and soft drinks, so consumers will demand less wine and more of the substitutes. Also, the real income, or purchasing power, of consumers falls as prices of consumer goods rise, so consumers purchase smaller quantities of almost *all* goods. These two effects of a price change on demand are known as the *substitution effect* and the *income effect.*

The demand curve considerably narrows the possible values for the quantity and price of wine—only points on the line, not those off the line, could prevail (in the absence of government interference such as rationing or pricing ceilings). But to uniquely determine quantity and price, we need to also consider the "supply side" of the market—wine producers.

Suppose that there are 100 wine producers. For simplicity, assume that they have identical facilities, costs of labor, capital, and technology—they are simply clones of one another. Each producer is therefore faced by the same *cost function*—the relationship between total cost of production and quantity produced. Total cost is assumed to be a strictly increasing function of output: To produce more, the firm will have to hire greater quantities of inputs (land, labor, machinery, and so on), thus increasing costs. In the following analysis, we will need to make use of another relationship, the *marginal cost* curve, which can be derived from the (total) cost function. Marginal cost (MC) is simply the *additional* cost of producing the *last* unit of output. For example, if it costs $20 to produce 10 bottles of wine and $23 to produce 11, the marginal cost of the 11th unit is $3. The marginal cost *curve* is the relationship between the number of units and the marginal cost of the last unit. Again for simplicity, we will assume that MC is strictly increasing. The MC schedule in Table 4.1 will be used for illustrative purposes.

TABLE 4.1.   Total and marginal cost schedules
of typical producer.

Number of Units Output	Total Cost	MC of Last Unit
1	$ 3	$ 3
2	7	4
3	13	6
4	20	7
5	28	8
6	38	10

We assume that each producer's objective is to maximize his profit, where profit is defined as revenue minus cost. Revenue is the number of units sold times the price per unit. For the moment, we also assume that each producer considers himself to be a "price taker": He can sell as many units as he likes at a price determined by the market, and his output decision has no influence on the price. (We relax this assumption later when we consider the case of monopoly.)

Under these conditions, the producer can maximize profit by producing the quantity of output at which $MC = P$, where P denotes price. Suppose, for example, the price were \$6, and the MC schedule is given in Table 4.1. Then the profit-maximizing level of output is 3. (Actually, the firm is indifferent between producing 2 and 3 units). If the firm increased production from 3 to 4 units, its revenue would increase by \$6 ($= P$) but its costs would increase by \$7 (the MC of the fourth unit); hence, its profits would decrease by \$1. Similarly, if the firm reduced production from 3 units to 1, it would save \$10 in costs but would lose \$12 in revenue, so its profits would decline by \$2. At $P = \$6$, the firm cannot do better than a profit of \$5 by producing 3 units. This analysis reveals that *the supply curve of the firm*—the relationship between price and profit-maximizing quantity—*is identical to its marginal cost curve*. That is, we can determine from the marginal cost curve, the number of units of the goods the firm would be willing to supply at different possible prices.

The *market* supply curve is the ("horizontal") sum of all of the individual firm supply curves. It indicates the total quantity that *all* firms in the market would be willing to supply at various prices. If there were 100 firms in the market, each faced with the cost schedule in Table 4.1, then the market supply curve would be

Price of Output	Quantity Supplied by All Producers
3	100
4	200
6	300
7	400
8	500
10	600

The market equilibrium price and quantity of wine—the price and quantity that would occur in a competitive market—are determined by the intersection of the market supply and demand curves. In Figure 4.2 this is the point (Q_o, P_o). P_o is the only price at which the quantity of wine

FIGURE 4.2.   Determination of market equilibrium quantity and price.

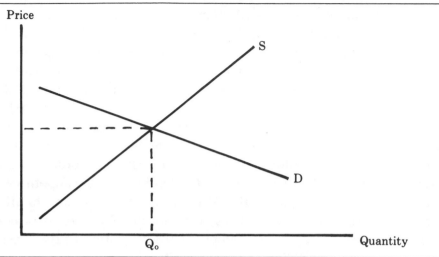

producers are willing to supply is equal to the quantity consumers are willing to purchase. At prices above P_o, there is *excess supply* of the product. If one producer tried to charge a price above P_o, other producers would find it profitable to charge a slightly lower price ($\geq P_o$) to draw away his customers. Competition among producers ensures that the market price is driven down to P_o.

This exercise is a *short-run* analysis, in the sense that we have assumed that the number of producers in the industry is fixed. In the *long run,* however, new firms may enter or existing firms may exit the industry. Whether or not entry and exit will occur depends upon how the rate of profit earned by firms in the industry compares to that earned by firms elsewhere in the economy. Suppose that $P_o = \$7$, so that each firm is producing 4 units and earning $\$8 [= (4.7) - 20]$ in profit, and that each producer has invested $\$100$ of capital in his firm; his rate of profit is therefore 8 percent. If the rate of profit available elsewhere in the economy is only 5 percent, in the long run, new producers will enter the industry, shifting out the market supply curve, driving down the market price, output, and profits of each producer. Entry will cease once the profit rate in this industry is equal to the economy-wide profit rate.

One of the most important properties of the competitive market equilibrium is that the quantity produced is the *socially efficient* quantity: The cost of producing the last unit of output just equals consumers' marginal willingness to pay for it. Any level of output below Q_o would be inefficient since it would cost less to produce the marginal unit than consumers would be willing to pay for it. Since all firms receive the same price for the product, the distribution of output across firms is also efficient. Instead of assuming that all firms have the same marginal cost schedules, suppose that there are two types of firms, "high-cost" and "low-cost." Because of poor land or access to water, high-cost firms have a greater MC at every level of output. Because both high- and low-cost producers equate their MC to the price (uniform across producers), low-cost firms operate at a higher level of output. This arrangement is socially efficient: If both types of firms were producing at the same rate, total costs of production could be reduced by transferring production from high-cost to low-cost firms. As noted, the tendency of a competitive market to produce the socially efficient quantity of a good and to allocate production efficiently across firms, without the direction of a central planner or coordinator, is an example of the operation of the "invisible hand"—a term immortalized by Adam Smith.

The supply-and-demand framework just outlined enables us to analyze or predict the effects of various events and government policy changes on the price and quantity of wine. Suppose that advances in biotechnology result in increased grape yield—more grapes can be grown with given amounts of land, labor, and capital. This hypothesis implies that each producer's MC schedule will be shifted down—the MC of producing any given level of output has declined. Consequently, the market supply curve shifts down, and there is a reduction in price and an increase in total quantity produced and consumed.

Even seemingly remote events can have an impact on the wine market. At many social functions, wine and cheese are served together, suggesting that they are *complementary* goods. If two goods are complementary, then an increase in the price of one good reduces the quantity demanded of the other good. Hence, an increase in the price of cheese might be expected to reduce the quantity of wine demanded, that is, to shift the market demand curve for wine toward the origin. For many years, the U.S. government has supported the income of cheese producers (dairy farmers) by purchasing enormous quantities of cheese and other dairy products at a "support price" above the market equilibrium price. At the end of 1984, the government had accumulated stockpiles of over 1.4 billion pounds of cheese, butter, and nonfat dry milk, amounting to more than 40 percent of the total production of cheese and butter in that year. If the government were to sell its stockpiles, it would drive down the market price of cheese, which would (assuming complementarity of wine and cheese) increase the demand for wine, thus raising the price and quantity of wine. Wine producers might not lobby for the sale of government dairy stockpiles, however, since such sales would probably also depress the price of milk; if milk and wine are *substitutes* in consumption, a fall in the milk price would trigger a decline in wine demand. The net impact of the government's action on wine demand would depend on the relative strength of the cheese and milk price effects.

The final scenario affecting the wine market is the imposition by the government of a $1 per bottle tax on wine, payable by suppliers. This tax acts to shift up by $1 the MC schedule of the typical producer, since in addition to paying his factors of production (workers, suppliers of materials), the producer must make payments to the government. Now, the marginal cost *to the producer* of the fourth unit of output, for example, is $8 rather than $7. The *social* cost or value of the resources used to produce the fourth unit is still $7, however; the additional $1 is a *transfer* from the producer to the government.

Since each producer's MC curve is shifted up by the tax, the market supply curve is also shifted up (see Figure 4.3). The equilibrium quantity will fall from Q_o to Q_1. In discussing the effect of the tax on the price of wine, we must be careful to distinguish the *gross* price (inclusive of tax)— the price paid by the consumer—from the *net* price (exclusive of tax)— the price received by the producer. The gross and net prices may be denoted P_g and P_n and are related by the equation $P_g = P_n + 1$. Figure 4.3 shows that as a result of the tax, the price paid by consumers will increase, but by less than $1, and the price received by producers will decrease, also by less than $1. The "burden" of the tax is shared by consumers and

FIGURE 4.3.   Effect of a $1 per bottle tax on the wine market.

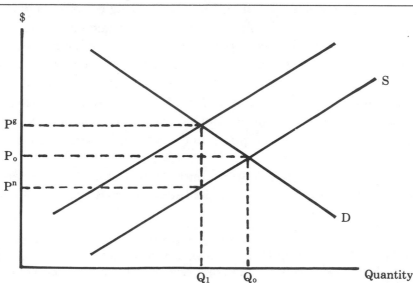

producers; the fraction of the burden borne by each group depends upon the slopes of the demand and supply curves.

The amount of revenue the government raises is equal to the equilibrium quantity (Q_1) times the tax per unit ($1). The flatter the demand curve—the more price sensitive consumers are—the less revenue will be raised by imposing the tax, since consumers will reduce purchases more (shrinking the tax base) in response to the tax-induced price increase.

Q_1, the amount of wine that is produced and consumed after imposition of the tax, is not a socially efficient quantity. Suppose $Q_1 = 500$. Consumers would be willing to pay more—but less than $1 more—for the 501st unit than the value of the resources required to produce it; therefore, it should be produced. However, in the presence of the tax, they would have to pay the full dollar above the resource cost, which they are unwilling to do; hence, the 501st unit will not be produced. The tax, by driving a "wedge" between the price paid by consumers and the price received by producers, causes an insufficient quantity of the good to be produced, reducing economic welfare (even though the resources appropriated by the government via the tax are presumably used to increase the output of some other product or good). The sum of the losses borne by consumers (in the form of reduced consumer welfare) and those borne by producers (in the form of reduced profits) exceeds the government's gain in tax revenue.[1] Using taxes of this sort to transfer income or resources from one use to another resembles using a leaky bucket to transfer water; some of the intended benefits of the transfer are dissipated due to imperfections in the transfer mechanism.

We conclude our analysis of the hypothetical wine market, and our brief sojourn into microeconomics, by investigating the effects of monopolization of an industry's supply on price, quantity, and economic welfare. Suppose all of the productive capacity (firms) in the industry were under the control of a single decision maker (monopolist) whose objective is to maximize profits. The market demand curve and MC schedule of the typical firm are just as they were before. Now, however, because there is (by assumption) no threat of competition from other suppliers, the monopolist is free to choose that point on the demand curve that maximizes his profit.

To understand how price and output are determined under monopoly, we first need to define *marginal revenue* (MR). Marginal revenue

---

[1]The geometrical measure of "excess burden" is the area of the triangle bounded by the vertical line at Q_1, the original supply curve, and the demand curve. All commodity taxes are subject to some excess burden; the degree of excess burden depends upon the slopes of the supply and demand curves.

is the increase in a producer's revenue resulting from a one-unit increase in output. If a producer is maximizing profits, he will produce output up until the point at which the marginal profit earned on the last unit equals zero. Since Profit = Revenue − Cost, the condition that marginal profit equals zero is equivalent to the condition MR = MC. Thus, the general condition for profit maximization is that the firm produce the level of output at which MR = MC. Recall that in the case of a competitive firm, we assumed (because the firm is "small" relative to the market) that the firm could sell as much output as it wanted without influencing the market price; the firm was a "price taker." Hence, marginal revenue is identical to price (MR = P) and the condition MR = MC reduces to P = MC. (This equality between price and marginal cost was one reason we found the competitive market to be efficient.) In contrast, because he controls the entire industry supply, the monopolist is *not* a price taker— he is a price setter. The demand curve facing the monopolist is the *market* demand curve. The monopolist recognizes that if he wishes to increase the quantity of output that he sells he will have to lower the price of *every* unit of output. Suppose that two points on the market demand curve are

Price	Quantity Demanded
$10.00	9
9.50	10

If the firm sells 10 units, the price of the tenth unit (and of the first nine) is $9.50; however, the MR of the tenth unit is $5 $[= (10 \times 9.50) - (9 \times 10.00)]$. The firm lost $.50 on each of the first nine units when it lowered its price to enable the tenth to be sold. Because demand curves slope down, the MR curve always lies below the demand curve (see Figure 4.4). Indeed, MR can easily be negative, as it will be if demand is very *elastic* (price sensitive). The quantity produced by a monopolist, therefore, is always lower than that which would be produced in a competitive market, and the price will be higher. In Figure 4.4, the output produced is equal to Q_M and is determined by the intersection of the MC and MR schedules. This number is lower than the competitive output level Q_o, which we argued is the socially efficient level. The value to consumers of units of output $Q_{M+2}, \ldots, Q_o$ exceeds the cost of producing them, but given the incentives facing the monopolist, he or she is (rationally) unwilling to produce more than Q_M units.

This theoretical demonstration that monopolists tend to restrict output below the socially desirable level has long been a cornerstone of antitrust policy, which attempts to ensure that industries do not become monopolized. But some prominent economists, notably Joseph

FIGURE 4.4. Output and price determination under monopoly.

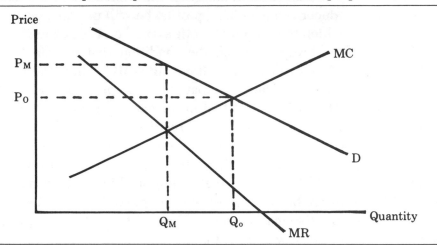

Schumpeter, have made a case that monopolies (or more generally, firms with "market power" (the ability to influence price) are not necessarily entirely, or even mostly, bad for economic welfare. Schumpeter maintained that, in the long run, economic well-being depends as much on "dynamic efficiency" (the rate of introduction of new and improved products and processes) as it does on "static efficiency" (efficiency in the sense just discussed). Moreover, he claimed that large firms with command over extensive resources are more likely to produce important innovations than smaller, more competitive firms. This latter claim is quite controversial and largely untested. Nevertheless Schumpeter's critique of the standard (static) theory of monopoly is worth noting.

MACROECONOMICS

We have indicated that microeconomics is concerned with the issue of how the quantity and price of output of individual firms or industries is determined. In contrast, macroeconomics addresses the determination of the *entire economy*, or *aggregate* output and price. Economists are often more interested in analyzing the *changes* or *rates of growth* of aggregate output and price than they are in analyzing their *levels*.

The most widely used measure of aggregate output is *gross national product* (GNP)—the market value of all final goods and services produced in an economy within a given time period. (The market value of a good equals the quantity produced of the good times its price.) Since

GNP in each year depends both on that year's quantities and that year's prices, part of the change in GNP from 1986 to 1987, for example, was due to a change in quantities, and partially was due to a change in prices. It is important to distinguish between these two sources of change. We can do so by calculating what GNP *would have been* in 1987, if prices had remained at their 1986 levels, and comparing this to actual GNP in 1986. That is, we will use the *same year's* (1986) prices to compute the value of output in both years. The increase in GNP we calculate when we use a constant set of prices (base year prices) is called an increase in *real* GNP. The increase in GNP we calculate when we use a changing set of prices is called an increase in *nominal* GNP. The difference between nominal and real GNP growth is due to *inflation,* that is, to a change in the average level of (or *index* of) prices:

$$\text{Inflation rate (percentage increase in average price level)} = \frac{\text{Nominal GNP}}{\text{growth rate}} - \frac{\text{Real GNP}}{\text{growth rate}}$$

One of the major challenges in macroeconomics is to explain—and *predict*—fluctuations in the overall rate of economic activity (real GNP) and in the price level. (In the remainder of this chapter, the term GNP will refer to *real* GNP, which will be denoted by the symbol Y.) Table 4.2 presents data on the annual growth rate of GNP during the period 1970

TABLE 4.2.   Annual growth rate of real U.S. GNP, 1970–1986.

Year	Percentage Change in GNP from Previous Period	Below (−) or Above (+) Average Growth
1970	−0.3	−
1971	2.8	+
1972	5.0	+
1973	5.2	+
1974	−0.5	−
1975	−1.3	−
1976	4.9	+
1977	4.7	+
1978	5.3	+
1979	2.3	−
1980	−0.2	−
1981	1.9	−
1982	−2.5	−
1983	3.6	+
1984	6.4	+
1985	2.7	+
1986	2.5	−
Average, 1970–1986	2.6	

to 1986. Several features of the data are noteworthy. GNP has tended to increase over time: The mean rate of increase during this 16-year period was 2.6 percent per year. However, the growth in aggregate output is far from steady: The growth rate ranged from a minimum of −2.5 percent in 1982, to a maximum of 6.4 percent just two years later. These data also point to the existence of *business cycles:* Years of below average (2.6 percent) growth in GNP (indicated by a minus sign in the last column of Table 4.2) tend to be bunched together, as do years of above-average growth (indicated by a plus sign). The path of GNP over time can be described as cyclical fluctuations around a long-term upward trend. In order to explain or predict movements in GNP, we will need to answer two questions: (1) Why does GNP have an upward trend, and how is the magnitude of this trend determined? (2) Why are there sizeable short-run fluctuations of GNP around this long-term trend? The first question is of primary concern to economists studying *long-run economic growth,* the second to economists concerned with *short-run economic fluctuations* or business cycles.

To answer these questions, it is useful to define the concept of *potential GNP* and to contrast it with actual (observed) GNP. Parents and teachers sometimes complain that students are "underachievers"—that their actual level of performance falls short of their potential for achievement. Similarly, economists postulate that during certain periods (lasting up to several years) less output may be produced than an economy is capable of producing. The economy's potential output (like the potential achievement of a student) is usually not directly observable—it must be inferred indirectly on the basis of available data. To infer an economy's potential output, we need to make use of a fundamental economic relationship known as a *production function.* A production function is a relationship between output and input (labor, capital) that indicates the maximum amount of output it is possible to produce from given quantities of input, using available technology. Potential output is defined as the level of output that would be produced if the labor and capital resources available in the economy were "fully employed." Hence, the economy is operating at potential if, and only if, resources are fully employed. What does full employment mean? Let us consider the issue of full employment of labor. In 1983, there were 174 million persons 16 years of age and over in the U.S. population. Does "full employment" mean that all 174 million should be working? No, some of these individuals were in school, retired, ill, taking care of families, or otherwise not interested in working for pay. Only 112 million people were in the civilian *labor force*—either employed (101 million) or unemployed (11 million). The unemployed are people who are not working, but who are seeking work. The *unemployment rate* is the ratio of the number of people unemployed to the number of people in the laborforce (the sum of the employed and the people seeking work). Should "full employment" of labor mean that the entire *labor force* is employed, that is that the unemployment rate is zero? While this might seem sensible, economists do not think zero is the value of the unemployment rate that corresponds to full employment of labor. It is natural and even desirable for some individuals, such as people changing jobs and new entrants into the labor market (e.g., high school graduates), to be unemployed for a time while they search for an appropriate job. Thus, even an economy producing at its potential would have a positive amount of unemployment. The appropriate value of the natural or full-employment rate is a matter of considerable debate among economists. The consensus value of the natural rate of unemployment (denoted U∗) in the 1980s is about 6 percent. If the actual unemployment rate (denoted U) exceeds the natural rate, less than full utilization of the economy's labor resources occurs, and actual output falls below potential output. These data indicate that in 1983, the unemployment rate was 9.6 percent, 3.6 percent above the natural rate.[2]

When the unemployment rate exceeds the natural rate, some fraction of the output the economy was capable of producing will not be produced. Economists refer to this fraction as the *output gap* (YGAP).

> YGAP < 0 if the economy is below full employment
> YGAP = 0 at full employment
> YGAP > 0 if the economy is above full employment

In addition to noting that YGAP and the unemployment rate U are inversely related, we need to know *how much* YGAP will decline (increase in magnitude) when U increases 1 percentage point—from 6 to 7 percent, for example. On the surface, it might seem that there should be a one-for-one (inverse) relationship between U and YGAP—that lowering the utilization rate of the laborforce by 1 percent (a 1 point increase in U) should cause 1 percent less output to be produced. However, as demonstrated by the late macroeconomist Arthur Okun, the slope of the relationship between U and YGAP is close to −3:

$$YGAP = -3 \ (U - U^\circ)$$

---

[2]Just as the unemployment rate measures the rate of utilization of the laborforce, the *capacity utilization rate* (as measured by the Federal Reserve Board) reflects the utilization rate of the nation's capital stock. The "natural" or full-employment rate of capacity utilization is in the vicinity of 85 percent.

This relationship is referred to as *Okun's Law*. Therefore, a 1 percentage point increase in U is associated with a 3 percent reduction in output. For several reasons, output falls dramatically when the unemployment rate rises. First, when U increases, the laborforce contracts, since some workers who otherwise would have searched for jobs become discouraged and drop out of the laborforce. Second, average weekly hours of work tends to be lower during periods of high unemployment (recessions), partially because employers cut back on the use of overtime. Third, labor productivity (the average amount of output produced per hour of work) is lower during recessions than it is during periods of high unemployment, because the pace of work is slower.

The cost to society of unemployment, in terms of the amount of output foregone, is high. Okun's Law implies that if the economy had been at full employment in 1983 (if U had been 6 percent rather than 9.6 percent), almost $400 billion worth of additional output would have been produced. As a benchmark, this is slightly greater than the total purchases of goods and services by all state and local governments in that year.

Why does unemployment occur, that is, why do modern industrial economies sometimes fail to fully utilize available resources and realize their potential for producing output? Is there anything the government can do to reduce unemployment? If so, does the reduction of unemployment entail sacrifices with respect to other economic goals, such as maintaining a low rate of inflation? These are some of the fundamental questions that macroeconomics attempts to answer.

Providing complete answers to these questions is beyond the scope of this chapter; we will instead sketch some answers using a simple model of supply and demand. Some crucial differences, however, distinguish the model we will develop here from the one used previously in the section on microeconomics. There the quantity and price determined by the model were those of a single commodity (wine). Here, the quantity refers to real GNP—the sum of the quantities of all goods and services produced—and the price refers to the aggregate price level—an average (or index) of the prices of all goods and services. (The Consumer Price Index is probably the most familiar example of a price index.) When quantity and price are defined in this way, the supply and demand are referred to as *aggregate supply* (AS) and *aggregate demand* (AD) curves.

The AS = AD model is depicted graphically in Figure 4.5. We shall consider the AS curve first. In contrast to the usual (microeconomic) upward-sloping supply curve, the AS curve is *vertical*, and it is vertical at the value Y*. This orientation signifies that the amount of output producers wish to supply does not depend upon the (average) price level, and this

FIGURE 4.5.   AS-AD model of real GNP and price-level determination.

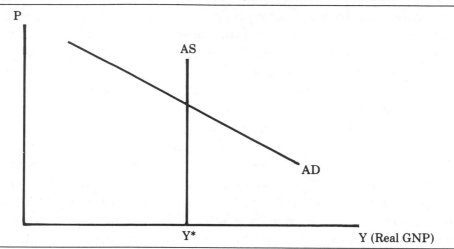

amount is equal to potential output. Why does the aggregate supply of output not increase when the price level rises? The supply remains constant because the price level is an average of *all* prices, including prices paid by producers for inputs (like materials and labor). When the price level goes up by, for example, 5 percent, we assume that all prices increase 5 percent, and that *relative* prices remain unchanged. If the prices of a producer's output and inputs go up by the same percentage amount, the producer's profit-maximizing level of output remains unchanged. The reason the microeconomic supply curve derived earlier sloped upward was that we implicitly assumed that when the price of output increased, the price of inputs remained unchanged, so that the *relative* price of output increased. Since relative prices are assumed to remain unchanged when the aggregate price level P changes, the quantity of aggregate output supplied is independent of P.

Now we turn to the AD curve, which shows the total amount of output that consumers, investors, the government, and foreigners would want to purchase at different values of P. Like the microeconomic demand curve, the AD curve slopes down, *but for different reasons.* One reason the microeconomic demand curve had a negative slope was that reductions in price were assumed to reduce the *relative* price of the good, inducing substitution toward the good; in the AS = AD model, relative prices are unaffected by changes in P. Why, then, does the AD curve slope down? The descent is due to the effect of changes in P on the *real stock of money* in circulation, hence on *interest rates,* hence on the desired amount of *investment.* Let us briefly consider these linkages. Investment, which includes purchases by businesses of buildings and machinery, and by households of houses, is a very important (and volatile) component of aggregate demand. The amount of investment (I) that businesses and consumers wish to undertake is sensitive (and inversely related) to the level of the market interest rate (R), since the latter determines the cost of borrowing. (The rate of investment in residential housing is particularly sensitive to interest rate fluctuations.) The level of the interest rate—which may be thought of as the *price* of (borrowing) money—depends in turn on the *quantity* of money in circulation. It is the *real* quantity, or purchasing power, of money, not simply the number of dollar bills in circulation, that determines the level of interest rates. Suppose the (nominal) amount of money in circulation (M) is $1 million. If the price level is 2, that money would purchase only half as many goods and services as it would if P were equal to 1: Money would be scarcer, and the interest rate would be higher to "ration" the smaller supply. For a given nominal stock of money, then, the higher P is, the lower the real stock of money; the higher is the interest rate, the lower is desired investment, and the lower is desired total spending. This relationship can be summarized as:

$$P{\uparrow}{\rightarrow}\frac{M}{P}{\downarrow}\ {\rightarrow}R{\uparrow}{\rightarrow}I{\downarrow}\ {\rightarrow}Y{\downarrow}$$

It is this effect of P on interest rates and investment that accounts for the negative slope of the AD curve.

We can now use the AS = AD model to explain how real GNP and the price level are determined, and consequently why output may deviate from its potential level. Suppose that the AD curve were initially at the position indicated by AD_0 in Figure 4.6, and that the price level were equal to P_0, the price at which the quantity of output demanded equals the quantity supplied; the economy would be at full employment. Suppose further that there were a sudden downward shift (to AD_1) of the AD curve; there is a decline in the quantity of output demanded at any given price level. Such a decline could occur as a result, for example, of a severe downturn in the stock market (like the one that occurred in October 1987) which might cause consumers to feel poorer (due to capital losses) and more apprehensive about the future economic outlook, and therefore to curtail expenditures, particularly on "big-ticket" items such as automobiles and major appliances. What impact would this kind of AD "shock" have on real GNP?

Observe that if the price level were to immediately fall to P_1, then the quantity of output demanded would again be equal to Y∗, and the economy would remain at full employment. If P were extremely *flexible*,

FIGURE 4.6   Effect of a decline in aggregate demand on output and price.

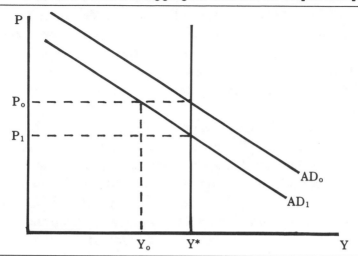

tending to fall rapidly whenever demand declined, then the decline in demand would not cause output to fall below potential; YGAP would remain equal to zero, and U would remain equal to U*. According to the "classical" school of economic thought (which prevailed throughout the nineteenth and early twentieth centuries until the Great Depression of the 1930s), there was every reason to believe that prices *were* extremely flexible. In the face of a general decline in demand, producers would lower their prices enough so that full employment would be maintained. Price flexibility essentially guaranteed that the economy would continuously remain at full employment.

The problem with this view of the macroeconomy became apparent in the early 1930s, when it was grossly at odds with the facts. Between 1929 (the year of the historic stock market crash) and 1933, real GNP declined almost 30 percent. Moreover, it was clear that this collapse was due to a decline in demand (and an increase in the magnitude of YGAP), not due to a reduction in potential output. The unemployment rate increased from 3 percent in 1929 to 25 percent in 1933; by 1940, it was still as high as 15 percent. The British economist John Maynard Keynes observed that these facts were blatantly inconsistent with the hypothesis of flexible prices. Such high and persistent unemployment, argued Keynes, could only be explained by the tendency of prices and wages to be *downwardly rigid.* Keynes believed that workers would refuse to accept wage reductions, even if failure to do so would result in mass layoffs. Producers would not reduce the prices of their products unless their labor (and other) costs declined. The consequences of price rigidity may be seen in Figure 4.6. If the price level remains "stuck" at P_0 after AD has shifted from AD_0 to AD_1, output will fall from $Y*$ to Y_1: The economy enters into a recession (or even a depression) and operates below its potential. Moreover, *deflation*, a decline in the price level, could not be counted upon to eliminate unemployment. Although prices and wages might ultimately fall, Keynes was fond of saying that "in the long run, we're all dead."

Keynes rejected the classical doctrine that price flexibility could be relied upon to "automatically" keep the economy at full employment. He did not, however, believe that society had to simply accept the existence of prolonged periods of unemployment. Full employment could be achieved, not as a result of automatic price adjustment, but by deliberate and intelligent use by the government of *monetary policy* and particularly *fiscal policy.* Monetary policy refers to the government's control of the nominal stock of money, fiscal policy to its control over government expenditure and taxation. In terms of Figure 4.6, the basic idea is that when AD shifts down from AD_0 to AD_1 and the price level is stuck at P_0, by judicious use of fiscal and monetary policies, the government can shift AD *back* to AD_0, thus restoring full employment. When the AD curve is located at AD_1 and the price level is P_0 there is *insufficient demand* to keep the economy's resources fully employed. There are three ways the government can attempt to increase demand for goods and services. The first, and most direct, is for the government to increase its expenditures on highways, education, national defense, and other items. The second is by lowering taxes on consumers (thus increasing their disposable income) or on firms (thus increasing their after-tax profits); such tax reductions would tend to increase consumption and investment expenditure, respectively. (Either increasing government expenditure or lowering taxes could also have the undesirable side effect of increasing the government's budget deficit, the excess of expenditures over tax revenues.) The third way is to increase the nominal money supply. As discussed earlier, if P remains fixed at P_0 this measure would result in an increase in the real money supply, a fall in interest rates, and an increase in desired investment expenditure. Keynes believed that an increase in government spending was likely to be the most effective of the three techniques for stimulating aggregate demand.

Keynesian macroeconomic theory amounted to a revolutionary advance over previous thought, but there have been many further important developments since Keynes published *The General Theory of Employment, Interest and Money* in 1935. The classical and Keynesian models adopted completely polar assumptions about the process of price adjustment: In the first model, prices are perfectly flexible; in the second, they are perfectly rigid (at least in the downward direction). An intermediate view of price adjustment (in some sense a synthesis of both extreme views) underlies much contemporary macroeconomic analysis. According to this *"sticky price"* model, prices are rigid in the short run— they do not decline immediately in response to a decline in AD—but they are flexible in the long run—they tend to gradually decline when the economy is below full employment. They do not decline immediately because some individuals (such as workers and firms covered by collective bargaining agreements) have previously signed long-term contracts that lock them into price and wage levels. As time passes, however, those contracts expire and new wage and price negotiations can take account of changes in economic conditions.[3] As prices decline, the real stock of money increases, interest rates fall, and investment and output increase, until output has returned to potential. As in the Keynesian model, the economy has undergone a recession (due to the failure of prices to instantaneously fall), but in the sticky price model, the recession was temporary, and the economy recovered from it without intervention by the government. This is not to say, however, that government intervention would not have been desirable. Although the recession was temporary, it was not painless—output was lost during the period of adjustment to the new, lower price level. In principle, the government could have reduced the duration and depth of the recession by appropriate use of its fiscal and monetary policies.

In practice though, it may be difficult for the government to provide the right amount of stimulus at the right time so as to keep the economy at full employment. While the scenario of a one-time downward shift of the AD curve is a convenient one for illustrating how GNP is determined, in reality the AD curve is constantly (and unpredictably) shifting up and

---

[3] An important element of the sticky price model is the *price adjustment equation:*

$$\eta_t = \frac{P_t - P_{t-1}}{P_{t-1}} = f \cdot YGAP_{t-1}$$

where η is the rate of inflation between year $t-1$ and year t, $YGAP_{t-1}$ is the output GAP in year $t-1$, and f is a parameter (number) greater than zero. This equation says that when output is below potential ($YGAP < 0$), prices will tend to fall in the coming year, and that when the economy is above full employment, prices will tend to increase. According to the sticky price model, the response of the economy to the decline in AD from AD_0 to AD_1 would be as follows. In the short run (before contracts have expired), the price level remains at P_0 and output falls below potential to Y_0. As times passes, old contracts expire and new ones are negotiated at prices that are below P_0. Prices continue to fall until they reach the value P_1.

down as the economy is buffeted by various economic and political disturbances. Consequently, the target that economic policymakers are (or should be) aiming for is moving rather than stationary. Moreover, it takes time for changes in policy, such as expansions in the money supply, both to be implemented and to have an effect on the economy. There is evidence, for example, that the peak effect of changes in the money supply on GNP takes about $1\frac{1}{2}$ to 2 years to occur. Suppose the AD curve shifted down from AD_0 to AD_1, and the government increased the money supply to combat recession, but that AD for unrelated reasons (an increase in investor confidence, for instance) quickly shifted back to AD_0. The monetary stimulus would eventually cause the economy to "overshoot" full employment as AD shifts past AD_0 and prices are stuck temporarily at P_0. The problem with going above full employment (YGAP > 0), as indicated by the price-adjustment equation, is that inflation will result. The recognition that the position of the AD curve is highly unstable and that it takes considerable time for fiscal and monetary policies to have an effect on aggregate demand has made many contemporary macroeconomists more skeptical about policymakers' ability to *fine tune* the economy (maintain it continuously at full employment) than Keynes was half a century ago.

The last aspect of macroeconomic fluctuations considered here is the existence (or lack thereof) of a *trade-off between unemployment and inflation.* Although the costs to society of a high rate of inflation are less obvious and amenable to measurement than the costs of high unemployment, inflation is regarded by policy makers and the public as just as serious an evil as unemployment. Two pieces of legislation (both lacking enforcement provisions)—the Full Employment Act of 1946 and the Humphrey Hawkins Act of 1978—commit the federal government to the twin goals of *full employment* and *price stability* (absence of inflation). The question is whether these objectives are consistent: Can they be simultaneously achieved or does greater achievement of one entail less achievement of the other?

The price-adjustment equation given implies that there *is* a long-run trade-off between unemployment and inflation: Society can achieve a permanently low rate of unemployment by maintaining a permanently high rate of inflation, and vice versa. We can see this relationship by substituting for YGAP in the price adjustment equation, using Okun's Law:

$$\eta = -3f(U - U*)$$

For a given value of $U*$, the higher U is, the lower the inflation rate η. Prior to the early 1970s, this theoretical relationship "fit" observed data on unemployment and inflation very well: The inflation rate tended to be low (or even negative) during years in which unemployment was high. The inverse relationship between U and η was first established empirically by A. W. Phillips using British data spanning many years; for this reason, this relationship has come to be called the *Phillips Curve*. Taken at face value, the Phillips Curve indicated that (1) it would be difficult or impossible for the economy to simultaneously achieve low unemployment and low inflation, and (2) policymakers could bring about a low rate of unemployment by maintaining a high rate of inflation—by adopting a policy of rapid monetary growth, for example.

In the early 1970s, however, the Phillips Curve relationship began to break down—it no longer fit the data. In 1975, the unemployment rate reached 8.5 percent, the highest rate since the Depression, and the inflation rate reached 9.3 percent, the highest rate since the late 1940s. Contrary to the dictates of the Phillips Curve, the economy was experiencing a period of both stagnation (low output) and inflation: *stagflation*. Economic theory had to be reformulated to attempt to explain this new and unpleasant phenomenon.

It turns out that a relatively simple reformulation (generalization) of the price-adjustment equation can account for the existence of stagflation and other aspects of observed macroeconomic behavior. Though simple, this reformulation has dramatically different implications concerning the nature of the unemployment-inflation trade-off and the effectiveness of economic policy in fighting these two scourges. This reformulation, proposed independently by Milton Friedman and Edmund Phelps, consisted of respecifying the price adjustment equation as:

$$\eta_t - \eta_{t-1} = f \cdot YGAP_{t-1}$$

YGAP is now related to the *change* in the rate of inflation, rather than the *level* of inflation, as it was in the original price adjustment equation. This revision implies that if YGAP = 0, the rate of inflation will be *constant*—it will not, in general, be *zero*. If the economy is below full employment (YGAP < 0), the *inflation rate* will decline, but the *price level* will not necessarily decline. (If the inflation rate falls from 7 to 5 percent per year, prices are still increasing, but at a slower rate.)

The revised price adjustment equation implies that there is *no long-run trade-off between unemployment and inflation, only a short-run trade-off*. The absence of a long-run trade-off is signified by the fact that *as long as* $\eta_t = \eta_{t-1}$ (the rate of inflation is constant), $YGAP_{t-1} = 0$ (the economy is at full employment), *regardless of the level of* η_t. If the economy had a permanent 10 percent rate of inflation, it would have no less unemployment (or more output) than it would if it had a permanent rate of inflation of zero—in both cases, the economy would be at full employment. The existence of a short-run trade-off is due to the fact that $(\eta_t - \eta_{t-1})$ is proportional to $YGAP_{t-1}$. For *disinflation*—a reduction in the rate of inflation—to occur, the economy must undergo a recession. The greater the desired extent of disinflation, the deeper the recession required. Suppose that $f = 2$, each percentage point reduction in $YGAP_{t-1}$ reduces the inflation rate by 2 percentage points. If the rate of inflation in year $t - 1$ is 10 percent and policy makers want to reduce it to 4 percent in year t, then they will have to use fiscal and/or monetary policies to force output 3 percent below potential in year $t - 1$.

Policymakers "engineered" a recession to lower the rate of inflation in the early 1980s. In 1979 and 1980, the rates of inflation were respectively 13.3 and 12.4 percent—considered too high by the administration and many Americans. The government allowed the unemployment rate to rise from 5.8 percent in 1979 to 9.7 percent—a postwar high—in 1982, primarily via tight monetary policy. By 1983, the inflation rate had fallen to 3.8 percent. Once the "inflation dragon" had been tamed, the economy was allowed to gradually return to full employment, and the rate of inflation remained moderate.

We observed two salient attributes of the growth of real output: an upward long-term trend, and cyclical fluctuations around this trend. Economists postulate that the tendency of actual output to increase in the long run is due to steady growth in potential output, and that the cyclical fluctuations are due to transitory deviations of actual from potential output. The preceeding discussion explains why such temporary departures from full employment may occur. We conclude this chapter with a brief introduction to evidence and theory pertaining to long-run growth of potential output.

Table 4.3 presents data on the average annual rates of real output growth of the United States and of five other countries during four intervals of the period 1870 to 1984. During the first two intervals, the United States experienced the highest rate of output growth, but it had the second lowest rate in interval III. Every country experienced a sharp acceleration in output growth from interval II to interval III, and a dramatic slowdown from interval III to interval IV. How can we account for these substantial differences across both countries and time in the rate of economic growth?

To begin to answer this question, it is useful to define the notion of *productivity*. The general definition of productivity is the quantity of output per unit of input:

$$\text{Productivity} = \frac{\text{Output}}{\text{Input}}$$

TABLE 4.3. Real output average annual growth rates, six countries, 1870–1984.

Country	Period				Acceleration from Period II to Period III	Slowdown from Period III to Period IV
	I (1870–1913)	II (1913–1950)	III (1950–1973)	IV (1973–1984)		
United States	4.2	2.8	3.7	2.3	+0.9	−1.4
France	1.7	1.1	5.1	2.2	+4.0	−2.9
Germany	2.8	1.3	5.9	1.7	+4.6	−4.2
Japan	2.5	2.2	9.4	3.8	+7.2	−5.6
Netherlands	2.1	2.4	4.7	1.6	+2.3	−3.1
United Kingdom	1.9	1.3	3.0	1.1	+1.7	−1.9

Beyond this general definition, two more specific concepts or measures of productivity differ with respect to the definition of input. First, *labor productivity* is defined as output per unit of labor input:

$$\text{Labor productivity} = \frac{\text{Output}}{\text{Labor input}}$$

The conventional measure of labor input is the total number of hours worked by all persons employed. Recall that according to the production function, another input besides labor—capital—determines the quantity of output produced. Hence, labor input is only a *partial* measure of the amount of resources utilized in production, and labor productivity is a partial productivity measure. The second concept of productivity is *total factor productivity* (TFP), which is defined as output per unit of total input (the terms factor and input are synonymous):

$$\text{TFP} = \frac{\text{Output}}{\text{Total input}}$$

Total input is a weighted sum of the quantities of labor and capital employed, similar to the way in which GNP is a weighted sum of the quantities of all of the commodities produced in the economy. TFP is the best measure of the productive efficiency of the economy: If TFP increases, more output can be produced with the same quantity of input (or a given level of output could be produced with less input).

To facilitate our discussion of long-run economic growth, adopt the following notation:

$$\begin{aligned} Y &= \text{Output} \\ L &= \text{Labor} \\ K &= \text{Capital} \\ T &= \text{Total input} \\ \theta &= \text{Total factor productivity} \end{aligned}$$

Since $\theta = Y/T$, then

$$Y = \theta \cdot T$$

The amount of output produced is determined by the quantity of total input times total factor productivity (output per unit of total input). This is a relationship among the *levels* of Y, θ, and T. However, we are primarily concerned with the *growth rate* of Y and its determinants. Let a dot over a variable denote the growth rate, or percentage rate of change, of that variable; for example, $\dot{Y}$ denotes the growth rate of output. The following relationships among growth rates is implied by the previous equation:

$$\dot{Y} = \dot{\theta} + \dot{T}$$

This means that output growth is the *sum* of total input growth and total factor productivity growth.[4]

We are close to having a simple model which can account for long-run output growth. To complete the model, one more point must be addressed. It concerns the definition and measurement of $\dot{T}$, the rate of growth of total input. Economists have shown that the correct way to define $\dot{T}$ is as follows:

$$\dot{T} = \lambda\dot{K} + (1 - \lambda)\dot{L}$$

where λ is the ratio of capital costs to aggregate costs of production, and $(1 - \lambda)$ is the ratio of labor costs to aggregate costs of production. $\dot{T}$ is therefore a *weighted average* of the growth rates of capital and labor input, weighted by their relative importance in the production of output. For the U.S. economy as a whole, λ is approximately equal to 0.3: Capital accounts for 30 percent, and labor the remaining 70 percent, of total production cost. We will therefore set $\lambda = 0.3$. Substituting this value into the previous equation and rearranging terms,

$$\dot{T} = \dot{L} + .3(\dot{K} - \dot{L})$$

The growth in total input may be expressed as the sum of labor input growth ($\dot{L}$) and the growth in capital per unit of labor ($\dot{K} - \dot{L}$) multiplied by capital's share in production costs. Substituting this expression for $\dot{T}$ into the output growth equation, we obtain our final model of output growth:

$$\dot{Y} = \dot{L} + .3(\dot{K} - \dot{L}) + \theta$$

This equation reveals three sources of output growth in the long run: (1) growth in labor input; (2) growth in capital-intensity, that is, increase in the amount of capital employed per worker; and (3) growth in total factor productivity or efficiency. Let us briefly consider each of these sources of output growth in turn.

Population increase is the major reason for long-run growth in labor input. Between 1950 and 1973, for example, the U.S. population increased at an average annual rate of 1.4 percent, from 152 million to 212 million. However, labor input growth also depends on changes in the *labor force participation rate* (the fraction of the population in the

---

[4]This follows from the mathematical fact that the growth rate of a product of two variables equals the *sum* of the growth rates of the variables. For example, revenue-price × quantity, so if price increases 5 percent and quantity increases 3 percent, revenue increases 8 percent.

labor force) and in average weekly hours of work. The participation rate remained essentially constant between 1950 and 1973, although it has increased somewhat since, due to the increased presence of women in the labor market. Average weekly hours of work declined fairly steadily during 1950 to 1973, at an average annual rate of −0.3 percent. The average growth rate of labor input was therefore about 1.1 percent (= population growth rate + growth rate of average hours). This figure is well below the output growth rate of 3.7 percent reported in Table 4.3, and implies that labor productivity—output per hour of work—was increasing at a rate of 2.6 percent.

One reason for the high rate of growth of labor productivity was that during this period, the amount of capital per worker was increasing at a rate of almost 2.2 percent per year. Society was saving and investing enough to provide each worker with more machinery and other capital with which to work, not merely enough to equip a growing laborforce with the same average amount of capital per worker. As indicated by the last equation, to determine the contribution of capital accumulation to output growth, we multiply the increase in capital per worker by 0.3, which reflects the relative importance of capital in production. Thus "capital-deepening"—the increase in capital intensity—was responsible for about 0.7 percent per year of the growth in output. The *sum* of the contributions of labor input growth and capital deepening to output growth is 1.8 (= 1.1 + 0.7) percent. This is only about half of the 3.7 percent rate of increase of output during the period. About half of the increase in total output was due to an increase in efficiency (total factor productivity), rather than an increase in the amount of capital and labor employed.

Economists have identified a number of the sources of this growth in efficiency; two important sources are investment in education and investment in research and development (R&D). Education tends to increase the quality, or skill level, of the labor force; the effective quantity of labor input depends on the skill level of persons employed as well as on the number of persons. The average level of educational attainment of the laborforce has increased substantially over the long run. For example, the fraction of workers employed in manufacturing who had at least some college education increased from 17 percent in 1960 to 27 percent in 1980.

Investment in R&D contributes to efficiency and output growth by adding to the stock of useful knowledge and by yielding new and improved processes and products. Abundant evidence indicates that industries which perform the most R&D per dollar of sales tend to have the highest rates of TFP growth.

Unfortunately, the rate of TFP growth has fallen substantially since the early 1970s. The rate declined from 1.9 percent during the period between 1950 and 1973, to 0.5 percent during 1973 to 1984. In fact, the entire slowdown in output growth documented in Table 4.3. can be attributed to this deceleration of productivity. A large number of studies have attempted to determine why the productivity slowdown occurred. They have investigated the role of such factors as the sharp energy price increases of the 1970s, the increase in environmental regulation, and a possible decline in the rate or efficacy of industrial innovation. For the most part, however, these studies have failed to provide a compelling explanation for the post-1973 slowdown. The decline in the rate of productivity growth remains a mystery waiting to be solved by future research.

FOR FURTHER READING

Baily, Martin, and Arthur Okun, (eds.), *The Battle Against Unemployment and Inflation.* 3rd ed. (New York: Norton, 1982).

Feldstein, Martin (ed.), *The American Economy in Transition.* (Chicago: University of Chicago Press, 1980).

Hall, Robert, and John Taylor, *Macroeconomics: Theory, Performance, and Policy.* 2nd ed. (New York: Norton, 1988).

Hirshleifer, Jack, *Price Theory and Applications.* 4th ed. (Englewood Cliffs, NJ: Prentice-Hall, 1988).

Okun, Arthur, *Equality and Efficiency: The Big Tradeoff.* (Washington: Brookings, 1975).

PART TWO

THE FUNCTIONS OF A BUSINESS

5 ACCOUNTING AND MANAGEMENT DECISION MAKING

John Leslie Livingstone

THE ROLE OF ACCOUNTING IN ORGANIZATIONS

Accounting for Management Control Purposes

Seluk was the Keeper of Pharaoh's goats. His position was one of great honor, and also of great responsibility. It was to Seluk that Pharaoh looked for goats' milk for the royal table and for the beauty baths of his many wives. Pharaoh looked also to Seluk for goat meat to feed his army, for goat wool to make rugs, and for goat leather to fashion whips, camel reins, and sandals. In modern words, Seluk was manager of the Goat Division of Pharaoh, Inc.

Seluk had charge of some 2000 goats. At the time of each full moon, he met with Ebis, the High Priest. To Ebis he gave a report of how many billy goats, nanny goats, and kids there were in the flock at latest count. To Ebis he reported also how many ewers of milk had been delivered this period to the palace, how many carcasses to the army, how many skeins of wool to Pharaoh's rug weavers, and how many goatskins to the royal leather workshop. All of this Ebis set down on his papyrus, asking questions of Seluk as he wrote:

My faculty colleagues at Babson College offered many helpful comments on earlier drafts of this chapter. For their warm interest and generous assistance, I would like to thank Professors Allan Cohen, Michael Fetters, Carolyn Hotchkiss, William Lawler, Clinton Petersen, and Srinivasan Umapathy.

Seluk, how is it that your flock is now larger than before, but the ewers of milk have become fewer? Seluk, at the rising of this moon, the goats numbered 1991, and there were 2013 at the setting of this moon. Kids born this moon were 240, and 98 carcasses were delivered to the army. Should not your ending goats be 2133 rather than the 2013 which you reported unto me? Where are the remaining 120 goats?

Seluk, you claim that you delivered to the army this moon 98 carcasses. But the army reports to me that only 87 carcasses were indeed received. Explain to me where are the 11 missing carcasses.

What Seluk was recounting to Ebis each moon were the monthly financial statements for Pharoah's flock of goats. Ebis, by his questioning, was performing an audit of these financial statements. Why were they doing these things?

Seluk was entrusted by Pharaoh with the royal flock of goats. His responsibility as a manager made him *accountable* to Pharaoh for the goats, for their natural increase, for their yield in milk, wool, meat, and hides. This accountability required Seluk to report monthly on how well he had carried out his duties to his king. His report was the scorecard on his administration. It also served to direct attention to matters requiring explanation or decision.

Ebis was a highly educated bureaucrat, able to read, write, and count. These rare abilities made him Pharaoh's business manager, and the auditor of Pharaoh's enterprises. His audit was designed to ensure that Seluk was competent and diligent in his duties, and also honest—resisting any temptation to steal goats, milk, wool, meat, or leather.

If Seluk became incompetent, Pharaoh would want to know, in order to remind Seluk of his duty, or to coach him, or to rebuke him, or to replace him. If Seluk were found to lack in diligence or in honesty, Pharaoh would certainly wish to find out in order to punish his disloyal lieutenant and to set an example for any other of his followers who might be slacking off or perhaps even stealing royal property.

In this story, we see one essential role of accounting in organizations: to make those placed in authority and given the responsibility over resources accountable to the people they serve. Managers are held accountable for being competent, diligent, and honest. Accounting provides the scorecard, and auditing is designed to ensure that the scorecard is correct.

This is the *control* function of accounting. Now we turn to the *planning* function of accounting.

Accounting for Business Planning Purposes

Pat Jacobs (PJ) was applying for a loan to start her new business, McSoft. She described her concept to the bank loan officer (LO): a store selling computer software to small businesses.

LO: How much money will you need to get started?

PJ: I estimate $40,000 for the beginning inventory; $18,000 for store signs, shelving, a cash register, and a counter; and $12,000 working capital to cover operating expenses for about two months. That's a total of $70,000 for the start up.

LO: How are you planning to finance the investment of $70,000?

PJ: I can put in $50,000 of my savings, and I'd like to borrow the remaining $20,000 from the bank.

LO: Suppose that the bank lends you $20,000 on a one-year note, at 15 percent interest, secured by a lien on the inventory. Let's put together *pro forma*, or projected, financial statements by rearranging the figures you gave me. Your beginning balance sheet would look like this:

McSoft: Balance Sheet as of 1/1/1991

Assets		Liabilities and Equity	
Cash	$12,000	Note payable	
Inventory	40,000	(bank loan)	$20,000
Current assets	52,000	Current liabilities	20,000
Fixed asset: equipment	18,000	Owner capital	50,000
		Total liabilities and	
Total assets	$70,000	owner equity	$70,000

The left side shows McSoft's investment in assets. It splits the assets into current (turning into cash within a year) and noncurrent, or fixed (not liquid within a year). The right side shows how the assets will be financed—the note to the bank (payable in a year) and your equity as the owner.

PJ: Now I see why it's called a balance sheet. The financing on the one hand must be equal to the assets on the other hand. It's like both sides of the same coin. I also see why a distinction is made between current and noncurrent assets and liabilities: The bank wants to see whether assets turning into cash in a year will provide sufficient funds to repay the loan. Well, will you approve my loan?

LO: I don't know yet. We need more information. First, how much do you think your operating expenses will be?

Here's what I estimate for year 1:

Store rent	$18,000	
Utilities and phone	7,200	
Assistant's salary	20,000	
Interest on bank loan	3,000	(15% on $20,000)
Depreciation	1,800	(10% of $18,000 equipment)
	$50,000	

PJ: My understanding is that the store equipment will last 10 years. Therefore, the depreciation for wear and tear is 10 percent each year.

LO: Good. Now how much do you expect your year's sales to be? And your gross profit?

PJ: I'm confident that we can reach sales of $360,000. The cost of the software from suppliers will be $240,000. That will give us gross profit of $120,000 using the customary markup in the industry. Add this gross profit onto the cost of $240,000 and we get back to the sales figure of $360,000.

LO: Excellent. Let's organize this information into a pro forma income statement. We start with the sales, then deduct the expenses, and end up with the famous bottom line: net income. [The loan officer began to write on her yellow tablet. She put down the following figures:]

McSoft:
Income Statement for the Year Ending 12/31/91

Sales		$360,000
Less cost of goods sold		240,000
Gross profit		$120,000
Less expenses:		
Salaries	20,000	
Rent	18,000	
Utilities & phone	7,200	
Depreciation	1,800	
Interest	3,000	$ 50,000
Income before taxes		70,000
Income tax expense (40%)		28,000
Net income		$ 42,000

Pat, this looks fine for your first year in business. Many new businesses find it difficult to make a profit at all in their first year. They do well just to break even and stay in business. Of course, I'll need to go over all of your sales and expense projections with you, to make sure that I agree they are realistic. But so far, so good. Now we are ready to do the year-end pro forma balance sheet. I need to ask you how much cash you are planning to draw out of the business in the first year for living expenses.

PJ: Well, my present job pays $38,000 and I plan to keep to this same standard of living with McSoft for year 1.

LO: Let's see how that works out after we complete the pro forma financial statements. Now for the year-end balance sheet. [Again, the loan officer wrote on the yellow tablet and this is what she put on the paper:]

McSoft:
Balance Sheet as of 12/31/1991

Assets		Liabilities and Equity	
Cash	$17,800	Note payable	$20,000
Inventory	40,000	(bank loan)	
Current assets	57,800	Current liabilities	20,000
Fixed asset:			
Equipment	18,000	Owner capital 1/1	50,000
Less depreciation	(1,800)	Add net income	42,000
		Less drawings	(38,000)
Net equipment	16,200	Owner capital 12/31	54,000
		Total liabilities	
Total assets	$74,000	and owner equity	$74,000

LO: Pat, let's go over this balance sheet together. You'll see that the asset side has changed, compared to the beginning balance sheet. Leave cash aside for the moment. I just put in a *plug number* that kept the balance sheet in balance for now. We'll come back to it later. The equipment has the depreciation deducted, to write it down to $16,200. On the other side, your equity is increased by the net income, and reduced by what you drew out to live on. Getting back to cash, here's a problem. Cash is only $17,800 but the bank note of $20,000 is due for payment. We have hit a snag.

PJ: I realize that McSoft will need cash to repay the $20,000 on the loan, and I'll still need to keep $12,000 cash on hand for about two months' operating expenses. That's a total of $20,000 plus $12,000, which adds up to $32,000. With only $17,800 cash on the balance sheet, it seems I'm about $14,000 or $15,000 short on cash. Do you think I'll have to cut my drawings down from $38,000 to $23,000 to come up with the difference? Here I am, opening my own business, and it looks as if I'm going back to what I earned five years ago!

LO: That's one way to do it. But here's an alternative that you may find easier. After your suppliers get to know you, and do a few months' business with you, you could ask them to open credit accounts for McSoft. If you pay on the usual 30-day basis, then your suppliers would be financing one month's inventory. That would be $1/12$ of annual cost of goods sold, which is $1/12$ of $240,000 or $20,000. In essence, accounts payable of $20,000 would replace the bank loan of $20,000 on your balance sheet. The cash payment of $20,000 that you would normally make to suppliers in December 1991 would be used to pay off your loan instead of your suppliers.

PJ: That sounds like a perfect solution. But could we first see how the balance sheet would look with your suggestion?

LO: Good idea. Also, we still need to work through the cash flow statement. First, let's tackle the revised balance sheet. [Once more, the pen moved over the yellow tablet as the loan officer wrote:]

McSoft:
Balance Sheet as of 12/31/1991

Assets		Liabilities and Equity	
Cash	$17,800	Note payable, bank	$ 0
Inventory	40,000	Accounts payable	20,000
Current assets	57,800	Current liabilities	20,000
Fixed asset:			
Equipment	18,000	Owner capital 1/1	50,000
Less depreciation	(1,800)	Add net income	42,000
		Less drawings	(38,000)
Net equipment	16,200	Owner capital 12/31	54,000
		Total liabilities	
Total assets	$74,000	and other equity	$74,000

When you pay off the note to the bank, it disappears from the balance sheet, and accounts payable of $20,000 appears in its place. Cash remains at $17,800 and is enough to cover a couple of months of operating expenses. Now we move on to the cash flow statement.

McSoft:
Cash Flow Statement for the Year Ending 12/31/91

Sources of Cash	
From operations: Net income	$42,000
Add depreciation	1,800
Add increase in accounts payable	20,000
Total cash from operations	63,800
Less: Withdrawn by owner	38,000
Cash reinvested to grow the business	25,800
From financing: Bank loan repaid	(20,000)
Total sources of cash	5,800
Uses of Cash	
Invested in equipment	0
Total sources less uses (increase in cash)	5,800
Add cash at beginning of year	12,000
Cash at end of year	$17,800

Pat, do you have any questions about the cash flow statement or the balance sheet we have just put together?

PJ: Actually, the cash flow statement makes sense to me. I guess in the last analysis there are only two places where a business can get cash: from the *inside,* by making a profit, and from the *outside,* by external financing like bank loans or owner's capital. In this case, the outside financing is negative because it is a repayment of a loan.

I also see that the use of cash is to invest in equipment to grow the business, even though this happens to be zero for McSoft in 1991 because no further new equipment is acquired. But the part of the cash flow statement that I find a little unfamiliar is the cash from operations section. Can we talk about that some more?

LO: Sure. As you said, profit is the source of internal cash generation and so we begin with net income. But we have to convert it to a cash basis. First, we add back depreciation to net income. Remember that we deducted depreciation as one of the expenses in order to arrive at net income. Adding back depreciation just backs it out of net income. In short, we ignore it in figuring cash flow. Why do this?

Here's why. Since the depreciation is just a portion of the total cost of the equipment, the total cost of equipment is a cash outflow that should not be counted twice: once when the equipment is purchased and again when we write off part of it as expense, for depreciation. We don't write a check for depreciation, so it should not be treated as a cash outflow.

We also add back the increase in accounts payable for this same reason. In arriving at net income, we deducted all of the cost of goods sold, even the part we have not yet paid for: Remember the $20,000 we talked about before? We add back the $20,000 because that amount of cash has not yet been paid out.

With these adjustments, cash from operations is $63,800. The business has generated $63,800 of cash and can invest it for future growth. But your withdrawal of $38,000 reduces the amount available for reinvestment of $25,800 as the statement shows.

Also, notice that the statement ties in with our balance sheet cash figure: It reflects how the beginning cash amount changed into the ending cash amount.

PJ: Thanks. Now I understand. Am I right that you want to review my projections, and that you will then let me know about the loan?

LO: Yes. I'll be back to you before the end of the week. By the way, would you like me to make you a photocopy of the pro forma financial statements to take with you?

PJ: Yes, please, I'd appreciate that. They certainly do put the finances of the business into clear focus. I am grateful to you for putting them together with me.

As Pat walked out of the bank, she reflected that she had a good interview with the loan officer. She had also learned some accounting skills that would be valuable to her as an entrepreneur.

Points to Remember About Financial Statements

When Pat got home, she sat down and summarized on paper what she had learned about balance sheets:

1. The basic form is Assets = Liabilities + Owner equity
2. Assets are the investments, such as inventory and equipment, made by the firm to operate its business. The liabilities and owner equity reflect how the assets are financed.
3. Balance sheets summarize financial position at a given moment in time and change as each transaction is recorded.
4. Every transaction is an exchange, and both sides of the transaction are always reflected. For example, when the bank loan is paid off with cash, the loan vanishes from the balance sheet and cash decreases by the same amount.
5. Only transactions measurable in money are recorded: We cannot put a transaction onto the balance sheet if it does not have a definite monetary amount. For example, if McSoft gains favorable publicity through a TV news interview, nothing is reflected on the balance sheet, since no definite money value can be assigned to this event.
6. Profits increase owner equity, and cash withdrawals by the owner decrease equity.

These simple rules and the example of McSoft, provide you with a beginning of understanding of the basic structure of an actual balance sheet for a major corporation.

Next, Pat noted what she had learned about income statements:

1. The basic form is Revenues – Expenses = Net income
2. Net income is not the same as cash from operations.
3. Some expenses are never cash outflows (depreciation, for example), and some expenses may be partly paid in cash this period and partly in the next period (cost of goods sold, for example).
4. Owner withdrawals are not an operating expanse, but are a distribution out of net income.
5. Profit, after being adjusted to a cash basis, is how cash is internally generated.

While Pat was summarizing what she had learned about balance sheets and income statements, the loan officer was preparing for her next day. She knew that she would be analyzing the cash flow for a well-established large company, so she reviewed some guidelines that the bank had given out on reading cash flow statements.

In reading a cash flow statement, be alert to the following indicators:

1. Is cash from operations positive? Is it growing from one period to the next? Is the increase in working capital growing faster than sales, and if so, why?
2. Are cash withdrawals by owners (or dividends) only a small fraction of cash from operations? If cash withdrawals are too large a share of cash generated from operations, then the business is being milked of cash and will not be able to finance its future growth.
3. Of the total sources of cash, how much is generated inside the business through operations, and how much is obtained from outside financing? There are exceptions, but it is normally wise for businesses to rely more on internal cash generation than on outside financing to fund their future growth.
4. Of the outside financing, how much is equity and how much is borrowed money? While there are exceptions, it is wise to use more equity than debt funds for growth.
5. How much of its total sources of cash is the company using to invest for growth, and how much to increase its cash resources, or liquidity? Is it overinvesting (total uses greater than total sources of cash) or underinvesting (total sources greater than total uses) by too wide a margin?
6. Just what is the company investing in? Is it likely that these investments will be profitable? How long will it take for these investments to repay their cost, and then to earn a return?

These sample questions reminded the loan officer that the cash flow statement supplies valuable information that goes to the core of the company's business strategy and to the effectiveness of its management. She felt ready for tomorrow and decided to end her business day.

The Auditor's Report

In our opening story, Ebis received the account of Seluk's management of Pharaoh's goats. Ebis checked Seluk's report by asking important questions. Ebis served Pharaoh as a true watchdog, by verifying that Seluk had made a full and fair report. This valuable watchdog function remains alive and well in our times. It is performed today for the investors in the company by the outside independent auditor, whose report must accompany all annual financial statements published by companies with publicly traded securities.

The auditor's report follows a standard format. The first paragraph says *what the auditor did,* namely, that the auditor has examined the financial statements by following generally accepted auditing standards, which include tests (rather than 100 percent examination) of the accounting records. The second paragraph gives the *auditor's opinion,* based on the audit examination performed.

The key words in the opinion paragraph are *present fairly* and *in conformity with generally accepted accounting principles applied on a consistent basis.* This opinion provides comfort to users of the financial statements that the information is fairly and consistently presented. If this were not the case, the auditor would say so in the auditor's report. Phrases such as "subject to" or "except for" are often used in such situations. In other words, this phrasing indicates that the watchdog is barking.

Companies with publicly traded securities must publish annual audited financial statements. Other firms are not required by law to do so. However, they may still need to provide audited financial statements in order to borrow from banks and other lenders, or to satisfy large investors, major suppliers, or major customers. Unaudited financial statements are not as reliable as audited statements.

Before you review any set of audited financial statements, first read the auditor's report to see if the auditor has flagged anything in the examination. Do not remain asleep when the watchdog is barking!

We now have obtained a basic understanding of the three main financial statements and the auditor's report. It is time to put our knowledge to work in making decisions as managers.

USING FINANCIAL STATEMENTS IN MAKING BUSINESS DECISIONS

The following is a short list of some of the *users* and *uses* of financial statements. This list is by no means complete:

1. Equity and debt investors, to monitor the performance of management
2. Prospective investors, to decide in which companies to invest

3. Banks and other lenders, to decide on whether to make new loans, or continue existing loans

4. Investment analysts, money managers, and stockbrokers, to make investment recommendations or decisions for their clients

5. Rating agencies (such as Standard & Poor's, Moody's, and Dun & Bradstreet), to assign credit ratings

6. Major suppliers and customers, to evaluate the strength and financial staying power of the company as a long-term resource for their business

7. Labor unions and employee associations, to assess what the company may be able to afford to pay in upcoming labor negotiations

8. Management, to assess the company's standing with the present and potential investors, bankers, the financial community, customers, suppliers, and workers

9. Management, to review their effectiveness in running the business, and to plan the future of the company

10. Corporate raiders, seeking hidden value in companies with under-priced stock

11. Competitors, to benchmark their own progress in the industry against what the company has achieved

12. Potential competitors, to assess how profitable it may be to enter the industry, and how strong a competitor the company would be

13. Government agencies who are responsible for taxing, regulating, or investigating the company

14. Politicians, consumer advocates, single issue groups, lobbyists, environmental activists, foundations, and other parties who are either promoting or fighting a particular cause

15. Joint venture partners, trade associations, franchisors or franchisees, and other present or potential business associates who have an interest in the company and its financial position

This brief list shows how important and useful the roles are that financial statements play in the business world. It also shows how essential it is for managers to master the understanding, analysis, and use of financial statements for making business decisions.

How to Analyze Financial Statements

Imagine that you are a physician, working in the emergency room of a large hospital. Some patients arrive with serious injury or illness, some barely alive or even dead, some with minor problems, and some with only imagined ailments. Your training and experience have taught you to make a careful diagnosis, based on certain tests. In a case that appears serious, you check the vial signs: pulse, blood pressure, respiration, temperature, and EKG.

We check the financial health of a company in much the same way, using the financial statements for our examination. The tests that business doctors use are mostly based on *financial ratios*. It is convenient to classify these tests and ratios into three categories:

1. Short-term solvency
2. Long-term solvency
3. Profitability

We will describe each of these categories next.

Short-Term Solvency

We must emphasize the importance of sufficient cash resources or liquidity, which enables a company to pay its bills and to stay in business. Liquidity means survival, and insufficient liquidity means bankruptcy to a business. The essential nature of liquidity is why current assets (which turn into cash within a year) and current liabilities (which require cash payment within a year) are shown separately on balance sheets. In the short-term solvency test, liquidity is measured by means of the following financial ratios.

The *current ratio* is total current assets divided by total current liabilities. It indicates the company's ability to meet current obligations out of its current resources. It is expressed as "2.5 to 1," or "2.5:1," or just "2.5." A current ratio that is greater than one is needed to provide some margin of safety.

Bear in mind that the current ratio is not a precise measure. There is no point in calculating it to more than one decimal place. It is open to "window dressing," quite legitimately, as firms attempt to put their best foot forward in their financial statements (which they are tempted to do to present their management performance in the best possible light).

For example, suppose that current assets are hypothetically $200, and current liabilities are $100. Then the current ratio is 2.0. The financial year ends in one week. The firm decides to make early payment on $50 of accounts payable. The current assets are now $150 (cash decreased by $50), and current liabilities are $50 (accounts payable decreased by $50). The current ratio becomes 150/50, or 3.0 rather than

2.0: a great improvement on paper! Regard *all* financial ratios as rough figures and not as precise measures.

In some cases, inventories are not liquid in a crisis situation (except at "fire sale" prices). This condition is especially likely in a trendy or high fashion business, or where technological obsolescence is probable, or if the market is saturated. In these cases, the current ratio is modified by including only the more liquid items in current assets and excluding inventories and prepaid items.

This variation is called the *quick ratio,* or *acid test ratio.* It, too, is expected to be greater than one by some margin of safety.

Next, we consider turnover in relation to liquidity. Faster turnover of assets allows us to do more business without an equivalent increase in assets. Speedier asset turnover means that we tie up less cash in assets, which in turn helps liquidity. By the same token, slower turnover of liabilities assists liquidity. However, too slow a liability turnover may reflect lack of enough cash to pay the bills. Three ratios are commonly used to measure turnover of accounts receivable, inventories, and accounts payable, respectively.

Accounts receivable is:

$$\frac{\text{Accounts receivable}}{\text{turnover}} = \frac{\text{Credit sales}}{\text{Accounts receivable}}$$

Suppose that credit sales for the year are $120,000, and accounts receivable are $30,000. Then the receivables turnover is 120,000/30,000, or 4, which shows that receivables are "turning over" on average four times a year. It can also be expressed as *days' sales,* by dividing 365 days (in a year) by 4 to get an average of 91 days. This expression says we are carrying receivables averaging 91 days sales. That is fine if our credit terms call for payment 90 days from invoice. It is not fine if our terms are 60 days, and it is alarming if terms are 30 days. Unlike vintage wine or great works of art, receivables do not improve with age! Show receivables turnover signals danger to liquidity.

Inventory turn is *cost of goods sold* divided by *inventories.* Unlike receivables, the numerator here is cost of goods sold rather than sales. The reason is that inventories are carried on the balance sheet at *cost* (not selling price: check back to the McSoft balance sheets to verify this fact). So, to have a consistent "apples to apples" ratio, both numerator (cost of goods sold) and denominator (inventory) must be in the same terms, namely cost.

In this example, cost of goods sold this year is $100,000, and inventory is $33,333. Then, inventory turn is 100,000/33,333, or 3 times per year. This figure can be expressed as 365/3 = 122 days supply of inventory on hand. In the auto manufacturing business, 60 days supply of cars is about normal, and 122 days would be regarded an unacceptable. That oversupply would trigger a vigorous rebate campaign to clear out the excess vehicles. Slow inventory turnover is a serious red flag for liquidity.

Accounts payable turnover indicates the extent to which a firm is keeping current in paying its suppliers. This ratio is:

$$\frac{\text{Accounts payable}}{\text{turnover}} = \frac{\text{Cost of goods sold}}{\text{Accounts payable}}$$

Cost is used in the numerator for the same reason as in inventory turn: The accounts payable are owed to suppliers of goods for resale and are recorded at cost. To illustrate, cost of goods sold this year is $100,000, and accounts payable is $20,000. Accounts payable turnover is 100,000/20,000 = 5 times a year. It can also be translated into 365/5 = 73 days average. This average should be compared to a relevant yardstick (we shall discuss relevant yardsticks later).

We have now concluded all the ratios indicating short-term solvency. If your analysis of a company reveals poor liquidity ratios, you may have finished your work. This patient is almost dead, and only desperate measures can save the day. On the other hand, if your patient passes the liquidity tests, the business doctor is ready to make the next set of tests: long-term solvency.

Long-Term Solvency

The two tests of long-term solvency focus on a firm's ability to meet its obligations to pay interest and principal on the long-term debt. One test is for interest and one for principal.

The test of ability to pay interest on the long-term debt is based on a statistic known as *times interest earned.* This statistic is the ratio of earnings before interest and taxes (**EBIT**) to the interest on long-term debt. The numerator represents profit available to meet interest expense. Bear in mind that business interest is tax deductible so that income taxes are calculated on income after interest expense.

For example, assume that McSoft had a long-term loan payable of $30,000. Suppose that interest is 12 percent per year or $3600. Also suppose that McSoft had EBIT of $10,800 this year. Then, times interest earned is 10,800/3600 = 3.0. This ratio indicates that McSoft could meet its interest expense three times over, thus providing a safety cushion for the lender. However, if the ratio had been 1.0, there would be no cushion at all, a serious red flag.

The ratio to test the safety of principal on long-term debt involves the proportion of long-term debt in the total long-term capital structure of the firm. The long-term capital structure means long-term liabilities plus owner equity on the balance sheet. This ratio shows how the fixed assets plus the working capital (current assets less current liabilities) are financed out of long-term funds.

Returning to McSoft, suppose that the latest balance sheet showed the long-term capital structure as follows:

Long-term debt		$30,000
Owner equity: Owner capital	$20,000	
Retained earnings	9,000	29,000
Total long-term capital structure		$59,000

The item of concern may be measured as the *debt to equity ratio*, 30,000:29,000 which is approximately one. Alternatively, it may be measured as the proportion of long-term debt in the total capital structure, the *debt to debt-plus-equity ratio* of 30,000:59,000, which is approximately 50 percent. Either approach is commonly used. This option makes it important to clarify which method is being applied in a particular case to avoid any possible misunderstanding.

An acceptable level of this ratio causes little worry, but too high a level is grounds for concern. When it exceeds the comfort level, the larger this ratio (whichever way it is measured), the riskier the enterprise. This increased risk results because the debt is senior to the equity (meaning that interest must be paid before dividends can be paid). In liquidation, the principal and interest of the debt must first be paid in full before any cash remaining can be paid to the equity holders.

The comfort level of the debt to equity ratio varies from one industry to another and depends on the stability or volatility of the industry, and the value of the collateral (if any) securing the debt. So-called "junk bonds" are regarded as "junk" because their issuers often have poor debt to equity ratios. This discussion concludes the long-term solvency tests.

The third and final group of tests examines profitability.

Profitability Ratios

There are two categories of profitability ratios. The first category is *percentage of sales*. Consider the following income statements:

	1990	1991
Sales revenues	$8,976	$9,864
Cost of goods sold	5,296	6,017
Gross profit	3,680	3,847
Operating expenses	2,441	2,792
Selling, general, and administrative expenses	637	750
Operating profit	602	305
Interest expense	201	201
Income before taxes	401	104
Income taxes	160	41
Net income	$ 241	$ 63

What do these income statements reveal about the financial results for 1991 versus 1990? The good news is that sales *increased* by about $900; the bad news is that net income *decreased* by about $180. How did this frustrating situation develop where sales are up but profits are down? The reason is hard to see from the income statements. Is it due to increased expenses? The income statements do show that most expenses rose in 1991. However, sales were up too, so we would reasonably expect expenses to increase with the higher level of business activity. Why we gained sales but lost profits in 1991 is still vague.

Now, consider the same income statements again, but with added columns for percentages:

	1990	Percent	1991	Percent
Sales revenue	$8,976	100.0	$9,864	100.0
Cost of goods sold	5,296	59.0	6,017	61.0
Gross profit	3,680	41.0	3,847	39.0
Operating expenses	2,441	27.2	2,792	28.3
Selling, general, and administrative expenses	637	7.1	750	7.6
Operating profit	602	6.7	305	3.1
Interest expense	201	2.2	201	2.0
Income before taxes	401	4.5	104	1.1
Income taxes	160	1.8	41	0.4
Net income	$ 241	2.7	$ 63	0.6

The percentage columns show sales each year as 100 percent, and each line item on the income statement is shown as a percent of sales. In other words, out of every sales dollar we can see how much went to each type of expense and why we ended up with a net income per sales dollar of 2.7¢ in 1990, but with only 0.6¢ in 1991.

Now it becomes clear why we had disappointing results in 1991 and how they happened. Mainly, the gross profit ratio to sales fell by 2 percent (39 versus 41.0 percent), while the operating expenses ratio to sales rose 1.1 percent (28.3 versus 27.2 percent), and SG&A expenses increased by 0.5 percent (7.6 versus 7.1 percent). The combined impact of these effects was a 3.6 percent drop in operating profit, from 6.7 to 3.1 percent. This 3.6 percent drop was partially offset by decreases in interest expense (0.2 percent) and income taxes (1.4 percent), resulting in an overall fall of 2.1 percent in net income.

With the percentage columns, we have a clear picture of what happened. We can also calculate the dollar impact of events:

	Percent	Dollars
Sales revenue for 1991	100.0	9,864
Expected net income for 1991	2.7	266
Less deterioration: Gross profit	(2.0)	(197)
Operating expenses	(1.1)	(109)
SG&A expenses	(0.5)	(49)
Add improvement: Interest expense	0.2	20
Income taxes	1.4	138
Actual net income for 1991	0.6	63

The use of *percent of sales* ratios is a simple but powerful technique for examining the behavior of gross profit and the various types of expenses. The main ratios of this kind are:

1. Gross profit percent
2. Operating expense percent
3. SG&A expense percent
4. Operating profit percent
5. Income before tax percent
6. Net income percent

The second category of profitability ratios is the return on investment type. This category takes into account the amount of capital invested and indicates the profit earned on the investment as a percentage yield. It is a most important and widely used type of profitability measure. We explain it by using the following summary balance sheet, together with the example income statements that we discussed in dealing with the *percent of sales* ratios.

Summary Balance Sheet as of 12/31/90

Current assets	$1,200		
Less current liabilities	700		
Equals working capital	500	Long-term debt	$1,600
Fixed assets	2,500	Owner equity	1,400
Total assets	$3,000	Total equities	$3,000

Summary Income Statements for the Years Ended 12/31

	1990	1991
Operating profit	$602	$305
Less interest expense	201	201
Income before taxes	401	104
Income taxes	160	41
Net income	$241	$ 63

The first ratio we consider is *return on total assets before taxes* (ROTABT), which is *operating profit* divided by *total assets*. In 1990, this ratio was $602/3000 = 20.1$ percent. There are several points to keep in mind with ROTABT. Note that it measures the basic earning power of the assets of the firm, regardless of whether theses assets are financed by equity or by long-term debt. It focuses directly on the assets that are financed by equity and long-term debt, by calculating total assets as *fixed assets plus working capital* (which is current assets less current liabilities). This formulation makes the total assets consistent with, and equal in amount to, the long-term capital structure when calculating the return on investment-type ratios. The current assets, in relation to current liabilities and liquidity, have already been taken into consideration in the tests of short-term solvency. We do not need to duplicate those tests by again taking into account current liabilities when we test long-term solvency. The form of the summary balance sheet for this purpose is:

Assets		Long-Term Liabilities & Equity	
Working capital		Long-term liabilities	
Fixed assets	_____	Equity	_____
Total assets	_____	Total long-term capital	_____

Note that the numerator in ROTABT is EBIT. This formulation excludes any effect from the ratio of how assets are financed, by leaving out interest on debt and the tax impact of interest. Excluding the effects of financing enables us to compare ratios for more than one firm, regardless of how any particular firm finances its assets. Remember, the aim is to measure the basic earning power of assets, unaffected by methods of long-term financing. This same point is true for the next ratio also.

Return on total assets after taxes (ROTAAT) is:

$$\frac{\text{Net income} + \text{interest expense net of income tax deduction}}{\text{Total assets}}$$

This ratio allows for the fact that interest is deductible for income tax purposes. Therefore, the cost of debt to the firm, after tax, is the interest less the related tax saving. This tax saving is the tax rate (40 percent) times the interest of $201, which is $80. So, interest net of the tax deduction is $121 ($201 − 80). Then, our ratio is $241 (net income) + $121 (net interest after tax) divided by $3000 (total assets) = 12.1 percent.

Long-term debt is usually a less expensive form of financing than equity for two reasons. First, the interest on debt is deductible for tax purposes. However, dividends on the equity capital (stock) are not tax deductible. The advantage of tax deductibility makes debt interest relatively less expensive to the firm. Second, debt is senior to equity and is thus less risky to the investor. Investors are able to demand a higher return for riskier investment securities. This ability makes the required rate of return on a firm's equity securities higher than on its debt securities. For these reasons, debt is usually less costly to a firm than equity.

The example financial statements reflect such a tendancy. Note that interest after tax is $121 on the long-term debt of $1600 or 7.6 percent, but recall that ROTAAT was 12.1 percent. Therefore, the firm earns 12.1 percent, and after paying the holders of long-term debt their 7.6 percent, the firm benefits by the difference between the 12.1 percent earned and the 7.6 percent paid on debt financing. How much is this benefit? We measure it by the next ratio—*return on equity.*

Note that there are two kinds of equity. Preferred stock usually has a fixed rate of dividend, like a fixed rate of interest on long-term debt, and it is senior to the other kind of equity: common stock. Common stock has no fixed rate of dividend, and it is always the most junior form of long-term capital. Some companies do not have preferred stock, but all companies have common stock. When people use *return on equity,* they usually mean return on the *common equity.*

Return on equity (ROE) is probably the most important ratio to the common stockholders. It indicates the return on their equity investment in the company. *Return on equity* is the *net income* (less preferred dividends) divided by *common equity*, which in our example is 241/1400 = 17.2 percent. We recall that ROTAAT is 12.1 percent. Therefore, if there were no long-term debt, then ROE would also be 12.1 percent. However, the long-term debt, costing only 7.6 percent after tax, enables ROE to be boosted to 17.2 percent. The benefit to the owners is their higher ROE of 17.2 percent versus the 12.1 percent that they would have earned without the debt. This tactic is known as *leverage*.

Leverage is regarded by some investors as a turbobooster to earnings. Therefore, it is no wonder that debt financing is in vogue and that junk bonds have become so popular. Also popular are leveraged buyouts—purchases of businesses financed heavily by debt and with abnormally low equity. Leverage gives a higher return on equity so long as profits are large. On the other hand, if profits shrink, leverage has the opposite effect.

Recall in our sample income statement that net income fell from $241 in 1990 to $63 in 1991. The 1991 ROE is 63/1600 = 3.9 percent, compared with 17.2 percent in 1990. This is reverse leverage! 1991 ROTAAT is 6.1 percent, calculated as follows:

$$\frac{\text{Net income (\$63)} + \text{Interest after tax (\$201} - \$80 = \$121)}{\text{Total assets (\$3000)}}$$

Without debt, the ROE would have been 6.1 percent, but the cost of the debt after tax was 7.6 percent, leaving only 3.9 percent return to the equity owners. The *negative benefit* is −2.2 percent (3.9% − 6.1%) to the equity owners. This calculation illustrates the downside risk of excessive leverage. In summary, high leverage will make the good years better and the bad years worse for equity owners.

The financial markets reflect this relationship by demanding larger rates of return on both debt and equity as leverage increases beyond the comfort level. Investors willing to take greater risks ask for greater returns. However, once past a certain point, further increase of a firm's leverage is no longer economic because the rising cost of financing will outpace any further gain from leverage.

The next profitability measure is the well-known *earnings per share* (EPS). EPS is *net income* less *preferred stock dividends* divided by the *number of common shares outstanding* (excluding treasury stock, which is stock repurchased from stockholders by the company). If a company has issued convertible debt securities (where holders have the option of converting their debt securities into common stock), there are two versions of EPS—*primary* (or *undiluted*, as described above) and *fully diluted* (assuming that all of the conversion options have been exercised).

Stockholders are wary of dilution because when more stock is issued, the earnings per share must perforce go down. EPS reveals dilution by stating earnings in relation to a single share of common stock.

The next ratio is also on a single share basis. It is known as the *price earnings* (PE) *ratio*. It, too, applies only to common stock and is the ratio of the *market price* of the stock to *earnings per share*. The PE ratio is a return on investment-type measure, but (unlike ROE) it uses the market price per share as the investment base.

Two points are worth noting. First, the EPS used may be for the past year (actual), the present year (estimated), or the next year (projected). Past EPS is sometimes referred to as a "trailing" EPS. The PE ratio is an upside-down return on investment concept: The usual *return on investment* is the *return* divided by the *investment*. But the *PE ratio* is the reverse: *Investment* divided by *return*. Why is it done upside down? Who knows: It is simply a time-honored tradition!

All of the ratios discussed reflect the actual results of the *past*. But the PE ratio is by its very nature a *prospective* ratio, because the stock market builds future prospects into present stock prices. The same is true of all ratios based on market prices or projections, which includes our final ratio.

The final ratio is also a per share of common stock ratio. It is the ratio of the market price per share to the book value per share of common stock. Sometimes it is called the *market to book ratio*. *Book value per common share* is the *common equity* (total owner equity excluding preferred stock) divided by the *number of common shares outstanding*. It simply translates common equity into a per share basis. The ratio indicates whether a company is worth more in market value than the cost it paid for its assets (less its liabilities).

A ratio greater than one means that market value exceeds the book value. This excess may be taken as a sign that management (and possibly good fortune) have created stockholder value over and above the acquisition cost of the assets. Many experts in business strategy say that the ultimate goal of management is to maximize stockholder value. The market to book ratio is one indicator of success in achieving this objective.

For some regulated companies, regulation is based on a fair rate of return. Then, the market to book ratio indicates the extent to which regulation is indeed fair. A market to book ratio of approximately one indicates 100 percent fairness. (The regulator is allowing the company to earn the market rate of return.) A market to book ratio significantly above one suggests overgenerosity by the regulator (allowing an excessive return), and a ratio substantially below one is a sign of a regulator allowing an inferior rate of return.

We have now discussed all of the main financial ratios, and they are summarized in Table 5.1.

Practical Use of Financial Ratios:

Keep in mind a number of important points for the effective use of ratios. First, the ratios can never be more reliable than the data on which they are based. Therefore, it is essential to be sure that you have checked the reliability of the basic data. Remember: Garbage in garbage out! Beware of: Garbage in, gospel out!

Remember that our discussion of financial statements has dealt with fundamentals; some of the highly technical aspects can challenge even the experts. For example, financial statements include footnotes that can contain important information which can affect the interpretation of those statements. Some of these footnotes are complex, and you should seek professional advice if you come across anything that you do not fully understand.

Be aware of areas where the accounting treatment of certain items is not cut and dried. Two ways of accounting may be equally acceptable methods of treating the same item but give very different results. These diverse results can, in turn, affect the financial ratios and make them better or worse than they might otherwise be.

Often, the ratios will not provide a decisive answer. Do not be surprised if this happens. Uncertainty is a signal to investigate further by gathering more facts and by using other suitable techniques.

Ratios can be affected by seasonal factors. For instance, retailers commonly end their financial years on the 31st of January, when business is slack and the inventories are low. Since inventories are at their seasonal low, the inventory turnover ratios look faster than they normally are. Remember to keep seasonal effects on ratios in mind.

Few financial ratios are meaningful when considered in a vacuum. They need to be measured in relation to a standard or appropriate yardstick. The simplest yardstick is to compare ratios for a firm against its ratios for previous periods. One firm may be compared with another firm in the same industry, or against composite ratios for the entire industry as

TABLE 5.1. Summary of financial ratios.

Ratio	Numerator	Denominator
Short-Term Solvency:		
Current ratio	Current assets	Current liabilities
Quick ratio (acid test)	Highly liquid current assets	Current liabilities
Receivables turn days' receivables	Credit sales 365 days	Accounts receivable receivables turn
Inventory turn days' inventory	Cost of sales 365 days	Inventories inventory turn
Payables turn days' payables	Cost of sales 365 days	Accounts payable payables turn
Long-Term Solvency:		
Times interest earned	Operating income (EBIT)	Interest on long-term debt
Debt to equity ratio	Long-term debt	Owner equity
Debt ratio	Long-term debt	Total financial structure
Profitability: Profit to Sales Ratios:		
Gross profit	Gross profit	Sales
Operating expense	Operating expense	Sales
SG&A ratio	SG&A expense	Sales
Pretax income	Pretax income	Sales
Net income	Net income	Sales
Profitability: Return on Investment Ratios:		
Return on Total Assets:		
Before taxes	Operating income (EBIT)	Total assets (working capital + fixed assets)
After taxes	Net income + Interest after tax	Total assets (working capital + fixed assets)
Return on equity	Net income − Preferred dividends	Common equity
Earnings per share (undiluted or primary)	Net income − Preferred dividends	Number of common shares outstanding
Earnings per share (fully diluted)	Net income − Preferred dividends	Number of common shares outstanding (all conversion options exercised)
Price to earnings ratio	Market price per common share	Earnings per share of common stock
Market to book ratio	Market price per common share	Book value per common share

FIGURE 5.1.   Ratios included with financial statements for Prime Computer, Inc.

Operating and Capitalization Ratios		
Current ratio	3.92	2.94
Inventory turnover	4.90	4.56
Days sales in average accounts receivable	90	95
Tax rate	25.0%	25.0%
Long-term debt as a percentage of total capital	49.5%	3.1%
Research, development, and engineering expense as a percentage of total revenue	11.4%*	10.7%*
Productivity Ratios		
Operating income as a percentage of total revenue	8.6%	7.4%
Net income as a percentage of total revenue	6.7%	5.5%
Sales per average number of employees	$110	$103
Return on average assets	6.4%	7.3%
Return on average stockholders' equity	13.8%	11.4%
Operating Data		
Percentage—foreign sales	48%	47%
Employees—year end	8.818	8.621

*Includes the impact of Statement of Financial Accounting Standards No. 86 (SFAS 86), which requires the capitalization of certain computer software development costs. Excluding the effect of SFAS 86, RD&E expense as a percentage of total revenue would have been 12.5% and 12.1% in 1987 and 1986, respectively.

Source: Reproduced by permission of Prime Computer, Inc.

a whole. The industry ratios are often available from firms specializing in financial statistics, such as Dun & Bradstreet, Standard & Poor's, and Moody's, among others.

Keep in mind that the trend over time is critical in considering ratios. For example, a current ratio of 1.5 may seem barely satisfactory. However, if it were only 1.0 last year, then this year's 1.5 may be a substantial improvement. On the other hand, if the ratio last year were 2.5, this year's 1.5 is not good news.

Some companies helpfully include ratios with their financial statements. Figure 5.1 shows such an example from an annual report of Prime Computer, Inc. The two columns are for the latest year and the previous year.

FINANCIAL ANALYSIS AND BUSINESS STRATEGY

Financial ratios can be combined into a DuPont chart. The DuPont method was originally developed at the DuPont Company for financial planning and control purposes. It shows how the key financial ratios are logically interrelated. Also, it reflects how the ratios interact to determine profitability measured as return on equity. The brief form of the DuPont formula is:

Profit Margin		Asset Turnover		Return on Assets
$\dfrac{\text{Net income}}{\text{Sales}}$	×	$\dfrac{\text{Sales}}{\text{Total assets}}$	=	$\dfrac{\text{Net income}}{\text{Total assets}}$

Return on Assets (ROA)		Financial Leverage		Return on Equity (ROE)
$\dfrac{\text{Net income}}{\text{Total assets}}$	×	$\dfrac{\text{Total assets}}{\text{Common equity}}$	=	$\dfrac{\text{Net income}}{\text{Common equity}}$

In turn, these ratios can be broken down again into their component ratio parts for further analysis, as we shall see.

The DuPont formula is a financial X-ray of the business that reveals how the key ratios link with each other to govern total business profitability. As an illustration, Figure 5.2 shows summarized financial statements for American Stores, a well-known chain of supermarkets.

Figure 5.3 shows the financial information for American Stores in a DuPont format.

The DuPont formula is even more valuable than an X-ray. It also enables us to ask "what if" kinds of strategic questions. For instance, it can deal with issues such as:

1. If inventory turnover improves 10 percent, how much will **ROE** increase?
2. If price is cut by 4 percent, and volume increases by 12 percent, what will be the effect on **ROA**?
3. What would net income be if leverage is reduced by 25 percent?

These capabilities make the DuPont formula a useful technique for strategic analysis. With the added power of a computer spreadsheet, the DuPont formula can rapidly calculate the answers to a large array of "what if" questions.

Accordingly, to assess the effects on **ROE** of changes in the key ratios, we perform a "what if" analysis on American Stores as shown in Figure 5.4.

"What If" Analysis

The "what if" analysis asks how much **ROE** will increase if certain financial ratios could be improved. The following possibilities are considered:

1. Test the change in ROE for a 2 percent relative improvement in the ratios of gross margin and operating expenses to sales.

   Result: ROE proves to be highly *sensitive* to both of these ratios. The ROE of American Stores increases by 9.3 and 8.1 percentage points respectively, with a relative gain of 2 percent in either gross margin or the operating expense ratio.

2. Test the change in ROE for 5 percent relative improvement in each of the turnover ratios for accounts receivable, inventories, current liabilities, and fixed assets (net fixtures and equipment).

   Result: ROE turns out to be *insensitive* to all of the asset turnover ratios. For American Stores, ROE goes up only by 0.1 or 0.2 with a 5 percent improvement in any of the asset turnover ratios.

FIGURE 5.2.   American stores.

Summarized Balance Sheet

Average 19XX	$ Million	% to Sales
Accts receivable	140	1.0
Inventory	1235	8.9
Other current assets	107	0.8
Total current assets	1482	10.6
Less current liabilities	(1256)	(9.0)
Equals working capital	226	1.6
Net fixed assets	2017	14.5
Total assets	2243	16.1
LT liabilities	1266	9.1
Preferred stock	255	1.8
Common equity	722	5.2
Total liabilities plus equity	2243	16.1

Summarized Income Statement

19XX	$ Million	% to Sales
Net sales	13,890	100.0
Gross margin	3,343	24.1
Operating expenses	2,920	21.0
Operating profit	423	3.0
Interest	129	0.9
Other income	16	0.1
Income before tax	310	2.2
Income taxes	155	1.1
Net income	155	1.1
Preferred dividends	25	0.2
Net income: Common	130	0.9

FIGURE 5.3. DuPont chart.

American Stores

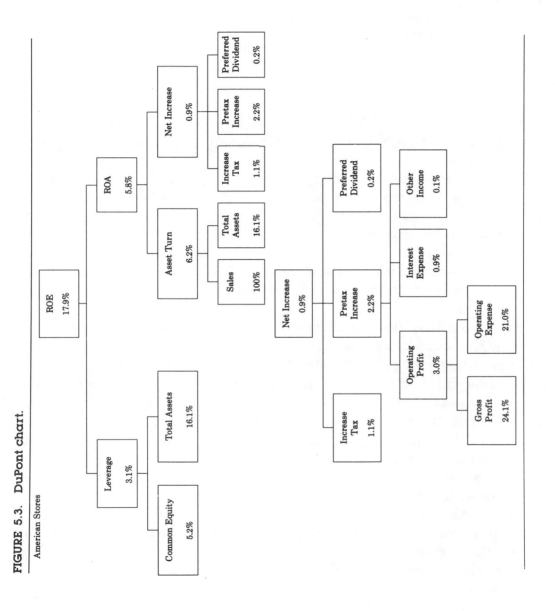

FIGURE 5.4. "What if" analysis for American stores.

% to Sales	Present Value (%)	Improve by (%)	To (%)	ROE Grows from 17.9% to (%)
Gross profit	24.1	2	24.5	27.2
Operating expenses	21.0	2	20.6	26.0
Accounts receivable	1.0	5	1.0	17.9
Inventory	8.9	5	8.4	18.0
Current liabilities	9.0	5	9.5	18.0
Fixed assets	14.5	5	13.6	18.1

Using the Results of the "What If" Analysis for Strategy

These results are most surprising! The ROE increases as the gross margin and operating expense ratios improve. This is predictable. However, the high degree of improvement is not so predictable: ROE increases more than 4 percentage points for each 1 percent relative improvement in the gross margin ratio. Specifically, with a gross margin increase from 24.1 to 24.5 percent (a relative rise of percent), ROE goes up from 17.9 to 27.2 percent (a relative increase of 52 percent). This rise is an extremely strong response.

Similarly, the operating expense ratio has a powerful effect on ROE. ROE goes up by 4 percentage points for each 1 percent relative decrease in the operating expense ratio. In precise terms, if operating expense is reduced from 21.0 to 20.6 percent (a relative fall of 2 percent), ROE increases from 17.9 to 26.0 percent. The response is strong, although not as dramatic as the response of ROE to a change in gross margin.

These results demonstrate that the *spread* between the gross margin ratio and the operating expense ratio is crucial in determining ROE. This spread is operating profit; operating profit is the main driver of ROE for supermarkets.

Also surprising is the lack of ROE response to asset turnover improvement. This absence is especially interesting because one of the main rules of thumb in retailing is to improve the asset turnover, most importantly for inventories. Then, why does a 5 percent asset turnover improvement for American Stores not result in a higher ROE?

Keep in mind that asset turnover is usually rapid for supermarkets. Therefore, additional improvement in the asset turnover is added onto already fast-turning assets. The small extra gain in the asset turn adds nothing to ROE, given the already rapid turnover of assets.

Does this mean that asset turnover is unimportant for ROE? Certainly not. It means only that a small improvement in the presently rapid asset turnover does not continue to increase ROE.

The "what if" analysis clearly shows that the key to improved ROE for American Stores is higher operating profit margin, rather than accelerated asset turnover. Thus, the "what if" analysis draws attention to the two highest profit strategies on which to concentrate: first, those which increase the percent of gross profit to sales, and second, those which decrease the percent of operating expenses to sales.

Examples of strategies for a supermarket to raise its gross profit percentage are to offer more high-profit items such as fresh produce, refrigerated cooked gourmet meals, hot and cold deli, and high quality fresh-baked goods. Note that use of the DuPont chart leads directly to important business strategy issues, and note also how it points out and prioritizes the most effective methods for raising ROE. This is a single example of the benefits a DuPont analysis can provide in dealing with business strategy. Financial ratios are useful in examining past performance, as discussed earlier. Now we see that they are also valuable for the design and the implementation of business strategy for the future.

FOR FURTHER READING

Anthony, Robert N., and James S. Reece, *Accounting: Text and Cases.* 7th ed. (Homewood, IL: Richard D. Irwin, 1983).

Davidson, Sidney, Clyde P. Stickney, and Roman L. Weil, *Financial Accounting.* 4th ed. (Hinsdale, IL: The Dryden Press, 1985).

Davidson, Sidney, and Roman L. Weil, (eds.). *Handbook of Modern Accounting.* 3rd ed. (New York: McGraw-Hill, 1983).

Horngren, Charles, and Gary L. Sundem, *Introduction to Management Accounting.* 7th ed. (Englewood Cliffs, NJ: Prentice Hall, 1987).

Needles, Belverd E., Henry R. Anderson, and James C. Caldwell, *Financial & Managerial Accounting* (Burlington, MA: Houghton Mifflin, 1988).

Seidler, Lee J., and Douglas R. Carmichael, (eds.). *Accountants' Handbook.* 6th ed., 2 Vol. (New York: John Wiley, 1981).

FINANCIAL MANAGEMENT: OPTIMIZING THE VALUE OF THE FIRM

6

James E. Walter

Financial management is a dynamic process which aims to maximize common stock value. The means to this objective is to invest in areas where anticipated returns equal or exceed the cost of the company funds that must be committed to generate these returns, and to disinvest when returns fall short of costs. Cash flow that cannot be invested profitably should be returned to shareholders or debtholders for investment elsewhere.

The dynamic character of the process is nicely illustrated by reference to the consolidated statements of changes in financial position shown in Table 6.1 for P.H. Glatfelter Co., a manufacturer of printing, writing, and specialty papers. Funds provided by operations consist of net income plus (or minus) such elements of operating expense (or income) as depreciation and depletion and deferred income taxes that do not require the outlay of cash. Funds provided by operations are supplemented by proceeds from the disposal of assets, issuance of common stock for employee stock plans, and additions to debt and other liabilities. Funds are used for capital expenditures, payment of dividends, repayment of debt, repurchase of common and preferred stock, acquisitions, and additions receivables, inventories, and other miscellaneous elements of working capital. Total funds provided in 1987 exceeded net income by about five times.

To facilitate discussion of the financial process, we organize the subject matter along the lines of: (1) guidelines for investing company funds, (2) adjustment for the time factor, (3) elements of asset management, and (4) financing decisions. The section dealing with guidelines for investing

TABLE 6.1. P. H. Glatfelter Company and subsidiaries consolidated statements of changes in financial position for the years ended December 31, 1987, 1986, and 1985.

	(in Thousands)		
	1987	**1986**	**1985**
Cash and short-term investments at beginning of year	$ 53,952	$51,232	$42,053
Funds provided by:			
Operations:			
Net income	55,027	41,474	39,731
Items which did not require funds:			
Depreciation and depletion	19,011	11,877	11,381
Interest income on long-term note	(15,342)	(13,495)	(11,868)
Deferred income taxes—noncurrent	16,771	12,229	12,047
(Gain) loss on dispositions of fixed assets	17	(448)	(274)
Total funds provided by operations	75,484	51,637	51,017
Proceeds from:			
Disposals of fixed assets	514	706	540
Issuance of common stock under employee stock ownership plan	72	69	65
Decrease in:			
Prepaid expenses and deferred income taxes and other assets	—	—	431
Increase in:			
Long-term debt	179,200	—	—
Federal, state and local tax liability	117	947	243
Other current liabilities	20,006	3,321	684
Total funds provided	275,393	56,680	52,980
Funds used for:			
Additions to plant, equipment, and timberlands	62,591	16,524	18,736
Dividends	13,383	12,566	11,340
Reduction of debt	—	500	500
Purchase of preferred stock	19	3	10
Purchase of common stock	11,827	19,272	10,463
Investment in Ecusta Division (including plant and equipment of $187,038)	222,984	—	—
Increase in:			
Accounts receivable	2,245	2,131	1,519
Inventories	6,838	2,706	1,233
Prepaid expenses and deferred income taxes and other assets	6,097	258	—
Total funds used	325,984	53,960	43,801
Cash and short-term investments at end of year	$ 3,361	$53,952	$51,232

company funds deals with company objectives, management incentives, and limitations imposed by the environment. The section relating to the time factor pertains to the valuation now of cash flows to be received or paid out in future years. The third section concerning asset management deals with financial planning and plan implementation, otherwise known as capital budgeting. The fourth section pertaining to financing decisions concerns itself with internal and external sources of funds and the appropriate mix of debt and equity.

GUIDELINES FOR INVESTING COMPANY FUNDS

The ultimate financial objective of most firms is to maximize common share value. The shareholder has title to whatever remains after prior claimants have been paid off and is the principal risk taker. As the contributor of risk capital, his or her point of view should prevail.

It follows that the *basic guideline* for investing corporate funds is that the anticipated rate of return on any given investment proposal must be sufficient at least to cover interest charges on borrowed funds and compensate shareholders for the risks associated with the commitment of equity funds or capital. Otherwise, the value of the firm is adversely affected. The stockholder, being last in line, bears the brunt of the loss when the realized return on any investment project falls short of the composite cost of the funds committed to that project. Conversely, the shareowner receives the windfall gain on a project when the return on investment surpasses the cost of funds employed.

The cost of any source of funds—whether debt or equity—is the rate of return that investors require for taking on the particular risk associated with the source of funds in question. The cost of debt varies with its location in the *pecking order* of priority and is typically lower than that for equity in the same firm. Interest on debt is also deductible for tax purposes, while the return to stockholders (i.e., dividends and appreciation in stock value) is not deductible as a company tax expense. Composite or overall cost of capital is simply the cost of each source of funds, weighted by the ratio of the respective source to total capital or funds employed, and tax adjusted where relevant.

Suppose company policy is to finance investment projects partly by debt to the tune of 30 percent of the funds needed and the remainder by equity. Assume further that the respective costs or required rates of return for debt and equity are 10 and 14 percent, and that the corporate tax rate is 37 percent. The composite cost of capital becomes:

Source of Capital	Weight		Cost		Composite
Debt	.30	×	.10 × (1 − .37)	=	.0189
Equity	.70	×	.14	=	.0980
Composite	1.00				.1169

Now, imagine a one-year investment of $1 million expected to return 20 percent before taxes ($200,000), over and above the original investment, and suppose that the investment is financed in the manner and at the costs assumed above. With the corporate tax rate at .37 and debt at 30 percent of the capital needed, the lender would receive repayment of the principal amount loaned ($300,000) plus interest ($30,000) for a total of $330,000; the equity investor would also get his money back ($700,000) and expect to receive his required return ($98,000) plus, in this case, a bonus of $9,100. The latter represents the base investment of $1 million multiplied by the difference between the after-tax return on investment, with interest excluded, of .20 × (1 − .37) or .126 and the combined cost of debt and equity of .1169. If less than the expected return is realized, the lender will continue to receive his $330,000 as long as the investment generates at least that amount of cash value, while the equity investor gets whatever remains.

The efficacy of the basic guideline stipulating that anticipated rates of return on prospective investments should at least equal the composite cost of capital depends upon management's ability to make unbiased revenue projections and to assess accurately the cost of capital. Strict adherence to the guideline, in turn, may run counter to the personal goals of management. Its application is also constrained by government regulation and other factors.

In the treatment that follows, attention is directed first to the theory that underlies the estimation of the cost of capital and to a critical assumption (i.e., market efficiency) on which it is based. Questions relating to: (1) the motivation of management to act in the best interest of shareholders, and (2) the limitations imposed by accounting conventions, government regulation, prior commitments, and the like, are then considered. Matters pertaining to the unbiased forecast of revenues are deferred until later.

Cost Estimation

The costs of debt and equity that enter into the calculation of composite cost are not arbitrary. Interest costs can often be objectively determined by reference to the yields on equivalent-risk bonds traded in the public markets. The cost of equity, in contrast, cannot be directly measured since it reflects investors' unspecified expectations of the future; it must be estimated on the basis of some underlying plausible model of investor behavior.

The *Capital Asset Pricing Model* (CAPM) is an accepted and sensible way of rationalizing the manner in which assets in general and common stock in particular are priced, and thereby assessing the minimum rates of return needed to compensate investors for choosing risky assets. Under the CAPM, investors are presumed to be rational, risk averse, and willing to accept expected rate of return and standard deviation of rate of return as measures of prospective reward and risk. Risk aversion implies that investors must be rewarded for bearing risk and will be motivated to minimize risk for any level of expected return through diversification.

In the model, the market in which assets are bought and sold is assumed to be highly competitive. Buyers and sellers are numerous, operate independently, and individually are unable to affect asset prices. New information is disseminated rapidly and cheaply, taxes are uniform, and transactions costs are minimal. Investors can lend and borrow at a riskless rate of interest, and the investment horizon is uniformly a single period (usually one year) in duration.

Investors have the choice of investing in a riskless asset, a risky portfolio, or a combination of the two. The expected return on the composite portfolio selected is the riskless interest rate *plus* the premium investors generally demand for investing in the risky market portfolio, weighted by the proportion of the investor's own wealth invested in the risky portfolio. If the riskless rate as approximated by, for instance, treasury bills is on the order of 8 percent, and the risk premium or added return for investing in risky common stocks is 5 percent, the investor with half of his wealth at risk can expect to earn 10.5 percent; that is:

$$8 \text{ percent} \times \frac{1}{2} + 13 \text{ percent} \times \frac{1}{2}$$

The standard deviation measures the prospective deviation of the actual from the expected return and, subject to some debate, is commonly regarded as an acceptable measure of portfolio risk. The standard deviation of any portfolio or package of securities is defined as the square root of the weighted sum of the individual variances and covariances.

Since riskfree assets have—by definition—zero variances and covariances with risky assets, the composite portfolio's standard deviation boils down to the standard deviation of the risky portfolio times the percentage of the investor's resources allocated to it. Substitution into the expected return equation gives rise to the capital market line that states that the expected return on any portfolio equals the riskfree rate plus the *market price* of risk multiplied by the portfolio's standard deviation. The market price of risk is the risk premium associated with common stock in general divided by the standard deviation of the risky market portfolio.

Risk-averse investors are motivated to be diversified to the degree that risks uncorrelated with the return on the market portfolio are washed out for the most part. The expected return or required rate of return on any security or package of securities, and, *by inference, the cost of equity for any given firm*, thus reduces in equilibrium to the return on the riskfree asset plus the market risk premium times the sensitivity of the individual security or portfolio to the market portfolio. The sensitivity measure is known as *beta*. Beta is the regression coefficient that relates the return on the individual security or portfolio to the return on the market portfolio. In effect, Beta measures—in a relative sense—that part of asset risk which cannot be diversified away. It establishes a straightforward basis for assessing the required rate of return on any asset to the degree that the underlying assumptions hold.

Market Efficiency

Competition in the marketplace is essential to the process of asset pricing and cost determination in the CAPM just described, as is rational behavior. Competition among investors helps to keep the rates at which money is offered in line with comparable investments and reduces the likelihood of discrimination. Competition also pressures management and employees to be efficient. Otherwise, the competitor lures the business away since he can offer the product at a lower price.

To the degree that the conditions necessary for competitive behavior prevail, funds flow and resources move from low return to high return areas. Barriers to entry and exit of any consequence are precluded. Values in the marketplace adjust to the point that, in the absence of further shifts, expected returns are uniform for each level of risk.

The financial markets in the United States are judged to be among the most efficient in the world. Sophisticated financial institutions pool the funds of individual investors. Secondary markets exist for all classes of securities and provide the basis for pricing new issues. Information sources and professional help abound for both the financial manager and the investor.

The financial markets are, however, less than 100 percent efficient as evidenced by the October 1987 market break. Institutions individually and collectively do have the power to affect security prices. Taxation lacks uniformity. Access to information varies directly with the size and character of the company. Spreads may be substantial for small, infrequently traded securities. Marketmakers lack the capital to maintain liquid markets under all circumstances.

Since the market-efficiency assumptions that underlie the CAPM are not completely satisfied, estimates of the cost of equity are somewhat ambiguous. The numbers derived are, however, generally believed to be acceptable and usable as ballpark estimates.

Whose Viewpoint?

On the surface, the shareholder appears to stand atop the corporate hierarchy. Holders of the corporation's common stock, along with any other parties entitled to vote, elect company directors. Directors, acting as agents of the shareholders, set policy and hire and fire chief executive officers (CEOs). The CEO, in turn, operating within policy guidelines has the power to hire and fire other members of management.

In practice, however, shareholders rarely exercise their right to "throw the rascals out." Management may nominate "friendly" persons to be members of the board; management may arrange for staggered boards, to preclude rapid change of control; shareholders may side with management or register disappointment by not submitting their proxies. Proxy battles are both expensive and difficult to win, as several corporate raiders have discovered to their chagrin.

Management, as personified by the CEO, frequently has de facto control of the firm and can—within broad limits—substitute its objectives for those of shareholders. For instance, management may emphasize growth at the expense of rate of return; management may choose to diversify even though shareholders can do it more effectively; management may choose not to borrow optimally despite tax advantages. In potential conflict with shareholder interests, management may opt for a management leveraged buyout when stock prices are depressed.

Efforts within the corporation to equate the objectives of management with those of shareholders revolve around compensation schemes. Top executives of major firms now receive a base salary plus (1) annual cash bonuses and (2) long-term performance compensation made up of stock options, stock appreciation rights, restricted stock, and performance awards. The underlying idea is to relate an increasing part of compensation to company earnings and to stock price behavior.

Help has also come from the outside, so to speak. Companies that underachieve in stock value open themselves to attack by corporate raiders. The latter create added-value through leverage and sale of under-performing assets and, in so doing, have pressured managements to restructure on their own.

Management has partly countered the threat of takeover by changes in corporate charters and bylaws, adoption of poison pills, lobbying for restrictive state legislation, and management buyouts. The implied argument is that the raider's short-term focus is antisocial and that those who speculate in takeovers are somehow less worthy than long-term investors.

Conflicts are certain to ensue no matter what is done. The fact is that numerous parties have stakes in the corporation. What is good for one may be at the expense of another! The upshot is that, while the basic guideline for investing remains more or less intact, management has—by virtue of its strategic position in the corporation—some leeway to substitute its values for those of the shareholder and to take account of the interests of other parties.

Conditioning Factors

Management is further constrained in its effort to apply the basic guidelines by accounting conventions, tax considerations, government regulation, and contractual agreements. Management may also be sensitive to public opinion, the need to maintain the corporate image, and other factors as well.

Accounting Conventions

Accounting conventions play an important role since they establish the basis upon which income is measured. Income or earnings per share and its period-by-period change may directly influence stock value. Investors rely upon the independent auditor to affirm the fairness of the accounting numbers.

Fortunately or unfortunately, management has considerable leeway in its reporting of income. Write-offs, in particular, have become the order of the day. One CPA explains that there are a number of different ways to measure income in a composite sense, permissible under GAAP.

In their emphasis upon historical cost, accounting conventions may not reveal realizable asset values, and thus lead to the incorrect valuation of the company and its common stock in the marketplace. In their failure to provide sufficient information about potentially significant off-balance sheet items, the future impact of certain risks and obligations remains unspecified. Future expenditures on health care for present and prospective retirees estimated by Aetna Life & Casualty for its personnel for the first time (in response to reporting rules being drafted by the FASB), for example, come to a "surprising" $900,000,000. Adoption of the cash flow statement in accord with FASB No. 95 assists the analyst in his own interpretation, but omissions and discrepancies remain with respect to asset and liability valuation.

The internal (cost) accounting system sometimes also leaves something to be desired. Costs may be imperfectly broken down. Costs can be allocated on an outmoded basis. The manager may thus remain uncertain or ignorant as to the true cost of individual products.

Deficiencies in income measurement and reporting of the kind just noted may contribute to market inefficiency in three ways: (1) Revenue projections may ignore or incorrectly assess certain relevant costs, (2) estimates of the cost of equity may reflect questionable market valuations, and (3) evaluation of project performance and assignment of responsibility under prevailing accounting conventions can be difficult.

Tax Considerations

Taxes on income shape behavior in at least two ways: (1) Rules for determining taxable income affect the manner in which income is measured for other purposes as well, and (2) all taxes take cash, have economic effects, and are rarely neutral.

Companies may partly negate tax-imposed accounting procedures by legitimately maintaining two sets of books—the first for reporting to investors and the other for the tax authorities. Note, for example, the deferred income-tax item that appears on many income statements. This item reflects the difference between the effective tax based upon accelerated depreciation and the like, and the tax that would have to be paid if, for example, straight-line depreciation were utilized. Limitations to separate bookkeeping nonetheless exist. The firm must, for instance, employ the same inventory valuation method for reporting purposes as it does for tax purposes. The consequences are similar to those attributable to accounting conventions.

Economic effects abound. Ability to deduct research and development as a current tax expense places it in a preferred status relative to expenditures on plant and equipment. The recently terminated investment tax credit favored equipment purchases over outlays on fixed plant.

Interest deductibility alters the cost of debt and thereby the cost of capital. The list could go on, but the point has been established that cash flows associated with prospective investments need to be valued on an after-tax basis. Capital outlays that appear attractive on a before-tax basis may or may not be acceptable on consideration of tax effects.

Government Regulation

Government is everywhere. The belief exists and is supported by hard fact that business, if left completely unfettered, would ignore social concerns unless the bottom line benefited. Land, water, and air pollution are all legacies of earlier neglect by both business and government. Regulatory agencies now press business to limit further damage to the environment. Government agencies also focus concern on employee and customer safety.

Competition itself, if left unchecked, can be destructive. The objective is to win, and winning may lead to gobbling up one's competition. Anti-trust thus has a role to play.

Furthermore, government aims to ensure that the competitive game is played fairly. Disclosure is the key word of securities legislation, since information processing is the name of the game in stock and bond valuation.

The intent of government, then, is to ensure that the basic guideline for investing heeds social costs and bypasses monopoly income. Some investment projects are rendered less desirable; some may be ruled out altogether. Disclosure, in turn, contributes to market efficiency and thereby to the more precise determination of cost of capital.

Contractual Agreements and Other Commitments

Management's ability to invest in projects whose expected return exceeds the cost of capital hinges, in the final analysis, upon the firm's flexibility. Companies that are committed to the hilt, subject to unduly restrictive covenants or threatened with massive litigation have reduced flexibility.

Firms are not short-lived organisms. They must commit themselves to the future to survive. This commitment to the future obliges management to enter into contractual and other less formal (but binding) agreements that limit flexibility and add to risk. Armco, a partner with LTV in a mining venture, was placed in jeopardy when LTV declared bankruptcy, and the venture's debt thereby immediately became due. Armco also worried about the mounting costs of its obligation to provide health benefits for retired employees.

Long-term debt commits the firm to a series of future cash payments. The same is true with respect to financial or capitalized leases and operating leases to a lesser extent. The penalty for failure to meet such commitments can be severe.

Firms must also live with the unintended consequences of past decisions. Confronted with an unending stream of suits arising from its disastrous Dalkon Shield product, A. H. Robbins declared bankruptcy. Johns Manville suffered a similar fate in connection with asbestos claims.

THE TIME FACTOR

In a very real sense, the principal function of the financial manager is to buy and sell claims to future cash flow in such a way as to create value *now* for the shareholder. Investments or capital expenditures represent the purchase of such claims, while debt instruments and equity shares constitute the sale of claims to future cash flow. Some investments generate cash quickly, some, over an intermediate term, and some, slowly over an extended period. The same holds true for debt and equity as well.

To make claims that are characterized by different cash flow streams and maturities comparable, we resort to discounting. The basic thrust of discounting is that the value of an asset or claim now (i.e., its present value) is that dollar amount which, given the firm's required rate of return, will generate the projected or promised stream of future cash flows. Thus, cash flow of $3.00 materializing one year hence is worth $2.61 today if the required return is 15 percent per annum; conversely, $2.61 put to work for one year at 15 percent will grow to $3.00 by year end.

Present Versus Future

The future value of one dollar depends upon the yearly rate (i) which that dollar can earn and the length of time (T) that the earnings are expected to continue. Thus, future value of one dollar (FV$1) equals $(1 + i)**T$. Note that "**" stands for exponentiation, so that (FV$1) equals $(1 + i)^T$. One dollar invested at 12 percent per annum for five years grows, for example, to $1.76 if the interest (i) is reinvested and compounded annually.

The present value of one dollar (PV$1) to be received T years in the future is simply the reciprocal of the future value equation; that is, $PV\$1 = 1/(1 + i)**T$. Present value is that amount which, if invested now at rate i, will grow to one dollar at the end of T years. Total present (PV) or future (FV) value equals PV$1 or FV$1 multiplied by the number of dollars (A) at stake.

Consider now an investment expected to generate cash flows of $1,000,000 per year for each of the next five years. Assume further that the minimum return required is 15 percent. Total present value is determined by summing the product of the cash flow (A) and the respective PV$1 for each year, as follows:

Year (T)	Cash Flow (A)	×	PV$1	=	Present Value
1	$1,000,000		.870		$ 870,000
2	$1,000,000		.756		756,000
3	$1,000,000		.658		658,000
4	$1,000,000		.572		572,000
5	$1,000,000		.594		497,000
Total present value					$3,353,000

In short, shareholders receive more than their minimum required rate of return from this project as long as the price paid for this investment is less than $3,353,000.

Annuities

In many instances, it is convenient to think in terms of a cash flow stream starting at one dollar per period, either remaining constant or growing at some rate, and continuing for a specified period of time. Should there be no maturity, as in the case of a special British bond or consol, the annuity's present value (PVA$1) equals $1/i$. Since the maturity is infinite, the cash flow per period is pure interest or income and there is no principal ever to be repaid. Should there be a finite maturity (T), PVA$1 equals the present value of an annuity of one dollar forever minus the present value of a perpetual annuity of one dollar commencing (T + 1) periods in the future. Thus,

$$\text{PVA\$1} = (1/i) \times [1 - (1 + i)** - T].$$

Consider the previous example of yearly cash flows of $1,000,000 continuing for five years and discounted at 15 percent. Viewed as an annuity, its present value equals $1,000,000 \times$ PVA$1 where PVA$1 equals $(1/.15) \times [1 - 1/(1.15)**5]$, or 3.352. The annuity value of $3,352,000 differs slightly from the prior PV solution due to round off. Unless otherwise specified, cash flows are presumed to occur at the end of each period.

For many valuation purposes, an appropriate assumption is that the annuity grows at some constant rate throughout its life. The present value (PVG$1) of cash flows starting at $1 and growing at rate g for T periods equals $[(1 + g)/(i - g)] \times \{1 - [(1 + g)/(1 + i)]**T\}$. If T is infinite, PVG$1 simplifies to $(1 + g)/(i - g)$, provided $i > g$.

Suppose that the cash flow of $1,000,000 in the above illustration grows at 10 percent per annum throughout the five years with the discount rate (i) remaining at 15 percent. Present value now equals $1,000,000 times PVG$1, where PVG$1 equals $[(1.1)/(.15 - .1)] \times [1 - (1.1/1.15)**5]$, or 4.384. Total present value is $4,384,000 and is well above the corresponding present value for the constant, nongrowth annuity.

Future values, where needed for the evaluation of pension programs or other purposes, can readily be derived from present values; the future values of a constant annuity (FVA$1) and an annuity growing at rate g (FVG$1), respectively, equal $PVA\$1 \times (1 + i)**(T + 1)$ and $PVG\$1 \times (1 + i)**(T + 1)$. The use of $(1 + i)**(T + 1)$ assumes that the initial cash flow is received or invested at the start—rather than at the end—of the initial period.

Adjustment for Uncertainty

Future values frequently are not known with certainty. The financial manager is, as a consequence, faced with a choice. Should he (1) discount each of the possible outcomes by the risk-free interest rate in order to obtain a set of risk-free present values for each project, (2) assign a utility index value that represents the trade-off between risk and return to each element of the set, and (3) weight each utility index value by its likelihood of occurrence and sum to derive a composite utility value that can then be used for ranking purposes? Or, should she form expected values for the cash flows in each future period and discount these expected values at a discount rate that reflects the degree of uncertainty?

The latter method seems preferable. It is more readily understood, and it allows one to view risk or uncertainty in a global, firm-wide respect, as opposed to an individual project sense. Risk-adjusted discount rates will be treated subsequently.

Internal Rate of Return (IRR)

Suppose that the project analyst has projected cash flows for each future period and has also estimated the investment outlay (I) that is required to

TABLE 6.2. Internal rate of return.

Assume that a $10,000 investment generates a net cash flow (after tax) of $3,000 per year for each of the next 5 years. What does an IRR of 15,238 percent mean?

Year	Remaining Investment	Cash Flow	Interest	Retirement of Principal
0	$10,000			
1	8,523.80	$3,000	$1,523.80	$1,476.20
2	6,822.66	3,000	1,298.86	1,701.14
3	4,862.30	3,000	1,039.64	1,960.36
4	2,603.22	3,000	740.92	2,259.08
5	(.10)	3,000	396.69	2,603.32

*The Internal Rate of Return (IRR) is a true rate of return in that it measures the return on the investment outstanding at each point in time.

generate the projected cash flows (CF). The financial manager now wishes to know the "true" rate of return on the project in question for comparison with the cost of capital. As illustrated in Table 6.2, the "true" or internal rate of return is that discount rate (i.e., .15238) which equates the positive cash flows with the negative cash flow or investment. The investment, I(0), of $10,000 is presumed in this case to be made in a lump sum at the outset.

Table 6.2 shows how the periodic cash flow of $3000 is divided between interest or income and retirement of the principal amount. Return on investment is always .15238 times the remaining investment at the end of the previous year. In brief, the return on investment is constant throughout the life of the investment, and the original investment is recovered. IRR thereby meets the test of being a constant rate of return over all periods of project life.

Valuation Models

Stocks and bonds are valued in much the same manner as capital expenditures. The typical bond is, for example, characterized by a coupon (c) representing the amount to be paid each period, an amount (M)—normally, $1000—to be paid at maturity, and a maturity (T) representing the life of the bond. The bond thus can be viewed as an annuity of c dollars for T periods plus a payment of M dollars at time T; its value (V) reduces to: $V = c/i + (M - c/i)/(1 + i)**T$. With c, i, M, and T respectively set equal to $120, .10, $1000, and 25, the bond value is equal to 120/.1 + (1000 - 120/.1)/1.1**25, or $1,181.54. If the coupon rate, that is,

120/1000 or .12, exceeds i, the bond value exceeds par (M), and vice versa.

The value of a share of common stock, in contrast, can be viewed as the summed present value of all future cash dividends. Since companies normally reinvest part of earnings at a positive rate of return, the expected internal growth rate (g) equals the portion of earnings retained times the rate of return. Since common stock has no maturity specified, the value of a share of common stock is the value of an annuity growing at rate g forever (in an expected sense) and is equal to $D(0) \times (1 + g)/(r - g)$, where $D(0)$ is the current dividend per share, r is the investor's required rate of return, and $r > g$.

The foregoing valuation model is especially applicable to mature firms that have attained a steady-state growth rate. The valuation of growth companies that have not yet achieved maturity must be modified to take account of changing growth rates. Two- or three-stage growth models can readily be derived.

ASSET MANAGEMENT

The three phases of asset management are (a) planning, (b) implementation, and (c) control and feedback. Planning establishes the ground rules for orderly development consistent with corporate aims. Implementation translates the plans into action. Control and feedback operates to correct mistakes, move forward along the learning curve, and assign responsibility.

Planning

Management normally tries to look forward three to five years as part of its capital investment planning process. The goal is to give profit center heads clues as to the availability of funds for capital investment and to assess what needs to be done to achieve corporate goals. Go or no-go decisions regarding capital investment frequently must be made well in advance.

Other planning cycles also exist. The short-term cash flow cycle is watched to ensure that cash is available to pay bills as needed. Product cycles are followed to determine the rate at which new products must be introduced to perpetuate growth.

Key policy variables for the investment planning cycle include: (1) identification of "core" business(es), (2) liquidity, (3) degree of leverage,

(4) internal versus external growth, and (5) dividends and stock repurchase. Amoco, for instance, stipulates that its two core businesses are (1) petroleum exploration and refining and (2) petrochemicals. Its financial objectives are long-term earnings growth of 8 to 10 percent annually, return on equity between 13 and 15 percent, a debt to debt-plus-equity ratio falling between 20 and 25 percent, and a dividend payout ratio of 35 to 45 percent. These variables, together with management's ability to attain its specific goals and the market's view of company risk, largely determine stock value.

Growth need not be the prime focus of the business. Exxon reports in its Annual Report for 1987, "The corporation continued to pursue a vigorous program of divesting low return operations, implementing work force reductions, and reorganizing into more effective operating units." Exxon also repurchased some 4.2 percent of its stock at a cost of $2.6 billion. Restructuring that stresses ROE and achieves growth in per-share earnings at least partially through share repurchase has become accepted practice for many firms.

Core Business(es)

The type(s) of business that management elects to emphasize influences the sales per dollar of assets, the profit margin, and the sensitivity of revenues to changes in the economic environment. Sales per dollar of assets multiplied by the profit margin gives rise to return on assets (ROA). Intersegment differences in profitability ratios can be substantial even in the case of strong product intercorrelation, as shown for three AMOCO business segments:

Ratio	Production	Refining	Petrochemical	Overall
Sales/Assets	.47	3.08	1.40	.946
Operating profit/Sales	.261	.056	.193	.124
Operating profit/Assets	.123	.172	.270	.117

Cash flow sensitivity, in turn, depends upon such product characteristics as price, durability, and market share, as well as upon operating leverage. High product prices imply sensitivity to interest rates; durability indicates ability to defer replacement, while market share and product price inelasticity afford management a degree of control over price. Operating leverage refers to the sensitivity of operating cash flows to the underlying percentage change in sales and has to do with the mix of fixed and variable costs; the formula boils down to:

$$\frac{(Sales - Variable\ cost)}{[(Sales - Variable\ cost) - Fixed\ cash\ cost + Tax\ rate \times Depreciation]}.$$

Management sometimes attempts to reduce cash flow sensitivity in particular and risk in general by means of diversification. Automobile manufacturers partly offset the volatility of new car sales by producing and selling automotive parts whose sales tend to be negatively correlated with new car sales.

Diversification benefits the firm in three ways: (1) Diversification averages across company-specific risks, that is, risks that are uncorrelated with each other. (2) Diversification diminishes correlated risks to the degree that the firm diversifies into areas that are less sensitive to the underlying economic environment. (3) Diversification may increase the likelihood of company survival in the long run since some products among a diversified set are likely to be winners.

Diversification at the firm level has at least two demerits: (1) Management may be unable to manage effectively a diversified set of businesses. (2) Investors are generally better able to diversify than are companies. The result is that diversification at the company level may be redundant and contribute little to enterprise value.

Liquidity and Degree of Leverage

Liquidity, measured by the ratio of cash items to total assets, and financial leverage, measured by the ratio of debt to debt-plus-equity, go hand in hand since the former could be used to retire the latter. General Mills, among others, thus subtracts cash items from debt in deriving its debt ratio. Exxon has even removed over $700 million of debt from its balance sheet since 1982 by placing sufficient government securities in escrow to cover the debt through a procedure called *defeasance*.

From the standpoint of planning, net leverage, that is, debt adjusted for cash items, affects profitability, growth, and risk. Return on equity (ROE) surpasses return on assets (ROA) by a factor that represents the tax-adjusted difference between ROA and interest:

$$ROE = ROA + [ROA - i(1 - T)] \times (D/E),$$

where i is the interest rate, T is the tax rate, and D and E are respective debt and equity. ROA is the after-tax return on assets. With i, T, ROA, and D/E respectively taken to be .1, .4, .12, and .5, for example, ROE becomes $.12 + [.12 - .1(.6)] \times .5$, or .15.

Dividend Policy

Dividends compete with capital investments for the available cash flow, as do stock repurchases. Companies that reinvest all of their earnings can be expected to grow at the rate of their normal return on equity, or ROE; those that reinvest half of their earnings grow at half their ROE, and so forth. The formula for internal growth (IGF) is $ROE \times (1 - p)$, where p refers to the proportion of earnings paid out in the form of cash dividends. Stock repurchases slow down internal growth in a total company sense, but not on a per-share growth basis since repurchases reduce the number of shares outstanding.

Internal Versus External

Based upon its financial targets enumerated previously and on assumed interest and tax rates of .1 and .4 respectively, Amoco must realize a before-tax return on assets ranging from 18.4 to 23.7 percent to achieve its growth objective of 8 to 10 percent internally. The alternative is to go outside the firm to achieve the desired growth through merger and acquisition. The latter, as Amoco has found in its acquisition of Dome Petroleum, is easier said than done.

Implementation

Implementation, like Gaul (for those who took Latin), is divisible into three parts. The first is management of working capital; the second, capital budgeting; and the third, merger and acquisition.

Management of Working Capital

Working capital, or more precisely, net working capital, is defined as current assets minus current liabilities. Current assets typically include cash items (i.e., cash and near-cash), accounts receivable, inventories at various stages of completion, and prepaid expenses. Current liabilities comprise notes and accounts payable and accrued liabilities. The dividing line between current and noncurrent is 12 months.

Waiving cash items, notes payable, and current maturities on long-term debt for the moment, the requisite investment in working capital depends upon customer and supplier credit policies and duration of the production and inventory cycle. Creditworthy companies buy materials, hire workers, and the like on credit, and likewise extend credit to worthy customers.

Working capital ratios, given below for USG, a building materials company, illustrate the point.

Ratio[1]	1987
1. (Accounts receivable/Sales) × 360	41.82 days outstanding
2. (Inventory/Cost of sales) × 360	34.95 days outstanding
3. (Currrent liabilities/ Operating expenses) × 360	54.70 days outstanding
4. (1 + 2)/3	1.40
5. Current ratio	1.25

The number of days outstanding for receivables and inventories taken together *minus* the number of days outstanding for payables largely determines the investment period for working capital. The current ratio, by its very nature, is closely identified with the ratio of these three variables.

Working capital is a mixed bag. It is, as noted above, a part of the permanent investment base due to its ongoing, revolving character. It is also, by virtue of its nearness to cash, a one-time source of funds. Accounts receivable can be used as collateral or sold with or without recourse. The finished goods part of inventories is available for the same purpose.

Decisions to extend more or less credit to customers and to hold larger or smaller inventories require the same assessment as any investment decision. The issue to be resolved is whether the return on the added investment exceeds or falls short of the cost of capital. Decisions to rely upon working capital as a one-time source of funds depend, in contrast, upon the availability and cost of alternative sources of funds.

Cash items, notes payable, and current maturities on long-term debt warrant separate treatment since they are not a part of the more or less automatic credit-inventory-credit cycle. Apart from so-called transactions cash, the level of cash items depends upon management's perceived need for liquidity. Short-term loans from banks and other financial institutions, designated as notes payable, bear interest; must be negotiated by management; and, if used consistently, should be viewed as part of the permanent capital base.

Capital Budgeting

Capital budgeting relates to the execution of the firm's long-term investment strategies. It entails (1) product development and search for feasible

---

[1] Notes payable and current debt maturities are omitted from current liabilities. Accounts receivable, inventory, and current liabilities are averaged.

projects, (2) cash flow forecasting, (3) project ranking, (4) risk assessment, (5) determination of cut-off point, and (6) process control. The focus here is upon items (2), (3), and (4). Item (1), however, is critical. No feasible projects means no company future! Cash resources and worthy projects are rarely in balance.

Profit center managers normally originate new investment proposals and rely on aides to prepare cash flow forecasts and follow company guidelines with respect to the project details, forecast horizon, and ranking criteria employed. The magnitude of the investment outlay determines the level in management hierarchy needed for approval. Major projects are reviewed by the finance staff and require approval by the executive committee.

The cash flow worksheet, together with appendices, constitute the basic document. The worksheet provides a year-by-year schedule of projected cash outflows and inflows. Outflows include outlays for both plant and equipment as well as working capital. Inflows consist of: (1) forecasted profit before taxes and such noncash charges as depreciation (EBDT), minus (2) the EBDT lost on related business due to the project in question, minus (3) the appropriate tax rate times the net EBDT, plus (4) the tax rate times noncash charges, plus (5) the tax-adjusted terminal value of plant and equipment and residual working capital. The schedule of inflows minus outflows, that is, net cash flows, is given in the final column.

Projects differ notably in the degree of reliability with which cash flows can be projected. The easiest to handle is equipment replacement since its profitability hinges on degree of usage and comparative efficiency of the "old" and "new." The next degree of forecast complexity relates to the expansion of facilities to handle increased demand for existing products. Although benefiting from past experience, the analyst must not only project underlying economic variables upon which demand depends but also consider the possibility of competition (especially if profit margins are high). Most difficult to forecast are the results of investing in plant and equipment to house new products. Aside from test marketing, perhaps, there is little past history; everything must be simulated.

Forecast errors are to be *expected*. The problem for management is to avoid foolish mistakes and to work toward unbiased forecasts. Foolish mistakes include the neglect of factors relevant to the outcome, the failure to check for internal consistency, and the application of flawed methodology. It is, for example, inappropriate to dismiss the possibility of competition when projected profit margins are high and entry into the business is easy; it is improper to have changes in working capital that are out of tune with the anticipated behavior of sales and EBDT, and it is methodologically deficient to deduct overhead expense in deriving EBDT unless cash flows are directly affected. The checklist of factors to be considered is substantial.

Sensitivity analysis is a useful way to sort out forecast items of major concern. The effect of forecasting errors on IRR, shown in Table 6.3, indicates: (1) Delays in cash generation alone can be devastating since the investment grows by $(1 + r)**T$, where r and T are, respectively, the cost of capital and the period of delay; (2) errors in forecasting the exact duration of long-lived investments need not be crucial; and (3) the effects of project overruns and overstatements of cash flow are about the same for comparable forecast errors. Sensitivity analysis helps to determine where to place the forecast effort.

The worksheet for developing cash flow, given in Table 6.4, is arranged somewhat differently from the breakdown just described. but leads to the same result. Can you explain the differences? The projections in Table 6.4 also appear to be based upon a number of questionable assumptions. What are they?

Unbiased forecasts are difficult to achieve despite the fact that management—conceptually speaking—should be able to compensate for a persistent tendency to depart from the predicted value. The difficulty lies in inadequate recordkeeping, the long-lived character of many projects, and the bureaucratic process itself. Projects tend to be evaluated on an IRR or net present value (NPV) basis, while records of performance—if kept—are maintained on a traditional accounting basis. Cash flow forecasts for long-lived projects in turn are commonly truncated at five or ten years. Project review likewise is often deferred until the responsible parties have moved elsewhere in the organization.

Methods of summarizing or ranking investment projects, once their cash flows have been estimated, include: (1) payback period, (2) accounting rate of return, (3) internal rate of return (IRR), (4) net present value (NPV), (5) discounted payback period, and (6) profitability index (PI). Payback period, defined as the number of years required to recover the investment from project cash flows, is easy to understand and is used as a secondary criterion in cases where risks and inflation are high, and the firm is short of cash. Payback period does not address profitability, is potentially discriminatory, and should not stand alone as a criterion for investment.

Accounting rate of return (ROI) relates accounting income (before or after depreciation) to gross or net investment; it may relate to a single year or be averaged. The concept of ROI is simple to comprehend, and the

TABLE 6.3. Effect of forecasting errors on IRR.

	Project Forecast	Project Overrun 10%	Actual Cash Inflow Overstated 10% per Year	Useful Life Overstated 20%	Cash Inflow Deferred 2 Years
Investment	$10,000	$11,000	$10,000	$10,000	$10,000
Annual net cash flow	$ 2,000	$ 2,000	$ 1,800	$ 2,000	$ 2,000
Example A:					
Useful life	10 YEARS	10 YEARS	10 YEARS	8 YEARS	10 YEARS
IRR	15.1%	12.7%	12.4%	11.8%	10.4%
Actual IRR variance from forecast	—	16%	18%	22%	31%
Example B:					
Useful life	20 YEARS	20 YEARS	20 YEARS	16 YEARS	20 YEARS
IRR	19.4%	17.5%	17.3%	18.7%	15.6%
Actual IRR variance from forecast	—	10%	11%	4%	20%
Memo: Third year ROI (assuming 10-year straight line depreciation)	10%	9%	8%	10%	10%

TABLE 6.4. Worksheet for developing *cash flow* (in $millions).

Year	Capitalizable Expenditures*	Working Capital Additions†	Investment Cash Flow	Pre-Tax Earnings Before Deprec.	Book Depreciation‡	Taxable Earnings	Net Earnings	Net Cash Flow from Operations	Net Cash Flow
1986	(4.5)		(4.5)	(2.0)		(2.0)	(1.2)	(1.2)	(5.7)
1987	(6.2)		(6.2)	(2.0)		(2.0)	(1.2)	(1.2)	(7.4)
1988	(5.8)		(5.8)	(2.8)		(2.8)	(1.7)	(1.7)	(7.5)
1989		(3.0)	(3.0)	(.3)	1.7	(2.0)	(1.2)	.5	(2.5)
1990		(1.0)	(1.0)	4.7	1.7	3.0	1.8	3.5	2.5
1991		(2.0)	(2.0)	9.7	1.7	8.0	4.8	6.5	4.5
1992		(2.6)	(2.6)	16.5	1.6	14.9	8.9	10.5	7.9
1993				16.5	1.2	15.3	9.2	10.4	10.4
1994				16.5	1.2	15.3	9.2	10.4	10.4
1995				16.6	1.1	15.5	9.3	10.4	10.4
1996				12.9	1.0	11.9	7.1	8.1	8.1
1997				12.9	.8	12.1	7.3	8.1	8.1
1998				12.9	.8	12.1	7.3	8.1	8.1
1999				12.9	.7	12.2	7.3	8.0	8.0
2000				12.9	.6	12.3	7.4	8.0	8.0
2001	.5	8.6	9.1	12.9	1.9	11.0	6.6	8.5	17.6
Total	(16.0)		(16.0)	151.7	16.0	135.4	80.9	96.9	80.9

*Working capital by 1992, when operating at 100% of capacity, includes:

Accounts receivable (30 days × sales)	$6.2
Raw materials (10 days × materials cost)	.5
Finished product (30 days × mill cost)	3.4
Cash (8 days × Cost of sales – Depreciation)	1.0
Current liabilities (25% of above items excluding cash)	(2.5)
	$8.6

†Investment includes:

Building	$ 2.0
Equipment	14.0
Land	.5
	$16.5

‡Depreciation accruals commence in year facilities start up operation.

numbers upon which it is based are the same as those reported to investors. The shortcomings are that a one-year ROI of 15 percent could turn into an 85 percent loss next year if no future revenues are forthcoming, averaging over project life fails to take the timing of cash flows into account, and expense allocations may be arbitrary.

The remaining four criteria cited take into account the arrival time of cash flow and, subject to slight qualification, are equally acceptable. Internal rate of return was previously defined to be that discount which equates cash inflows with cash outflows. The IRR is solved by trial and error, and there may be as many solutions as there are changes in sign. The rate at which funds are presumed to be reinvested is IRR.

Net present value represents the difference between the present value of the cash flow generated and the present value of the investment incurred. The discount factor is taken to be the cost of capital. An NPV of zero implies that the cost of capital equals the IRR. Net present value is deemed to be slightly preferable to IRR as a ranking device since it bypasses the problem of multiple solutions and makes the more realistic assumption that funds can be reinvested at the cost of capital rather than IRR. As a concept, however, IRR is easier to "sell" than NPV, and its difficulties can readily be rectified if necessary.

Discounted payback period is understood to be the number of years required for cash flows from the project to cover both the investment outlay and the cost of capital. It helps to resolve the question of the minimum forecast period required for a go or no-go investment decision. The profitability index differs from NPV in that it equals the ratio of the present value of cash flows generated by the project to the present value of investment outlays. Since it scales projects to NPV per $1 of investment, PI facilitates comparison among projects of different magnitudes.

Allowance for risk differentials among projects tends to be somewhat arbitrary. Management typically bases its judgement on so-called project risk; that is, the range of outcomes associated with each project. Management is prone to assign the lowest cut-off rate or equivalent to replacement of equipment and facilities, the median rate to proposals to expand facilities to meet increased demand for existing products, and the top rate for new product outlays.

Theory holds the cut-off rate or its equivalent should reflect the contribution of each investment proposal to the overall risk of the firm. The critical factor is the degree to which outcomes are intercorrelated, since management and shareholders are both motivated to diversify away noncorrelated or project-specific risks. The risk premium, defined as the minimum expected return net of the risk-free rate, should therefore vary directly with the sensitivity of the project's return to the underlying rate of return for the company as a whole.

Assessment of the appropriate adjustment for risk is complicated by: (1) the dependence of project outcomes upon several factors, (2) long-tailed liability distributions, and (3) just plain bias. Dependence upon the behavior of multiple economic or other factors reduces the benefit from diversification since each factor may deviate from its expected value and the sensitivity to each factor may vary from investment outlay to investment outlay. Product liability experience demonstrates that certain project risks—no matter how small in an expected sense—cannot be fully diversified away. Outlays to settle product liability suits have led such major companies as A. H. Robbins and Johns Manville to file for bankruptcy. Worse, insurance companies not only charge high fees to insure against such events, but also place caps on the liability assumed, and sometimes refuse even to write insurance. Litigation, moreover, is a growth industry!

In the matter of forecast bias, it is tempting simply to add a few points across the board to the cut-off rate, as some firms do. The problem with this approach is that those who prepare unbiased forecasts are penalized, while those who "lie" win acceptance of their proposals. Elimination of bias is really a matter for process control and feedback.

Process control and feedback, an integral part of financial management, unfortunately may be hampered by deficiencies in accounting data. Costs are sometimes allocated on the basis of arbitrary formulas; cash flows attributable to individual projects often cannot be separated from the totality of cash flows; project lives need not be uniform nor certain.

No comprehensive solution to the problem posed is available as yet, but awareness of the issues is fundamental. In the short run, the process can be measurably improved by stressing group, as distinct from individual, project performance and perhaps by modifying the depreciation factor to conform with that implicit in the IRR calculation. The end in mind is to assign responsibility in the light of sufficiently accurate measures of performance.

Merger and Acquisition

Firms that fail to achieve growth and performance objectives internally are motivated to enter the merger and acquisition arena. Acquisitions surpassed 3700 in 1987 and were valued in excess of $167 billion; the magnitudes were 15 percent or so below the nine-year peak in 1986, possibly due to the tax change starting in 1987 and the market break in October 1987.

Acquisition procedures parallel those of internal capital investment in certain respects, extend well beyond the internal capital budgeting process in other respects, require the participation of corporate planners, and generally involve *top* management. Search, cash flow forecast, and evaluation have their counterparts in acquisition analysis. Furthermore, there are complicating factors such as negotiation, competition with other would-be acquirers, target management, employee reaction, and unspecified liabilities.

The first step in acquisition analysis is to examine the appropriate fit between the two firms. As a rule, the target firm must contribute something over and above its stand-alone value. In times past, the contribution has ranged from accounting flexibility in the late 1960s to underpriced assets relative to replacement costs due to low stock values in the late 1970s. The plus factor in recent acquisition activity appears to be addition to market share, with diversification to spread risk lagging far behind.

The second step is to determine the upper bound or limit for the value of the target firm. Cash flows must be projected; synergy possibilities explored; a terminal value set, and an appropriate discount factor derived. A major risk is that the available record may not tell the whole story.

Assets not needed in the business and particularly coveted by others add value to the target since they can be sold. Costs of integrating the two companies, in turn, subtract from value. Golden parachutes and other attempts to make the acquisition process expensive have become the order of the day.

The third step is to negotiate an acceptable—if not favorable—acquisition price. The price offered must be in line with prevailing premiums over market price and often turns out to be excessive. Fees paid to merger brokers and advisers hinge upon successful conclusion and vary directly with the price paid. Tender offers also invite competitive bidding. The party that puts the target in play frequently loses out in the final bidding.

The list of factors that lead to overpricing is long. Executives, for example, may tend to involve their egos and then hate to lose. Relevant information is concealed, overlooked, and misinterpreted. Leveraged buyout specialists base price upon bust-up value and availability of junk bond financing.

FINANCING DECISIONS

Asset management is but half the battle. The way in which operating cash flows (net of capital expenditures and additions to working capital) are allocated among financial claims, cash dividends, and stock repurchases also affects total enterprise value and thereby the worth of common stock. Management must determine the proper level of prior financial claims (debt and preferred stock) in relation to the firm's expected cash flows, the mix of such claims, strategies for selling and modifying financial claims, and dividend policy.

Prior Financial Claims

Prior financial claims refer to all legally binding commitments to pay cash that have priority over the residual or ownership interest in the business. The bulk of such claims is summarized on the balance sheet under current liabilities and long-term debt. Prior claims not shown on the balance sheet include operating leases, pension benefits, take-or-pay agreements, and so on.

Debt Instruments

Apart from accounts payable and accrued liabilities that arise in the normal course of business, short-term debt or notes payable typically represent draw downs under multiyear revolving credit agreements with banks. Rates may be fixed but are more likely to be floating. Commitment fees of, for example, 25 percent per year are paid on the unused portion of the bank's commitment. Should the firm's creditworthiness be in question, the credit agreement may, for instance, require the borrower to: (1) maintain certain minimum levels of tangible net worth and working capital, (2) meet certain ratio requirements, (3) restrict capital expenditures, and (4) collateralize the debt. Failure to meet these and other requirements that may be imposed could result in termination of the bank's commitment.

    Debentures, the traditional long-term debt instrument, are characterized by: (1) a fixed coupon rate usually payable semiannually; (2) specified maturity dates of 15, 20, or 25 years; (3) a principal amount to be paid at maturity or earlier, if called; (4) a so-called sinking fund provision for periodic retirement of the debt; and (5) a call provision that permits the company to buy back the bond at par for sinking fund purposes and at a declining call premium for other purposes. The bond indenture or agreement may restrict the firm from taking a variety of actions, including the sale of assets and the payment of dividends.

Tradition notwithstanding, the variety of long-term debt instruments is now virtually unlimited. The breakdown of long-term debt given in Table 6.5 for IC Industries points to the international character of the market for debt, reveals the presence of substantial subsidiary—as well as parent—debt, shows a mixture of fixed rate debt, floating rate debt, and even zero coupon debt that reinvests interest until maturity and features differences in maturities, degree of seniority, and other respects as well.

TABLE 6.5.   Breakdown of long-term debt: I C Industries.

Long-term debt at December 31 consisted of the following:

	(in $ millions)	
	1987	**1986**
Parent Company:		
Equipment notes due 1993 to 1996, 10.97% to 13¼%	$ 61.3	$ 66.4
Swiss franc bonds due 1988, 7%	—	24.1
Swiss franc bonds due 1994 and 1995, exchanged for U.S. dollar liabilities, 12½% and 12.2%	104.3	104.3
Canadian notes due 1995, exchanged for U.S. dollar liabilities at 12.2%	38.1	38.1
Loans and notes due 1991 and 1995, effective rates 12.2% to 13½%	124.9	124.9
Bank loans due 1988 to 1992, floating rates	989.0	33.0
IC Industries Finance Corporation, N.V.:		
Guaranteed notes due 1990 and 1991, 8¾% to 12%	185.8	268.2
Split currency bonds due 1993 and 1997, 9.9% and 11½%	144.8	139.1
Retractable notes due 1998, 11⅞%	75.0	75.0
Swiss franc bonds due 1992, 6½%	75.2	104.0
Floating rate notes due 1991	36.6	58.7
Zero coupon bonds due 1994, 14¼%	73.9	64.7
Other Subsidiaries:		
Sinking fund debentures due 1992 and 1995, 5⅞% and 10¼%	25.9	32.7
State and local industrial development bonds and mortgages due 1988 to 2014, 7¼% to 12¼%	36.8	37.2
Various, due 1988 to 2002, 4% to 17.2%	30.6	28.4
Obligations for capital leases	16.0	15.9
Notes payable by foreign subsidiaries due 1989 to 2012, 2.67% to 13.25%	47.3	48.0
Subordinated sinking fund debentures due 1995 to 1999, 10.2% and 12%	32.3	52.1
Total	2,097.8	1,314.8
Less: Amount due within one year	201.2	93.5
Unamortized discount	10.5	14.7
Long-term debt	$1,886.1	$1,206.6

Subordination of debt has been given new meaning with the emergence of the high yield, junk bond market. In response to a takeover threat, USG, a building materials company, proposed on May 2, 1988, to recapitalize the firm by exchanging each share of USG stock for $37 in cash, $5 in face amount of redeemable 16 percent junior subordinated debentures due in 2008, and one share of stock in the recapitalized firm. The recapitalization was to be financed by a term loan of $1.6 billion to be repaid over 17 installments, $550 million of senior subordinated debentures and $260 million of junior debentures. Interest on the junior debentures could be paid either in cash or in junior debentures through 1993. The book value of the stockholders' equity in USG would become a negative $1.57 billion. It would appear from this case, FMC, and others like it, that the amount of leverage possible is almost unlimited.

Firms that wish to reduce the interest cost may issue debt that is convertible into common stock or offer warrants to buy stock as inducement to purchase debt. Convertibility and warrants both imply that shareholders are surrendering part of their residual interest in future cash flows in return for lower explicit interest cost now. Collateral may also have to be offered. Payment in some cases has even been in kind.

Investment bankers have devoted considerable effort to new product development in recent years. Almost any combination of rate schedule, priority, and maturity is possible.

Leasing

Leasing represents one of several alternatives to borrowing. *Financial leases* are capitalized and recorded on the balance sheet as both an asset and a liability. *Operating leases* involving less stringent terms are merely reported in footnotes to the financial statements.

Much could be said about leasing, but the purpose here is to contrast the financial lease with other debt forms. Leasing is somewhat perplexing in that it represents the combination of: (1) a sale of assets, and (2) the sale of a prior debt claim. The assets sold include the future value of the underlying equipment of facility and the privilege of depreciating the asset. The debt claim carries with it the obligation to make certain cash payments. The value of the debt claim is the present value of the payment stream discounted at the appropriate rate for comparable debt claims.

Motivation for Leverage

The incentive to leverage the company derives from interest deductibility for tax purposes, inflation expectations, and market segmentation or inefficiency. Consider first the case of firms X and Y confronted by zero income taxes and an efficient capital market. Suppose that X and Y differ only in the respect that X is leveraged, while Y has no debt. Should the summed market value of debt and equity for X initially surpass the market value of Y, arbitrage activity will bring the values in line. The lower valued Y will be bought financed partly by debt and partly by the short sale of X's equity. The arbitrager gains from the offsetting transactions as long as the differential in values exists. The process terminates when the values are brought in line and no benefit is derived from the use of debt.

Once taxes are introduced and interest is made deductible for tax purposes, the situation changes. The after-tax combination of interest plus net earnings for firm X exceeds the after-tax earnings of the all-equity firm Y by the tax rate times the interest cost. Since the composite risk of holding both debt and equity in X can be no different from holding an equivalent share of equity in Y, the discount rate must be the same for the composite cash flow of both X and Y. It follows that the total value of X will exceed that of Y by the tax rate times the magnitude of the debt incurred.

The motivation to borrow varies directly with the expected rate of inflation. The point is simply that nominal interest contains both "real" interest and an inflation component. The latter measures the anticipated decline in "real" principal value and thereby constitutes a partial repayment of principal. The borrower gains to the extent of the tax rate times the inflation or principal element inherent in nominal interest.

Differential taxation at the investor level may either augment or negate the benefit of tax deductibility at the firm level. Assuming that taxes cannot be shifted or passed along, the investor bears the burden of taxes imposed at the corporate and individual level. Should the shareholder be taxed at a lower rate on his dividends and capital gains than the lender is on her interest income, the differential tax at the investor level may offset, in part or in whole, the reverse differential at the corporate level.

Debt Policy

The optimum mix of debt and equity ultimately hinges upon the likelihood of bankruptcy and the costs associated therewith. The direct costs are bankruptcy filing fees together with legal, accounting, and other professional service charges. Indirect costs comprise lost managerial time, lost sales and profits, and lost ability to obtain credit at reasonable rates. Side effects of bankruptcy include records that may be in shambles, assets that turn out to be nonexistent, and fire sales of good assets.

The costs of financial distress can be significant even in the absence of outright bankruptcy. In its efforts to remain solvent, Armco sold its profitable Aerospace and Strategic Materials Segment and its Fabricated Products and Services Segment. It also incurred restructuring charges of $335.6 and $103.6 millions respectively in 1985 and 1986 in scaling back its Carbon Steel, Speciality Steel and Oilfield Equipment divisions.

Optimality is achieved when additions to debt no longer add to the value of the firm and when the tax benefit derived from debt is just offset by the incremental costs in an expected sense associated with an additional $1 of debt. The precise location of the optimum point is subject to considerable debate and depends upon one's estimate of indirect costs.

Despite the existence—conceptually speaking—of a "best" mix of debt and equity, it appears that degree of leverage actually adopted by the firm hinges upon which of three points of view dominates. The vantage points are those of: (1) management, (2) lenders, and (3) raiders. Factors taken into consideration include: (1) operating cash flow in relation to fixed financial outlays, (2) cash flow sensitivity, (3) asset composition and liquidity, and (4) company size.

Shareholders can diversify, while management (with job continuation, salary, and stock option values, all depending upon the successful continuation of the business) cannot. It follows, therefore, that management—unless pressured from outside—will opt for less debt than shareholders might elect.

Lending institutions, in turn—unless stretching for fee income as some are—require at least two ways out of each loan. The strongly preferred way is through free cash generated in the normal course of operations. The secondary way is by means of asset liquidation.

Pressure to leverage the firm in extreme fashion comes from corporate raiders. Corporate raiders combine cash flow and bust-up value to create the leveraged buyout situation. Banks and insurance companies take sizable senior debt positions in LBOs, while junk bond specialists absorb the junior, subordinated debt needed to provide the equivalent of an equity cushion. Segments of the business are sold to reduce the debt quickly; expenses are cut and capital outlays slashed to provide additional cash flow to service the debt.

In the attempt to avoid takeover, potential targets feel obliged to restructure on their own. USG, mentioned above, represents the extreme case, since it was confronted with an actual tender offer by Desert Partners. No wonder an array of debt policies exists.

Financial Strategies

Numerous opportunities exist for the astute financial manager to add to profitability by altering the composition of debt in response to changing market conditions. Interest rates can be hedged. Bonds can be refunded by debt of equal rating or different rating. Fixed interest payments can be swapped for variable interest payments, and vice versa. Bond maturities can be lengthened or shortened.

Nothing stands still! Earnings retained in the firm, periodic retirement of debt, and changes in cash items continuously reshape the capital structure. Bond ratings rise and fall as prospects vary.

The manager can move quickly. Large companies typically register with the S.E.C. their intention to issue debt or equity at some time over, for instance, the next two years. Once the so-called shelf registration is in place, the firm can then take advantage of rate "windows" without the traditional waiting period. Swaps and hedges can be arranged with a phone call. Here, as elsewhere, the decision rule is based upon cost versus benefit.

Residual Claims: Equity

Residual claimants to the business include holders of preferred and common stock. Preferred stock has priority over common stock in liquidation and normally receives a fixed or floating dividend rate—in the case of money markets preferreds—irrespective of how well the company fares. Preferred dividend arrears typically must be removed before cash dividends can be declared on common stock. High-quality preferred stock is attractive to corporate investors by virtue of the intercorporate dividend exclusion of 80 percent.

Common stock occupies the bottom rung of the priority ladder, carries with it the right to receive whatever is left after other claimants have been satisfied, and features voting rights. More than one class of common stock may exist, each with differential voting (and sometimes dividend) rights.

Residual interest in the firm is measured—in a bookkeeping sense—by shareholders' equity whose component parts comprise preferred stock (if any), common stock, capital received in excess of par, deferred currency translation, and reinvested earnings. Additions to shareholders' equity result from the issuance and sale of stock and the retention of periodic earnings. The outstanding shares of publicly traded companies usually grow in number through time as a result of dividend reinvestment programs and exercise of stock options by management, whether or not public offerings are undertaken. Changes in number of shares outstanding due to splits and stock dividends that do not affect the investors' position must be reversed when making interperiod comparisons.

Unless the stock market is deemed to be "high," as it was alleged to be during the first half of 1987, management prefers to augment equity through the retention of earnings rather than through public offerings of common stock. For one thing, management tends to believe that its stock is underpriced in the market. For another, management dislikes the initial dilution occasioned by the offering.

Dividend Policy and Share Repurchase

Cash dividends and share repurchase both represent a partial liquidation of the firm in the sense that assets and net worth are concurrently diminished. Most public companies pay cash dividends; the exceptions are firms that are growing rapidly and firms that are losing money. Many public firms also repurchase stock from time to time.

Cash dividends per share typically depend upon past dividends per share and current earnings per share. Management hates to reduce dividends unless other firms are doing likewise for fear of investor misinterpretation. Management likes to raise dividends when sustainable earnings rise.

Consistent dividend behavior signals that conditions remain relatively unchanged in the opinion of management. Deviations from past behavior signify that something is awry. The market responds quickly.

Academicians have previously favored share repurchase over cash dividends due to the differential between the tax rate on dividend income and that on capital gains. The differential has been eliminated for the moment at least, but capital gains remain slightly favored since the tax is not imposed until the gain is realized.

Share repurchase serves several purposes. In the 1970s, it reflected managements' belief that common shares were undervalued and represented good investments in their own right. In the 1980s, share repurchases pointed to managements' efforts to restructure and to readjust leverage. Share repurchases offer management notably greater leeway in terms of magnitude and timing than do dividends.

Whether dividends or share repurchase, the ultimate decision rule seems clear cut. Cash can legitimately be retained in the business as long as management can employ the cash as effectively as the shareholder with due allowance for risk and taxes.

Cost of Capital

Cost of capital is understood to refer to the minimum compensation required by investors for assuming a given class of risks. In the context of the corporation, it is the weighted sum of the after-tax costs of the diverse components that make up the capital structure. The weights are the ratios of the market value of each component to the total market values of all elements.

Costs for the publicly traded debt components are simply the effective yields at which the securities are trading in the market. Costs of privately held, nontraded debt can be estimated by reference to publicly traded issues belonging to the same risk class. The cost of preferred stock is the dividend divided by market price where there is no maturity.

The cost of equity cannot be known with certainty since the price per share represents the present value of an uncertain stream of future cash flows. The cost of equity can be estimated by reference to the CAPM model which states that the cost or required rate of return associated with any risky asset should be equal to the risk-free rate plus the relevant Beta times the market risk premium. The Beta for any stock measures the sensitivity of that stock's return to the market and is estimated by reference to historical market data. Alternatively, should the market be judged to be efficient, the required rate of return can be estimated by solving the dividend discount model for the discount rate r; that is, r equals the long-term growth rate in dividends plus the ratio of dividends for the coming year to the current stock price.

As an allocator of corporate resources, cost of capital varies with the contribution of each capital investment project to total enterprise risk. The expected return for each project minus the hypothetical risk-free rate should vary in direct proportion to the project's sensitivity to the underlying economic environment relative to that for the firm as a whole.

Cost of capital is not calculated to the tenth decimal place, or to the fifth, or even to the third. The end purpose is to come up with reasonable numbers that make adequate allowance for significant risk differentials.

SUMMARY

The role of the financial manager is to allocate limited company resources among competing fund uses to optimize the value of the firm. The scarce or limited resource is internally generated cash flow, supplemented by additions to debt and equity from external sources. The alternative uses are capital expenditures, additions to working capital, dividends and share repurchases. The balancing item in any period is change in cash or debt position. The allocating device is cost of capital.

Asset management, the traditional focus of financial management, is only part of the task. Financing decisions also contribute to shareholder value. The idea is to "sell off" portions of anticipated cash flow in such a way as to maximize total company value and to adjust capital structure quickly as windows open. The manager of a creditworthy firm has virtually unlimited choice.

Most decisions are made under uncertainty, and many decisions relate to cash flows several years hence. Uncertainty is partly resolved by diversification at either the firm or investor level, but there remains the tie-in of the firm with the underlying economic environment. Sensitivity to economic conditions cannot be diversified away and is reflected in estimates of cost of capital.

The timing of cash flows is often critical to the decision process. Delays in cash flow generation can affect IRR significantly. Understanding of the discount process is essential to the comprehension of finance.

APPENDIX: DEFINITION AND DERIVATION OF FORMULAS

1. Expected Return: Sum of individual returns, each value weighted by its relative frequency.

2. Variance: Sum of squared deviation from group mean for each observation divided by the number (N) of observations, or by $N - 1$.

3. Covariance: Sum of deviation from the mean for the tth observation in the ith group times the corresponding deviation from the mean for the tth observation in the jth group, divided by N or $N - 1$.

4. Variance of a Portfolio: Weighted sum of individual variances and covariances.

5. Present Value.

    a. Annuity of $1 per year: $1/(1 + i) + 1/(1 + i)**2 + ... + 1/(1 + i)**T$
    $= 1/i - (1/i)[1/(1 + i)**T] = (1/i)\{1 - [1/(1 + i)]**T\}$, where T is the the number of years.

b. Annuity of $1 growing at rate g: $(1 + g)/(1 + i) + (1 + g)**2/(1 + i)**2 + ... + (1 + g)**T/(1 + i)**T = [(1 + g)/(i - g)] \{1 - [(1 + g)/(1 + r)]**T\}$.

6. CAPM.

a. Expected return $E[Rp] = Rf + (E[Rm] - Rf) \times w$, where $E[Rm]$ is the expected return on an efficient set of risky securities, Rf is the risk-free rate, and w is the ratio of the investment in the risky asset to the investor's total equity.

b. Standard deviation (S.D.) = sq. rt. of $(w[Rf]**2 \times Var[Rf] + w**2 \times Var[Rm] + 2 \times w \times w[Rf] \times Cov[Rf, Rm]$, where $w[Rf]$ is the percentage of net worth allocated to Rf, Var and Cov are variance and covariance respectively. Since $Var[Rf]$ and $Cov[Rf, Rm] = 0$, S.D. of $Rp = w \times S.D.$ of Rm, or $w = SD[Rp]/SD[Rm]$.

c. By substitution for w into $E[Rp]$, $E[Rp] = Rf + (E[Rm] - Rf) \times SD[Rp]/SD[Rm]$.

d. For any security i, $E[Ri] = Rf + Beta(i) \times (E[Rm] - Rf)$, where $Beta = Cov[Ri, Rm]/Var[Rm]$ and Rp is fully diversified.

ADDITIONAL READINGS

Altman, E. I., ed., *Handbook of Corporate Finance*, 6th ed. (New York: John Wiley, 1986).

Brealey, R. A., and S. C. Myers, *Principles of Corporate Finance* (New York: McGraw-Hill, 1988).

Ross, S. A., and R. W. Westerfield, *Corporate Finance* (St. Louis, MO: Times Mirror/Mosby College Publishing, 1988).

7 MARKETING MANAGEMENT: BECOMING A MARKET-DRIVEN COMPANY

Robert T. Davis

A useful start to this chapter is to contrast two frequently used words—though often employed incorrectly—namely *markets* and *marketing*. The unexperienced might think that the two are interchangeable, but this is not so in practice. The two refer to very different dimensions of the subject. A company can be *marketing oriented* without being *market oriented*. How can this be?

Marketing describes a business function, like production, finance, research—or marketing. These functions are the key organizational components of any company. Marketing's essential responsibility is to create customers—just as production creates products. The marketing executive, in this role, employs an assortment of marketing variables to craft an effective marketing strategy. His selected variables are known as "the marketing mix"—the manager's blueprint for action.

The specifics of the mix can be combined in dozens of ways to stress, for example, product differentiation, market segmentation, or personal selling. Marketing, when viewed as a function, is action centered. It focuses on what marketing managers *do.*

The word market, on the other hand, has different implications. It is not internal in its focus nor does it "belong" to the company. A market is external: It is "out there." A market in its fundamental posture is a collection of buyers, actual or potential, external to the company. The market is the ultimate source of the company's income. If the buyer does not buy, there is no business. The seller may activate the market but he does not necessarily originate it. He adapts as much as he creates. He designs his marketing strategies for selected markets.

Markets come in all shapes and sizes: large or small; simple or complex; technical or nontechnical; repetitive or intermittent; consumer, industrial, or service specific. Thus, senior citizens, Texans, small businesses, and policemen are all markets. Some are better developed than others. Regardless, markets are fundamental and are the targets for marketing strategies.

We have marketing companies and market-oriented companies. The latter concentrate their attention on a particular array of customers. Lever Co. sells mostly to homemakers, Varian to chemists, Hewlett Packard to electrical engineers, and Stanford to college and graduate school students.

Whereas the market-driven organization keys itself to the user segments, the marketing company in the final analysis is predisposed toward the in-house or functional environment.

The distinction is profound; it explains how the firms choose to compete. A market-driven company tries to provide what the buyer wants; a marketing company, on the other hand, prefers to sell what it already makes. It has, if you will, a selling bias.

A benefit to being market-driven is sometimes overlooked. Everyone (management and other) shares a common mission: The customer comes first. Having such a shared mission means that all company activities are responsive to the consumers' well-being. A common drumbeat throbs in such organizations. The mission is clear and shared by all. Nordstrom and Walmart, two rapidly growing specialty retail chains, have gained their preminence by delivering superior customer values.

As far as Nordstrom employees are concerned, customer service is the raison d'etre for every company action or program, and the fulcrum is the salesperson on the floor. To facilitate this philosophy, sales personnel are expected to make most of the service decisions that are restricted to management in other companies.

To reinforce this philosophy, senior management depicts its organization as the upside down triangle (Figure 7.1).

All of the superstructure has a single-minded purpose—to reinforce the salesperson-consumer interface. Service is the operative byword; service is the all-consuming passion of each employee. It is not easy to think of any other company that centers so much responsibility on the floor salesperson.

Once you acknowledge this business philosophy, it is evident that the only way to succeed in business is to make sure that every aspect of your

FIGURE 7.1. Organization as depicted by senior management.

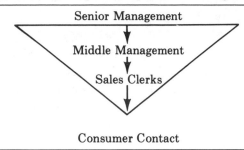

operation has but a single purpose, namely, to deliver better values to the consumer, at a profit. This dedication holds no matter which part of the company is considered, be it warehousing, the credit department, manufacturing, or research—the ultimate test for each is whether it enhances consumer satisfaction. It follows needless to say, that everyone is *in* marketing.

Consumer satisfaction is the sum total of a large number of benefits and activities. Let one fail, and the entire structure is threatened. Consider a restaurant with dirty menus or unwashed windows. All of their expensive advertising would be for naught.

CONSUMER BENEFITS

You can hardly know too much about consumer needs and associated benefits. Indeed, one of the most fertile dimensions of market research is that of consumer behavior. What causes buyers to behave the way they do? Why are they not all rational?

Every buyer wants the benefits, not the intrinsic raw material in each product. Yet, the temptation is for the inexperienced observer to concentrate unduly on product features. "Let's differentiate the product," "Let's modify the specs," "Let's add some extra features." These comments all imply an instinctive reliance upon product attributes. We do buy many things because of product characteristics, including soft drinks, convertible automobiles, or disposable pens. Moreover, we are inclined to think that if two products have the same features, nothing important differentiates them. Price will determine the purchase. Hence, we quite naturally focus on specialty items (differentiated) and commodities (not differentiated) and view price as the major competitive variable.

However, this myopic approach assumes that the typical customer is a robotlike character who is interested only in product specifics. What, on the other hand, about other buyer values such as product reliability, service, postsale reinforcement, prestige and status, convenience, availability —the list could go on and on. The possible buyer values available to the seller are almost limitless. Different markets, to be sure, will prefer different attributes, so there must be a careful match between the elements of the offer and the separate market segments. As already noted, many specifics of the selling/buying interface are linked—they are interdependent. For example, the inefficient warehouseman can severely curtail the sales manager's promise to a critical customer. And, if the industrial designer substitutes plastic panels for oak, the marketing manager may have to lower the price ("it looks cheaper"), increase the warranty terms (to augment the selling offer) and change the shipping container.

In summary, customer values can be characterized as interdependent with value links to most parts of the company's operations. Simple changes in activities can result in chain reactions.

As a result, we define marketing as both a business function and a management philosophy. It is essential to a company's health in both its functional and philosophic dimensions.

MARKET SEGMENTS

We have noted that different submarkets favor different values and benefits. Their demand profiles are dissimilar. In marketing terminology, we define a segment as a group of buyers whose reaction to a particular marketing stimulus (an advertisement, a distribution system) is similar. Segments are homogeneous within the group but heterogeneous between.

Because segments have separate consumption patterns, what is a satisfactory service to one may not be to another. The doctor and the dentist are medical specialists. But what the doctor wants is not what the dentist prefers; likewise, the Yuppie suburbanite has desires dissimilar to the retiree from Bangor, Maine.

This disparity highlights the fact that segmentation is a significant marketing concept. It permits the manager to break his gross market into smaller, more manageable pieces. This possibility implies further that the manager must determine separate strategies for each piece.

For years, we boasted about the American economy as "a mass market" as opposed to the segmented European version. Costs were in our favor. However, is this position genuine? A truly mass market would behave in a consistent manner. A quick survey of the real world indicates that the American market is composed of many smaller pieces. "Niche-manship" is the credo of today's marketing managers.

The notion of segmentation allows us to subdivide our population into such representative subsets as "the economic buyer," "the retiree," and the "blue collar worker." It also suggests that we can gain differential advantages in the marketplace by better matching our strategy to appropriate segments. Even though we have a stagnant position in one market, we may well develop a specialty position in another.

MARKETING STRATEGIES

The mix, we can now appreciate, is the raw material for assembling a marketing strategy. The marketing manager picks and chooses from the various mix elements until he has a collection or strategy which he considers appropriate. This selection is no casual exercise: A marketing strategy must take into account the environmental pressures (both positive and negative), take advantage of the firm's strengths while avoiding its weaknesses, be responsive to the competitive scene, recognize the meaningful consumer values, and include channel of distribution alternatives. The purpose of a strategy is to build a sustainable competitive advantage—a so-called competitive edge. In street language the test of a marketing strategy is whether or not it allows its user to obtain "more than his fair share." Unfortunately, in this strategic creation process, the world rarely holds still. As manager, you struggle, adapt, and modify until you wonder how anyone can make sense out of this morass, but managers have been dealing with these elusive competitive issues for many years. The key is to develop a basic action philosophy, remain flexible, listen, and learn.

In both theory and practice, marketing managers have pretty well agreed that a marketing strategy is the agglomeration of fix mix elements—the irreducible minimum into which all the remaining marketing variables can be fitted. These elements are:

1. The product—what is its definition, its values or benefits, its positioning, its physical dimensions?
2. The segments—who are the target audiences, what are their requirements?
3. The delivery system—how will the product be brought to the user?
4. The communication strategy—how will the potential buyer be made aware, induced to try, and persuaded to rebuy?

5. The price—what is our relative cost compared to the alternative product choices?

Some summary illustrations of strategy are:

1. Pocket Books, Inc. turned the book business on its end about 40 years ago. The company successfully launched into mass distribution the now familiar softcover books. The initial strategy was simple but effective:

   - Offer well-known popular sellers and themes (cowboys, detective stories) reprinted in scaled-down size, softcovered, visually attractive, and made up of reasonably sturdy raw materials
   - Aim for the postwar mobile leisure time population of all ages and interests, who would buy on impulse
   - Set a selling price competitive with magazine and lending library alternatives and conducive to spontaneous purchase
   - Distribute through all kinds of traffic outlets reached through magazine and newspaper jobbers
   - Employ in-store display as the primary communicating inducement

2. McDonald's drastically changed the "eating out" business by:

   - Concentrating on the fast-growing hamburger segment
   - Setting up an in-store delivery system that provides for immediate service (precooked and stored in warming bins)
   - Pricing at a modest, impulse level—but allowing for trade-ups by means of bigger or different hamburgers
   - Insuring French fry "perfection"
   - Monopolizing traffic locations
   - Concentrating on the traveling and youth markets

3. IBM grew to dominate the computer business, not so much because it led technically or had the best salespeople, but because it offered reliability at a slight price premium. No matter what your circumstances, as a customer, IBM was always at your disposal if you needed their help. You could count on it, and it was worth the premium!

What is common to these strategies?

Each identifies the underlying logic but not the tactical details by which the firm expects to compete. These are long-term, not short-term concepts.

Each strategy delivers important values to the buyer: availability and choice to the reader, convenience and consistent quality to the hamburger devotee, and assurance to the computer user. Furthermore, every operating activity within these companies is designed to reinforce the core promise to the consumer.

Sound strategies are the manager's playbook for competing. They essentially differentiate competitors. A good strategy alone is no guarantee of success, however. For each, a myriad of implementation alternatives, or tactics, can be used. To be specific, mass media advertising could include television, radio, magazines or newspapers; frequent or infrequent insertions; different appeals and visual formats, and so on. Tactics may well change frequently as immediate circumstances dictate. Strategy, in contrast, is more likely to persevere until underlying changes occur in the environment.

Because of the ongoing need to fine-tune the strategy, it must never be inflexibly accepted as "God-given." Every strategy is based on assumptions that may shift unexpectedly. Contingency planning, as a result, is a necessary characteristic of market planning. The extent to which management can anticipate likely outcomes diminishes the possibility of surprise. Contingency scenarios, it would seem, often differentiate between success and failure.

In economic terms, the marketing strategy deals with the issue of resource allocation. "How does the manager intend to spend his money? What is the underlying logic by which these allocation decisions are to be made?" The allocation decision is complicated by the fact that marketing decisions must be compatible with the other specifics of company operations, otherwise the separate business functions might pull at cross purposes. One can easily imagine the conflicts in an organization where R&D stresses technology, marketing is inclined toward systems selling, and production is totally cost-oriented. To match these disparate pieces would be no easy task.

Because of its complex facets, strategy cannot be fully comprehended by reviewing a few simplified examples. The mental exercises by which alternative strategies are developed, the subsequent alterations over time, and the large array of alternatives considered are impossible to reduce to a few airtight formulas. In addition, and of greater significance, is the underlying constraint that the analytic approach can take us only so far. Creativity is far more powerful than analysis and profoundly shapes the strategic decision. The need for creativity greatly adds to the complications of the job.

A thoughtful summary of strategic possibilities is the subject of Lee Adler's book: *Plotting Marketing Strategy*. Each chapter delves into a specific variation:

- The end run
- Concentration
- Marketing segmentation
- Market stretching
- Multibrand entries
- Brand extension
- Product innovation
- International expansion
- Distribution breakthroughs

The reader can, no doubt, add to the list. How about repositioning? selected distribution? integration? downsizing?

Professors Kollat, Blackwell, and Robison have reduced the choice to the array of 11 shown in Table 7.1.

Strategy over Time

Marketing strategy is shaped by the passing of time. As new products age, and competition gains a foothold, the strategic alternatives must be reconsidered. The manager does not manage the traditional product as he does the new. This phenomenon of aging is known as the *product lifecycle*. Marketing students depict the cycle as an "S" curve, such as the one shown in Figure 7.2.

The innovative product can be positioned, at the outset, in the "embryonic" stage. Stirrings begin, the management team begins to form, and the early buyers begin to consider purchase.

In stage 2—the "take-off"—demand is more cohesive and the seller increasingly excited about his or her prospects. A greater degree of formality and systematic thinking develops in place of the initial informal "reactive" atmosphere.

During stage 3—growth—everything is advancing: product strategy, marketing expansion, manufacturing processes, control systems, market and segmentation development. Keeping up with the accelerating demands on company resources is time consuming.

With the entry and subsequent aggressive moves of competition, as well as the emergence of a more mature buying audience, the seller enters stage 4, maturity. Eventually, the problem of decline arises.

The lifecycle concept serves as a helpful framework for appraising the adequacy of the firm's marketing strategy. The manager's problems of implementation, for example, grow as the cycle progresses from left to

TABLE 7.1. Product-market scope and growth vector alternatives.

Products Markets	Present Products	Improvements in Present Products	New Products with Related Technology			New Products With Unrelated Technology
			Assortment Manipulation	Expansion of the Variety of the Product Line		
Consumption Markets: Same markets*	(1) Market-penetration strategies	(3) Reformulation strategies	(5) Replacement strategies	(7) Product-line extension strategies		(9) Horizontal diversification strategies
New markets	(2) Market development strategies	(4) Market extension strategies	(6) Market segmentation/ product differentiation strategies	(8) Concentric diversification strategies		(10) Conglomerate diversification strategies
Resource and/or Distribution Markets	(11) Forward and/or backward integration strategies					

Source: David T. Kollat, Roger D. Blackwell, and James F. Robeison, *Strategic Marketing* (New York: Holt, Rinehart and Winston, 1972).

182

FIGURE 7.2.   Typical product lifecycle curve.

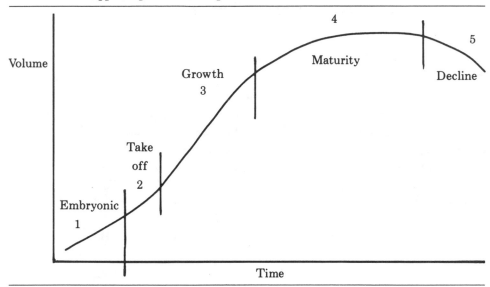

right. At the beginning, the business executive finds himself, for all intents and purposes, a monopolist. Nonetheless, he soon matures, with increasing speed, toward the commodity extreme.

What, one might ask, is acceptable behavior for the practitioner when confronting this product/market evolution? There are two choices: Lower the costs of operating in order to become more competitive, or innovate and re-establish a novel edge.

The first or productivity alternative demands a step-by-step analysis of the present cost structure. How much is being spent by major category—product, market, function—and how could these outlays be restructured? Should some activities be combined and others eliminated?

Cost cutting is undoubtedly the most pervasive management practice. But cost pairing is nevertheless a double-edged sword. Downsizing a company can create morale havoc with the employees: "Do we or don't we have jobs? Who will be the next to go?"

The more challenging management choice is to tackle the other half of the equation, increased sales. How can we improve our market position?

Products and markets *evolve;* for management to capture an increasing portion of the available market becomes a difficult task. The trick is to continue making profits while the commodity phase develops.

The manager inevitably inquires: "Why permit our market environment to migrate to the commodity extreme? Why not turn the arrow back and regain a specialty position?"

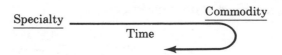

Specialty ——————————— Commodity
                   Time

This question suggests rich opportunities for improving our circumstances. How do companies, we ask, regain a sustainable competitive advantage? How do they re-establish a specialty position?

To start, we must recognize that significant differentiation can be developed from many competitive attributes, not mere product differences which is our normal mind set. Consider the following differentiation possibilities:

1. Product: Technical breakthrough (Nike airsole)
                    Cosmetic changes (perfume)
                    New ingredients (electronic devices)
                    New functions added (PCs)
                    Better dimensions and physical attributes (miniaturization)

2. Segment: Overseas markets (Japan)
                    Underserved markets (older population)
                    New segments (Levi and the casual user)

3. Price: Value pricing (systems selling)
                    Deeper discounts (grocery retailing)
                    Volume inducement (wholesalers)
                    Special deals and promotions (Frito Lay)

4. Distribution: New channels (health care)
                    In-store service (Nordstrom)
                    Company-owned outlets (IBM)

5. Communication: Uses of telemarketing (Goodrich, Clairol)
                    Catalog selling (Williams Sonoma, L.L. Bean)
                    Application-oriented advertising campaign (Nike —"Just Do It")

The conclusion? Essentially, the business executive must develop a unique approach, the alternative being reliance upon price concessions. Imitation, it would seem, is a sure path to poverty, as least in marketing strategy.

We often ignore it, but there is another differentiation possibility, probably the single most important so far. The strategist not only decides the program, he executes it. *Doing* is a far cry from *thinking*. Many a competitor pulls out ahead because he executes better than anyone else. Companies such as IBM, General Electric, and Pepsi Cola are superb doers. They can make average plans outstanding. Their impressive skills are in "the doing." Effective execution, it should be emphasized, is hard to imitate.

Market Differences

Do marketing strategies vary by market type—for example, as among consumer goods, industrial goods, and services?

In the macro sense, the answer is no. A number of marketing concepts are shared by all companies, regardless of market type. These concepts would include: business definition; mission statement; information systems. At this level of generalization, the common marketing requirements are easy to identify.

However, the answer is not so obvious when we move our sights to the operational level. Can the same manager supervise daily operations in the three markets? The answer is, not surprisingly, a bit involved. Specialists are usually essential in the lower echelons of any company—salesmen, sales supervisors, and field managers who understand intimately the particular demands of their individual markets. One cannot sell effectively to real buyers without possessing operating knowledge of products, applications, and territories. Senior executives, on the other hand, might find such details interesting but not essential. They need, primarily, a clearer understanding of such matters as business direction, market positioning, and strategic alternatives.

Marketing managers, during many class discussions, distinguish the three as shown in Table 7.2. Given these characteristics, it is a reasonable step to speculate what skills are required for each market. Here is one set of suggested conclusions:

Merchandising	Sales	Atmosphere
Mass Communications	Service	Presentation
Ability to influence the trade	Applications	Operations
Physical presentation	Team approaches to key accounts	

Note several modifiers:

1. The differences between markets are less obvious moving from top to bottom.
2. The believability of each category is greatest at the start.
3. The implications of these admittedly subjective judgments, suggest different management skills and attitudes.

TABLE 7.2. Some marketing differences—real and presumed.

Packaged Consumer Goods	Industrial Instruments	Air Service
1. Heavy pull (advertising) supplemented with point of sale and push efforts	Heavy push (salesmen) supported by service and some advertising	Pull (advertising plus word of mouth) plus reliance upon personal experience
2. Emphasis on mass markets	Highly segmented markets—limited customers	Concentration on business traveller—use other audiences for incremental income
3. Impersonal emphasis: advertising, brand names, perceptions, self service	Personal emphasis: service/backup support, confidence	Impersonal pull plus inflight personal attention
4. Purchaser's risk is in product satisfaction	Purchaser's risk is in product performance, service and technical support	Purchaser's risk is in ontime delivery of service, and personal satisfaction
5. Segmentation by groups	Segmentation by individual account with some group classification	Segmented by business and non-business grouping
6. Innovation includes more than product: package, promotions/deals, perceptions, communication	Innovation more product related: technology, financing, availability, support systems	Innovation lies in price deals and promotions, excellence of personal service, schedules
7. Communication efforts are highly leveraged (many customers see one ad)	Low leverage, essentially one-on-one relationship	Low leverage, complicated by fact that product can't be inventoried
8. Price focuses on volume-repeat purchases	Price focus on per-transaction profit	Price for repeat purchase and incremental income
9. Few influencers in buying decision	Many influencers; multiple roles	Few influencers: Less predictable
10. Short decision process	Long decision process	Short process
11. Heavy brand switching	Less likely to switch: institutional constraints	Loyal, but once turned off, difficult to recapture
12. Short memories	Long memories	Long memories
13. Customer may not be consumer	End user likely to be the customer	Customer is often the end user but travel agent a critical intermediary
14. Tangible product	Tangible product	Much intangibility

Perhaps, after all, markets differ more than first suggested. However, these differences are primarily micro in nature, our original hypothesis.

There are a number of reasons why marketing jobs differ in tactical details. First, as we have just indicated, are market and consumer variations. The packaged foods manager and his high technology counterpart have different requirements for their communication programs due to the nature of consumer expectations. Some buyers, for example, tend to be more sophisticated and require less help.

We can also look to the product lifecycle as an explanation of market differences. You will recall that the typical PLC develops as an S curve on its path from embryonic to decline. As a consequence, strategy must accommodate these different rates of change.

The Finnish economist, Mickwitz, has formulated an explanation based on the evolving elasticity of five competitive elements—product quality, advertising, price, service, and packaging—over the product lifecycle. In each of five stages (introduction, growth, maturity, saturation, and decline), he postulates the relative contribution to sales of each.

In stage 1, quality has the biggest impact on volume closely followed by advertising. In stage 2, advertising becomes crucial, quality assumes secondary importance, and price and service elasticity remain low. At stage 3 (during the keenest competition), pricing is critical, followed by advertising, quality, and service. In stage 4, packaging emphasis is important: At this stage, a high investment in packaging is necessary to generate more sales. Finally, in the last stage when the problem is to develop new product uses, advertising again assumes major importance. The Mickwitz explanation is in terms of consumer, not industrial, goods.

Phillip Kotler comments that this approach is not supported by empirical data; nevertheless, it is based on the compelling logic that changing competitive requirements and conditions result in an evolution in the strategic use of the different marketing variables.

Another thoughtful explanation of what happens to strategy throughout the lifecycle is sometimes labeled the *value theory.* This theory has to do with the shift in power, over time, from manufacturer to retailer (and channels). According to its proponents, consumers want values (or benefits) with every purchase, and they gladly give up their cash for these values. During the innovation stage of the cycle, the supplier is responsible for delivering the important consumer values—namely product distinction—and therefore controls the marketing process. The inventory of the new product—such as dehydrated soup—has the leverage to influence the trade during the early days of product monopoly. The innovator spends marketing dollars primarily upon awareness advertising and only secondarily upon trade promotions and deals.

Once the later stages of the cycle emerge, the consumer (and the customer) can choose among equally attractive brand alternatives—the original supplier has lost his product edge. The consumer, aware of a choice, selects particular supermarkets because of their shopping values (i.e., proximity to home, better meats and vegetables, bigger parking lot, et cetera). With the advent of product maturity, new consumer values (trade, or retailer, centered) become decisive. What we are experiencing is a shift of marketing control to the channels. As a product passes through the lifecycle, the significant values migrate from the manufacturer and are reborn as retailer values. Power follows values. The emergence of private labels, as well as the healthy increase in manufacturer-supported inducements (deals and promotions) to the trade, bear witness to this important transformation in power and strategy.

From the manufacturer's point of view, with product maturity the sales force (which must sell the deals) becomes the dominant marketing influence. Earlier during innovation, it was the advertising/brand managers. The strategic parallel to this power shift can be seen also in the industrial fields—values still govern. Merely substitute engineer/scientist for brand manager and the two explanations are virtually identical.

Most business executives try valiantly to keep their products from slipping into the decline stage. Hence, they constantly change the ingredients, the strategy, the segments. A product lifecycle curve might well resemble the diagram in Figure 7.3 over time. The jumps are caused by new products and/or markets. Rejuvenation is the hoped for payoff. On the other hand, repeated renewal poses a tough management dilemma—do these successive jumps put an unusual demand on management, particularly in the smaller companies? The answer is probably yes—the management must survive two pressures—growth of the new and maintenance of the old. The management requirements for each expand. It is all too likely that the marketing manager will be overwhelmed by the accumulation of lifecycle rejuvenations. Inevitably the large assortment of products and markets in different stages of development prevents giving each its necessary attention.

Market Research

The development and execution of marketing strategy does not occur, we all know, in a vacuum. The marketing manager requires lots of data on which to base his plans. Indeed, managers have begun to learn that "knowing the market" is an underrated marketing essential. The need for such specific knowledge runs counter to time-honored assumptions that

FIGURE 7.3.   Product lifecycle curve showing new products or markets.

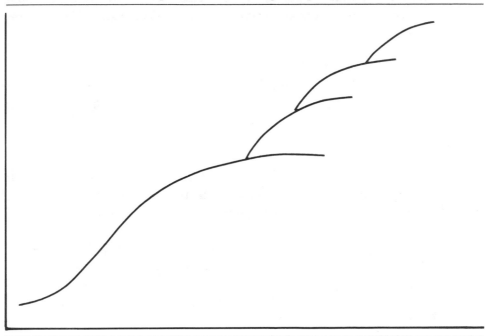

good managers can manage anything. They cannot: they must know the market in a very intimate sense. In his recent book *The Renewal Factor*, Robert Waterman begins by stating, "Renewing organizations set direction for their companies, not detailed strategy. They are the best of strategists precisely because they are suspicious of forecasts and open to surprise. They know the value of being prepared, and they also know that some of the most important business decisions they make are inherently unpredictable. They think strategic planning is great—as long as no one takes the plans too seriously.

Waterman summarizes his position neatly by referring to the effective manager as an "informed opportunist." The manager is familiar with the market, but does not yet know which particular piece is likely to pop up. Therefore, his need to be opportunistic does not mean that market research is superfluous. It does mean, however, that the practitioner needs a deep, formal or informal, understanding of the market. The best marketing managers, by this logic, spend considerable time talking, traveling, questioning, observing. They are forever in search of additional insights and market changes. They "network effectively," to use current language. For some, the acquisition of knowledge is a formal quest, but for others it is not as systematic. Either way, the manager is "information sensitive."

When new product decisions are necessary, several questions must be raised, and relevant facts and opinions obtained for each. These unanswered questions are straightforward:

1. Is the market really there? Is it real?
2. Is the product (or service) substantial?
3. Can we as an organization pull it off? Do we have the skills and resources?
4. Is it worth it? Is the payoff sufficient?

If the answer to any of these questions is no, then there is not much sense in continuing. Market information, in the sense that we have just described it, is a vital marketing requirement. Otherwise, the manager is engaged in a big crap shoot.

It is worth a few lines to dwell in more detail on this matter of market research. We live in an age that treasures abundant data. Formal market research can be classified as:

1. What people say
2. What people do
3. What people have done

The first category includes several well-known research approaches. Take, for example, surveys of buyers' intentions, composites of salesforce opinions, and expert advice. Buyer intentions have been used to predict the purchase of industrial goods as well as some consumer durables. The reliability of this technique is contingent upon how clearly the buyers have rationalized their intentions and, in fact, do follow through.

Salesforce opinions are likewise a mixed bag—you must balance the source of your data with the relevance of the information obtained. Salesmen know a great deal, though often in an unsophisticated form. Remember that they operate under an array of other pressures, including quota requirements, commission incentives, and other specified nonselling activities. Salesmen talk verbosely, and the listener must edit carefully what he hears. How many managers have heard the complaint, "Our price is too high!" "The product is not right!"

Third, there are the outside "experts"—dealers, distributors, the trade press, consultants, and so forth. These sources may be insightful, but the inquirer has difficulty in obtaining a balanced understanding of any separate parts of the market. Data shows up in "bits and pieces."

What people do is the second category of research approaches. We establish by this technique minimarkets which hopefully reflect the larger real world. The high-tech world refers to these as Beta Test Sites while the consumer goods specialists refer to test marketing and market tests. Once again, however, the transposition from the sample to the whole can be misread. If you doubt that, reflect on the Edsel automobile fiasco, or more recently, Coke's attempt to introduce a "new" version. Jumping from research sample to the market whole is not a routine process.

Finally, we can refer to what people have done. In this third category, we review history and interpolate from yesterday's facts. We surmise that history will repeat itself, however, that supposition is tenuous.

Another approach is to select some meaningful independent variables, trace their movement, and then transpose the results to the specific products in question. Tire sales can be predicted in that manner. The demand for automobiles is the independent variable: their sales estimates can be employed to forecast other auto-dependent products. Of course, one must still estimate the sale of autos. But the approach at least opens new measurements of research opportunities.

Forecasting, as we know, is not a precise science. The danger is that, because we use so many mathematical procedures and formula, the uniformed observer is inclined to assign more accuracy to the research procedures than they warrant. A memorable fundamental for the beginner is the caution: "What are the assumptions underlying the estimate?" In reality, the legitimacy of the assumptions far outweighs the niceties of the statistical techniques. The identification of critical assumptions is the highest priority when evaluating a forecasting program.

Nonetheless, as mentioned earlier, more knowledge and understanding is generally better than less when it comes to deciding marketing programs. To say that "he has great market feel" is to pay the highest marketing compliment.

The Buying Side

Implicit in our observations to this point has been our emphasis upon the seller over the buyer. We reviewed how to segment, how to price, how to obtain data. Now, we must broaden our perspective to include a greater understanding of the buying side of the equation. For every sale, there must be a buyer.

When dissecting buying behavior, it is hopefully obvious that our earlier comments about segments, benefits, and values are all relevant. We need to elaborate upon them. What are some of the segmentation alternatives, we might properly ask?

Marketing managers segment many ways—by age, income, sex, lifestyle, geography, application.

As we also noted, because different segments desire different benefits, and because products are essentially bundles of benefits, the fit between buyer and product is critical. Indeed, what may be a product to one segment may not be to another, which means essentially that there are products (people buy them) and nonproducts (people do not buy them). Examples of nonproducts would include:

1. Expensive solutions to inexpensive problems
2. Complicated solutions to simple problems
3. Clever solutions to marginal problems
4. Solutions directed at the wrong segment

Markets, as with products, are equally tenuous. People respond to different values, but it is not always easy to identify the relevant segments before the fact. To complicate the issue, segments usually cut across several classification categories, or vary as the individual's circumstances change. You and I will make specific purchases for any number of reasons. We might buy particular product attributes, for example, depending upon our motives at the moment. Consider the purchase of a book for self-consumption, as a gift to your child, to read on the airplane, to keep in the formal bookcase: the same general class of product, but different items due to contrasting motivators.

Customer buying patterns, moreover, may be broader and more flexible than imagined, and customers may be quite willing to adapt their preferences to whatever is available. Correspondingly, unless we marketing people begin to broaden our segment definitions, we may overfragment the markets and proliferate our bands—both options being low profit alternatives. A narrow market may be too small to cultivate; it will, at the least, limit the effectiveness of our advertising expenditures. Advertising is a mass notion: It is unlikely that each special customer segment can support its own advertising and promotional program, nor, for that matter, a high-priced selling effort.

Positioning

Management has long realized that it is one thing to decide about target markets, but an entirely different thing for the market to accept the distinction. Many a company has pioneered a tidy package of business definition, purpose, image, and positioning only to find that the customers do not buy the proposition. Consider the sales problems that beset Jaguar, Mercedes, Porsche, and BMW in 1988. The long-suffering consumer finally decided that the astronomical prices were too much!

A company's position and its consumer image are underlying considerations that management must continuously monitor. Visualize a simple "map" that bounds a hypothetical market as in Figure 7.4. We label, arbitrarily, the four corners.

The four market quadrants are defined by short descriptors and are numbered from 1 to 4. Incidentally, this model is only one "cut at the market"; other boundaries can be posited. To the marketing manager, it makes considerable difference which quadrant he assumes, particularly in contrast with how the customer sees the firm. The customer view, needless to say, is the one that counts.

Now, for an example. In the 1960s, the Head Ski Company was viewed by the market as being in quadrant 2 (functional product and limited distribution), while the new competitors were exploding into quadrant 3 (style and mass distribution). Each quadrant requires a unique marketing approach. Head's quadrant 2 image was shaky at best, however. The serious skier (quadrant 2) was being squeezed out by the social, fun-loving enthusiast. Quadrants 1 and 3 were more appropriate reflections of industry migration from "selective functional" to "mass style." The inevitable acquisition of the original Head Ski Company was reasonably

FIGURE 7.4. Map showing hypothetical market.

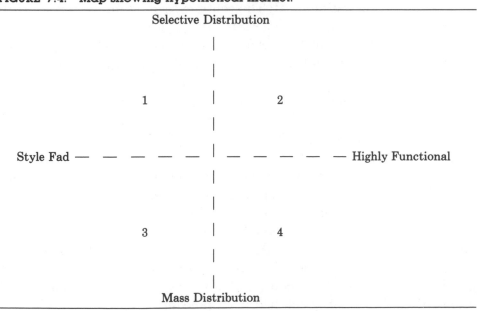

evident. (Nonetheless, Mr. Head recovered very well by starting a new firm that developed and sold Prince Tennis Racquets.)

Southwest Airlines in its early days of competition against Braniff and Texas Air deliberately chose an image of "fun, relaxation, and love" that set the tone for the subsequent marketing strategies. Strategies and image were self-reinforcing.

Surely, it would not make sense to select a business definition or strategy inconsistent with the market perception. On the other hand, changing the image or market position is no simple matter. Customer stereotypes are strong: It is not easy to persuade buyers that National Cash is famous for computers (isn't it cash registers?), Sears Roebuck for financial services, and Honda for automobiles.

Repositioning is difficult to accomplish for many reasons—inertia, frozen mind-sets, old company mores and informal relationships, territorial imperatives, long-established personal interactions, and self-satisfaction. Companies, of course, can change, but the process takes time and patience.

Saga, a contract food operator, ran into such a problem. The business had been built on a base of contract feeding—college students, hospitals, businesses. Saga grew well and profitably. Thus, it seemed a natural move to open restaurants. After all, restaurants are feeding operations. These entrepreneurs assumed that the contract feeding operation could supply the restaurants with a cadre of new managers for the expanding restaurant operations.

One problem was eminent: The contract feeding business dealt with a captive audience, and the restaurants with a transient audience. The two customer sets were significantly different. A contract manager, almost literally, would check out his business by "walking in through the kitchen door," the restaurateur "through the front door." The two feeding situations were actually dissimilar. The result, of course, were two quite different behavior patterns. Whereas the contract or institutional managers were oriented toward operations, the restaurant group was more concerned with markets.

Saga's senior management decided to generally strengthen the company's marketing skills. This step meant refocusing primarily the institutional group. They hired a major consulting firm to observe the situation and recommend a course of action. Their plan was adopted and launched. However, nothing happened; the one group remained operations inclined, the other marketing. A small company committee reviewed the problem and decided that a new point of view would require a number of basic changes, none of which had been recognized earlier. The changes listed were:

1. Get the attention of the key managers. Reading or hearing about a new program is no guarantee of understanding the message. Pains must be taken to have the new program heard and comprehended.

2. Retrain the individuals so that they can behave the new way. Do not assume that the adoption of a different behavior does not require different skills or attitudes. Unless this need is recognized, comprehension will suffer.

3. Restructure the jobs to provide time to incorporate the new expectations and position requirements. There is no such thing as an idle manager—the good ones put in 70-, 80-, or 90-hour weeks. They need time to adopt the new duties, which means redefining the various jobs (i.e., "Do this and drop that!")

4. Motivation for all is a key necessity. Top management may recognize the need for change, but similar urgency must extend to the lower echelons. Such techniques as involvement and/or incentive schemes can be vital.

5. Introduce a feedback and monitoring system so that ongoing progress can be measured. An organization, quite naturally, tends to pay attention to those job specifics that are being evaluated.

Changes of such magnitude are not simple, but they can be accomplished. The point to remember is that the change process is complex and takes time.

The Creation of Customers

Marketing managers make extensive use of two other processes which help to create buyers. Each maps how consumers progress from prospect to repeat buyer. One concentrates on individual buyers and we refer to this concept as "the adoption cycle." The other, "the diffusion process," is concerned about groups of buyers and in what order they will enter the market.

The adoption cycle traces the emerging buyer as he progresses through five states described as:

Awareness: The potential customer must be made aware that there is such a product or service. Without awareness, there could hardly be a purchase, except accidentally. However, awareness alone is not sufficient; we are all aware of many products that do not *interest* us. We must say, in effect, that is a good idea, I like it. Once again, that is not enough. Interest will not create a sale unless the buyer *internalizes it:* "I think it would work for me." Now, we have a chance to generate *trial.* If the trial meets the buyer's expectations, we can expect a *repeat purchase*, and we finally have a customer.

Although simple in logic, the adoption cycle is a much-used marketing tool. Not surprisingly, each of the five states requires a separate marketing strategy. In practice, the five outline a meaningful, useful way to structure the marketing strategy.

Suppose you are a manufacturer of personal computers (PCs), and at the end of your first year, you note, through market research, that your market has the following profile:

Awareness	75%
Interest and conviction	50% each
Trial	10%
Repeat	30%

Now you have some actionable data. Your awareness score is incredibly high: 75 percent of the potential buyers are aware of your product. Regular advertising is not your immediate concern. No, the problem seems to lie in the transition from conviction to trial, especially given the awareness level. Interest and conviction suggest that you have a strong potential market. The conclusions? Build into your marketing strategy some trial-inducing techniques. Obviously, the interpretation of real life data would be more complicated, but the suggested action is nonetheless clear cut.

The other customer creation approach is labeled as "the diffusion process." It explains how groups of initial buyers enter the market. Even though each individual in the group must evolve through the separate adoption phases, customer groupings appear to move into markets sequentially. Moreover, any one group in the market does not advance until the prior groups have converted. This group ordering is referred to as the diffusion of innovation. The general conclusion is that markets can be classified into five segments whose relative importance holds for a wide range of products:

Segment	Total (%)
Innovators	2.5
Early adopters	13.5
Early majority	34.0
Late majority	34.0
Laggards	16.0
	100.0

Each segment can be separately described in terms that distinguish it from the others. Conclusion?

1. Find the opinion leaders in each market.
2. Seek the innovators when launching a new product or service.
3. Vary your strategy by segment.
4. Do not try to jump ahead of the natural progression.

Simply because there is a bell-shaped pattern, not all products will succeed and progress through the cycle. Acceptance can collapse at any point, including the unwillingness of even the innovators to give the innovation a try.

Checking Your Strategy

Suppose you have just put to bed a novel marketing strategy but are worried about its effectiveness. Will it work or not? You can, of course, expose the strategy to a test market—often a wise course of action. Or, you may prefer not to tip your hand. Do you have any other useful alternative?

Ask yourself this question? "If my strategy is to work, how must the ideal customer behave?" You may, for example, conclude that such ideal buyer behavior is so foreign to normal reactions that continuing is pointless. Needless to say, when preparing a strategy, the marketing manager should be armed with knowledge about the buying requirements of the target segments. The segment definition should always precede the strategy selection.

Distribution and Pricing

Although we have referred to them at various times, we have not said much about distribution and pricing, two fundamental elements of marketing strategy.

Distribution concerns how the product gets to market. Shipment and warehousing might be through company owned distribution outlets (a company store, for example) or independent outlets. Delivery might be made to a central location or to decentralized destinations. In practice, the distribution system must satisfy two important requirements: the logistics of moving goods and services, and the creation of a unique strategy that reinforces a sustainable competitive advantage. McDonald's, for example, is primarily a unique distribution system (fast food) which not only moves product to the point of sale, but also gives McDonald's, the innovator, a competitive edge. Other innovators are the first automats, bank

ATMs, self-service stores, facsimile equipment and Sears Roebuck financial services.

Debate simmers these days about the desirability of suppliers attempting to "partner" with their channels. Arms-length relationships are no longer sacrosanct. The argument is that each party (buyer and seller) is dependent upon the other, thus justifying cooperative interaction.

At times, the desirability of such partnering is unquestionable. One has only to look at McKesson's retailer program which successfully integrates the company with its channel structure. Despite this exception, a powerful potential conflict between the buyer and seller reduces eventually to a power struggle. It is easy to appreciate why manufacturer and retailer operate often at loggerheads. The optimizing strategy is "opposites." The seller would prefer that his retailer carry the full line, not stock competitive items, sell at a competitive (low) price, advertise, display, and pay cash (in advance). The retailer's preference would be the reverse. Hence, an underlying pressure tenses between manufacturer and channel. What is good for one is not necessarily good for the other. They vie continuously for the upper hand.

Channels, it seems, are under severe strain these days. Long accepted definitions of appropriate product lines, acceptable competitive strategies, and personnel requirements are changing fast. Retailers engage in wholesaling, wholesalers engage in retailing. Discounts are rampant through the channels, and conventional margins nonexistent. Why?

1. A plethora of new competitors, some from within the industry, some not
2. Consolidation and merger
3. Supplier pressures for increased volume
4. A squeeze on margins due to excess production
5. Greater price volatility
6. The upgrading of personnel and facilities
7. Multiple buying levels

As noted earlier, the biggest gains in leverage belong to the retailers, not the manufacturers. Retailers have become increasingly sophisticated marketers. They offer an ever-expanding assortment of inducements including location, convenience, parking facilities, decore, merchandise, and style that more than offset the manufacturer's product virtues. Unless the manufacturer succeeds in pioneering a sustainable innovative edge, the retailer's value set pulls the consumer more than the product offer.

Buyers, it seems, shop more because of the retailers' shopping inducements than the manufacturers' product innovations. Thus, we see the shift in values to the trade.

Pricing

Pricing is one of the least understood marketing mysteries. Few companies, for example, have a "manager of pricing." Businessmen are inclined to price on a cost basis. However, as stated earlier, the consumer always seeks product values, a broad concept. A value is the basic benefit minus cost. The buyer, it is to be expected, always selects the best value, either real or perceived.

There are, therefore, two extremes for pricing, cost or value/benefit. By and large, value pricing has more attraction than cost pricing, but cost has a long history.

We talk, for example, about price elasticity—how many units will sell at different prices?—but we seldom include advertising, selling or merchandising elasticity. Yet, sales volume is, to varying degrees, dependent upon these other marketing variables.

Proper pricing, it follows, has two inputs—the value to the buyer and the cost of supply. The best value is meaningless if the product cannot be produced at a profitable figure.

The economists have played a significant role in the pricing world, although their bias has been toward rational models. Some of the major arguments of economists have included:

1. The rational buyer and seller model
2. The elasticity of price
3. The notion of marginal cost and marginal revenue
4. The models of perfect competition, pure competition, monopolistic competition and monopoly

Each theory, as one might expect, is carefully constructed and the theoretical determinants of price and volume spelled out. Although theoretical, the economic approach to pricing provides the marketing manager with a useful analytic device.

The last pricing observation is more pragmatic and is described as "marginal pricing." It separates variable costs from fixed costs. The proper use of these contrasting cost categories lets us calculate breakeven and the resulting cost behavior, assuming changes in volume.

Advertising

Advertising is one element of marketing communication. To many observers, it is the most important element of the marketing mix. It is probably the most obvious because of the dramatic nature of much advertising—illustration, size, media characteristics, number of insertions, dramatic headlines, persuasive copy. The fact, however, is that personal selling is equally significant but less familiar. Typical customers do not encounter salesmen every day. Furthermore, people usually associate salesmen with industrial marketing, and advertising with consumer marketing—though these are questionable generalizations. The underlying support for these assertions is that industrial markets are small and technical, suggesting a personal interface, while consumer markets are large and scattered, suggesting an impersonal interface.

Whatever your communication format, advertising is one of the essential ingredients along with promotion, personal selling, and such special media at catalogs, direct mail, telemarketing and public relations. In most instances, the communication strategy employees a combination of all of these.

Advertising, considered with some care, claims a number of advantages over personal selling. The message, to cite a single advantage, can be controlled and delivered in a predictable manner, and the message has longer-term impact because it is usually read and reread. In fact, the initial target audience grows in size over time. Moreover, an advertisement has high potential leverage. To illustrate, the first cost can be spread over many prospects, whereas a sales call is often a "one-on-one relationship"—it has low leverage. As an offset, however, the printed word does not command the same personal attention as a sales call.

A major distinction among communication media is contained in the words *effective* and *efficient.* A magazine insertion can be quite efficient (a low cost per message delivered) but not as effective (fewer sales are apt to materialize per transmission). The manager must always choose between efficiency and effectiveness: What may seem at first blush the cheapest way to communicate may, in reality, be the most expensive. A Super Bowl advertisement may cost approximately a dollar per listener, but it will not sell many golf club memberships.

When the manager shops for his advertising needs, he considers typically both "reach and frequency." Reach refers to the number of potential buyers to be covered, such as "the five million residents of City A" or the population of Switzerland. Exposure, it will be understood, is not effectiveness, though without exposure, no message can be delivered.

Frequency means exactly that: How many times will the target audience be exposed to the advertisement, every month? daily for three weeks? four times within the prescribed period?

When the marketing manager negotiates for space, he will find that this purchase will be tied specifically to the reach and frequency—those are what he buys!

One drawback to the printed word, on the other hand, particularly in comparison to radio, is its inflexibility. Schedules must be determined well in advance of the publication date, and there is not much room for adjustment. A personal message, in contrast, is easy to change or reschedule.

A question often argued at this point is "How much should we spend on advertising?" The answer is dependent upon the issues just introduced.

Not uncommonly, the advertising budget is based on one of four criteria (or close approximations):

1. Spend the same as last year.
2. Spend the same percentage as last year.
3. Spend enough to stay within reasonable profit or competitive guidelines.
4. Determine the communications task to be accomplished, and spend accordingly.

All but the fourth suggestion have serious drawbacks; nonetheless, each has its own real-life supporters.

The "last year" logic is easy to apply, and, at the least, earmarks an amount that has proven to be effective at least once. Unfortunately, this happy conclusion assumes no serious change in the environment, and it assumes that each element in last year's strategy is being used effectively.

A fixed percentage of sales is similarly attractive and essentially assumes that cause and effect (advertising percentage and sales) are easy to integrate.

The third approach is attractive because it singles out the competition and argues "Let's spend what we must to match the competition, but let's not throw our traditional ratios too far out of line!" At least this alternative ties the spending to some predetermined acceptable profit or competitive criterion.

The task approach is intellectually attractive and reasonably common in use, but its determination is hardly simple. If we understand truly the reasons for particular buying behavior, we could easily match advertising with results. Unfortunately, the explanation is not clear. On a happier note, however, the task argument forces the manager to think out, in the most fundamental way, the correct array of ingredients needed to produce a sale.

There are, as one might suppose, other audiences that advertising tries to influence. For example, for the publicly owned firm there are the omniscient financial markets—investors, bankers, the financial press, market makers, and so forth. These so-called specialists are also susceptible to advertising messages and inducements and represent, therefore, an attractive communication target.

Another useful consideration characterizes the technical press. Many of its publications will, and do, publicize in print selected products and applications. A second's thought will underscore how much adjacent editorial content can enhance an advertising campaign or may, indeed, feed a powerful word-of-mouth campaign.

Finally, in this complex arena of communication, are the immense expenditures by and for manufacturers and the channels of distribution. Visualize, if you will, the inside of a grocery store (or other popular retailer). All kinds of media displays are evident—posters, hang tags, duplicates of magazine ads, special price notices, displays. We can imagine in addition, a number of inducements aimed at the consumers, including contests, samples, give-aways, special deals (such as "three for the price of two"). We label this entire assortment of buying inducements "promotions." They are important: They deliver a buying inducement at the point of sale.

One last observation: The typical householder is barraged by another series of advertising alternatives, cooperative ads. Such ads are typically found in newspapers and promote special product offers and deals. They are cooperative because, in most cases, the manufacturer reimburses the retailer (or makes the material available at no cost).

In recent years, the promotion category has become for many manufacturers a considerable financial burden. The power of the retailers, as we noted earlier, has grown so considerably that the retailer will add a new item only if the manufacturer pays a fee, usually up front. These payments for being placed on the store shelves are called slotting allowances. They are a further reflection of retailer power and can add up to many hundreds (thousands) of dollars.

Sales Strategies

The reason for this section is to dig into sales, not marketing or advertising strategies, and to examine their ingredients, a somewhat elusive objective. The specific topics singled out include: the sales manager's variables, selling strategies, sales cycles, and individual selling techniques.

The question of semantics is an important aspect of this discussion. The definition of sales strategy is not the same from one part of the organization to another and from one market segment to another. For example, the brand manager in Pillsbury is usually described as a strategist, and sales is his or her execution arm. Implicit in this belief is the assumption that the brand manager deals with the consumer and tries to pull the brand through the channels.

Now, what of the sales to and through the channels? The supermarkets represent a different level of the same ultimate market and are driven by strategic needs of their own. Selling is more than the brand manager's execution tool; it is the retailer's communication strategy. In this context, advertising and selling serve the same purpose, one for the consumer (the user), and the other for the customer (the trade). Hence, we can conclude that both the marketing manager and the sales manager face the strategic problem of manipulating the appropriate variables to determine strategy, one at the first market level and the other at the second.

The Sales Manager's Variables

Assuming the prior determination of a marketing strategy and corporate goals and objectives, as well as an analysis of the environment, the sales manager can manipulate a collection of selling factors—combining them in varied ways. As a general rule the sales manager is one step more micro in his outlook than the marketing manager. Whereas the marketing manager identifies the target segment, the sales manager must deal with specific customers—names and addresses, in fact.

What then are the sales management variables? There are at least 12:

1. The names and addresses of possible accounts
2. The identification and selection of key accounts
3. The origination of appropriate selling strategies for each key customer
4. The determination of selling's role in the marketing strategy
5. The calculation of sales manpower needs
6. The organization structure for selling
7. The supervisory structure (such as span and duties)
8. The recruitment and selection of a salesforce
9. Training programs
10. Evaluation criteria
11. Incentives, both financial and other
12. Control techniques

A rundown of these sales management specifics suggests a great array of possible outcomes. The competent sales manager, one can see, must possess a rich assortment of abilities.

Selling Strategies

What are some of the more useful selling strategies? We will discuss the more frequently used strategies next.

Team Selling

It is easy to think of team selling examples such as the sale of a nuclear power plant, a communication system or a vocational school for the Third World. These selling scenarios are complex, requiring a variety of skilled selling and backup personnel: physicists, engineers, construction specialists, and systems experts, to mention but a few. A lone salesperson would be overwhelmed were he or she to try to duplicate these specialty resources. As a result, selling teams are assembled. Hardly surprising is the consequent need to coordinate the activities of the separate individuals. Coordination is the responsibility of the team captain, a selling task at the most complicated end of the "difficulty continuum."

Some of these teams, as in HP, GE, Northrop, and certain military contractors, will exceed 150 to 200 people. Usually, the target sale is for a complicated system that calls for extensive warranties and guarantees, service modification, and time consuming postsale follow up.

The reliance upon a team rather than individuals is a strategic sales decision of considerable importance. Its impact upon operations is monumental.

Key Accounts

Some customers are more desirable than others, be it due to size, profitability, prestige, or potential. To adapt from Pareto, 20 percent of the customers will produce 80 percent of the results. No matter what the exact percentage, in fact, critical accounts demand special treatment. This need complicates life for the sales manager who has two categories of accounts: the special and "the rest." The two cannot be handled similarly. The big ones, for example, want VIP treatment, special service, direct access, quantity incentives, fast response, and so on. As a result, the sales and support personnel, the traditional systems and procedures, the rules and regulations may all have to be modified. Business economics, alone, dictates that accounts cannot be treated as equals—small customers are expensive. Not surprisingly, it follows that the typical sales department starts with the needs of the special accounts and fits in the rest the best way possible.

Such favoritism may sound unfair, but it is the only workable way to nurture the key customers. Some organizations, for this reason, field two salesforces, one for the major accounts and one for "all others."

National Accounts

In this strategy variation, we deal with special customers whose operations are geographically scattered. The accounts, in addition, may be key. The rub comes because the territorial boundaries of buyer and seller are unmatched; Safeway's regions are not the same as General Foods. This overlap complicates the matching process between buyer and seller. The customer may want regional programs, while the seller is geared for a national campaign. Or, the seller prefers to deliver on Monday, but certain large accounts prefer Tuesday in selected regions. One solution in these cases is to assign national accounts to a dedicated group of sellers.

Executive Selling

When dealing with major accounts, it is natural for the seller to establish some executive-to-executive relationships. Although the salesforce continues to call on the regular buyers, the senior staff of each firm establishes personal contacts, not so much to sell but to facilitate communication up and down the line. At the executive echelon, many broader business matters that may not be appropriate for the sales force can be discussed. For instance: (1) future service and support alternatives, (2) the intermeshing of promotions and advertising programs, (3) possible new product and market introductions, and (4) better mutual logistical support. Furthermore, each executive has the comfortable knowledge that his equivalent is only a phone call away.

An interesting variation to executive selling in special cases has proven effective: namely, the use of the chief executive as the head seller. We need go no further, as illustrative, than Lee Iacocca, the CEO who transformed a weak consumer attitude toward Chrysler into a positive identification toward himself. The same transference of the company image can be noted in William Hewlett and David Packard, Steven Bechtel, Henry Ford, Henry Kaiser, and Harold Geneen. The great risk, of course, of such personal fealty is that the symbol will eventually disappear.

Nonetheless, a number of institutions have successfully survived a return to the corporate institution, including Disney, Ford, and some airlines.

Management Selling

A more debatable instance of sales strategy occurs when the field sales managers personally handle a sales territory. They double as salespeople.

The reasons given for such a selling role are time honored. In "thin" territories where the management load is light, it is cost-efficient to ask the manager to accept some accounts. Moreover, the manager is probably a more experienced salesperson and can bring a higher level of skill to the territory. Occasionally, as a final explanation, some accounts insist on management attention.

However, the cost of executive selling can be high. The selling manager is competing with his or her own subordinates. A neutral stance is hard to maintain. The salesforce will easily conclude that their manager "has the best accounts" or "gets favored treatment for customers from the home office." The issue of how selling managers will prioritize their time is a sensitive one. When the crunch comes, these managers may move instinctively to protect their own accounts before attending to their salesteam. And, finally, selling managers are apt to favor what they do best and fall back on sales prowess, which means they may never adequately develop their supervisory talents.

Multilevel Selling

Sales managers usually exhort their sales people to "sell high and wide," meaning many lateral and vertical contacts—the essential characteristic of team selling. The contented sales individual can easily settle on a few comfortable contacts or avoid calling higher because that is 'unfamiliar hard work and beyond the pale of us ordinary mortals." The strongest salesforces, to the contrary, establish a broad range of contacts and make a point of understanding what each customer level needs. Many a sure sale is lost because some senior manager has other competitive preferences and manages to substitute his own candidate for the sure thing.

Reciprocity (a.k.a. "Trade Relations")

Of dubious legality is the sales strategy known as reciprocity: "You buy from me, and I'll buy from you." Buying and selling organizations, using specialized personnel, used to crosscompare volumes of sales and purchases as the pressure for new orders. Practitioners included steel companies, railroads, and large can manufacturers.

Such systematic trade-offs have all but disappeared. Nonetheless, the practice continues informally. Reciprocity is usually associated with commodities and not specialty items, for which substitutes are uncommon. Interestingly, we have recently seen reciprocity practices at the national level as during the United States-Japan semiconductor negotiations in 1988.

Organizational Strategies

No comments about sales strategies would be complete without referring to the organizational structures. To illustrate, a salesforce can key in on geography, product, customer, task, or some combination. The implications of each are notable.

A geographic bent requires that each individual sell the full line within an assigned territory. Not bad, if the products and customers are homogeneous! Customer coverage, under these circumstances, seems to be better because the salesperson can usually sell something to somebody throughout the territory, so is encouraged to make more marginal calls.

In certain instances, an extensive product line includes some very technical items. This expanse means that the generalist salesperson is less in demand than the product expert, creating the practice of hiring separate salesforces for separate products.

In other circumstances, the company may opt to assemble the salesforces according to customer distinctions, such as utilities versus process control industries, large accounts versus small accounts, or integrated versus nonintegrated operations.

One last organizational alternative remains: to assign the salespeople by "task." Food companies, like General Mills, normally have direct sellers who call on the large accounts, and merchandisers who handle the small buyers, as well as in-store presentation requirements. Some technical firms, like Motorola and Northrop, employ "bird dogs" who develop leads but are backed up by highly trained specialists who close the sales. It is also possible to distinguish between prospecting and maintaining business.

Systems Selling

The sales transaction might revolve around essentially individual items or it might encompass entire systems. The system sale, which was mentioned earlier, is complex and requires a mix of skilled sales- and support-people as well as an unusually high degree of coordination. Some systems are categorized as "turnkey"—the buyer is supplied with a ready-to-use installation. Examples include a new robotic production line, a dam for flood control and recreation, and a finished office building.

As we said earlier, the single sales representative likely does not have the background or expertise to close the system sale but is rather more valuable as the quarterback for the team. In technical environments, this sales individual stresses the commercial requirements of the transaction, including such things as when to bring in support personnel, who to contact next, and when to move on the next phase of the sale.

Pooled Selling

When a number of separate divisions sell similar technologies to a spread of customers, the excessive costs of separate salesforces can be allayed by sharing a common team, a pooled salesforce. It certainly helps in pooling if the sales tasks are reasonably similar among the divisions.

The General Electric Company, as a case in point, has an Apparatus Sales Division that is shared among dozens of operating divisions too small to support their own dedicated sales units. A recurring sore point with a pooled operation is insuring that each division gets its fair share of the selling effort. Some firms go as far as to draw up formal contracts between sales and the divisions, specifying the effort being "bought" or paid for by each.

Sales Through Intermediaries

Another useful sales strategy is to use external intermediaries who specialize in one or more phases of the distribution chain. We are all familiar with retailers, wholesalers, manufacturers' reps, brokers, and sales agents, each of whom is an "outside expert."

The retailer, to make the point, is a specialist. Not many manufacturers can duplicate his retail merchandising skills. Just think of the unusual talents required of a Nordstrom, The Limited, The Gap, or L.L. Bean! The manufacturer is more often than not well advised to "hire" such go-betweens, the fee consisting of sales support programs and retail markups.

The preferred working relationship between the manufacturer and the outsider remains an issue for frequent debate. "Should we subcontract the function or do it ourselves?" "Should we grant an exclusive franchise or not?" "Do we treat the outsider as part of our team or on an arm's-length basis?" "Should we employ a mix pattern that makes use of outsiders and insiders?"

Third-Party Sales

The classic example of third-party sales is the ethical pharmaceutical house. The salesforce sells products into the wholesale and retail channels but depends upon the prescribing physician for consumer demand. The "sale" to the doctor is essentially educational. Without the doctor's recommendation the product will die.

NIKE, in its early days, offered another version of third-party selling. It sold to the specialty retailers but placed the shoes on the feet of expert performers whose victories and testimonials persuaded much of the public to imitate. Girl Scouts who sell cookies and ex-athletes who recommend a certain brand of beer are modern versions of third-party sales.

Back-End Processing

Volume selling would be impossible without an efficient, in-house servicing system. The compelling demands upon service and processing facilities are well illustrated in the typical brokerage firm. So volatile are the markets and so critical the logistics of handling each transaction that there would be no front-end sales if the back-end processing broke down. To illustrate, such support needs exist in banks, large warehouse facilities, and airline reservation systems. These "invisible" mechanisms are essential to the sales strategy.

Telemarketing

Telemarketing is the up-to-date version of telephone selling and has become a much discussed selling component. Telemarketing goes beyond historic telephone selling because it combines a number of selling variables: a computer and customer data bank, special telephone operators, advertisements listing an 800 call-in number, direct mail coupons, and so on. In the normal course of events, the seller places an ad, describes the product benefits, and includes a return coupon as well as an 800 number. When a respondent telephones in, the receiving operator "calls up" the stored customer data base and initiates the sales interview. After the call, the customer data file is amended by the new information. The result is a more efficient sales presentation, including the substitution of the telephone sale medium for the expensive face-to-face sales call. Whereas the traditional salesperson can make maybe 8 to 10 calls each day at an average cost of $150 to $200, the telemarketing sales expert can far exceed these call numbers and at significantly lower costs.

The underlying logic of telemarketing is that the scarce resource (a live salesperson) becomes far more productive, with only a small loss in personal selling relationships.

Door-to-Door Selling

In earlier days, the country was characterized by cowboys, Indians, and traveling salesmen—snake oil salesmen they were called. In contemporary language, the traveling salespeople are known as direct sellers.

There are dozens of direct sale organizations—Fuller Brush, Electrolux, Stanley, Avon, Mary Kay, Amway. They field large salesforces (full-time and part-time) who are paid strictly on commission and are motivated by a large assortment of incentives.

The legitimate direct sales organization sells good products for generous markups and pays out large commissions and overrides. As individuals rise in the organization, they begin to share in the commissions paid to the salespeople they have, in turn, recruited. Unfortunately, environmental developments have not all been friendly. For example, an increasing number of employed wives are without the time or need to supplement their finances. Additionally, people are increasingly nervous about opening their doors to strangers. For this reason, Avon and Tupperware parties have become an effective selling variation.

A few dishonest operators have given the industry a bad name. These pyramiding organizations sell the rights to sell memberships to new buyers. No products are involved—merely "rights to sell memberships." The worst offenders have presumably been put out of business, including "Dare to Be Great" and "Holiday Magic."

Product and Position Selling

Three vastly different strategic postures are possible: innovation, application, and low cost. These three pretty well describe the evolution of firms over the product lifecycle—from innovation through growth to decline.

Also, the three suggest major differences in sales strategy. Product innovation requires a product-oriented salesforce that pushes technical differentiation. The selling message is transmitted from selling specialist to buying expert requiring considerable technical interchange. A need exists for selling and technical expertise.

In contrast, the application seller needs a customer comprehension. She is selling solutions and applications. The hardware is of no intrinsic value except as it helps solve consumer problems.

The low-cost operator, in the economy slot, is dedicated first and foremost to volume and minimum costs. Low costs fuel increased sales and consequently even lower costs. The efficiency approach is less a matter of selling and more of cost manipulation.

Self-Service

By now, we take self-service for granted—after all, it has been around for 60 years, at least in the grocery trade. Self-service means what it says—there are no salespeople. Thus, the inducement to buy depends upon shelf location, package attractiveness, brand reputation, colors, photographs, displays, adjacent brands, and so on. When well executed, a self-service store is a marvel of silent persuasion.

Needless to say, a self-service selling strategy imposes a number of requirements upon the seller having to do with the presentation of the product and its advertising and merchandising support.

Full-Service Selling

Some sales strategies encompass a complete range of buyer services: wide choice, credit, delivery, trial, price concessions, options, replacement, postsale service, training brochures (ad infinitum). The salesforce is expected to offer a collection of values designed to differentiate the product and shift the buying focus away from price. Full service is quite expensive, but it gives the salesperson an arsenal of selling options.

Post-Sale Reinforcement

It is true, unfortunately, that most sales strategies concentrate primarily upon *before the sale* and *during the sale*. Their weakness is the failure to recognize the importance of *postsale reinforcement*. After the sale—unless it is a one-time-only transaction—is when the buyer's lingering reservations can be modified. The buyer, for example, may be unsure of his choice and, if it is a first time purchase, be concerned about its wisdom. He needs a dose of reassurance. "Harry, did you notice that we offer a five-year guarantee?" "Harry, did you know that IBM bought five of these!" Success in postsale reinforcement will pay off in increased "word of mouth."

Decentralized Sales Strategy

The seller's strategy depends considerably on where ultimate sales responsibility is lodged. A centralized company, for example, funnels all important sales decisions through the home office. Bureaucracy becomes a real bugaboo; response time stretches out. On the other hand, the centralized operation can better deliver a consistent set of operating decisions; local prejudices play a smaller role.

The Notion of Sales Cycles

The concept of sales cycles is critical for sales managers. It identifies the required steps—not necessarily in rigid order—for completing a sale. Successful sales representatives cycle through the steps, centering their objectives for each day on one or more of the cycle requirements. Each step has its own pre-requisites.

The easiest way to construct the sales cycle is to start with the planned result (a completed sale) and work backwards—somewhat like reverse engineering. The process resembles peeling an onion, layer by layer. A simplified example might appear as shown in Figure 7.5.

Part of the salespersons' preparation is to plan out the cycle, then use it as a guide and measure of progress. Sales objectives should be consistent with the cycle. This process is rigorous and time-consuming. Sales personnel can be judged by how well they understand their cycle and how well they move through the steps. The competent salesperson learns something on every call, that further facilitates his next moves. Meaningful information covers many facets—personality conflicts, corporate culture, personnel changes, power shifts, sales, and profits.

Early insightful data centers on the query, "How are profits made in the customer's business?" Understanding the answer to this question is fundamental to closing complicated sales. The buyer's rationale will reflect the profit-making formula. The salesperson who understands this formula knows which buttons to push, which appeals to make, and which concessions to grant.

FIGURE 7.5. Example of sales cycle.

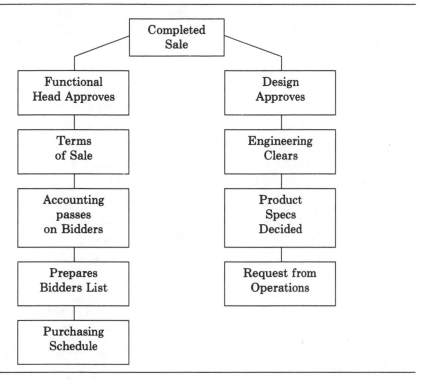

So much for selling strategies. What about the tactics of the individual salesforce?

INDIVIDUAL SELLING TECHNIQUES

Many writers have eulogized the selling secrets of outstanding salespeople—all the way from "Sell the sizzle and not the steak" to "Sell benefits not features." Unfortunately, there does not seem to be any single best way; different experts support various favorites. The woods are full of "master practitioners."

The following array identifies a reasonable sampling of the most oft-cited selling techniques. They are not entirely independent; there is some overlap.

1. *Naive* (or unprepared) probably does not warrant inclusion in our inventory, but a surprising number of salespeople's approach is "Here it

is. How many do you want?" Witness the old-time traffic representative for the railroads: "Here's a cigar. How many carloads are you shipping next month?" Or, the pushcart vendor on New York City's lower East Side.

2. *Canned* (or memorized spiel) is a time-honored technique. National Cash once had their sales representatives use a canned talk, as did the Encyclopaedia Britannica people ringing doorbells. Actually, most experienced sales individuals naturally develop some canned material. The trade-offs are obvious, but there is one underlying benefit: When faced with buyer resistance, the salesperson can think about the response while automatically reciting some memorized sales points. A canned talk, moreover, can include tested phraseology such as "Do you accept shipments on Fridays or Mondays?" or "Do you prefer the large size or the jumbo?"

3. *Stimulus-Response* is a close cousin to the canned talk. Such inviting phrases as "Did you ever want a totally guaranteed machine?" ". . . a million dollars?" ". . . a trouble-free air conditioner system?" hopefully will elicit an interested response. Artful salespeople pepper their phraseology with "yes-inducing" questions. The weakness? There is no meaningful customer involvement: The entire relationship is contrived.

4. *Features and Benefits* is probably the granddaddy of all selling techniques. Buyers want benefits, not product features. Salespeople are taught to differentiate product characteristics from buyer wants and to phrase their sales pitch from the benefits vocabulary. The features, if used, serve primarily as "proof" of the benefit. "Because we use Walker shocks, you get twice the comfort in your car."

5. *Needs and Benefits* is almost identical to 4. The real distinction here is that the seller begins to link the benefits of the product to the needs of the account. There has to be a linkage between needs and benefits, otherwise no sale.

Problem/Solution variation is essentially similar. It, too, centers on knowing the customer.

6. *Mental States* is the title for this well-recognized category. The salesperson pushes (or pulls) the prospect along from awareness → interest → conviction → trial → repeat. It is a manipulative procedure. A "typical" sales call might start: "Mr. Jones, I'm John Smith of Universal Incorporated. It is nice of you to see me, Mr. Jones, and you will be pleased to know that my proposal will be of real benefit to you. You are under no obligation to buy. In fact, my call will take only a few minutes of your time."

7. *Selling Steps* describes another common technique. This variation translates the sales call into a number of sequential procedures, including:

Prospecting
↓
Qualifying the Prospect
↓
Presenting
↓
Closing
↓
Servicing

Not a bad sequencing for the neophyte. Each of the steps, of course, has requirements of its own.

8. *Consultative Selling* boils down to "do your homework and adapt your presentation and offer to the client's specific situation." The proficient salesperson is the one who knows more about the client than the client does. Without in-depth knowledge, the seller cannot convincingly approach the buyer. The seller needs to know about the decision makers, the internal politics, the product direction, the executive influences, the in-house environment. Selling, under these conditions, is hardly a matter of luck.

9. *Psychological States* is the attempt to have the salesperson play psychologist on each call. The customer whose psychological state is understood by the sales individual can be handled more appropriately. Thus, the selling approach will not be the same for the timid, the self-styled expert, the introvert, the social animal, and the aggressor.

Most of these social science formulas employ simplifying descriptors to identify the many real-life types. Suggestions about sales techniques are provided for each. Among the better known psychological offerings are those of SRI and Wilson Learning.

10. *Account Development* is a well-publicized sales-training approach that distinguishes between *Need Satisfaction Selling* and *Strategic Account Planning*. Xerox pioneered this approach.

11. *Match Salespeople to Buyers* is an additional selling suggestion that works on the assumption that like people are more apt to do business together.

12. *Party Selling* is a technique that concentrates on group interaction and the ambience of the selling environment. The technique creates an informal, related setting. Tupperware and Mary Kay Cosmetics rely primarily on such sales parties held in private homes.

Many industrial trade shows are similar to the party setting—social gatherings, often with food and entertainment, where the seller can display the line informally for the buyers.

13. *Personal Relationships,* usually in conjunction with one of the above selling techniques, provide a useful selling approach. Salespeople acquaint themselves with the buyers and build a relationship over time, based on confidence and mutual respect. Once the empathy is established, a volume of business is executed. After all, most of us would prefer to do business with our friends.

14. *Call in Depth* is our next illustration. The admonition here is not to neglect potentially important customer personnel—the receptionist, the secretary, the administrative assistant, the assistant buyer. Who knows who the next buyer will be or the influence that present junior employees can exercise?

15. *Selling Tools* are discount structures, terms, guarantees, and "freebies." It often seems that, aside from its selling skills, the salesforce has very little flexibility in creating a sale. It is faced with the task of selling products whose prices are set by marketing, whose features are determined by product development, and whose markets are circumscribed by its competitors. Looking behind the scenes, however, sales often uses numerous tools to make a product more attractive.

Discounts can take many forms, from the simple "two for the price of one" to complex formulas based on volume, average order size, weight (if transportation costs are significant), and other factors. Generally, these are set out in standard forms for different markets (by type of customer) or products (by volume); however, they can be varied in the extreme to "meet the competition." While antitrust laws have stifled some creativity, there is still significant incentive to discount just to the maximum price at which each customer will buy, thus maximizing overall revenue. For new products or in new markets, one-time "try it, you'll like it" discounts are common, as are discounts to influential "reference" customers.

Terms can be varied to affect the timing of payments. Traditional terms are either cash on delivery (e.g., shopping at the supermarket) or 30 days (business-to-business sales). However, by varying the timing of payments, the salesperson can effectively change the price to the customer. Sixty-day terms, for instance, are often viewed as equivalent to a small discount. Leasing or other financing schemes can also affect the customer's ability to pay for (hence, willingness to buy) the product. Finally, for new, untried products—especially expensive ones—a brief trial or pilot period for free or at a reduced cost can increase the probability of a sale.

Guarantees are another tool to increase the customer's comfort with buying a product. To the extent that guarantees can be extended for additional time (e.g., an extended warranty) or are unequivocal (money-back) guarantees, they either increase the perceived value of the total product package or reduce the customer's concerns about the utility of the product.

Freebies can take many forms. In selling to retailers, salespeople not uncommonly include attractive promotional displays or racks with large orders (or to high-volume customers). In wholesaling, the "baker's dozen" concept of extra product at the same price is part of normal short-term sales promotion. In all sales areas, it is typical to include either additional products (such as add-on peripherals or software with a computer sale) or services. Additional services can range from free consulting before the sale to after-sale training, seminars, user groups, service and support, or even free freight. Finally, incentive programs (often called "spiffs") can encourage customers to buy (or to buy more) in order to qualify for prizes and other benefits.

A RECAP

Sales management is multidimensional. How can we best capture its many elements? Diagrams are easier than words. Figure 7.6, redrawn from Porter Henry, depicts the sales management world.

FIGURE 7.6. The environment (external and internal).

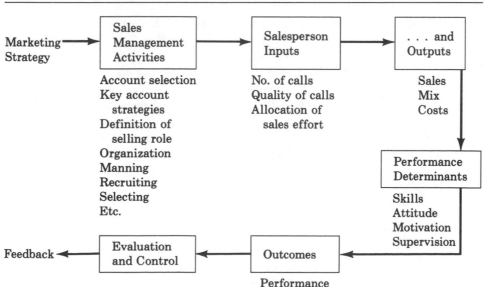

Given the environment and the marketing strategy, sales management evolves from left to right. The dependence upon system and coordination is evident. The diagram summarizes nicely the essential interface between buyer and seller.

The model introduces two implementation ideas: situation management and territory management. Situation management focuses on the personal relationships between seller and buyer. Managing successfully this aspect of the sales process is the essence of salesmanship. Territory management, on the other hand, deals with allocating company effort and resources among customers, products, and tasks. It is primarily logistic, and we normally label it "time and territory" management.

From this base, it is meaningful to construct the two extremes of a sales management balance.

Implementation is represented by the salesforce, although it is not independent of the plans and strategies. The idea of a balance suggests that the sales manager would be in error to approach his selling problems entirely from the right: "Sell more"; "sell better"; "train the salesforce." More often than not, poor results come from poor plans.

FOR FURTHER READING

Bonoma, Thomas V., *Marketing Management* (New York: Free Press, 1984).

Davidson, William, and Bro Uttal, *Total Customer Service: The Ultimate Weapon* (New York: Harper & Row, 1989).

Kotler, Philip, *Marketing Management: Analysis, Planning and Control.* 5th ed. (Englewood Cliffs, NJ: Prentice Hall, 1984).

Levitt, Theodore, *The Marketing Imagination: New, Expanded Edition* (New York: Free Press, 1986).

Settle, Robert, and Pamela Alreck, *Why They Buy: American Consumers Inside and Out* (New York: John Wiley, 1986).

HUMAN RESOURCE MANAGEMENT: COMPETITIVE ADVANTAGE THROUGH PEOPLE

8

Mary Anne Devanna

Few managerial processes offer the opportunity to leverage employee behavior and organizational performance as effectively as the human resource function. Yet, human resource management continues to occupy very little of the manager's time and attention. This lapse is true despite the intellectual interest and debate that has been triggered by numerous books on Japanese management, leadership, and strategy implementation. Many of these books offer concrete suggestions for improving managerial performance, but most organizations have yet to back up their frequently espoused belief that "people are our most important asset" with the control systems needed to insure managerial behavior consistent with that belief.

In most organizations, managers are empowered to select, appraise, reward, and develop people. Problems arise either because insufficient time is devoted to these functions, or because they are carried out without consideration of their impact on organizational strategy. In addition, many managers have not received adequate training in this important area. A human resource planning system can help managers do a better job in developing and maintaining a superior workforce which has taken extensive organizational resources to achieve.

In this chapter, we will first discuss the human resource cycle as a process, examining each of the functions in detail. We will then focus on the managerial skills needed by managers to fully implement a strong human resources planning system. Finally, we will deal with the organizations within which the managers operate. What is it about such organizations that can help or detract from the manager's success in human resource management.

THE HUMAN RESOURCE CYCLE

Figure 8.1 shows how the four generic human resource functions—selection, performance appraisal, rewards, and development—impact organizational performance. The dependent variable in this model is behavior. This series of managerial tasks will impact performance at both the individual and organizational levels.

Let us examine how it works. A person is selected for a job in the organization with the idea that he or she will be able to carry out the responsibilities of that position. To insure that this objective is met, the organization monitors the individual's performance in the position and evaluates his or her ability to meet these responsibilities. Based on this appraisal, the organization rewards the individual who is able to meet or exceed the standards for performance in that position, thus reinforcing the desired behavior, while simultaneously providing developmental help to correct weaknesses in the individual's performance. Over time, the reinforcement of the positive behavior and the correction of weaknesses results in increased performance levels for the individual and the organization.

These activities seem relatively simple to explain and understand, but they are difficult to execute, because as Allen Cohen explained in Chapter 2, people behave in unpredictable ways. Each one comes to the organization with different levels of training and capacities for learning new skills, different rewards that they seek to obtain from the organization, as well as a set of life experiences that determine both how they give feedback and

FIGURE 8.1. The human resource cycle.

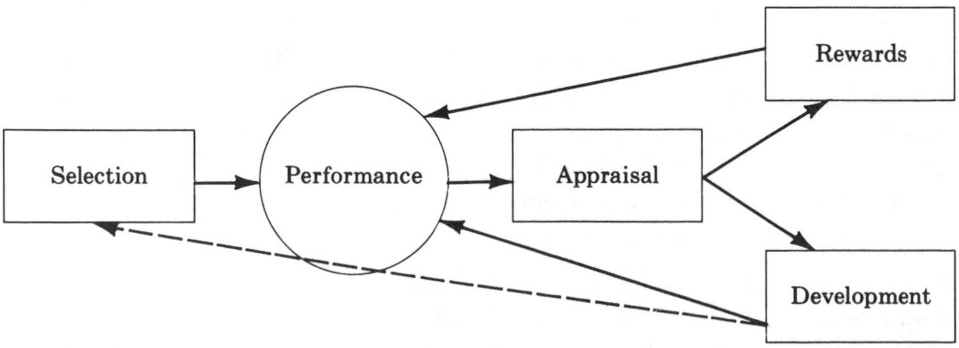

how they take it. The organization's challenge is to provide an environment that enhances the positive inclinations of its employees and provides close links between the personal goals of individuals and organizational objectives.

These managerial tools—selection, appraisal, rewards, and development—encompass effective and ineffective practices in each area.

Selection

Selection includes not only hiring but also moving people across positions internally. The time and resources that an organization or a manager devotes to this task will reveal whether they truly believe people are their most important asset. Compare the hiring practices of two automobile manufacturers operating in the United States.

When a blue collar worker applies for a job on the assembly line at the Honda plant in Marysville, Ohio, he or she is asked to write an essay about life goals and how working at Honda will help to achieve them. Ninety percent of all applicants are screened out when the managers who read these essays find no link between the applicant's desire to work at Honda and his or her personal objectives. The remaining 10 percent now pass to the next phase of the process where they are interviewed to determine how well they will fit in with the Honda way of doing things. Those who are selected undergo three weeks of intensive training before they are allowed on the assembly line. Their initial placement on the line will be next to the most experienced workers so they will not learn bad habits.

In contrast, a manager for one of the big three automobile firms told me that they sometimes took a van to Detroit and asked people on the street if anyone wanted to work on the line. Volunteers were taken back to the assembly plant to fill out forms. Those who wanted to start immediately could work the night shift the same evening. They were assigned the poorest jobs on the assembly line, next to the second most recent hires!

One does not need to conduct scientific research studies to form an opinion of which method is most likely to result in better employees.

Another outcome frequently not considered is the belief of workers at the bottom of the hierarchy about the importance of their performance on the job relative to the overall success of the firm. One could argue that the firm that devotes significant resources to the hiring and training of all workers will convey the message better than one that simply gives lip service to the idea.

Historically, as we move up the hierarchy in the organization, more resources are devoted to assessing the qualifications of candidates for jobs. The number of firms that are forced to look outside the organization to fill senior level positions bears eloquent testimony to the lack of depth in the management ranks that exists in many organizations. The implicit message of the way resources are allocated to the selection process in these organizations is that only a few jobs at the very top of the pyramid count.

An organization that devotes 90 percent of its resources to 5 percent of its population should not be surprised to find that they have been beaten in the marketplace by one that allocates resources to insure strength at every position. One result is technical—better matches between the individual and the job to be done. The second result is psychological. People at every position understand that the way they do their jobs plays an important part in determining organizational performance. They cannot escape their own role in its ultimate success or failure. Indeed, in periods of high uncertainty, insisting on good people at each position is more likely to produce a talent pool containing the managerial characteristics the organization will need to meet future competitive challenges. For example, in many organizations where the power is concentrated in one strong function like finance or marketing, the organization has not spent a great deal of time worrying about the quality of people in its "minor" functions.

Two problems are likely to arise. The first is the absence of a balanced business debate in these organizations—frequently, little debate arises at all since senior management approaches the issue with the same functional perspective. The second problem accompanies a shift in the competitive environment. Firms without bench strength have difficulty adjusting because no one is available with the necessary expertise to meet the need to become more market driven or more focused on quality. Forced to turn to outsiders, they must hope to find someone with industry savvy at a critical moment, a Chrysler was able to do when it hired Lee Iacocca. This method of staffing is highly risky—the man on the white horse is not always available to ride into town when the organization is threatened.

Thus, when an organization is forced to go outside to fill a key position, the odds of making the right match become longer. Not only must they locate someone who has the necessary technical skills, but they must also find someone who will fit in with the organization's culture. The business landscape is littered with those who did not make it. For example, AT&T had difficulty absorbing the type of marketing expertise they needed in the postdivestiture period. General Motors' ability to meet the challenge of global competition was hampered by the dominance of the finance function in an era that cried out for manufacturing and marketing expertise. Talent grown in another environment cannot always be successfully transplanted. Superb managers form companies like IBM and GE do not always flourish in companies that cannot provide the excellent staff support that played a key role in their managerial development.

The perils of devoting insufficient resources to the selection process are evident. The danger for those who are diligent in this area is more subtle. They must learn to be self-conscious about the criteria they use to screen people for jobs. Ability and commitment to the organization's objectives are not only legitimate but desirable. The danger is that the screening process will result in homogeneity of perspective that works against the organization's ability to innovate and change. Successful organizations not only hire the best people, but they also create a culture in which a diversity of viewpoint can flourish.

Performance Appraisal

If you spend time in organizations, you will soon come to the conclusion that the most despised and avoided of all managerial tasks is that of performance appraisal. Billions of dollars have been spent on appraisal systems in an attempt to encourage managers to give their subordinates feedback on how they are performing. The problem, however, is not in the form but in the process.

In most organizations, performance appraisal is an annual ritual in which the manager evaluates the subordinate's performance and the evaluation is used to determine how much of a merit increase the subordinate will receive. The manager is concerned that negative feedback will be demotivating and that subsequent interaction with the subordinate will be difficult. The subordinate knows that valued organizational rewards are riding on the outcome of the appraisal and tends to focus on the bottom line rather than the reasons behind the bottom line.

This ritual has little to do with a manager's primary responsibility to coach and counsel subordinates. This role includes frequent doses of praise for the things that are done well and instruction either on the job or in a more formal training program to correct deficiencies in performance. Appraisal should be an ongoing process of open and honest exchanges between manager and subordinate. There should be few surprises when the two sit down for a summary of what has taken place since the last formal appraisal.

The time to correct an employee's mistake is when it happens so that an error does not become a habit. The value of this managerial process cannot be overstated. Senior executives from various companies identified working for a tough but fair manager who gave them feedback as the single most important developmental experience they had.

Organizations attempt to deal with the mixed feelings that both parties bring to the appraisal process by providing increasingly greater structure. Thus, we have forced distributions which maintain that performance will be normally distributed in a group and that a manager's performance appraisal of his subordinates fit into a bell curve. This assumption is not valid in evaluating performance in an organization which has done a superior job of selection and development. Assuming the purpose of a performance appraisal system *is* appraisal of current performance and not of potential for higher level positions, we should not see a wide disparity in the spread of performance evaluations in a high-performing company.

The reason for trouble with performance appraisal systems is people frequently are promoted to managerial positions not because they were good at managing people, but because they were good individual contributors. When promoted to managerial positions, they are evaluated by how well they get results rather than how well they manage (get work done through) people. In the short term, the two are not the same.

The performance appraisal process provides an opportunity to fix the employee's attention on the things that really matter. If employees are informed of the organization's goals and how their jobs fit those objectives, they have the ability to determine for themselves what is important and to set priorities among tasks of differing value to the overall organizational effort.

Again, this sounds simple. However, in looking at the results of a study conducted by the Management Institute at Columbia University, more than 60 percent of the middle managers and professionals working in successful companies complain about lack of goal clarity. Few were able to tell us what the organization's strategic objectives were. These intelligent and well-educated people had few clues that would have enabled them to manage themselves—they had to be told what to do! They tended to spend an inordinate amount of time analyzing the behavior of those who advanced to see if they could divine the rules that led to success.

Contrast this scenario with the managerial process at Honda where top management tells middle management what the organization must accomplish and then says they do not know how to get there—this plan is middle management's job to figure out. With a clear sense of the goal, those closest to the problems are free to experiment with possible solutions until they find one that works.

Rewards

Two important issues are of interest in the area of rewards. The first is to determine what we are trying to reward: membership or performance. The second is to identify the full range of rewards the organization can use to motivate its employees. Some reward categories go to people for membership. For example, most employees at certain levels of the organization receive the same benefits regardless of performance, while most organizations say that pay is based on merit. Historically, most organizations on merit pay systems did not use the system to leverage performance. There was usually little play in the range of pay increases that differentiated the superior performers from the average performers, and, in most cases, increases were not made public so people did not know if a real difference based on performance existed.

Some movement has been made in this area. For example, General Electric has in recent years been using lump sum bonuses to reward long service middle managers and professionals for superior performance. These bonuses are tied to overall company performance and do not become part of the base nor do they increase pension of other salary related benefits. *Fortune* magazine described a number of companies who have strengthened the link between organizational performance and pay.

In the long run, we would not expect a true merit pay system in a high performing company to be marked by large differences in merit increases within a group. Performers who are not delivering superior performance should be developed so they approach the ideal. If they have difficulty meeting the criteria for a particular position, they should be transferred to jobs that better match their abilities. Managers who maintain that this is the reality underlying their distribution of the merit pool must be scrupulously honest with themselves. If large differences in performance levels exist, they must be reflected in the distribution of rewards.

The second important issue in reflecting on organizational rewards is to think beyond pay and promotion. Not only is the list too limiting, but it also provides few points of leverage in organizations faced with the need to control costs. Besides, pay rarely makes the top three motivators in employee surveys. The following list demonstrates the variety of rewards that employees value:

1. Career opportunities, a long-term chance for growth and development
2. Opportunity to learn, to develop new competencies

3. Promotion, both upward mobility and lateral transfers to desirable developmental positions
4. Pay in its many forms such as salary, bonuses, stock options, and benefits
5. Responsibility
6. Autonomy
7. Personal sense of well-being from doing a job well
8. Managerial praise
9. Job security, especially important in tight economic times and at lower levels of the organization
10. Positive feedback from customers and clients
11. Respect from co-workers

Most of these rewards are underutilized by organizations who want to leverage employee performance, and the consequences of the way reward systems are administered deserves special attention in the current competitive environment.

The Definition of Success

Organizations have an enormous ability to define success for their members. Indeed, many of the human resource problems that managers wrestle with today emanate from an attempt to maintain a reward system that is at odds with the economic realities that their organizations are facing.

The reward system was designed to meet the human resource problems American companies encountered in the post-World War II era. There were significant shortages of qualified managers during a period of vibrant economic expansion. Most companies dealt with these shortages by adopting the crash training methods used to develop officers during the war when newly minted lieutenants, ensigns, and pilots were known as "90-day wonders." If they showed a flair for leadership, they were quickly rewarded with battlefield commissions or promotions to higher rank. Similarly, organizations relied heavily on on-the-job training and those who showed any aptitude for management were quickly promoted to more responsible positions. Driven by necessity, organizations experienced little harm in the practice since their growth hid a multitude of sins, and the greatest danger that these companies faced was not a lack of experienced managers but a failure to take advantage of the enormous opportunities generated in the postwar economy.

Since the organization wanted to encourage employees to take on the challenge of new positions, often before they had mastered the skills needed to do their present job, they created pay systems where the largest pay differentials were not accessed by mastering the present position but by moving to another organizational level.

In this environment, managers learned to avoid big mistakes in any assignment since they would soon be promoted if they avoided serious gaffes in their current jobs. Also, the beginnings of a short-term orientation emerged. Since a manager would be in the job for only one to two years, she did not have to worry about the long term. She had to make the short-term results appealing. If there were long-term pitfalls in the strategy employed, some successor would pay the price.

Thus, the definition of success was one of rapid promotion from one job to another, always on an upward trajectory.

The problems engendered by this definition of success became more evident as organizations faced a less forgiving environment where growth was not available to hide mistakes, and mistakes became ever more costly.

Despite the almost universal acknowledgment that the world has changed dramatically, most organizations still try to struggle along with the old definition of success. Indeed, the problem has been exacerbated since the pace of advancement for those who would be stars has accelerated, and the differences in pay and other forms of recognition between those who succeed and those who are left behind has widened.

This career system also had implications for the way jobs were designed. Jobs had to be narrow enough that someone could move into the position and perform adequately in a short time. Many people rose to high levels in the organization without a clear picture of the work of the whole organization. Furthermore they became the victims of the skill that brought them to the top: analysis, breaking an item down to its component parts. They should also have developed the skill of synthesis which would have enabled them to better understand the impact of the component parts on one another and on the goals of the organization.

DEVELOPMENT

The need for a more systematic development process poses a significant challenge to many organizations today. The problem is that most of the development that occurs in organizations takes the form of on-the-job training coupled with an informal mentoring system. Thus, both blue collar workers and managers tend to be insufficiently trained to perform their jobs and achieve corporate objectives.

To go back to our selection example of Honda and one of the American car manufacturers, we find that Honda puts assembly line workers through a three-week training program before they are permitted to work on the line, while its American competitor permitted people to work on the line the day they were hired. Honda workers have a clear understanding of the importance of their roles in quality and productivity because this orientation is part of the socialization process of every new hire.

In stark contrast, an American shop steward who had worked on the line at Chrysler for 27 years said that he had never understood the car business until Lee Iacocca explained the importance of certain actions when the company was in danger of bankruptcy.

On the managerial level, a study conducted by the Strategy Research Center indicates that more than 90 percent of the developmental experiences of key line executives in eight companies came from on-the-job training and informal mentoring as opposed to formal training and development. The effectiveness of this approach depends upon a number of conditions.

First, the organization must think about job rotation as a developmental sequence aimed at producing people to fill key positions in the company. In the past, the typical managerial career progression involved movement from first line supervisor through middle management ranks and on to top management. Among the skills stressed in this progression were interpersonal or leadership skills. As organizations are restructured to make them more competitive and responsive to environmental pressures, layers of management are being removed, and many positions that provided developmental opportunities for general managers are being eliminated. Middle managers frequently find themselves managing information or resources rather than people. As a consequence, managerial career progression is less of a continuous flow in which leadership skills become ever more critical. Rather, it is increasingly a discontinuous progression where the opportunity to develop leadership skills is constrained. To the extent that the skills needed at different levels of the organization are not part of a continuum, it will be necessary to supplement job experiences with more formal development opportunities.

The second condition needed for on-the-job training and informal mentoring processes to be effective tools for developing key successors is that the management processes and leadership characteristics currently composing the corporate culture must be the ones that the organization wishes to perpetuate in support of its future strategic direction.

Few organizations have been satisfied that their succession systems provided an adequate supply of corporate talent in relatively stable environments. Most are confounded by today's challenge—developing people whose skills are significantly different from those of its current executives. Yet, we frequently hear of the need for more risk taking, more entrepreneurial behavior, more willingness to make decisions.

The major issue is how to develop a new generation of leaders whose characteristics differ from those who have gone before. The growing consensus is that this cannot be accomplished solely through on-the-job training and informal mentoring activities.

Our aim is not the development of a small cadre of heroic figures to keep the organization safe from the threats of a hostile environment. Rather, the goal is to develop broad leadership capabilities that enable the firm to survive. This brand of leadership is a behavioral process capable of being learned and managed. It is supported by systems that push accountability and responsibility down in the organization.

In *The Transformational Leader*, Noel Tichy and I used the metaphor of drama to describe the challenges facing today's managers. In Act I, the leader must find a way to make the organization aware of the challenges it faces; in Act II, leaders must create new visions for the organization and mobilize commitment to those visions; and, in Act III, leaders must find a way to institutionalize organizational changes by designing management systems to support the new organizational reality.

The framework is useful with respect to the skills that managers need to operate in today's competitive environment and to consider how these skills can be developed.

Act I: Developing Heightened Awareness

The developmental challenge in Act I is to give managers the tools to make them more externally focused. The objective is to lower the threshhold of awareness to possible danger from competitors, technological change, and other environmental factors. The acid test for learning is: Does this give the manager a competitive edge?

Achieving these developmental objectives inside the company is difficult. Programs in which managers have their beliefs challenged by both formal presentations and the experiences of peers from other organizations will have the greatest impact in developing an external focus. To make these experiences more salient, organizations must find ways to develop more sensitive measures of effectiveness. In the search for means to lower the threshold of awareness to possible environmental threats, the important question to ask may not be "Can I use what I learned on Monday morning at the office?" but "Did I learn anything that makes me uncomfortable about the way we do things around here?" The leader's ability to spot a problem is certainly as important as its solution, since few people attempt to fix what they do not believe to be broken.

Act II: Developing Diagnostic Skills and Motivating Vision

Act II makes heavy demands on the leader's ability to use both left brain, analytical skills and the frequently dormant intuitive and emotional capacities associated with right brain activities. Healthy organizations have the ability to capitalize on the good times and to survive the bad times because their leaders spend their time working essentially as a team to face the competition outside the firm. They start by observing unstructured situations filled with uncertainty, and they work to "frame the problem."

In most organizations, the problem is not the absence of data. Indeed, for most executives, the problem is deciding what data warrants attention: How should they allocate their time and resources? The developmental challenge is to provide corporate executives with diagnostic models and conceptual frameworks that help them to organize a competitive world filled with uncertainty. These tools enable leaders to develop a coherent view of the world and to focus on the data relevant to the organization's future survival. In addition to these relatively familiar analytical problem-solving approaches, today's leaders also need to develop the ability to create motivating visions that enable employees to leave the relative safety of the past and embark on the new strategies needed to insure survival in the future.

The challenges for today's managers are to find and communicate a vision of an organization that is in some way better than the old one and to encourage others to share that vision. Creating motivating images is in no way akin to black magic. Some professions use both right brain and left brain activities in the execution of their work. For example, architects work in two modalities: They create artist's renderings of projects as well as the blueprints needed to execute them. The artist's renderings are frequently the reason people commit resources to embark upon a building project. Few people can visualize the project from blueprint. The ultimate success of the project, though, depends upon the execution of a set of blueprints that will insure the structural integrity of the project. Commitment to embark on a time-consuming and costly venture comes, however, not from the blueprints but from the idealized images of what can be.

Act III: Learning to Make the Bureaucracy Behave

In Act III, managers must learn to create the right social environment so that leadership and innovation can flourish. Resistance to creating organizations capable of ongoing renewal comes both from the top and the middle—rarely from the bottom—of the organization. The reason for resistance is that organizational forms most conducive to survival in competitive environments redistribute power and responsibility in the organization. The redistribution of power is frequently resisted by the top since it represents a significant attack on status and privilege. The redistribution of responsibility is also resisted by the middle who have been selected and groomed for their ability to execute detailed instructions and who feel threatened by an ambiguous environment in which they are expected to make decisions.

This rearrangement of power means that the development of leaders in organizations can rarely be accomplished by educating the few. Indeed, the education of the few is likely to result in the highest levels of frustration as executives take their newfound skills and return to relatively hostile environments. The ideal process is to start at the top of the organization and to cascade the learning as far down in the organization as possible.

This developmental process is alien to many of us who spent years on the technical, rational aspects of strategy and structure. However, it is becoming increasingly clear that zero-sum games require more than thoughtful analysis if we are to commit large organizations to the challenges they face today. Leaders must learn how to pay attention to the hearts as well as the minds of their subordinates if they are to develop widespread competitive capabilities throughout the organization.

These four activities—selection, performance appraisal, rewards, and development—are the generic organizational processes that enable managers to leverage change. The human resource system has received increased attention because of the growing awareness that employees' participation in organizational productivity is determined by how well this system is managed.

THE CORPORATE GOVERNANCE SYSTEM

The organization is a social system, and like all social systems, there are "laws" that tell the members what behavior will be rewarded and what behavior will be punished. In some functional areas, like accounting, the organization is specific about the rules and carefully monitors the control systems that guarantee their enforcement. As discussed in Chapter 5, there are many controls in place to insure that managers meet their fiduciary obligations to external constituencies. In addition, most organizations have carefully monitored internal controls to insure that managers are using an organizational asset—capital—in a way that benefits the organization and its shareholders. The laws are spelled out and enforced through a variety of control systems with the objective of insuring that individuals are not tempted to use organizational assets for their own gain at the expense of the organization.

Over the years, the government has also placed a number of constraints on organizations in terms of the way they use another organizational asset—people. Starting with a societal concern centered on health and safety, the government passed a number of laws regulating the use of child labor and safety standards in mines and factories. In consideration of economic justice, laws set a minimum wage. In the 1960s, recognizing the role that organizations played in distributing wealth and opportunity in the society, the government transferred its concern to the area of social justice: Did all citizens have equal access to the jobs in large organizations that offered the best opportunities for economic mobility? These laws were meant to insure that access to the organizational opportunity structure and advancement through it would be accomplished on the basis of merit.

These laws initiated a change in the way organizations viewed the management of human resources and the function that served as its internal watchdog—the personnel or human resource function. Triggered by increasingly complex regulations such as EEO and OSHA, organizations began to staff the personnel function with more sophisticated managers. Despite the recent neglect by the government agencies charged with the enforcement of the equal opportunity legislation, the focus on the management of human resources intensified during the 1980s as organizations faced a decade of increased global competition. Books appeared attributing the stunning success of the Japanese as global competitors to their methods of management. The major difference between Japanese management and American management was in the way *people* were managed.

Unfortunately, the pressures of global competition also made the job of corporate governance more difficult since a significant percentage of American companies found their labor costs out of line with those of their international competitors. Many resorted to massive layoffs to bring these costs into line, and in the process, they lost the faith and trust of many of the governed.

Organizations have paid a price for a lack of clarity about the corporate governance system. In most organizations, it is difficult to find written "laws" that govern. Yet, in the absence of a clear message, employees infer—sometimes correctly and sometimes incorrectly—those"laws" by observing what happens to people in the organization. Every organization has made a decision either explicitly or implicitly to answer basic questions that play a vital role in determining commitment to and effort for the accomplishment of corporate goals. The first of these two questions is:

What Is the Nature of the Psychological Contract That We Hold with Our Employees?

In the United States, organizations have had a broader range of alternatives in specifying the nature of the employment contract than European or Japanese firms enjoy. In Europe, government legislation complicates the process of employee termination. In Japan, tradition plays a strong role in determining practice. Indeed, if a Japanese manager finds it necessary to lay off workers, traditionally the expectation is that he will resign since he has failed in his responsibility to them.

In the United States, we have companies that have adopted a "Japanese" orientation. Companies like IBM, where the concept of lifetime employment was developed in the 1930s, are at one end of the spectrum. They, along with other institutions such as university faculties and law partnerships, explicitly lay out the terms under which lifetime employment is granted to employees. This contingency usually occurs after a lengthy trial period, during which the organization reassures itself that they will be able to "predict" future performance based on past and current observations. On the other end of the spectrum are companies (and in some cases whole industries, such as advertising and television) where the link between company and employee is more tenuous.

Unfortunately, companies where the nature of the psychological contract has been made explicit are in the minority. Most organizations never defined the nature of the contract, and employees were left to deduce its nature by observing what happened to people in the organization over time.

If we observed the practices of most American companies, we would discover two psychological contracts operating—one for the "high potential" people, often referred to as corporate property, whom management would go to extraordinary lengths to bind to the organization, and another for all other employees. At many of these companies, managers who early careers had been marked by rapid advancement found that in midlife their own opportunity structures had contracted along with the organization's growth rate. Other smaller companies could have provided new challenges, but they found that the financial sacrifice involved in leaving the organization would be high. Golden handcuffs in the form of back-loaded compensation systems kept them tied to the organization long after the promise of increasingly challenging assignments could be kept. These extraordinary measures were not extended to the rest of the workforce but the implicit promise of job security was given. It is these organizations, where people came to believe that they had lifetime employment, granted by virtue of tenure and good citizenship, that experienced the major assault on trust. For, when faced with the challenge of global competition, many of the organizations violated this implied psychological contract and layed off thousands of workers—creating a credibility crisis which many have yet to solve. As a result, managers in these organizations inherited the worst of situations—a promise of job security that could not be kept.

The short-term fallout of this bimodal system was that a significant part of the workforce were perceived as being cared for—not critical to the organization's success, but guaranteed job security if they performed adequately. When the economic pressures hit, they became the scapegoats for the organization's woes—first blue-collar workers were deemed to be lazy and indifferent to quality, and then middle managers were characterized as less committed to their organizations than their foreign counterparts.

Given the difficulty of maintaining full employment, are organizations better off if their contact with employees is in the nature of a "fair day's pay for a fair day's work"? Or, are they better off if they can find a way to forge a psychological contract guaranteeing lifetime employment?

Searching for answers, we realize that the Japanese experience offers us few clues to the right answer. In Japanese organizations, the psychological contract works both ways. Not only does the organization promise job security, but also the employee faces major structural impediments if he or she attempts to leave the firm to find employment with another established firm. Thus, the well-being of the employee is inextricably entwined with that of the organization. If the company should go bankrupt, job security ceases to exist for its employees.

In American companies, job security is viewed as a promise by the organization to the employee without any reciprocal constraint to prevent the employee from leaving the organization. Thus, in good times, the promise of job security probably does little to influence employee behavior either around membership issues or performance issues. The irony is that job security as a motivator works best in tough times when there are fewer external opportunities for employees. Perhaps it is sufficient to argue that job security does influence employee behavior positively when the organization most depends on it.

In addition, recognition is growing that quality can be demanded in the boardroom, but it is produced on the shop floor, and that the office of the chairman can never be sufficiently enlarged to handle all the critical decisions that must be made in organization.

Thus, the traditional bimodal American human resource system designed to worry about the few rather than the many will become obsolete. The companies that persist in that old pattern will be at a competitive disadvantage with those companies who understand that strength at *every* position is critical to success.

If organizations want to confirm their commitments to the entire workforce, they must manage their human resources differently. What changes must be made?

1. Organizations must be particularly self-conscious about staffing levels. Sometimes the addition of staff is not only justified but even desirable. The acid test for any position should be "if the work this person is hired to do were not done, would the customer know the difference?" If the answer is no, an organization should rethink incurring the additional salary expense.

2. Organizations should consider how long this particular job will exist. Employers with seasonal needs, for example retailers at Christmas, are usually sophisticated about the need to discriminate between long-term and short-term staffing needs. Other companies may find that they have allowed staffing levels to grow because of the assumption that future growth will equal past growth. The link between staffing and planning is critical, and the need for short-term staffing should be met by adding employees whose tenure with the organization is for a specified period of time.

3. Organizations must invest in developing and maintaining the skills of its entire workforce, not only a few people at the top. This commitment puts a premium on training and development. This measure is especially critical in companies which decide that a promise of lifetime employment is a crucial component of a committed workforce. Not only must skills be updated, but also plans must be made to shift employees from declining parts of the business to those which are growing.

4. The nature of the reward system must be examined closely. If everyone is important to the success of the organization, it becomes more

difficult to push for lower wages for blue-collar workers, marginal or no increase for the people in the middle, and concurrently higher salaries for a few at the top.

How and by Whom Will Decisions Be Made in This Organization?

Companies tend to reflect one of two images—authoritarian or participative. This dimension reflects the extent to which employees are involved in the decision-making process. If we know which option an organization has chosen, we usually can predict the direction information flows as well. Authoritarian firms tend to centralize information, while participative ones would distribute information widely through the organization. Participation does not mean that all employees are involved in all decisions—it more closely approaches Ackoff's concept of representative democracy in which all have a voice in deciding matters that affect them. Most companies, whether they be American, European, or Japanese, tend to be more authoritarian than democratic in practice if not in theory. The exceptions are the organizations that have moved closer to the goal of self-directed workforces. This group of organizations includes companies such as Honda, Cray Computer, and SAS. Therefore, they are not "Japanese," "American," or "Scandinavian," but rather companies whose management style and systems can be characterized as information age rather than machine age. The benefits they derive from their management process are speed in adapting to shifts in the marketplace, the ability to attract more entrepreneurial people, and a higher level of commitment from their workforces.

One can argue that this fundamental shift in corporate governance enables some firms to take on and outperform established competitors. Furthermore, this belief pushes us to a normative rather than a contingency view of how organizations should be structured. It enables better understanding of how a company like Honda can enter a mature auto industry in 1965, and not only survive by taking market share away from the giants, but also set the standard against which others are being measured.

This trend toward flatter organizations staffed with self-directed workforces continues to confound many organizations. They are discovering the difficulty of matching the competitive advantage of organizations who have spent their time developing superior management processes with the goal of achieving strength at every position. The difficulty in moving organizations to this ideal is one of the great paradoxes of economic activity in the West. The paradox arises from the two strong beliefs in the industrialized world: (1) free markets are more efficient than centralized planning because they minimize the cost of information. (2) Democratic social systems are inherently more stable than authoritarian ones, yet the organizations that serve as the producers in the marketplace historically have constructed systems of corporate governance that violate both of these principles.

The pressure in organizations today is toward more democratic systems, because they can respond more rapidly in the marketplace. The battle will be won by the organization that can transform itself from a machine age to an information age company designed to deal with environmental uncertainty and staffed by a self-directed workforce. It will have mastered the modern paradox by becoming an organization of entrepreneurs! It will succeed because its leadership understands that the primary mission of organizations is not profit but development, and that in highly developed organizations, profit is the byproduct of superior performance.

FOR FURTHER READING

Beer, Michael, et al., *Managing Human Assets: The Groundbreaking Harvard Business School Program* (New York: Free Press, 1985).

Fombrun, Charles, Noel M. Tichy, and Mary Anne Devanna, *Strategic Human Resource Management* (New York: John Wiley, 1984).

Fortune, "So What Is the Best Way to Pay," June 5, 1989.

Galbraith, Jay, *Organizational Design* (Reading, MA: Addison Wesley, 1977).

Kanter, Rosabeth Moss, *The Change Masters* (New York: Simon and Schuster, 1983).

Tichy, Noel, and Mary Anne Devanna, *The Transformational Leader* (New York: John Wiley, 1986).

THE STRATEGIC USE OF INFORMATION TECHNOLOGY

9

N. Venkatraman with Akbhar Zaheer

Over the last two decades, information technology (IT) and its impact on various facets of business and the economy have been subject to considerable speculation and discussion. The popular press has glorified IT as a buzzword. Futurists have painted provocative but perhaps Cassandra-like scenarios of the information society in the twenty-first century, while several are beginning to draw parallels between the emergence of the information age with that of the industrial age. Still others have called IT the most significant force yet in the transformation of society. The following quote from John Diebold is particularly telling:

> Information technology . . . is becoming increasingly the key to national economic well being, affecting virtually every industry and service. One would be hard-pressed to name a business that does not depend on the effective use of information: to design products and services, to track and respond to market demands, or to make well-informed decisions. Information technology will change the world more permanently and more profoundly than any technology so far seen in the history and will bring about a transformation of civilization to match.

While one may not subscribe to these somewhat extreme views, the fact is inescapable that information technology is currently a major force with the potential to affect a range of organizations in fundamental ways. Recently, management professionals as well as academic researchers from a variety of disciplines have increasingly focused their attention on this amorphous subject, attempting to arrive at useful theoretical and practical implications of IT applications, and to distinguish these from a mass of merely anecdotal "noise." For example, the impact of IT on how work is performed at different levels of the organization and its influence on organization structure, management process, and labor force displacement, have concerned many observers. Similarly, several striking examples of IT-induced strategic advantages realized in the marketplace by some innovative companies attest to the critical linkage between strategic management and information technology in appropriate contexts.

CURRENT TRENDS IN IT

The current and potential impact of information technology on the economy is driven home by the observation that in 1983 itself, the information processing industry revenues were a staggering $200 billion, which made it the second largest industry in the United States after oil; three times as large as steel, and almost twice as big as automobiles. Furthermore, the industry is growing at a fast clip of 20 percent compound growth per annum, at which rate it will reach one trillion dollars by the early 1990s to become the world's leading business. Inevitably, the impact of information technology on business operations will increase substantially.

Consider the shift from an industrial economy to an information-oriented service economy. Table 9.1 presents a model that powerfully illustrates the changes in products and services that will increasingly occur as the shift from an industrial economy to a service-oriented information economy gathers momentum. In essence, scale and the conventional dimensions of time, space, and mass will no longer be constraints on the products of the information age. Unlike the standardized product created for the mass market of the industrial age, the electronic delivery of banking services, for example, is scale-independent and intangible, provides instantaneous service, and is not bound by the physical location of the bank.

TABLE 9.1. Nature of products/services in an industrial and service economy.

Characteristics	Industrial Economy	Service Economy
Scale	Economies of scale	Flexible
Time	Lagtime	Realtime
Mass	Tangible	Intangible
Space	Bounded	Unbounded

Environmental trends like globalization and heightened international competition are speeding the movement toward increased IT use by corporations. The exigencies of worldwide coordination of operations and the need to react rapidly to global competitive threats have emphasized the importance of IT in the current business context. Dramatic technological developments in hardware, software, databases, and telecommunications have simultaneously pushed the utilization of IT further along. For example, the quality-equalized price of computer hardware has been estimated to be dropping at the rate of 25 percent *per year*. The phenomenal increase in the power and capabilities of desktop microcomputers, which match the computing power of the mainframes of the not-too-distant past, have doubtless been a factor in their rapid diffusion, leading to an explosion in "end-user computing." Software development has been a bottleneck in this process of fast-paced change, but even here CASE (Computer-Aided Software Engineering) tools may favorably impact productivity. The easy availability of diverse databases and developments in database design have further contributed to their widespread use. Perhaps most noteworthy has been the change in the telecommunications element of the new IT architecture: The phenomena of Local and Wide Area Networks, electronic data interchange (EDI), and electronic (E)-mail, among others, are rapidly becoming the vehicles of inter- and intraorganizational connectivity, with all its strategic ramifications.

At the same time, several factors are militating *against* the rapid deployment of IT. Among these are the still-slow development of appropriate software, long-standing difficulties in *quantifying* IT benefits (for justifying IT investment), issues of database integration, and the lack of standards (for the purposes of interorganizational connectivity).

IT and Strategic Management

This chapter is primarily concerned with the likely impact of information technologies on the practice of strategic management. The reason for adopting such a perspective reflects a fundamental belief that information technologies can potentially influence the core of a firm's activities: Choices pertaining to products, markets, and technologies (the corporate strategy level), as well as competitive methods within each of the product-market segments (the business strategy level). Since strategic management is concerned with the fundamental tasks of organization—environmental alignment and arrangement—the impact of IT on the organization can best by analyzed from the vantage point of strategic management rather than from that of operating functions such as the management information systems, marketing, or production. More importantly, the role of information technology is becoming broader than that of the traditional Information Systems (IS) function, and is becoming a general management concern and challenge.

The chapter is divided into two major sections. In the first section, the emerging interrelationships between strategic management and information technology are examined using a set of three linkages that have developed over a period of time. Four critical areas of the impact of IT on the fundamental strategic choices of the firm are detailed in the second section. A synthesis and managerial implications are developed, supplemented by an annotated bibliography of key books and papers for interested readers to pursue this topic.

STRATEGIC MANAGEMENT AND INFORMATION TECHNOLOGY: THREE LINKAGES

This section provides the necessary background to conceptualize the nature of the interconnection between strategic management and information technologies. The discussion is framed around three linkages that interconnect three important concepts—strategic management (SM), information technology (IT), and the management information systems (IS) function. The last concept is critical both from an historical point of view (IT was traditionally viewed as belonging to the IS function) as well as an organizational point of view (to discuss the changing roles and responsibilities for the various tasks). The linkages are diagrammatically represented in Figure 9.1 with the numbering scheme reflecting the historical (chronological) evolution of the linkages.

FIGURE 9.1. Strategic management and information technology:
Three linkages.

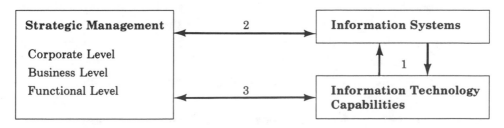

Link 1: **Management Information Systems ⟷ Information Technology**

Link 1: Management Information Systems ⟷ Information Technology

This link is best understood against the backdrop of the classic role definition of the management information systems (IS) function. According to the traditional view, IS is a service function (just as accounting, human resources, or industrial relations) which is charged with the task of efficient data processing and administration of the management reporting and control systems. This function is exemplified by numerous definitions found in the IS literature. For instance, MIS can be viewed as a set of facilities and personnel for collecting, sorting, retrieving, and processing information which is used, or desired, by one or more managers in the performance of their duties; or as a computer-based organizational information system which provides information support for management activities and functions. According to such views, systems are designed to cater to the informational requirements of different managerial roles and are identified using standard informational requirements assessment methodologies. In consequence, systems are evaluated using criteria such as timeliness, format quality, and reliability, reflecting the *technical capability* of the system. The implication is that the role of IT was conceived largely as the *technical core* of the MIS function.

Consequently, the important characteristics of this linkage were hardware and software support for the information architecture, and flexibility of design to support minor modifications in the information requirements or to respond to the fast-changing technical core of the system's hardware. Thus, in terms of the three traditional levels of management activities—strategic planning, management planning and control, and operational planning and control—IS largely supported the third level, and to some extent, the second level. The strategic planning level, by virtue of its unstructured nature of decision making, received minimal support from the traditional conceptualizations and role definitions of IS.

Systems designers and managers were thus essentially concerned with managing this link from an efficiency perspective, namely that of the best possible configurations and operations of the system given the level of resources allocated. Thus, IS can be likened to a *service* function that can be viewed independent of the strategic management context, and IT viewed as the technical infrastructure of this service function.

Link 2: Strategic Management ⟷ Information Systems

The description of Link 1 reflects a view that the charter of the IS function was derived directly from the informational resource assessment and had no explicit linkages with strategic choices at the corporate and business levels. This view was representative of the actual situation until the late 1960s and early 1970s, when the need to tailor the design of MIS to the requirements of the organizational strategic context gained currency. In 1968, McKinsey & Co. published a report titled, *Unlocking the Computer's Profit Potential* that called for a formal link between the design and implementation of MIS and the firm's strategies and objectives. This publication urged managers to visualize the role of computers in business organizations as something beyond a data processing resource at the operational level of the organization and more as a mechanism that supports their strategy.

Nearly a decade back, the link between strategic management and information systems emerged as a critical determinant of management success. William King proposed that the "IS-strategy set" (composed of IS objectives, IS constraints, and IS design strategies) should be derived from the "organization's strategy set" (composed of organizational mission, objectives, and strategies). This view is implemented in the IBM's Business System Planning (BSP) methodology that served as a popular approach toward ensuring that managers designed their information systems to support the strategic tasks. This approach involves a four-stage sequence as follows: (1) definition of the business objectives, (2) definition of the business process and activities, (3) definition of the data class, and (4) definition of the information architecture. These four stages reflect a fundamental concept of BSP in that information systems should support the goals and objectives of the business, and that BSP should be viewed as a vehicle for translating business strategy to IS strategy.

The importance of the systemic linkages between strategic planning and MIS planning gained further currency as preliminary empirical support of its importance has been forthcoming. For instance, Pyburn's study of the planning practices in a select set of companies established the criticality of the link between MIS planning and the firm's corporate strategy. Broader support for this position is provided by a large-sample study of MIS planning practices of over 300 leading U.S. corporations. Specifically, we found that the variable capturing the linkage between IS planning and business planning was an important determinant of IS planning effectiveness, which was conceptualized as the degree of support that IS provides for the strategic management activities of the firm.

Transformation of the Role

While this link represents concern within the MIS discipline to ensure that MIS is designed in accordance with the strategic contexts of the firm, the link in the other direction, from the corporate strategic context to MIS, was largely ignored. The strategic context for a firm is commonly conceptualized as a three-level hierarchy—the corporate, business, and functional levels. These levels are formally linked through planning and control systems. Here, the functional-level strategies are derived from the "higher level" strategies. Thus, information systems strategies are derived in line with the business and/or corporate strategies, and it is not surprising that much professional attention has focused on the higher levels, namely corporate and business strategies.

Over the years, there has been a growing feeling that the subordination of functional strategies to the business-level strategy may be too restrictive to exploit potential sources of competitive advantage that may lie within the various functional areas. Accordingly, functions are increasingly being viewed from a strategic perspective. In this emerging tradition, the key themes include "strategic marketing management," the linkage between the marketing function and strategic management, "strategic human resource management," highlighting the explicit consideration of human resource profiles and capabilities in the formulation and implementation of strategies, and the notion of manufacturing as a competitive weapon to illustrate the potential sources of strategic advantages that lie within the production and manufacturing function.

Similarly, several authors have called attention to the possibility of exploiting information and information systems for strategic advantages. As William King noted in an editorial comment in the *Management Information Systems Quarterly,* "Information (and IS) has the potential to be a primary source of (competitive) advantage in the marketplace rather than merely as a resource to be efficiently managed or a service that is periodically turned on and off as needed." Indeed, many see the link between strategic management and IS today as a bidirectional, mutually interconnected link, implying a strategic role for the IS function.

Strategic Information Systems

In a transition toward a strategic role, the goals and tasks of the management information systems function undergo an important transformation. The systems are no longer viewed in terms of informational support for operational decisions, but rather in terms of the realization of the organization's strategic objectives, especially the achievement of competitive superiority in the marketplace. For clarity, information systems with a charter to achieve competitive superiority are called "strategic information systems" and differentiated from the more operationally focused MIS. Indeed, MIS has been traditionally concerned with the operational control systems for relatively structured decisions based on readily available, internal data. In contrast, strategic information systems are designed to support relatively unstructured decisions, especially those that are intricately tied to the activities of the marketplace. Usually such decisions require a combination of internal and external data that are neither well structured nor completely specified. Although a perfect demarcation between management information systems and strategic information systems cannot always be made, the conceptual distinction is important enough to be recognized just as the conceptual distinction between strategic and operational decisions.

Anecdotal evidence and trade publications indicate that the number and diversity of the strategic information systems are on the increase. A partial listing of such systems with their corresponding benefits (from a strategic advantage point of view) is provided in Table 9.2.

TABLE 9.2.   An overview of popular strategic information systems.

Firm	Description	Ascribed Benefits
American Airlines	SABRE Reservation Systems—installed in over 11,000 travel agents for booking airline, hotel, and rental car reservations.	Provides American Airlines with critical operating data that can be used for strategic decisions; travel agents hooked on to SABRE are likely to book on American more than other airlines.
American Hospital Supply Co.	ASAP-order entry system—installed in over 4500 medical establishments to order supplies on-line. The system is internally interconnected to several supporting systems.	Streamlined order processing operations; captive customers—who are likely to place orders through ASAP than using competitors.
Bancone Corp.	Several systems that support their strategies for electronic banking services.	Helped Bancone to differentiate in a fiercely competitive marketplace and perform well.
Citicorp	Extensive use of automated teller machines and global transaction network.	Streamlined operations; supported Citicorp's strategy for global banking.
McKesson Corp.	Economost—order entry system that supports customers with inventory control and analysis of sales.	Fully integrated system that allows McKesson to be an efficient, low-cost player in a fiercely competitive industry.
United Airlines	APOLLO—Travel agency reservation system with several augmented services installed in about 7700 agencies.	Broadly similar benefits as SABRE provides to American (with additional revenues because of augmented services).

Strategic information systems achieve their objectives through several mechanisms, but two deserve special attention. These are: (1) the reconfiguration of the information flows within an organization to provide competitive advantages relative to competition, and/or (2) development of *interorganizational* systems that extend beyond the traditional boundaries of a single focal organization. These modes are not mutually exclusive, but are discussed independently in the following paragraphs using illustrative examples.

Reconfiguration of Information Flows

Let us consider the case of an airline that uses timely data to increase its load factor—perhaps the single most critical factor for achieving success in the airline industry. By developing a strategic information system designed not only to continually collect data on flight bookings, but also to compare current sales against historical patterns, the airline can recommend to its own ticketing agents (as well as travel agents) to modify the number of discount seats available on a particular flight depending on the current level of advance bookings. Similar benefits can accrue to a hotel, where a key determinant of competitive performance is the occupancy ratio. Using a system that provides data on current occupancy, historical patterns, and anticipated bookings, pricing levels can be modified and communicated to the travel agents to derive additional bookings through tour packages. In both these cases, the *perishability* of the service makes the *timeliness* of the availability of information (in addition to its accuracy and reliability) a critical determinant for achieving success in the marketplace. Indeed, one can generalize this mode of achieving competitive advantage to any service which has perishable inventory and can be sold at price levels close to the marginal cost.

The basic notion of timeliness of information can be extended from the context of the service sector to the manufacturing sector. Consider the case of an oil company which is able to communicate with its dealers directly and instantaneously as oil prices change to ensure minimum delay between the setting of prices in the headquarters and its realization at retail outlets. While the concept may appear intuitively obvious, the advantage realized can be better understood by comparing this method of communication to the traditional system—that would have required that the headquarters communicate this to the regional offices, which in turn would pass on the information to sales representatives and finally to the outlets.

These illustrations share a common theme: In these cases, IT does *not* influence the fundamental strategic business choices. However, the implementation of such decisions through organizational hierarchy and channels is facilitated through the use of IT, leading to improved strategic results. Indeed, such examples reinforce the importance of IT in strategy implementation, by highlighting the possibilities opened up by recent developments in information technology.

A fundamental question at this stage is: Why should such a system provide any source of strategic advantage in the marketplace? The answer perhaps lies in the *differential capability* of the players to reconfigure their informational availability for obtaining an additional (favorable) lever in the competitive game. A "me-too" strategy is unlikely to yield any sustainable long-term advantages. Since informational asymmetries (relative to other players) can be purposely created using strategic information systems, their use translates into potential sources of competitive advantage in the marketplace. Beath and Ives have discussed the reconfiguration of information flows, in the context of pricing decisions, in terms of information's *timeliness, content,* and *format:* Each of these aspects of information can be impacted upon IT to yield favorable asymmetries for an organization. Rapid response time and frequency of information, for example, can be significant competitive strengths when communicating price changes through several middlemen. For airlines analyzing traffic patterns to offer discounted fares on certain routes, both timeliness and detailed market information (content) can be key data. For real estate appraisers, data accessed through newly available databases enable comparisons (format) on important characteristics which determine price, giving them an advantage over competition not using such formats.

Interorganizational Systems   The discussion has thus far focused on informational efficiency through reconfiguration of systems which could provide sources of competitive advantage in the marketplace. It is necessary to recognize that the domain of the operations of the systems has been limited to the focal organization. While such reconfiguration is not novel, it is now possible to design and deploy such innovative systems more inexpensively than ever before because of a rapid decline in the cost of computing and communication. In contrast, interorganizational IT applications highlight the potential to achieve competitive success that extends beyond intraorganizational informational flows to the deploying and exploiting of information-based links with diverse actors in the marketplace.

In simple terms, an interorganizational strategic information system can be thought of as a system that extends beyond the boundaries of a single focal organization to link multiple organizations. The potential to develop such links (and the consequent benefits to achieve competitive advantage) is perhaps the single most important reason for the increased attention to informational systems from a strategic management point of view.

Stephanie Barrett and Benn Konsynski have developed a framework to view the different levels of participation in interorganizational systems. The (V) five levels are: Level I—Remote I/O Node, Level II—Application Processing Node, Level III—Multiparticipant Exchange Node, Level IV—Network Control Node, and Level V—Integrating Network Node. As the level of participation increases, so do the responsibility of the participant, the cost commitments, technical complexity, and the potential for realizing strategic benefits.

A Level I participant acts only to receive and enter information through a basic interface device linked to a mainframe of the higher level participant. The higher level partner determines the communication standards and protocols to be employed. In the airline industry, the travel agents, as well as suppliers, would be at this first level of participation, for several of them are linked to the higher level participant, the airline, by means of interface devices for data entry and receipt.

A Level II participant sets the standards and develops the software to be used by Level I participants, dealing simultaneously with a number of participants at this level. The airlines that have deployed interorganization systems would be classified in this category of participation. They interface with travel agents and suppliers according to specialized software developed by the airlines themselves.

A Level III participant manages and maintains a network linking itself and any number of lower level participants with whom it has an established business relationship. Such a participant's network is used by different types of lower level participants and allows for both direct company-to-company communication as well as processing.

A Level IV participant "develops and shares a network with diverse applications" which could interconnect many different types of lower level participants. A participant in an interorganizational system at this level may not have a business relationship with any of the lower level participants. Given the substantial cost commitment participation in an interorganization system at Level III involves, specialized network operators (McDonnell Douglas' Tymnet, GE's GEISCO, for examples) are usual participants at this level. These "value-added networks" often also offer a set of additional services such as protocol (communications standards) conversion (i.e., "translation") and "mailboxes."

A Level V participant is normally a data communication utility executing multiple applications in real-time at multiple sites. At this level, ownership of the network is central for strategic benefits and not merely for efficient processing of information for its participants. The ownership is a central decision to be made by the participants, as it implies how the economic rents are distributed among the various players.

The Railroads as an Example   The railroad industry, which has one of the highest levels of "penetration" of electronic data interchange (EDI) among all industries, displays several levels of interorganizational systems use. Most railroad customers, including both shippers and shippers' agents, are at this first level of participation. Most major railroads that have deployed interorganizational systems in the form of EDI, are at Level II, with some progressing to Level III. In these modes, railroads have developed networks with their suppliers for diverse applications in this information-intensive industry. For example, railroad customers can use personal computers to access railroad mainframes to obtain instant prices, send electronic waybills, and keep track of their shipments in real-time. By dramatically improving the levels of service in the goods transportation industry, the railroads are mounting a strong competitive challenge to the trucking industry, which had hitherto a clear lead in the service dimension. The Association of American Railroads (AAR) has set up a subsidiary, *Railinc,* which operates as a Level IV participant for interorganizational systems: It maintains a network that connects railroads (Levels II and III participants) to each other as well as customers and suppliers to the railroads, providing diverse applications without a noninformational product/market relationship with any of its participants.

A Schematic Representation

Figure 9.2 is a drawing of a focal organization with specific links to its suppliers (input) and buyers (output) as interconnected business processes. Traditionally, the focal firm has maintained communication links with the buyers and suppliers using media such as telephone, telex, and postal service. However, due to the increase in the computing and communication capabilities and the reduction in their cost structure, several firms have found it attractive to develop electronic links with their key suppliers and/or buyers. The underlying question is: Does this connection imply improvements in efficiency (due to reduction in errors and the substitution of machines for human interface), or does it provide an

FIGURE 9.2.   The role of IT in the interrelated business processes: A schematic representation.

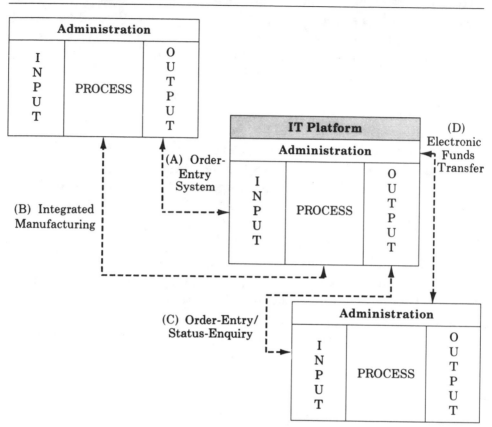

entirely different set of mechanisms for achieving strategic advantages in the marketplace? It is difficult to argue convincingly that such linkages alone provide sources of superior advantages in the marketplace. However, organizations can (and have) creatively leveraged such systems to transform business processes. The expected benefits from the design and use of such a strategic information system can be exemplified through three cases: (1) American Hospital Supply Corporation—the ASAP system, (2) McKesson Drug Company—the Economost system, and (3) Airline Computerized Reservation Systems (CRS).

Case 1: American Hospital Supply Corporation

The company's Automated System for Analytical Purchasing (ASAP), deployed in 1967, is often cited to illustrate the potential for achieving relative competitive advantage in the market. When this system was designed, the general view was that systematic capabilities can be used only to improve informational capability for operational decision making. ASAP was the first conception of potential marketplace advantages from such systems.

American Hospital Supply Corporation manufactures and distributes healthcare products to hospitals, laboratories, and medical specialists. Given the increasing cost of order transactions, they considered the use of dedicated electronic terminals at the location of their major customers. The introduction of electronic terminals can be visualized at one level as substituting fixed costs (electronic terminals) for variable costs (operators who manually take down orders)—where the benefit accrues because of the high volume transactions. If this were the case, this system serves to illustrate mainly the operational efficiency of the transaction processing tasks. However, an added strategic benefit accrued to them (which, incidentally, they had not envisaged), namely, that the hospitals that had these terminals installed in their locations were virtually locked into the purchasing system installed by American Hospital Supply Corporation. The customers found it easier and more convenient to send their order through these terminals than choose the relatively inefficient option of using the telephone ordering systems of the competitors. By 1984, over 4500 customers were electronically linked into the American Hospital Supply system with the facility to electronically place orders for any of their full line of over 100,000 products. It is widely accepted that this arrangement has given American Hospital Supply Corporation a formidable advantage in the competitive healthcare business.

Such a system not only provided operational efficiency for American Hospital Supply Corporation, but also provided a mechanism to differentiate its services from those of its competitors. Through the use of this system, it was possible for American Hospital Supply Corporation to guarantee better service (reliability in terms of deliver, and confirmation of orders after ascertaining the stock availability). In addition, this system serves as a barrier against the possibility of the customer's switching to a competitor because of the level of initial investment in training and use of the system. While one can conceptualize the role played by such a system in their overall strategy, a larger question that remains is: What benefit did it provide for the company's bottom line?

The accrued benefit to the company can be evaluated in terms of increased market share. Specifically, (1) It was found that hospitals that were linked to their system were more likely to buy from American Hospital Supply Corporation than from their competitors; (2) the average hospital purchase order over this system averages 5.8 items compared to the industry average of 1.7 items per order; and (3) the revenues during 1978 to 1980 were as much as three times greater than the corresponding three-year period before the introduction of the system, according to *BusinessWeek* in 1980. Furthermore, during 1981 to 1986, the company has doubled the number of such systems at its client locations, while there has been a steady increase in the proportion of its total sales received through these systems. Now, this system—or more precisely, the entire IT infrastructure that is built around this core system—is a central strategic lever for Baxter Healthcare (the newly formed organization that is the result of the merger between American Hospital Supply Co. and Baxter Travenol).

Case 2: McKesson Drug Company

The case of McKesson is frequently quoted as one of the most successful examples of business transformation using information technology capabilities. McKesson is a national pharmaceutical distributor that receives close to 100 percent of its orders electronically from drugstores through its *Economost* systems. A customer orders by making a single pass through the store with a hand-held order entry device, keying in a product identifier or using a bar code scanner. Reorder quantities are indicated on shelf tags. When the complete order has been entered, it is transmitted by telephone to a data center where it is acknowledged by voice synthesizer units. Orders are consolidated and passed onto a mainframe, from which the regional distribution centers pull them at regular intervals. The orders are delivered the same of following day in cartons that match the aisle arrangement of the drugstore. Price stickers are provided.

McKesson originally introduced the system as a defensive move, in order to improve operating efficiencies by reducing personnel and cost. The reduction in the numbers of customer orders was also expected to cut costs. However, McKesson further wanted to prop up the independent drugstores, its major customers (which were losing out to drug chains), by passing on many of its savings to them in the form of lower margins. Lower distribution margins would also reduce the incentives for drug companies and drugstores to deal with one another directly.

Since the systems were first introduced nationally in 1975, McKesson's drug sales have grown from $922 million to $4.8 billion in 1987, an increase of 422 percent, but its operating expenses have gone up by only 86 percent. While the company's market share—net of acquisitions—has not grown, industry concentration has, and so has the proportion of drugs supplied by distributors relative to that supplied by manufacturers. McKesson has also sizably reduced the number of personnel in order entry and sales.

McKesson's retail customers have gained by lower prices, lower inventory carrying costs, and lower transaction costs. However, Clemons and Row observe that "it is not clear that these systems have provided any one company with profitability superior to similar competitors," as McKesson's major competitors have also grown at the same time. In fact, one of them (Bergen) has an equivalent order-entry system, and most surprising, customers did not feel that switching costs were significant. Clemons and Row conclude that "for this industry, information technology, skillfully and aggressively applied, seems to be more a strategic necessity than a source of competitive advantage."

However, a closer analysis allows us to draw a more optimistic conclusion. McKesson clearly achieved its original operational efficiency benefits to improve its profitability. Although the company apparently did not gain share relative to its major distributor competition, it achieved significant strategic benefits in sales and market share gains *relative to its larger competition* (i.e., direct distribution by drug companies). The system also achieved "increased tying of the customer to McKesson" which is a substantial strategic advantage. Moreover, McKesson has begun to offer a number of other services based on the data it has obtained from the order entry system—such as management reports and drugstore credit cards. As a McKesson employee phrased it, "These value-added services are now profit centers." This, too, is a classic, and initially unforeseen, spinoff from IT—the leveraging of the database for the creation of new products, as will be discussed in greater detail later.

Case 3: Airline Reservation Systems

Another illustration is seen in the airline reservation systems—where the customer is the travel agent and the airlines are the providers of service. During the period of regulation, when price was not a differentiating factor, the travel agents played a key role in influencing the choice of the traveler. At that time, American Airlines introduced its SABRE reservation system that was accessed through terminals from the desks of travel agents. Although such systems displayed nearly all flights, it gave priority to American flights in terms of the order of display on the screen. This feature was critical because estimates reflect that between 70 and 90 percent of the airline bookings are made from the first screen, and more than 50 percent are made from the first line. While some question such a practice as a violation of fair trade practices, others consider it to be a significant strategic move that has parallels with the American Hospital Supply system. American Airlines' argument is that the inbuilt "bias" in the display of flight schedules over that of the competitors is justified given the level of investment (over $300 million) it committed to this venture.

Such a system helped American Airlines in its relative market position in the airline market. Although exact data are not available, it is widely acknowledged that the proportion of tickets booked through the SABRE system was much higher for the American Airlines' flights than for any other airline whose schedules were also displayed on the system. A similar pattern could be observed with the United Airlines' APOLLO system, where the travel agents linked through this system booked more flights on United than on any other airline. Thus, IT not only helped the airlines that deployed such systems (ahead of the others) to compete more effectively in an era of regulation, but also gave them a significant headstart when the industry was deregulated by providing them with critical market data on travelers. These data could be used as key inputs for strategic decisions pertaining to pricing and promotional packages. Realizing the importance of such a system, several other airlines developed and even tested pilot versions before deciding that it would be difficult to compete against SABRE and APOLLO.

Similar interpretations can be made for the other systems that are summarized in Table 9.2. The common underlying theme in the successful use of these systems appears to be that one organization develops and deploys a strategic information system with a view to create favorable asymmetries in the marketplace. Such systems—either confined to the boundaries of a single organization or more often extended beyond a single organization—usually provide the organization that deploys the system with significant operating (efficiency related) benefits as well as strategic (marketplace or competitive) advantages. While it is too early to predict the long-term benefits from such systems (especially in view of possible standardization of systems configurations which may offset firm-specific advantages), the indications clearly support the realization of short-term benefits by the pioneering organizations that create favorable disequilibria in the markets through such systems.

However, the discussion thus far is limited to those strategic management issues that do not involve significant changes in the product-market scope of operations. Also, the emphasis has been on the link of information *systems* and business strategy. Indeed, these examples largely serve to illustrate the role that strategic information systems play in developing and implementing more effective business level strategies (or, domain navigation) rather than on corporate level issues (i.e., domain choice).

Information technologies, however, also play a critically important role in strategic choice issues pertaining to domain choice (i.e., changing product-market definition). The implications of the impact of information technology on strategic choice issues, as well as issues arising from the direct interplay of information *technology* and business and corporate strategy, are discussed in detail in Section Two, "Impacts and Challenges." This section follows a brief description of the third link, that between strategic management and IT.

Link 3: Strategic Management ⟷ Information Technology

Peter Keen, writing in 1981, noted that "as yet there is no field entitled 'telecommunications and business policy.' Discussions on the impact of communications technology usually focus on hardware, public policy, and regulation or on specific applications as office automation, teleconferencing, and electronic banking." However, over the last six years, several new and powerful forces in the technological and market environment compel one to recognize the link between strategic management and information technology in terms of the fundamental role played by IT in influencing the formulation of a firm's strategy rather than merely supporting its implementation.

IT Push versus Competitive Pull

The radical transformation of the nature of this link can be viewed as a combination of two concurrent (and perhaps equally powerful) forces, labeled here as *technology push* and *competitive pull*. Over the years, rapid advances and the merging of constituent technologies have resulted in continuous improvements in the sophistication and price-performance ratio of information technologies. Robert Benjamin and Michael Scott Morton underscore this improvement by casting it in terms of the relative prices of capital and labor (the ratio of the cost of a technology to the cost of labor). Over the three decades from 1950, they find that for six product groups (cars, processed foods, appliances, furniture, machinery and equipment, and photographic equipment) there have been improvements of up to a maximum of 1.7 times in this ratio at the end of a typical decade (i.e., a decrease in the price-performance of capital versus labor). In sharp contrast, over the same period, the performance of the IT industry has shown an improvement of as much as 25 times. These developments now make it possible for managers to utilize IT-based applications at a fraction of the cost that would have been just a few years ago.

FIGURE 9.3. Forces contributing to the emergence of a strategic role for
            information technology.

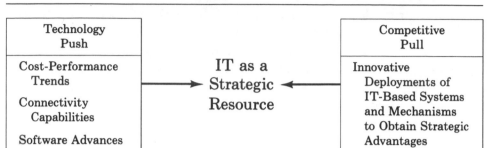

The nature of the second force can be explained by focusing on the degree of competitiveness in the various markets. Managers are constantly looking for ways to compete in today's fast-changing and complex marketplace. The macroeconomic imperatives of international competition and deregulation have intensified competitive pressures and increased the turbulence of the business environment, compelling firms to search harder for novel competitive strategies. The sharp rise in the number of strategic alliances, mergers, and acquisitions in the last few years are further indicative of these trends. The potential for innovative modes of competing as well as new products and services made possible through IT provides managers with an entirely different spectrum of opportunities and threats. Given the general explosion of computing power and communications capabilities (integrated voice and data), several new business applications can be (and have been) developed in those areas that directly enhance efficiency and effectiveness in the marketplace. Figure 9.3 is a schematic representation of these two forces and their influence on strategic management.

IMPACTS AND CHALLENGES

This section discusses critical areas of IT impacts and challenges which emerge from the link between strategic management and IT. These impacts are highly significant, from the point of view of both recency and of potential pervasiveness in the "information age."

The strategic management and information technology interconnection is detailed here using four crucial strategy issues, with appropriate examples. These are: The impact of IT on (1) changing industry boundaries, (2) business definition and redefinition, (3) competitive mechanisms and new sources of competitive advantage, and (4) the creation of new business opportunities.

The Impact of IT on Changing Industry Boundaries

The pervasive impact of IT in today's economic context is evidenced by the blurring of traditional industry boundaries. Once clear demarcations between even manufacturing and service industries have turned fuzzy, with a greatly increased service input into manufacturing—and information "bundling" with manufactured products—witness the on-board computers now common in many cars. Distinctions within the service sector are eroding still faster, notably in the financial services industry (as the following example of Merrill Lynch illustrates.)

Example: Merrill Lynch

Merrill Lynch's strategy demonstrates the potential offered by information technologies to develop superior substitute products (or services) as well as altering the definition and domain of business operations. The introduction of Cash Management Account (CMA) by Merrill Lynch in 1978 represented a revolution in terms of redefining the concept of financial services in a marketplace that was dominated by the traditional banking institutions. The new business concept was built around integrating diverse financial instruments under one common umbrella such that the individual investor is able to enjoy the convenience of moving money across them as well as benefit from the "float" that the banks traditionally enjoyed. This account permitted the integration of four basic services to investors: (1) automatic investment of cash and dividends in a money market account, (2) credit through a standard margin account, (3) cash withdrawal by check or debit card, and (4) investment advice in managing and diversifying the account.

The strategy could not be implemented without the use of information technology, for it requires daily swaps across different accounts to post the credit card charges, checks, securities, and deposits, as well as to develop a daily updated credit limit for each account holder. This complex data processing operation is not incidental to the business concept but is fundamental to its conceptualization and operation. The importance of IT in this strategy is perhaps best emphasized by the fact that Merrill Lynch obtained a patent for the cash management account system in 1982. The annual fees generated by this product for Merrill Lynch were around $60 million in 1983. Although several variations (circumventing the patent protection) of this basic concept have appeared in recent years, none has so far matched the success of Merrill Lynch's product.

Other firms which have utilized IT to break down traditional industry borders in the services sector include Sears, now an integrated financial services provider; Citicorp, now an investment and realty firm as well as a bank; and American Express, always strong in the travel business, now making a play in international banking, insurance, and securities, in addition, to becoming a financial and information supermarket. Indeed, the entire industry is being transformed due to parallel but related forces: deregulation and technology.

Information technology, while possibly causing the most apparent changes to the financial services industry, is also influencing the basis of competition in the air travel industry. In recent years, American Airlines has forged ahead with its commitment to exploit its system for competitive advantage over others. Recently, it has announced a personal computer version of the reservation system that enables travelers to book directly rather than use travel agents. Indeed, the automation of ticketing process through personal computers and the use of automated ticketing machines at airports (similar to banks' automated teller machines) could seriously transform the basis of competition in the airline industry and threaten the existence of the present form of travel agents in the next decade. American is thus beginning to use IT to muscle its way into the travel agent industry, and in the process redefining its business position.

Example: Electronic Markets

Another significant IT-induced development at the macro level, which potentially improves what economists call society's allocative efficiency, is the appearance of numerous "electronic markets" and the instantaneous exchange of price, demand, and supply information. The most obvious instances of these are the stock and commodity exchanges, where electronic trading allows brokers, buyers, and sellers to overcome barriers of geography and time. Regional electronic markets too are springing up and achieving the same result. As Beath and Ives report:

> A cooperative of cotton farmers in Texas has established Telcot—an electronic cotton trading system—"to facilitate swift, convenient, and competitive bidding on the cotton produced by the association's 20,000 members." Before Telcot, only a small number of potential buyers would bid (by phone)

on a farmer's cotton. Now scores of potential buyers vie for the cotton through "blind bidding" on a computer network. . . . The farmers . . . believe the Telcot system gives them consistently higher returns.

Malone, Yates, and Benjamin have argued that a move to electronic markets (buyers and sellers interconnected electronically), and away from electronic hierarchies (economic activity coordinated within the firm), will be accelerated with the current capabilities of IT. They base this analysis on the emergence of faster and cheaper telecommunications and the capabilities of computers to handle more complex information. Together, these give rise to forces which, in essence, lower coordination costs relative to production costs, as well as deal with the complexity of product descriptions more easily. Both these phenomena will lead to markets being preferred in certain cases where hierarchies were previously favored. There are incentives for buyers, sellers, distributors, and IT vendors to establish electronic markets.

For firms, the implications of the appearance of an electronic market implies that the "transaction costs" of dealing with external suppliers are lowered. Strategic choice decisions of whether to conduct certain economic activities in-house or through markets will need to be made anew as the trend toward electronic markets accelerates. Again, this development highlights the critical links between IT and corporate level strategy. The important message is that IT represents a new spectrum of opportunities and threats for managers. Creative application of IT capabilities proactively is the key to success in the new marketplace.

The Impact of IT on Business Definition

As the boundaries between industries blur, the proverbial question that is the logical starting point for strategy analysis at the corporate level— "What business(es) are we in?"—takes on greater significance. The objective in asking the question is to define the organization's position with respect to its products, markets, and technologies to identify an underlying logic in its portfolio composition and strategic thrusts. This task has become much more challenging as a result of the power and capabilities of IT to change not only product characteristics and definitions, but also market and industry boundaries (as discussed earlier). The rapidly changing industry-competitive maps introduce a new element in traditional corporate strategy: to adequately delineate the present and potential scope of their business and competition *in a dynamic context.*

Classic examples of such redefinitions are those of Merrill Lynch (discussed earlier) which not only changed its business scope but also the competitive map of the financial services industry; *USA Today's* successful use of satellite technology to create a national newspaper as well as its innovative use of fax technology for distribution is another market redefinition that changed the competitive map in the publishing industry. McKesson's addition of value-added services by leveraging its computer links is again illustrative of the potential of IT for redefining the business scope.

IT-Induced Shifts in the Business Domain

A major task for corporate strategy in the context of IT-induced shifts in the business domain is that of ensuring that the organization's core technologies are not rendered obsolete by a shift in the product or business definition. For example, traditional typesetting skills have become outdated by the advent of desktop publishing. American Express has transformed the handling of its receipts from paper to electronic imaging, thus setting new standards for its industry. Therefore, the core technology of businesses is changing rapidly with the increased IT component in many industries, requiring appropriate strategic responses. Nearly every aspect of a firm's technological and task base is likely to be impacted by IT. Firms must consider the implications of business redefinitions proactively and adopt IT-based functionalities if they are not to find themselves bypassed by the fast moving tide of IT-induced change.

The Impact of IT on Competitive Mechanisms and Sources of Competitive Advantage

IT's impact on the competitive marketplace can be viewed from several complementary angles. Over the last five years, several descriptive and normative frameworks have been proposed to enable managers to conceptualize and exploit information technology for strategic advantage. Robert Benjamin and his colleagues discuss the strategic opportunities presented by IT using two basic dimensions—domain of change (competitive marketplace versus internal operations) and domain of influence (structural change versus traditional products and services)—and the four cells of the two-dimensional matrix imply differences not only in terms of the nature of opportunities but also in terms of the modes available for exploiting them. Charles Wiseman proposed an options generator using four basic questions—What is the strategic target (supplier, customer, competitor)?

What is the strategic thrust (differentiation, cost, innovation, growth, alliance)? What is the mode (offensive, defensive)? and What is the direction (use, provide)?

Michael Hammer and Glenn Mangurian have developed what they term a "Impact—Value" framework which enables managers to conceptualizes IT applications. The framework characterizes the business *value* of an information system in terms of three major areas: the potential scope of *efficiency, effectiveness,* or *innovation,* "a basic transformation of a firm's business functions." The *impacts* on the organization occur through time compression, overcoming geographical limitations, and altering both inter- and intraorganizational *relationships.* Each cell entry "represents a unique kind of business change . . . a vehicle by which impact is translated into value," and a specific IT application may yield more than one kind of value. The framework allows a firm to analyze current and potential IT applications for sources of strategic advantage.

Another perspective builds on the well-known competitive forces model explicated by Michael Porter. Warren McFarlan uses the model to pose five questions (one for each force) for assessing the impact of IT on the business strategy of a firm and notes that "If the answer to one or more of these questions is yes, information technology represents a strategic resource that requires attention at the highest level."

Parsons also using Porter's framework, although more broadly, identified three levels of impact of IT. At the industry level, IT can cause a change in the industry's products and services, for example by reducing the product development life cycle. IT can lead to changes in the markets in other industries, such as financial services, by removing barriers of geography and time. IT can also alter the basic economics of production in some industries, such as with the use of flexible manufacturing practices. At the firm level, each of the five competitive forces enumerated by Porter—buyers, suppliers, substitutes, new entrants, and rivals—can be favorably altered by the strategic use of IT. Parson's third level is that of generic firm strategy, which can be supported or shaped by IT.

Yet another perspective for identifying sources of competitive advantage from IT deployment is from that of the firm's value chain. (For a fuller description of the value chain, see Michael Porter's book, *Competitive Advantage.*) Both greater efficiency and effectiveness may be realized within the organization by carefully evaluating IT use in various stages of the value chain, and reconfiguring it for competitive advantage. IT can be utilized to functionally restructure the value chain of an organization by combining and rearranging certain activities and processes of the value chain. The elimination of these activities could result in a decisive cost advantage to a firm, which may translate into a marketplace competitive advantage.

While such frameworks allow management to identify and assess the impact of IT on competitive mechanisms, they should not be used as providing "sure-win" applications for exploiting IT. The final choice of integrating IT capabilities with the other complexities of the business context is a true challenge for the strategists.

IT's Impact on the Creation of New Business Opportunities

Potentially, the most profitable impact of IT is in the creation of new goods and services, innovative moves into new industries, and the repositioning of the firm itself—in other words, domain redefinition.

Among the ways in which new business opportunities are grasped, notes Peter Keen, are *preemptive strikes* and *piggybacking*. Preemptive strikes occur when a business move changes the "competitive dynamics of the marketplace." However, for a preemptive strike to be genuinely innovative, it must not be easily replicable. Only then will strategic benefits accrue. Innovative IT applications sometimes maintain their headstart over competition, partly due to the long lead times competitors face in developing the technology base and the databases to match the innovation.

Even if IT-based advantages are realized by the first mover in the short run, the larger question pertains to the long-term *sustainability* of such advantages. Given that such advantages have accrued because of innovative ideas—which are difficult to protect using patents—little prevents competitors from imitating such operations and nullifying the advantages. The proponents argue that the leadtime is sufficiently long for the pioneer to reap supernormal profits, by citing the example of Merrill Lynch's Cash Management Account, which had a lead of over four years before being swamped by "me-too" products (despite the patent). Nevertheless, the company sill has the lion's share of the market and $70 billion from over a million affluent consumers. However, the ubiquity of IT capabilities may make it difficult for other pioneers to emulate Merrill Lynch's success. So, the question is: What determines the level of sustainability of strategic advantages through IT in the marketplace? Is it uniform across all types of IT innovations? No unambiguous answers are available at this time, but among the possibilities must count the continual upgrading of the IT application with software increasingly useful to the customer. American Hospital Supply is apparently a success in sustaining its competitive advantage over competition by such upgrades, building ever-stronger umbilical cords with its customers.

Piggybacking, another route to new business opportunities, involves the addition of new traffic on an existing delivery network. At relatively low cost, new products and services can be sent down the already installed "electronic highway" to the customer. In certain cases, even entirely new industries can be created.

Dun and Bradstreet

The example of Dun and Bradstreet serves as an example of an organization that has transformed its portfolio significantly over the last decade. Indeed, the additions and deletions to its portfolio can be best understood in terms of the notion of dominant logic and a strategic vision of the role of IT in the larger economy.

In 1978, Dun and Bradstreet was a $763 million dollar diversified information services company with four major divisions, with the business information services division contributing 38 percent of revenue but only 27 percent of operating revenue. By 1983, it had become a $1.5 billion dollar information services giant with 45 percent of revenues and 34 percent of operating income derived from the business information services. The changes in the composition of its portfolio is an interesting example of a fundamental commitment to the information technologies as a central pillar of their strategic choices and redirection. In 1979, it acquired a computer services company and a software company to develop new product offerings based on the basic data that it collects as a part of its traditional operations, but which can be sold through different channels. It divested its portfolio of its broadcasting stations and merged with A.C. Nielsen & Co., to exploit economies of scale and scope in its collection, packaging, and marketing of data for different purposes. Other new product offerings that are rooted in IT include the official airlines guide (electronics edition) as well as the creation of DunsPlus— an alliance with IBM and Lotus, and the development of DunsNet that enables the Dun and Bradstreet users to access their wide range of databases. So, in essence, the basic data of credit rating—which was sold in one standard form without IT could be converted into 30 different products (such as Dunsquest, Duns Million Dollar Lists, Duns Financial profiles, et cetera), each targeted at specific customer groups. Thus, while none of its services was sold electronically in 1978, over 70 percent of the businesses are carried out through IT.

STRATEGIC MANAGEMENT CHALLENGES

The last few years have been dramatic in terms of not only the technological developments within the IT arena but also in terms of managerial uses and exploitation of IT for obtaining efficiency and effectiveness gains in the marketplace. Even if we have to make a conservative assessment of the future trends, we arrive at two conclusions: (1) acceleration of technological developments, and (2) increased emphasis to the IT function within modern corporations.

Thus, managers—irrespective of specific industry—must seriously assess the specific potential of IT within their operations. Although it might appear that IT may not have any significant role in one particular industry at a specific time, this observation may be short-lived as creative managers find innovative uses and roles for IT and IS in the marketplace, thus changing the basis of competition.

The specific response calls for a movement away from treating the developments within the IT arena as a technological problem needing technological solutions, but toward dealing with them as business challenges that can be best solved through emerging IT capabilities. The impact of such technological trends is on the *business* domain—loss of competitive position, declining functionalities, new substitute products or processes, as well as new entrants. Thus, the domain of IT is fast emerging as a serious lever for developing and shaping strategies at different levels—corporate, business, and functional. Success will accrue to those that can creatively harness the power of IT to solve business problems.

The good news is that technological capabilities and favorable cost—performance position is upon us. The bad news is that managers have not realized the potential and exploited the technological capabilities to its fullest potential. It is beyond the scope of this chapter to even begin treating the complex issue of business transformation using IT. However, Table 9.3 is an attempt to synthesize and recapitulate the key issues made throughout the chapter that might serve to explore these issues in detail. The main thrust of this Table 9.3 lies in a movement away from traditional conceptualization of IT towards recognizing its centrality for strategic level management.

As managers begin to make the necessary changes to exploit the capabilities offered by IT, we will witness an increasing level of benefits emerging from the IT domain. As a final note, we would like to conclude that the impact and potential of IT needs to be viewed as qualitatively and quantitatively different from the past.

TABLE 9.3. Exploiting information technology: The management challenges.

Characteristics	Emerging View		
Focus	Information technology platform	NOT	Isolated information systems
Investment vision	Business transformation	NOT	Technological sophistication
Investment criteria	Business criteria	NOT	Cost-benefit numbers alone
Scope of impact	Business domain	NOT	Technological or systems domain
Executive Responsibility	Strategic (line) manager	NOT	Information technology manager
Guiding principle	Dynamic alignment between strategy and information technology	NOT	IT as a vehicle for implementing strategy

FOR FURTHER READING

Barrett, Stephanie, and Benn Konsynski. (1982), "Inter-organization information sharing systems," *MIS Quarterly*, Special Issue, 1982.

Benjamin, Robert I. (1982), "Information Technology in the 1990s: A Long Range Planning Scenario," *MIS Quarterly*, 6:11–32.

_____ and John F. Rockart, Michael S. Scott Morton, and John Wyman (1984), "Information Technology: A Strategic Opportunity," *Sloan Management Review*, 25(3): 3–10.

BusinessWeek (1985), "Information power," October 14.

_____ (1986), "Information business," August 25: pp.82–90.

Clemons, Eric K., and Michael Row (1988), "McKesson Drug Company: A Case Study of Economost—A Strategic Information System." *Journal of Management Information Systems*. Summer 1988 Vol 5 No. 1.

Fombrun, Charles, Noel Tichy, and M. A. Devanna. (1983), *Strategic Human Resource Management*. (New York: John Wiley).

Hayes, Robert H., and Steven C. Wheelwright (1982), *Restoring our Competitive Edge: Competing through Manufacturing*. (New York, NY: John Wiley).

International Business Machines Corporation (1981), *Business System Planning*. (New York: IBM Corp.).

Ives, Blake S., and G.P. Learmonth. (1984), The information system as a competitive weapon. *Communications of the ACM*. 27 (12): 1193–1201.

Keen, Peter G.W. (1981). Communications in the 21st century: Telecommunications and business policy. *Organizational Dynamics*. Autumn.

———— (1986). *Competing in Time: Using Telecommunications for Competitive Advantage.* (Cambridge, Mass.: Ballinger).

King, William R. (1978). Strategic planning for management information systems. *Management Information Systems Quarterly.* 2(1): 27–37.

———— (1983). Information as a strategic resource. *Management Information Systems Quarterly.* 7(3): iii–iv.

Malone, Thomas W., Yates, JoAnne, and Robert I. Benjamin (1987). "Electronic markets and electronic hierarchies". *Communications of the ACM.* June 1987, pp. 484–497.

McFarlan, F. Warren (1984). Information technology changes the way you compete. *Harvard Business Review.* 62(3): 98–103.

McFarlan, F. Warren, and James L. McKenney (1983). The information archipelago-governing the new world. *Harvard Business Review.* 61(4): 91–99.

McKinsey & Co. (1968). *Unlocking the Computer's Profit Potential.* (New York: McKinsey & Co.).

Porter, Michael E. (1980). *Competitive Strategy,* (New York: Free Press).

———— (1985). *Competitive Advantage,* (New York: Free Press).

Porter, Michael E., and V. E. Millar (1985). How information gives you competitive advantage. *Harvard Business Review.* 63(4): 149–160.

Rockart, John F., and Michael S. Scott-Morton (1984). Implications of changes in information technology for corporate strategy. *Interfaces.* 14(10): 84–95.

Venkatraman, N., and T.S. Raghunathan (1986). Strategic management of information systems function: Changing roles and planning linkages. Working Paper #1743–86, Sloan School of Management, MIT.

Wheelwright, Steven (1986). Manufacturing strategy: Defining the missing link. *Strategic Management Journal.* 5(1).

Wiseman, Charles (1985). *Strategy and computers: Information systems as competitive weapons.* (Homewood, IL: Dow Jones-Irwin).

10 OPERATIONS MANAGEMENT: PRODUCTIVITY AND QUALITY PERFORMANCE

Linda G. Sprague

Severe competition in world markets has focused attention on productivity and quality performance, particularly within American firms. The operations function within an organization bears the responsibility for output and, hence, for productivity and quality, as well as for cost and delivery performance. The result has been a heightened awareness of the operations function and its contribution to the effectiveness of the organization and, ultimately, for the success of its strategic plans and marketing strategies.

In well-managed organizations, this awareness leads to the development of an effective operations function that becomes part of the competitive arsenal. In too many organizations, the awareness comes too late—when the marketing campaign is strangled by lack of product, when market share slips because the competition is offering superior service, or when a financial crisis looms.

Operations management encompasses the fundamental action of an organization—the provision of goods and services. This chapter reviews a number of the concepts, techniques, and methodologies used in the design, development, analysis, and management of operations, and relates them to the strategic mission of the organization. The basic concepts of capacity, standards, inventory, scheduling, and control will provide a basic framework for the analysis of strategic options available to an organization. Central to effective operations within an organization is an understanding of the key tasks of the operations manager.

OPERATIONS FOR PRODUCT AND SERVICE ORGANIZATIONS

The United States today is the first economy in history dominated by service delivery instead of manufacturing or agricultural activity. The concepts that influenced the development of management based in the manufacturing industry are now being adapted for application to service operations. At the same time, manufacturing organizations are learning that market success requires integration of customer service with the product itself. Successful management of operations therefore requires effective management of the physical product's manufacture as well as of the services that complement it.

While it is commonplace to characterize an entire business or industry as either "manufacturing" or "service," this distinction is not useful for operations analysis. For example, International Business Machines (IBM) and Digital Equipment Corporation (DEC) are usually categorized as *manufacturing* firms. Yet fewer than 10 percent of their workforces are directly engaged in manufacturing activities. Even within a manufacturing facility, the service functions that support the actual manufacture of product often dominate the direct manufacturing workforce. Production control, quality assurance, data processing, maintenance, manufacturing, engineering, and methods—organizations that serve the manufacturing core—are service operations that demand excellence if the central mission of the firm is to be achieved.

Therefore, the focus here is on operations whether within a service industry or a manufacturing firm. In fact, at the product planning stage it makes sense to develop the combination of product and service that will be delivered to the customer. The marketing phrase *bundle of benefits* is a good description of the complete package that is being offered for sale. With this comprehensive definition of product, it is possible to better design and develop the set of operations required to carry out the marketing mission.

Examples of the product/service package being offered to the customer are common in industrial sales. Large-scale computer systems and custom-designed machine tools require substantial presale design and development and considerable engineering development of both hardware and software. After-sale service and maintenance can be more profitable than the original sale. The operations functions within the firm include service delivery in the form of the pre- and postsale activities as well as the manufacturing of any physical product.

The potential involvement of the customer in the production process sets the stage for the critical differences between service and manufacturing operations. In general, the less direct contact the customer has with the mechanisms for delivery of the product or service, the greater the opportunity to employ factory methods emphasizing high productivity and efficiency. When the customer becomes part of the process, efficiency must often be traded off against the customer's perception of quality. Extreme examples of this dichotomy include automatic tellers versus a personal banking service, a fast-food restaurant versus a chef-owned and operated restaurant, or a high-volume furniture manufacturer versus a cabinetmaker.

A FRAMEWORK FOR THE ANALYSIS OF OPERATIONS

The abundance of techniques and methodologies employed in operations easily overshadows the central problem—the provision of goods and services to the customer. Five basic concepts, interconnected, provide a framework for understanding the basic management task, as well as for selecting and exploiting the many analytic techniques and methodologies available today. They also describe the key managerial activities that comprise an organization's operations function.

These concepts drive and support the methodologies and permeate the fundamental vocabulary of the field:

- Capacity
- Standards
- Scheduling
- Inventory
- Control

The most powerful insights for management derive from first understanding these basic concepts and, then, understanding their interrelationships. Just-in-Time (JIT) systems are good examples: These are often described as methods for driving inventories down, yet no explicit attention is given to inventory in the development and implementation of a JIT system. The focus is on improved control over capacity and its arrangement, on careful attention to the design of standard methods and procedures, on elimination of schedule variability—on everything except inventory itself. Successful JIT programs result in dramatically reduced inventories through concerted attack on all four of the other basic notions. It is the relationships among the fundamental concepts that provide an organization with a framework for the design and constant development of effective operations.

Capacity and Its Management

Capacity is the ability to yield output. It is a measure of capability, a statement about the load limits of an operational system. Capacity is determined from a complex mix of the organization's resources relative to the demands on those resources, but essentially capacity is a description of the system's limitations.

In most organizations, the operations function is uniquely charged with the responsibility for developing and maintaining capacity. Given the fact that productivity is, in its simplest form, a ratio of outputs to input, management of capacity—the denominator in the productivity equation—must be the source of any substantial and sustained productivity improvement.

While capacity is often viewed as a relatively straightforward notion —"We can turn out 15,000 units a week" or "We can handle 350 customers an hour"—it is, in fact, a complex concept. For example, these statements about two organizations' capabilities are simple shorthand measures which can effectively mask important operational and customer service issues. Such brief statements about capacity are acceptable only as quick sketches: The process of definition and establishment of the organization's ability to achieve its objectives must be a continual effort.

Defining an organization's capacity requires identification of those inputs and resources that place limitations on the ability to produce—to yield product and/or service. Such an analysis of capacity can be broken down into analyses of the common components of capacity—the *determinants of capacity*. The four determinants of capacity are: *manpower, machinery, materials,* and *money*—sometimes called the "4 Ms of Manufacturing."

The idea is straightforward: The ability to yield output depends on the right mix of these elements, and whichever is in shortest supply—the key determinant—determines the capacity of the organization. Ensuring the right mix of these determinants over time is the fundamental task of capacity management. As such, capacity management is a key element in the marketing program, particularly where service is being provided.

The mix of manpower, machinery, and materials is critical for effective operation of an organization. To make matters more difficult, however, the mix within each of the elements is crucial. For example, hospital manpower must include the appropriate mix of physicians (and the specialty mix within that set), nursing personnel, technicians, housekeeping, maintenance, and so on.

As automation increases, the mix of personnel required changes dramatically. With relatively low levels of automation, the skill level profile for a manufacturing organization approximates a bell-shaped curve. However, the skill level profile required to support this increasing automatic environment changes radically. Figure 10.1 shows both profiles: The bimodal distribution of skill needs in highly automated environments consists of a number of unskilled jobs promising little growth potential for the incumbents. Examples would be general lugging and toting, opening boxes that are not delivered ready for introduction onto an automated line, and, perhaps, housekeeping and cleaning. At the other end of the job-skill spectrum are the people who maintain and support the automated equipment. Here, the job description could easily include mechanical, electrical, electronic, and computer hardware and software capabilities—all in one person.

Where service is being provided, the customer's direct experience with the process of service provision becomes a major factor in the design of capacity. As extreme examples, consider a dirty, noisy, smelly manufacturing plant staffed by surly employees, contrasted to a spacious, nicely decorated, air-conditioned, modern branch bank staffed by friendly people. Ignoring for the moment the fact that the plant is probably not meeting its productivity potential, both organizations could produce "high quality" as perceived by the customers. The perceived "quality" at the bank would drop dramatically if any one of its capacity elements were to change. If you have ever dealt with a bank or restaurant during an air-conditioning breakdown in August, you are familiar with the customer service implications of a capacity determinant failure in a service operation.

Technology—Manpower and Machinery

Manufacturing firms tend to describe their capacity in terms of physical technology, whether or not this is strictly true. From an operations perspective, "technology" means humans and their machines. A machine shop, for example, might be described as having "1000 machine hours of capacity per week" or a stamping operation as capable of "100 smacks per minute." Another common statement about capacity focuses on the output rate in terms of finished product—65 cars per hour, 100,000 gallons per day, and so on. The immediate image is of physical technology—machinery, hardware, capital equipment.

This emphasis on physical technology carries over into service operations where hotels are described by their number of rooms, hospitals by their number of beds, and banks by their dollar assets.

Such simplified capacity descriptions that focus on a single aspect of the physical technology are in common use because people in these

FIGURE 10.1. Product structure: Product life-cycle stage.

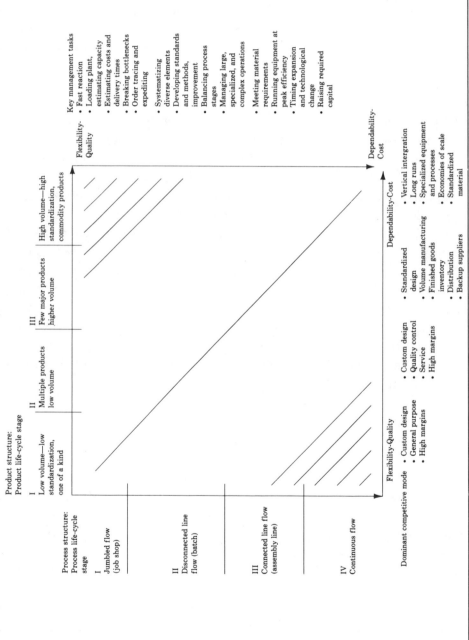

From: "Link Manufacturing Process and Product Life Cycles," R.H. Hayes and S.C. Wheelwright, *Harvard Business Review,* January-February 1979.

businesses can quickly envision their implications. An experienced hospital administrator, for instance, can almost instinctively recite the personnel implications of change from 275 to 350 beds. Similarly, a plant manager will be able to quickly provide rough estimates of the labor impact of a growth in output from 10,000 to 14,000 boards per day. These managers understand the relationships between single process or output definition and the rest of the capacity determinants.

In both instances, however, the physical technology alone does not constitute capacity. The physical technology must be matched with the appropriate labor-embodied technology—people with their skills, training, and talents, as well as "manpower" in the list of determinants. It is the mix of physical technology—machines, equipment, buildings, the physical assets—and labor-embodied technology that establishes the organization's capacity.

It is commonplace to associate physical technology with manufacturing operations, and labor-embodied technology with service operations. This association has some merit, particularly if one views extremes: The steel industry's capacity seems dominated by the massive scale of its physical equipment, and the hospital's operations expenses are dominated by personnel costs. Yet, steel industry capacity and productivity are equally determined by its steelworkers, and when a power failure occurs in a hospital, its ability to provide care can quickly drop to a life-threatening level.

The *mix* of physical and labor-embodied technology determines productive capacity for an organization. How much and what kind of each of the forms of technology are required to meet customers' needs is an increasingly complex question. This is the arena in which the economists' "substitution of capital for labor" concept becomes the issue of level of automation.

This description of technology—consisting of both the machinery and the people—is not the popular definition. To many people, "technology" implies inhuman (and likely inhumane) machinery working with a "mind" of its own. Managers who deal with the most sophisticated machinery available know only too well that an effective operational technology is possible only if the physical technology is matched with labor-embodied technology.

Technology is often the key determinant of capacity for an organization. While capacity can mean simply the raw ability to generate output, it also can mean the ability of the organization to yield variety, quality, and delivery performance. The design of an organization's capacity is indeed a competitive tool.

Material Resources

It is a rare organization that has not had to cope with the results of a material shortage. The business press focuses regularly on the extreme shortage of one type of computer chip or another, and its impact on manufacturers of products ranging from personal computers through cars, toys, and kitchen appliances. The threat of fuel shortages causes headlines because of the potential effects on medical service delivery as well as on manufacturing capability.

These dramatic shortages of raw materials critical to a particular industry make good press. Yet, on a daily basis, small crises caused by material shortages occur that do not make the evening news: Shortage of a particular blood type can halt critical surgery; delay in the delivery of the right forms has brought governmental agencies and some insurance companies to a standstill.

A vital segment of operations management focuses directly on maintaining a consistent supply of all materials necessary to achieve productive capacity, ensuring that materials will not become the key determinant of capacity.

Ensuring material supplies to operations (while part of the capacity determination) involves both the inventory and scheduling functions in an organization. Whatever the organizational structure and relationships, these functions must be carried out:

1. In a large organization, this separate department, typically staffed by purchasing professionals, has the responsibility for *materials acquisition*. The tasks range from the establishment and maintenance of vendor relationships through product and process evaluations in light of material availabilities.

2. Materials tend to be widely dispersed throughout an organization, making critical the need for sound information and control systems. *Materials storage* generates the large inventory numbers shown on many balance sheets.

3. There are three basic aspects of materials logistics—distribution from the supplier to the firm, internal movement, and physical distribution to the customer. Distribution of finished product in a manufacturing organization is often a responsibility shared between operations and marketing. This latter function, which is a critical part of the marketing plan, often requires special expertise in transportation, routes and rates, distribution channels, and so on.

Material resources are vital to effective operations. By its nature, a manufacturing operation is visibly dependent on material availability. A service operation is generally not thought to be critically dependent upon material resources. However, the result is often vast oversupply of "nonessential" materials that are loosely managed (and overstocked) because of their perceived low priority. This peculiar logic results in such phenomena as a $6 million inventory of pharmaceuticals and supplies at a large teaching hospital: That figure translates to $6000 worth of linens, disposable supplies, drugs, and so forth, per patient available at all times. As you will see in the later discussion of inventory, too much material on hand is as bad as too little.

Money

The scale and form of an organization's capacity is substantially constrained by the availability of capital. This is dramatically apparent in small, relatively new companies where a corporate form of Catch-22 is at work: To lure a large order, the firm must have substantial new equipment, but to finance this capital expenditure, the firm is required to show that the order is already in hand.

Larger, more mature organizations are more likely to have access to the funds necessary for expansion and/or replacement of physical technology through combinations of retained earnings and external funds sources. In recent years, it has become apparent that some of the techniques for justification of new technology are wanting: Justifying modern technology through labor saving alone does not allow for the incorporation of such critical market needs as product flexibility, improved quality, and delivery performance. Capital budgeting, nominally a part of the organization's financial function, can play an important role in capacity determination. In addition, if the capacity determination activity is executed effectively, the result will be improved productivity and profit performance.

Aggregate capacity planning is the first phase in the process of capacity planning. At this stage, the overall scale of operations decisions are made. It is therefore usually carried out for the longer range: The common planning horizon for aggregate capacity planning is beyond the maximum lead time of the elements of capacity. Given the long-term nature of aggregate planning, and the high cost usually associated with changes in the amount or kind of capacity, it is no surprise to find this activity as part of the strategic planning process at a high level in the organization.

Since aggregate capacity planning is a crucial part of the organization's long-range strategy development, it cannot be carried out in isolation. Market forecasts and marketing strategies, in particular, must be developed concurrently with operations plans and strategies. The operations function is dependent on the marketing function for sound information about the competitive situation and alternatives for responding to the market. Similarly, the marketing function is dependent on accurate capacity planning if products and services are to be delivered in a manner consistent with the market strategy.

One of the most difficult aspects of long-range capacity planning is the matter of technological forecasting. Typically, considerable enthusiasm for such forecasting is applied to new product development. Equal attention should be given to the impact of technological development on processes for manufacturing and for service delivery.

Capacity Configuration

Capacity configuration encompasses the philosophy of operations reflected in the spatial arrangement of physical space and equipment. This design is often embedded in architecture, where it can become an overwhelming force preventing needed change in an organization. If poorly understood, physical arrangements can be the source of serious material and information flow problems and, as a result, the source of major productivity loss.

Capacity configuration, scale of operation, and effectiveness are closely linked. As Figure 10.1 shows, two combinations of scale and configuration type are not productive—the northeast and southwest corners of the Hayes/Wheelwright product/process matrix. Maintenance of the proper balance between volume and configuration is a constant managerial challenge. Drifting off the diagonal in this matrix without understanding the implications of the situation often causes major output and efficiency crises.

The extremes of philosophies of operation are shown as the end points of the "process structure" axis in Figure 10.1. Pure end-point cases are relatively rare in practice: Mixed-mode or middle ground configurations are much more common. To appreciate the trade-offs involved, it is useful to first understand the ends of the spectrum.

In a *job shop*, the operational processes themselves set the dominant theme for the organization. This *process-dominated* capacity configuration results in groups of similar process capabilities. Traipsing through an outpatient clinic in an older hospital—from admitting (in the old building)

FIGURE 10.2.   Material requirement planning (MRP).

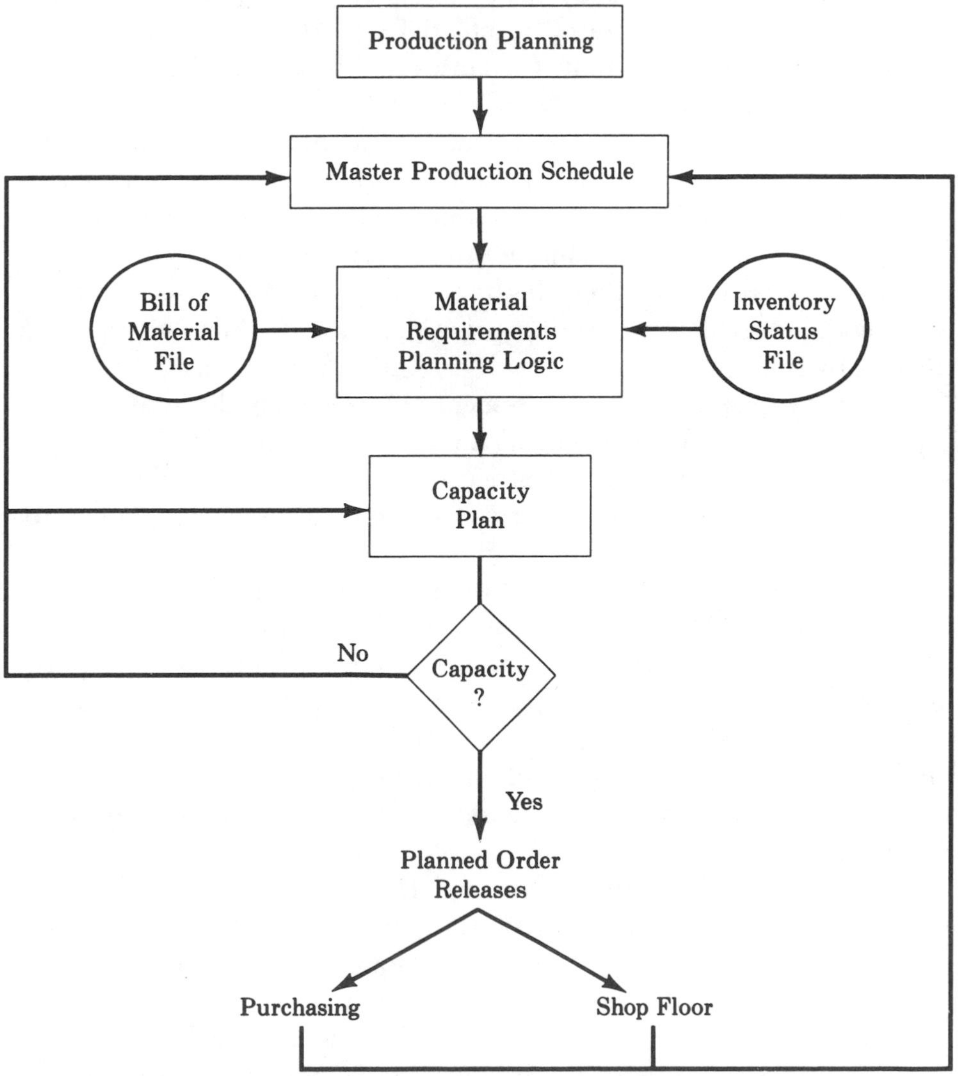

to X-ray (in the basement of the new surgical building) to the lab (on the second floor of the annex), you personally experience a job-shop configuration. Similar equipment and specialized personnel cluster in a single place, with substantial advantages: all related expertise together, permitting more effective professional supervision, training, and control. Customer service is not a primary issue.

An important characteristic of such an arrangement is the flexibility provided by the process-dominated capacity configuration. In theory, such a structure can accept any product request: Since there is no standard flow pattern through such a process, any sequence can be developed and implemented. The phrase "jumbled flow" describes the result—each "product" has its own route through and around the available capacity. For example, while you went from admitting to the lab to an examining room because of your unique treatment requirements, I went directly to X-ray, then to the lab, back to X-ray, and then to the orthopedic clinic. In a manufacturing environment with this configuration theme, any product can be manufactured in any sequence: Products requiring a sequence of milling, drilling, and grinding can be as readily accommodated as those requiring grinding, then drilling and turning, followed by finish grinding.

Capacity planning and management are extremely difficult in a job shop. Material handling and control is a constant problem, as is management of the work-in-process inventory level. Because of the diversity of demand facing each process department, high skill levels are generally required.

In an *assembly line,* the product requirements dominate and form the process structure. This "product-dominated" capacity configuration results in the regular movement of the product past the capacity requirements which are arranged in proper sequence. A physical examination at a "multiphasic screening center" or at a military induction center, provides experience with the important characteristics of this arrangement of physical and labor capacity. All incoming "clients" go through the same sequence.

In a product-dominated structure, the physical facilities are arranged in the sequence required by the product. So, if the product requires milling, then drilling, then milling again, milling capacity will be split to accommodate the requirements of the product.

The automobile assembly line is probably the most widely known—and least understood—example of this form of capacity configuration. The advantages include smooth, logical, and efficient flow of product, leading to reduced in-process inventory needs and limited material handling. Since the assembly line is dedicated to the production of a high volume of the same product, and since the work is typically broken down into very small tasks, relatively unskilled labor can be used, and training can be simple and inexpensive.

On the other hand, an assembly-line style of operation has severe limitations, the most severe of which is the line's lack of flexibility: Once a line is designed and established for one product, it is very difficult for that line to produce any other product; change in the product means change in the design of the line. A further, and often more serious, lack of flexibility is the insensitivity of an assembly line to volume changes. The classic response to a drop in volume requirements is a shutdown of the line in order to balance supply with demand.

As product volumes increase, most organizations attempt to gain the efficiencies of the product-dominated capacity configuration without losing the flexibility of the process-dominated structure. In manufacturing, modern equipment technologies have pushed the range of the effective beyond the band shown in Figure 10.1. Programmable machinery, for example, can provide flexibility along with the premium efficiencies associated with higher volumes.

The phrase *assembly line* carries a quite specific meaning in manufacturing. The essential characteristics of an assembly line are: (1) continuous uniform movement of work, (2) sequence of balanced operations, and (3) simultaneous performance. If any of these features is missing, the work is not being accomplished by a true assembly-line method.

A fundamental notion in the design of an assembly line is the concept of balance—ensuring that each station on the line has exactly the same amount of work to do in order to maintain the steady and productive flow of output. In a perfectly balanced assembly line, each worker contributes the same amount of work to the product, resulting in smooth flow and complete productivity for each person. This basic notion can also be applied at a more global level in the analysis of, for example, the movement of product through all steps from the generation of raw material to distribution to the ultimate customer.

Whether the analyses are carried out at the micro or macro level, the same rule applies: The capacity of the entire system is determined by the element with the least capacity availability, or the largest amount of work to be done. The word for this point is also the most descriptive—the bottleneck.

Two essential issues affect the management of capacity—capacity mix and capacity balance. Given the dynamic nature of demand, maintaining the most effective mix and balance is a constant struggle. It is commonplace to find, for example, an organization with its capacity perfectly mixed for last year's demand. In the determination of the organization's capacity, theoretical concepts such as economies and diseconomies of scale, learning and experience curves become the realities of brick and mortar, and of people with their talents, skills, education, and training.

Standards

Standards are the detailed time estimates that permit planning of capacity requirements for labor and equipment, and the yardsticks by which the amount and quality of output are measured. The language of the firm is generally taken to be that of accounting, measuring activity in dollar amounts. For the operations function, time is the essence of the matter— the time it takes to make something, to do some task, to provide some service.

At its heart, the establishment of standards for performance can, and often does, involve time-and-motion study. When properly performed, such a study encompasses job design as well as work and operations analysis. These techniques, often associated in the public mind with exploitation of labor and the struggles of the union movement, are widely misunderstood. Until recently, they were downplayed in most organizations. The recent corporate enthusiasm for so-called Japanese methods has brought a number of these techniques for the analysis of work back into favor.

The use of standards for planning and estimating costs, delivery, and service promises is difficult, sometimes exasperating, but it rarely causes profound organizational distress. The use of standards for evaluation and control, on the other hand, is at the heart of the majority of labor disputes.

Scheduling

Essentially the act of detailed planning, scheduling is generally understood to mean the scheduling of work to be done, either from incoming orders or from forecasts of future demand. It is the function of coordination of resources, of their allocation and arrangement, of their organization by time or place. Scheduling is the task of appointing or designating in advance a particular arrangement of manpower and physical resources to ensure that the demands of the customers are effectively and efficiently fulfilled.

An important first element of this activity is the conversion of incoming information about demand into the impact of that demand on the available capacity. In one sense, the operations function in an organization is less concerned about the demand itself than in the load that that demand imposes on the capacity. Customer service, productivity, and, ultimately, profitability depend upon the matching up of supply and demand. If capacity management can be characterized as the generation of supply, scheduling can be viewed as the linking of demand with that supply.

There are three levels at which scheduling is carried out:

1. *Aggregate scheduling:* generally done concurrently with the development of the aggregate capacity plan, this establishes the overall capability of the organization for the longer term—typically one to three years
2. *Master scheduling:* assignment of work to specific time periods, using a combination of real orders and forecasts, with a shorter time horizon—typically three to nine months
3. *Dispatching:* decision making at the point of service provision or product manufacture to match up supply and demand at execution

This hierarchy of scheduling activities sets constraints that limit the possibilities available to the shorter range activity, particularly evident when the organization links up scheduling activity with capacity planning. At the moment of execution—when dispatching occurs—the dispatcher can react only within the limits set by the capacity availability which is linked to the previously developed master schedule.

Service operations add several complications to this already difficult management task. In many situations, the "job" being scheduled is a person who will perceive the schedule, and may even resist it. The schedule itself then becomes a critical factor in the customer's perception of the service delivered and of its quality. Queue management in a manufacturing operation is the essence of work-in-process inventory control: In a service operation, it is as important to customer satisfaction as is the delivery of the service itself.

Material Requirements Planning (MRP) systems are the most widely used scheduling tools in manufacturing organizations. These computer-based information systems merge information about the structure of a manufactured product, the availability of its subassemblies and parts, and lead times with the needs imposed by forecasts and customer orders. The result is information about when parts orders must be placed, and when work on parts manufacture and assembly must begin, in order to satisfy demand.

The straightforward logic of an MRP system looks simple enough:

1. What does my customer want?
2. What do I have?
3. What do I need?

However, as Figure 10.2 suggests, this simplicity masks fundamental decisions that will affect the organization's ability to compete effectively.

FIGURE 10.3. Manufacturing resource planning (MRP II).

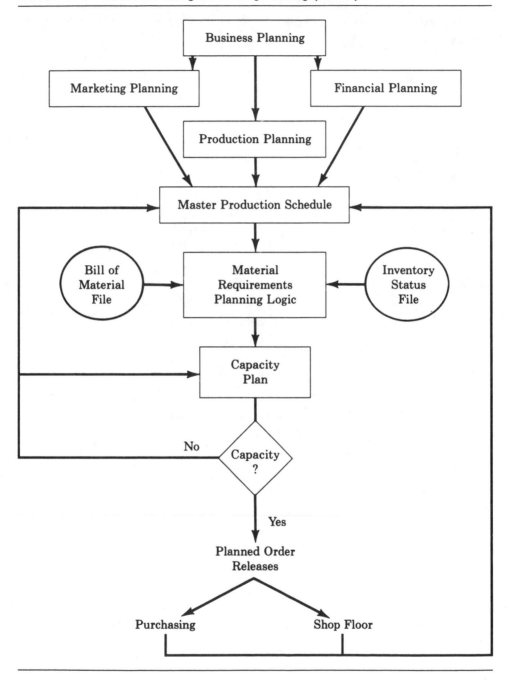

Each segment of the flow diagram represents a set of management decisions, often regarding the nature of the available capacity, which must continually evolve in order to provide complete customer satisfaction. Overall inventory positions as well as customer service performance are essentially determined by the decisions implied in the MRP system flow diagram.

More recently, Manufacturing Resource Planning (MRPII) has become popular. MRPII is the evolution and extension of an MRP system to encompass the organization's financial and market planning and, ultimately, the complete business plan. (See Figure 10.3.)

Manpower Scheduling

Most commonly, scheduling means job scheduling—routing an order through the production process, thereby generating work-in-process inventory. Difficult as this task is, it pales by comparison with a less publicized side of scheduling: scheduling customers and personnel. In job scheduling, the item being scheduled—whether a steel shaft or a circuit board—is inert and insensible to its own schedule. While any number of people may become agitated about the route, or, more likely, the amount of time it takes, the item itself remains mute.

When people are the "items" being scheduled, however, the entire picture changes dramatically. If it is customers whose schedules are being planned—through a set of medical clinics, for instance—these *people* will experience the routing and any travel or delays, as well as the service being directly rendered. The customer's perception of service quality will be affected by the schedule itself. Further, the customer will not necessarily remain inert and insensible to the schedule: Rather than waiting patiently in a queue as would a metal part, the customer may demand to be moved to the head of the queue or may resent not being so moved;

FIGURE 10.4. **Framework for operations management in a product operation.**

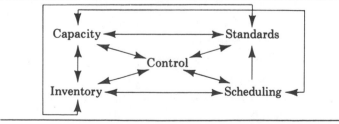

the customer may not follow instructions, and may arrive early or late; in general, the customer may not willingly participate in execution of the planned schedule, thus having an impact on the effectiveness, efficiency, and productivity of the service operation.

Any operation that does not work a regular 8-hour day, five days a week, finds itself involved in the complexities of manpower scheduling as part of capacity determination.

Inventory

Inventory is, after plant and equipment, a manufacturing firm's major asset. In certain analyses, it is treated as a "liquid" asset, although, in fact, it has no cash value to speak of if the firm is badly in need of cash. The dominant view about inventory within the financial arm of an organization is that it is money tied up—money that has been converted into an asset which should be generating returns, money that could be put to more productive use, money that is being transformed into an apparently uncontrollable form. Given this perception, it is no surprise to find that the financial arm of an organization has a simple attitude toward inventory—there is too much of it.

On the other hand, the existence of inventory permits the immediate sale of goods that take considerable time to produce. In this way, the customer is not directly exposed to the true manufacturing cycle time. The fact that a customer can order a customized product for delivery within three weeks, while the actual time to manufacture such a product is closer to three months, means that inventories are being used to provide improved customer service in the form of rapid delivery. Those closest to the customer in an organization—typically sales and marketing—will argue forcefully, therefore, for more inventory to better support the customer base.

These competing views—both of which have validity—help explain why inventory is so often an organizational "hot potato." One part of the organization sees inventory as a questionable use of the firm's money, another views it as a major contributor to the marketing strategy. Inventory management—as distinct from inventory control—involves the resolution of this dilemma to provide the best inventory system to support the organization's strategic and profit objectives.

Another view of inventory deserves mention—that of the people responsible for the physical stock itself. Inventory is composed of things— real items which must be picked up, put down, found, retrieved, moved, handled, assembled, air-conditioned, disassembled, cut, glued, stacked, and shipped. These items get misplaced and lost, they deteriorate and go out of style, rust, and rot. The physical care of stock is a nightmare that feeds directly into the enormous work-in-process inventory positions in many firms.

Those responsible for the physical stock have ambivalent feelings about it. On the one hand, the less physical material there is, the easier it is to control. On the other hand, the less there is, the more likely that whatever someone else needs will not be there. When that lapse occurs, considerable grief is usually poured onto the heads of those in charge of physical stock. The result is no surprise: From the point of view of the person well below the level of the balance sheet, more is better.

Classical theory has formed the basis of American inventory management systems and practice for decades. In the past 20 years, this theory has taken a considerable beating. It was the original target at the beginning of the MRP crusade in the early 1970s. It continues to be blamed for the magnitude of manufacturing's work-in-process stock positions in many firms.

The recent enthusiasm for Japanese methods of inventory management suggests further attacks on the traditional theory. It is worth asking if the basic rules of the game have changed. Have the earlier successes of the MRP crusade and the more recent results of Japanese-style systems confounded theory and established new rules for the management of that most pervasive and inconvenient of assets—the inventory?

This review of inventory fundamentals will begin with what we have "always known" about inventory (the classical model) and evaluate that against its decades of testing in manufacturing firms here and abroad. This history will provide the opportunity to state what we now know about both the theory and practice of inventory management. It will also show what is and is not unique about the currently popular JIT (Just-in-Time) approach.

The Classical (that is, old-fashioned) Model

Classical inventory theory, which has been the underpinning for most production and inventory control systems for more than 40 years, holds that an organization's inventory is primarily a cost generator. The profit potential of inventory has received virtually no attention, and that almost exclusively at the hands of those in distribution management. The focus has been on the use of inventory to serve a number of basic organizational functions. To put this another way, inventory has been viewed as the appropriate solution to certain manufacturing and distribution problems.

Within this context, the basic theme of inventory management and control has traditionally been to seek the lowest combination of all associated costs while solving these inevitable problems.

Cost, in this regard, has come to mean those costs captured by the firm's accounting system. Some costs and benefits of inventory are not captured or recorded in the normal cost accounting system, but these are typically ignored in favor of those readily available. Introduction of the profit implications of inventory is ordinarily accomplished through invocation of the concept of customer service with procedures for discovering the costs of service failure.

The newer approach makes a fundamental shift: It states that inventory is so powerful a cost generator that it is to be avoided. Whether any benefit can or cannot be properly recognized and ascribed is not at issue, since the basic presumption is that total associated costs of inventory will inevitably dominate these benefits.

The effect of this primary assertion is to focus attention on the problems that must be attacked directly in order to prevent the creation of "problem solving" inventories. The following examples demonstrate this approach when applied to the basic functions of inventory—or more specifically, to some problems of manufacturing and distribution that can indeed be ameliorated or solved through the use of inventories.

Variability

Variability is anathema to production processes. Whether the variability is the result of forecast error, human variety, "acts of God" or Murphy's Law, the result is the same—lowered efficiency, disruption of workflow, deterioration in customer service, and, in the end, higher cost.

The variability occurs in two forms—the predictable and the uncertain. Management responses to the problems of variability have tended to focus on inventory as the solution to the problems caused by variability. A company with basically smooth production schedules all year in the face of marked seasonal demand is building and draining an inventory to compensate for this predictable form of variability. Wherever safety stocks are set, inventories are being used to protect the firm from uncertainties in demand or in supply.

Most organizations have become so accustomed to these variability inventories that they rarely attack the sources of the variability directly. The variability is viewed as beyond the organization's control, so the resulting inventories are deemed inevitable.

Much of traditional inventory theory is devoted to the proper calculation of these inventory levels. Unquestionably, from this arithmetic, variability is costly: The cost/cost trade-offs that go into the figuring make this expense clear. Moreover, the behavioral implications will lead to even greater inventory positions than those calculated. Crises over stockouts have caused more than one inventory planner to fudge the numbers a bit, adding a "safety lead time" here and there "just in case."

Variety

The form of variability that deserves separate mention in inventory management is variety—product variety in particular. Simple arithmetic, not to mention complex mathematics, clarifies the inventory implications of increased product variety. The more options and variety available to the customer, the greater the geographic availability of the product, the greater the resulting inventory positions. There is no news here: This basic notion has been understood for decades. A central tenet of traditional inventory theory states that product and geographic proliferation causes inventory growth.

This form of variability, which will translate directly and quickly into inventory growth, generally is hidden from view. Decisions to add to the firm's product line or to widen its distribution net are typically made in an environment in which inventory implications are not carefully considered.

Permanent decreases in inventory levels require the removal of variability and variety from the product as well as from supply and demand. It is no surprise to find aggressive quality improvement and vendor relationship development programs, in addition to comprehensive management of product design, as critical elements of inventory reduction programs.

Economy

In the realm of economy, classical inventory shines. From the working hypothesis that setup, or other one-time charges, are immutable facts of life, scale economies are balanced against the costs of inventorying the resulting overproduction. This is the thrust of the Economic Lot Size (ELS) or Economic Order Quantity (EOQ) calculation.

While considerable hand-wringing transpires over the fact that data for such calculations are highly suspect, elation abounds in the end because of the robust nature of the EOQ model. The model is, in fact, insensitive to data quality, can (and does) absorb substantial error and fiddling, and still produces usable results. Delight with the model's robustness may have helped obscure the merit in attacking the data sources, in particular the realities of setup and order costs.

It takes minimal analysis to show that if setup times are directly attacked, calculated lot sizes drop. So, if inventories are to be avoided, setup and other one-time charges become natural targets.

Decoupling

Using inventories to "decouple" stations on an assembly line is the common solution to the problem of close dependency of one work site on earlier sites. The objective is to prevent the entire line from having to stop if one station on the line stops, and to compensate for individual variability at each work station.

At a larger organizational level, this phenomenon is replicated in order to permit better decentralized control of separate operations. Again, the objective is to reduce the dependency of one element on other preceding elements. The overriding concern is the specter of an idle line or entire organization because of upstream supply problems.

If, however, the cost of an idle line may be less than the cost of defects, decoupling is to be avoided. The more decoupling, the slower the response to problems—and the greater the number of defects that will likely be produced before corrective action can be taken.

Pipeline

Geographic spread as a cause of inventory build up is so well-known and understood as to be generally ignored in practice. Our colleagues in physical distribution and logistics wage the constant fight against this pervasive inventory, the more so as business moves into the international arena. One may therefore expect to find a predilection for proximity to supply embedded in newer inventory management systems.

Manufacturing inventories, however, are only part of the story. Fully developed competitive strategies include all outbound and inbound inventories from raw materials supply through to the final consumer. While American inventories continue to hold at historically low levels, remember that the sheer physical dimension of the United States will limit the drop in overall inventory levels.

Summary on Inventory

Two recent studies, one based on computer simulations and one on a survey of manufacturing firms, have come to similar conclusions. Computer simulation and analysis show that overall manufacturing performance is substantially improved through:

- Setup and lot size reduction
- Process yield improvement
- Capacity smoothing
- Increased worker flexibility
- Product structure improvement

A long-term study of American factories led to several conclusions about what factors lead to improved productivity and overall factory performance. A sustained level of capital investment in physical technology was important, but systematic programs for waste reduction and the removal of work-in-process inventory were as critical. This study also pointed to the reduction of confusion on the factory floor as a key to productivity improvement.

The attitude that inventory is so powerful a cost generator that it is to be avoided has substantial merit where manufacturing inventories are concerned. This viewpoint means that the use of inventories to solve fundamental manufacturing problems is not warranted. This decision, in turn, means that those problems must be attacked directly. Direct attack on such fundamental problems as variety and variability characterizes the Japanese production methods.

A classic example of the difference between the traditional approach to inventory control and that of the Just-in-Time (JIT) programs are evident in the Economic Order Quantity (EOQ) model. One can respond to the result of an EOQ calculation by accepting the calculated (and probably high) order quantity, or, if the theme of inventory avoidance is predominant, observe that this high number comes from a high setup, then attack the high setup.

In short, the rules of inventory management have not changed. If anything, the successes of "new" systems for inventory control have served to confirm the wisdom and rules which have been around for years. However, this substantiation is not necessarily good news: Management have not been avid adopters of the "older" methods. When it becomes apparent that the present enthusiasm for JIT and Japanese-style methods is masking the same old facts, the real risk is a return to business as usual. This reversal will signal the return to good old "Just-in-Case" inventories.

Control

The basics so far—capacity, standards, scheduling, and inventory—are determined beforehand. Capacity is configured and its scale determined, expectations about output are turned into standards, schedules are developed and posted, and inventory positions are set. The point of this is execution: making refrigerators, producing cornflakes, serving a party of four, delivering a package in 24 hours, providing emergency service to a heart-attack victim. The strategic question is: Did it work?

Control is an after-the-fact evaluation. Was the capacity there and was it properly utilized? Was the objective of avoiding any customer's waiting more than three minutes achieved? Did the shipment go out at 4:00 P.M. as promised? Was the inventory able to meet the needs of the customers? Without a control system to answer such questions, planning activities, even at the strategic level, make little sense.

There are three steps to control:

1. Observe—see what actually happened
2. Compare—study what did happen with what was supposed to happen
3. Decide—if the comparison shows that the objectives were not met, determine what needs changing, and change it to ensure success next time

This deceptively simple notion is at the heart of competitive success: the standards for comparison are closely allied with what the market demands. The most common error organizations make is to evaluate performance against historic or other more convenient standards. Reliable delivery 95 percent of the time is not the point if the competition is offering 100 percent reliability.

As Figure 10.4 shows, the five basic concepts are inextricably interrelated: For example, capacity utilization is a function of scheduling; scheduling is affected by inventory policy and practice, and inventory control can lead to improved capacity utilization. Indeed, inventory is often defined as "stored capacity," reflecting the close relationship between these two fundamental notions.

The art of operations management is working with these basics to achieve the organization's goals and objectives over time. The manager can orchestrate these concepts to meet quality, cost, and delivery performance targets.

FIGURE 10.5.   Framework for operations management in
a service operation.

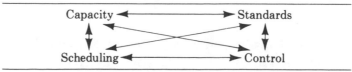

Service Operations

The operations manager in a service operation struggles against a profound problem. Since service cannot be stored, the concept of inventory has no meaning. Particularly where labor-embodied technology is involved, nothing can substitute for "production/consumption simultaneity" (the economist's term for "producing" at the same time that you are "consuming" for a successful appendectomy to occur). The manager of a service operation has neither inventory nor any of its relationships with the other four basic notions to work with. (See Figure 10.5.)

Eliminating inventory from the framework leaves a substantially curtailed set of conceptual relationships; these remaining relationships are necessarily more tightly interconnected. Managers of service operations lack an important shock absorber available to their counterparts in manufacturing operations. This helps to explain some of the productivity problems peculiar to service operations.

Effective management of service operations is in many ways more difficult than management of manufacturing. The most difficult of all is the most prevalent—management of operations comprising both service and manufacturing functions. Managing the design, development of a product—the combination of product and service performance to meet customer demands—requires continuous work with the basics. This is the famous "blocking and tackling" mentioned so often in news reports of American efforts to regain international competitiveness.

The operations function bears direct responsibility for the organization's output, productivity, and quality. Increasingly severe global competition is focusing attention on operations management and its role in positioning the organization for response to customers' changing demands. Success in the marketplace and overall profitability of the organization are dependent on operations excellence.

FOR FURTHER READING

Hayes, Robert H., and Steven L. Wheelwright, *Restoring Our Competitive Edge: Competing Through Manufacturing* (New York: John Wiley, 1984).

Ishikawa, Kaoru, *The Guide to Quality Control.* 2nd rev. ed. (Tokyo, Japan: Asian Productivity Organization, 1986). Can be purchased through Quality Resources, White Plains, New York (1-800-247-8519).

Schonberger, Richard J., *Japanese Manufacturing Techniques: Nine Hidden Lessons in Simplicity* (New York: Free Press, 1982).

Vollman, Thomas E., and D. Clay Weinbark, *Manufacturing Planning and Control Systems* (Homewood, IL: Richard D. Irwin, 1984).

11 STRATEGIC MANAGEMENT

Richard G. Hamermesh

Strategic management had its genesis in the concept of corporate strategy that was developed in the early 1960s. Faced with data from many companies in the same industry, researchers had to develop a way of understanding why some companies with very different approaches could succeed and why others that followed approaches similar to each other were not equally successful. The concept of corporate strategy provided an explanation.

These early thinkers, Edmund P. Learned, C. R. Christensen, and Kenneth R. Andrews, who were all at the Harvard Business School, formulated three major propositions to explain the data they had observed.

1. Strategy is "the pattern of objectives, purposes, or goals and major policies and plans for achieving those goals, stated in such a way as to define what business the company is in or is to be in and the kind of company it is or is to be."

2. Strategy entails two equally important and interrelated tasks: strategy formulation and strategy implementation.

3. The formulation of strategy requires the general manager to create a fit among:
   - Opportunities in the external industry environment
   - Strengths and weaknesses of the firm
   - Personal values of the key implementers
   - Broader societal expectations of the firm

As illustrated in Figure 11.1 the concept of how to formulate a strategy is both succinct and powerful. It is succinct in that it concentrates attention on the four major areas listed in proposition 3. It is powerful in that it helps to explain some of the anomalies that were suggested by the industry case studies. For example, companies can succeed with different strategies in the same industry by pursuing different opportunities (niches) within the industry that uniquely match their own internal strengths and weaknesses and the talents of their key managers. Conversely, a firm with a similar (but "me too") strategy would not be as successful if its strategy were not as consistent with the skills and resources of the firm. In the home appliance industry, for example, General Electric (GE) and Design and Manufacture are both very successful, even though General Electric's approach has been to produce a full line of high-quality branded products, whereas Design and Manufacture has produced a narrow line of private-label products. Westinghouse followed a strategy similar to GE, but lacked GE's skills and resources. Eventually, consistently low returns prompted Westinghouse to exit this business.

The power of the concept of strategy did not go unnoticed by other academics or within industry. The 1960s witnessed the first round of explosive growth in long-range planning. By the 1970s, long-range planning was renamed and reconceptualized as *strategic planning*. Soon, a number of consulting companies were formed that specialized in this activity.

In academia, Alfred D. Chandler's historical studies of the development of the modern corporation revealed important links between a

FIGURE 11.1.   Formulating a strategy.

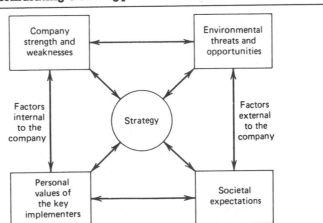

company's strategy and organization structure. Chandler's work not only inspired important subsequent research, but also underscored the important interrelationship between strategy formulation and implementation.

From these rather humble beginnings have come a wealth of research and ideas that has changed the way top managers think about and approach their task. Today strategic management is thought of as a way of managing a company whereby the overall strategy and purposes of the firm dominate decision making at all levels and in all functions of the company. No longer is it sufficient for the chief executive alone to have a sense of where the company is headed. Strategy must be communicated with sufficient clarity so that it can dominate action throughout the organization.

This chapter describes one of the most common approaches to strategic planning used in companies today and then examines some of the tough issues that arise when managers start to develop and implement strategy. First, however, observe what can happen to a company that has not carefully analyzed the nature of its business, and what that means for its ability to compete.

A COMPANY WITHOUT A CLEAR STRATEGY

On May 14, 1970, Fred Borch, the chief executive officer (CEO) of the General Electric Company, was preparing to address his senior management group about some changes he wanted to make in how the company approached strategic planning. Though Borch did not know it at the time, the changes he was about to announce not only would have a profound effect on GE but eventually would also influence the planning practices of most large, diversified American corporations. For Borch, however, the changes represented what he hoped would be the first steps in a solution to some problems that had plagued him since he became CEO in 1963.

The most immediate of Borch's problems was the profitless growth General Electric had experienced throughout the 1960s. In 1970, GE's sales were 40 percent higher than they had been in 1965, yet profits were slightly lower. This lackluster profit performance came at a time when three major new business ventures—commercial jet engines, mainframe computers, and nuclear power plants—were demanding more and more of the company's financial resources. Pressure on Borch and senior management was mounting: GE's "sacred Triple A bond rating" was in jeopardy. In response to these financial pressures, Fred Borch began to look for a new form of strategic planning.

Improving GE's financial situation and developing new planning approaches were not easy tasks. In 1970, GE was widely diversified, competing in 23 of the 26 two-digit standard industrial code categories, and the company was decentralized into 10 groups, 46 divisions, and over 190 departments. Under decentralization, the 190 departments were the basic organizational building blocks, each producing its own long-range plan and each with its own product/market scope and its own marketing, finance, engineering, manufacturing, and employee relations functions.

While decentralization had led to tremendous growth at General Electric, it presented series difficulties for Fred Borch, who not only had to comprehend and review the plans of 190 different departments, but who also had to approve or reject the ambitious investment plans that most of these departments were proposing. On what basis was he to make these decisions, when all of the departments could present convincing arguments and figures justifying investment in their businesses?

Reginald Jones, who succeeded Borch as CEO in 1972, offered me the following diagnosis of GE's problems at the time:

> Our performance reflected poor planning and a poor understanding of the businesses. A major reason for this weakness was the way we were organized. Under the existing structure with functional staff units at the corporate level, business plans received only functional reviews. They were not given a business evaluation.
>
> True, we had a corporate planning department, but they were more concerned with econometric models and environmental forecasting than with hard-headed business plan evaluation. Fortunately, Fred Borch was able to recognize the problem.

To help unravel these problems and to obtain an outside perspective, in 1969, Borch commissioned McKinsey & Company to study the effectiveness of GE's corporate staff and of the planning done at the operating level. The outcome of their report Borch was about to report to his most senior managers on May 14. He told them:

> They [McKinsey & Company] were totally amazed at how the company ran as well as it did with the planning that was being done or not being done at various operating levels. But they saw some tremendous opportunities for

moving the company ahead if we devoted the necessary competence and time to facing up to these, as they saw it, very critical problems.

In their report, they made two specific recommendations. One was that we recognize that our departments were not really businesses. We had been saying that they were the basic building blocks of the company for many years, but they weren't. They were fractionated and they were parts of larger businesses. The thrust of the recommendation was that we reorganize the company from an operations standpoint and create what they call Strategic Business Units—the terminology stolen from a study we made back in 1957. They gave certain criteria for these, and in brief, what this amounted to were reasonably self-sufficient businesses that did not meet head-on with other strategic business units in making the major management decisions necessary. They also recommended as part of this that the 33 or 35 or 40 strategic business units report directly to the CEO regardless of the size of the business or the present level in the organization.

Their second recommendation was that we face up to the fact that we were never going to get the longer-range work done that was necessary to progress the company through the 1970s, unless we made a radical change in our staff components. The thrust of their recommendation was to separate out the ongoing work necessary to keep General Electric going from the work required to posture the company for the future.

While McKinsey's recommendations addressed the problems of inadequate review of too many long-range plans, even with the reduction in the number of plans from 190 departments to 43 strategic business units (SBUs), Fred Borch still faced the formidable tasks of reviewing all of the plans and determining which of the SBUs' investment requests should be approved and which should be cut back. One GE manager noted that "Borch had a sense that he wasn't looking for lots of data on each business unit, but really wanted 15 terribly important and significant pages of data and analysis." To meet this need, GE, working in collaboration with McKinsey, developed a simple three-by-three matrix that distinguished both the growth and the profit potential of its SBUs. Depending on an SBU location on this matrix, Borch could make an independent judgment on investment proposals. The three-by-three matrix is described in greater detail later in this chapter.

The three innovations developed under Fred Borch's guidance at General Electric—SBUs, corporate review capability, and the matrix to differentiate resource allocation—formed the basis of a new approach to strategic planning at GE. Today, these concepts are commonly referred to as *portfolio planning* or the *portfolio approach to strategic planning,* and they have begun to dominate the planning practices of large American corporations.

PORTFOLIO PLANNING

What is portfolio planning and why has it been so helpful to American companies trying to define their businesses and enhance their competitiveness?

The Theory of Portfolio Planning

The portfolio approach to strategic planning was first developed in the late 1960s in work done independently at the Boston Consulting Group, at McKinsey & Company, and at the Strategic Planning Institute. Today, numerous other consulting firms and academics have developed their own versions of portfolio planning. While these differing versions can lead to different classifications of a company's businesses, on a conceptual level, the similarities among them are more noteworthy than their differences. As Bettis and Hall have concluded:

> Regardless of the particular layout for the matrix, the basic idea behind the portfolio concept remains the same: the position (or box) that a business unit occupies within the matrix should determine the strategic mission and the general characteristics of the strategy for the business.

In this study, the portfolio approach to strategic planning is defined as those analytic techniques that aid in the classification of a firm's businesses for resource allocation purposes and for selecting a competitive strategy on the basis of the growth potential of each business and of the financial resources that will be either consumed or produced by the business. While numerous portfolio planning approaches exist, only four of the most commonly used are considered here. In addition, the experience curve will be discussed because the theory underlying it was instrumental in the development of portfolio planning.

The Experience Curve

The *experience curve* was conceived by the Boston Consulting Group. Conceptually, it is closely related to the learning curves first identified in the aircraft-manufacturing industry, where the manufacturing costs of a particular airplane fell as more aircraft were produced. The underlying reason for this decline in costs was that, as greater volumes of a particular product were produced, workers and management learned to produce the product more efficiently, hence, the term *learning curve*.

The experience curve differs from the learning curve in that it applies to all costs. The hypothesized relationship underlying the experience curve is that average total costs will decline as the accumulated experience associated with selling, producing, engineering, and financing that product increases. In numerous industries, average total costs per unit (in constant dollars) have declined at a predictable rate with each doubling of accumulated production. Figure 11.2 shows the experience

FIGURE 11.2. Comparison of experience curves for two products. (a) Crushed and broken limestone. Data from U.S. Bureau of Mines. (b) Integrated circuits. Data published by Electronics Industry Association. Slopes show that costs of integrated circuits declined more rapidly with accumulated experience than did costs of crushed limestone.

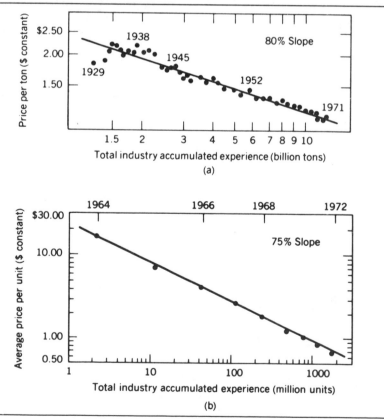

curves for two separate products. The different slopes of the curves indicate that the costs of one of the products declined more rapidly with accumulated experience than was the case with the other.

Although experience curves have been derived for numerous products, the reasons for the underlying relationship are not understood precisely. Among the most commonly cited are economies of scale in manufacturing, marketing, engineering, and financing: labor efficiencies, product standardization, and process improvements. The strategic implications of the learning curve are clearer—the company with the most accumulated experience can have the lowest costs, and therefore a company should invest rapidly and early to accumulate experience.

The Growth-Share Matrix

The growth-share matrix is a logical extension of the experience curve relationship. Its major contribution has been the conceptualization of a company as a portfolio of businesses that can be classified according to their potential for cash generation or cash usage.

The growth-share matrix uses marketshare as a proxy for accumulated experience. In theory, when competitors can exploit similar experience curves, the company with the highest marketshare will have the greatest accumulated experience and the lowest costs. With lower costs, high marketshare businesses should be more profitable, and thus should generate more cash than businesses with a smaller marketshare. Therefore, marketshare is one axis of the growth-share matrix and is a proxy for the cash-generation potential of a business.

The other axis of the growth-share matrix is market growth, which predicts the cash use of a business. Here, the posited relationship is that a rapidly growing business, with its attendant needs for new plants, equipment, and working capital, will require cash to finance its growth.

Combining marketshare and market growth has led to the development of the growth-share matrix shown in Figure 11.3. The matrix is divided into four quadrants with the following *hypothesized* characteristics:

High Share/High Growth

These businesses are in the most advantageous positions, such as those enjoyed by IBM in main-frame computers and Southland Corporation (7-Eleven stores) in retailing. They require heavy investments to sustain their growth, but their high marketshares provide high profits to finance

FIGURE 11.3.   Growth-share matrix. A business with a high market share and a
high growth rate is a "star"; one with a high market share but a
low growth rate is a "cash cow"; one with a low market share but
a high growth rate is a "question mark"; and a business low in
both factors might be called a "dog."

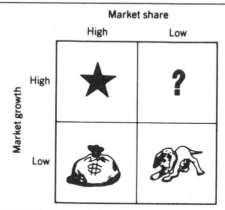

expansion. As a result, these businesses often produce as much cash as
they consume. Such businesses are often termed *stars*.

High Share/Low Growth

With their high share, these businesses produce large profits and cash
flow. However, because their industries are not growing rapidly, there is
little need to reinvest the profits for expansion. These businesses produce
a large positive cash flow; they are frequently labeled *cash cows*. An
example would be the leading department store in a slowly growing
metropolitan area.

Low Share/High Growth

Because they compete in rapidly growing markets, these businesses require large amounts of cash to finance growth. Nevertheless, their low
market share and, hence, low profitability, means that the business does
not generate much cash. These businesses are often referred to as *question marks*, *wildcats*, or *problem children*.

Low Share/Low Growth

These businesses do not require much investment but also do not produce
much cash flow. Overall they tend to use modest amounts of cash and are
commonly labeled *dogs*.

The Company Position/Industry Attractiveness Screen

Another technique for classifying businesses is the company position/industry attractiveness screen developed by McKinsey & Company in conjunction with the General Electric Company as described at the beginning of the chapter.

The company position/industry attractiveness screen is similar to the growth-share matrix with some subtle yet important differences. As can be seen in Figure 11.3, the two axes in this matrix are industry attractiveness and company position. Industry attractiveness includes market growth, as in the growth-share matrix, but also reflects such considerations as industry profitability, size, and pricing practices. Similarly, company position includes market share as well as technologic position, profitability, and size, among others. Finally, the company position/industry attractiveness screen is usually displayed as a three-by-three matrix, often referred to as a nine-block matrix (Figure 11.4).

Both matrices seek to categorize a company's cash flow position. However, the company position/industry attractiveness screen, which has a number of variables that must be factored into a single measure, is generally a more subjective tool than the growth-share matrix, a feature that its adherents applaud and its critics deride.

FIGURE 11.4. Company position industry/attractiveness screen.

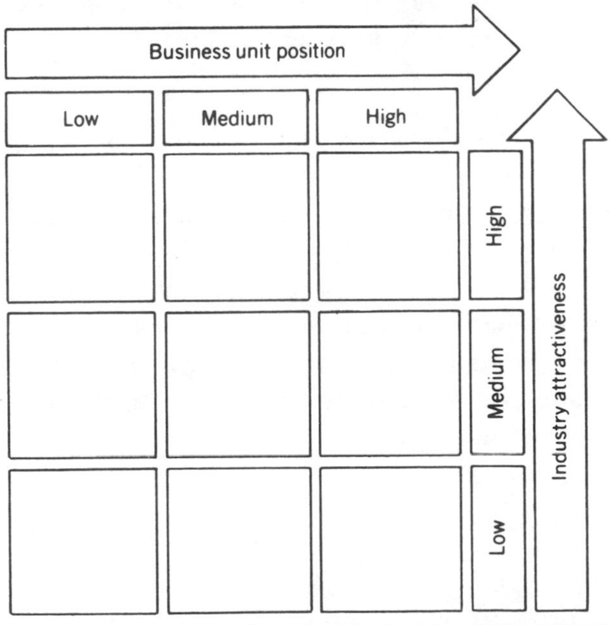

Strategic Mandates

Portfolio planning techniques can be used to classify a firm's businesses on the basis of their tendency to produce or to consume cash. These techniques can also be used for selecting a strategic mandate or basic, overall objective for the competitive strategy of a business.

If one accepts the assumptions that large corporations attempt to finance their growth from internally generated cash flow and debt (which is a generally valid assumption discussed in greater detail later), and that most markets eventually reach a mature state of slow growth, strategic mandates can be specified for each category of business. In the growth-share classification, the following strategic mandates are prescribed:

- *Stars* should receive their full share of capital and should be encouraged to invest capital to grow and maintain their strong market share positions.
- *Cash cows* should be suppliers of cash to other businesses (stars and question marks). Investment in them should be minimized, to maximize their cash flow.
- *Question marks* should be invested in, to improve their market share. Given the large amounts of capital required to move a question mark into the star category, however, most corporations can afford to support only a limited number of question marks.
- *Dogs* should be divested. With their low profitability and low growth potential, dogs are considered cash traps. Resources should not be squandered on them.

The strategic mandates for a firm using the company position/industry attractiveness matrix are similar and are shown in Figure 11.5. In both approaches, the purpose of the strategic mandates is to create a pattern of capital spending whereby a business receives funding early in its life so that it achieves a strong (i.e., profitable) competitive position. Then, as its market matures, the business will produce the cash flow that will fund other, more rapidly growing businesses. Significantly, the strategic mandates also facilitate the creation of a portfolio of businesses in which the sources and uses of funds are nearly balanced.

The PIMS Approach

On the basis of an analysis of a database containing information on the characteristics of more than 1,000 separate businesses, several PIMS

FIGURE 11.5. Strategic mandates: company position/industry attractiveness
screen.

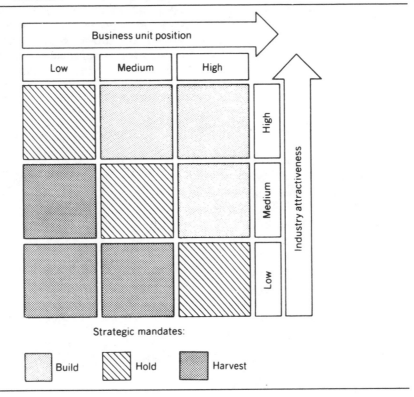

Strategic mandates:

Build   Hold   Harvest

(profit impact of marketing strategies) models have been developed that
are an additional portfolio planning tool.

The best known of these is the PAR report, which compares the
profitability (return on investment or ROI) of a particular business with
that of the other businesses in the PIMS database. It then determines
whether the ROI of the business in question is greater or less than that of
other businesses in similar circumstances. The underlying logic of the
PAR report is rooted in an equation that determines ROI on the basis of
about 30 variables. After quantification of these 30 variables for a particular business, a PAR report can be generated (Figure 11.6).

Although several PIMS models produce reports that provide strategic mandates, for our purposes, we can simply note that investment is
encouraged in those businesses whose actual and PAR ROI are high. In
other words, if a business has the characteristics of high return businesses
and is indeed earning high returns, it should be fully funded. On the
other hand, if a business's ROI is low but its PAR is also low, there is little

FIGURE 11.6.   PAR report. ROI: return on investment; PIMS: profit impact of
                marketing strategies. The average PIMS business has an ROI of
                16.7%. Business 12345 has an ROI of 33.9%. The PAR report
                explains that only 0.6 percentage point of the business's superior
                performance is attributable to the attractiveness of its business
                environment. Most of the superior performance can be attributed
                to the effective use of investment and discretionary spending to
                achieve a differentiated position.

Category	Impact on PAR ROI (pretax)%
Attractiveness of business environment	0.6
Strength of your competitive position	1.9
Differentiation of competitive position	4.1
Effectiveness of use of investment	4.5
Discretionary budget allocation	5.4
Company factors	0.2
Change, action factors	0.5
Total impact	17.2
Average ROI, all PIMS businesses	16.7
PAR ROI, Business 12345	33.9%

reason to expect much improvement in ROI, and subsequent investment is
discouraged.

The Chief Executive's Problem and Portfolio Planning

The previous discussion highlights the major features of the *theory* of
portfolio planning. This theory has been the subject of considerable
investigation as researchers have collected data and debated the existence of the experience curve and the characteristics of businesses with
different market shares and growth rates. Yet, despite these debates,
portfolio planning has persisted as one of the most widely used planning
techniques in diversified corporations. This level of acceptance can be
explained not because the entire theory of portfolio planning is beyond
question, but because key parts of the theory are responsive to one of the

major problems facing chief executives of large diversified companies: the allocation of resources. Reginald Jones described this benefit of portfolio planning as follows:

> You see, regardless of the size of a company, no company can afford everything it would like to do. Resources have to be allocated. The essence of strategic planning is to allocate resources to those areas that have the greatest future potential This is what General Electric had been lacking and what portfolio planning provided us with.

While chief executives may have difficulty telling some of their division managers that the division will not receive much new investment, portfolio-planning theory points to this necessity, so that other businesses with better prospects can be fully funded. One of the major implications of the experience curve is that if management does not invest aggressively and manage in ways that bring costs down or that make technologic breakthroughs in its strong businesses, it risks losing its advantage in those businesses to competitors that do. Significantly, this tough-minded approach toward weaker businesses enables CEOs to use portfolio planning, as Fred Borch and Reg Jones have done, to control resource allocation and to ensure that businesses with the greatest future potential are fully funded.

A broader perspective of what strategy is and what forces influence its development and implementation, then, suggests that the techniques are not (and probably never were) remedies for all strategic problems, nor are they relevant for all companies. Their effective use begins with a CEO who knows his or her own objectives, who understands the company's administrative inheritance, and who appreciates the financial constraints and strategic issues facing the company. With this as a starting point, portfolio planning techniques can be modified to fit the CEO's agenda and the company's situation.

Portfolio planning techniques never were the cure-all that some claimed. However, when properly used and modified, they can be important tools for the chief executive in administering the processes of strategy formulation and implementation.

STRATEGY: DEVELOPMENT AND IMPLEMENTATION

In 1976, the Norton Company was reassessing the strategy of its Coated Abrasives Domestic business. Beginning in 1971, the company had made extensive use of portfolio-planning techniques with outstanding results. Robert Cushman, President and CEO of Norton, commented, "Our strategic planning has made a tremendous difference in the way the company is now managed. It gives us a much needed handle to evaluate strategies for each of our many businesses."

The much needed handles to which Cushman referred were the requirements that the strategic plans of each of Norton's 30 business units be reviewed in light of a PIMS (profit impact of marketing strategies) analysis of the business and that the appropriateness of the mission to build, maintain, or harvest the business be reviewed in light of portfolio analysis.

When these tests were applied to Norton's Coated Abrasives Domestic business, the results were at odds with what both division and corporate management were inclined to do with the business. For example, the PIMS analysis revealed that the low ROI of the business was at PAR. In other words, the business was performing as well as could be expected in light of industry conditions and its competitive position. The PIMS analysis concluded that the business should be managed to lose market share gradually to maximize its cash throw-off. Similarly, a growth-share matrix analysis of the business placed it well within the dog quadrant, with the implication that the business should be liquidated or divested.

What these portfolio techniques did not take into account was the Norton Company's commitment "to remain a worldwide leader in abrasives," which originated in Norton's long-standing presence and leadership in the abrasives field. Also overlooked was the judgement of the division manager that the business faced numerous operating problems (high wages and cost structure) that could be corrected. Since Norton's planning process emphasized the involvement and commitment of line managers, the opinion of the division manager was not taken lightly.

When the time came to make as decision, these latter factors concerning Norton's traditions prevailed. Rather than the business being harvested for cash as suggested by the planning analyses, investments improved the division's cost structure and the business was given the strategic mandate to maintain market share. In discussing this decision, Norton executives indicated that, although the portfolio analyses were compelling, other strategic factors also had to be considered. Donald Melville, executive vice president, summarized this view when he explained that "We are not yet in a position where we can harvest a major segment of our abrasives business, because *that is the major guts of our company*" [emphasis added].

Three Levels of Strategy

The situation involving Norton's Coated Abrasives Domestic (CAD) business was a difficult one for top management because a number of different considerations, all strategic in nature, affected the decision. Not only did top management have to consider what approach would lead to the most success for the CAD business, but also whether the company could afford the investment required and how CAD related to the overall concept of what the company was. It is the presence of multiple strategic considerations that not only makes the job of top managers, such as those at Norton, so difficult, but that also leads to serious confusion about the definition of the word *strategy*.

The term *strategy*, or *corporate strategy*, is one of the most widely used and abused expressions in business today. As with most popularized concepts, its meaning has become more and more distorted as its popularity has grown. Today, we can read about corporate strategy, marketing strategy, functional strategy, and strategic control. Unfortunately, the result often is confusion rather than insight. For example, one common area of confusion is the relationship between financial goals and strategy. While one can debate endlessly which should come first, in practice, the two exist in a reciprocal relationship wherein strategy both shapes and is shaped by financial goals. For example, a financial goal to grow at a rapid rate will stimulate strategies to enter growth markets and either to exit mature industries or to build market share within these industries. On the other hand, commitment to a strategy of being a major player in a particular market will often result in financial goals that reflect conditions within that market.

More germane to this research is the confusion caused by the numerous definitions of strategy. This multiplicity is most unfortunate because, as we saw in the Norton example, often, different sets of strategic considerations affect an issue. What is needed is a precise definition of strategy that can distinguish among the full range of strategic issues. Moreover, a precise definition is necessary to assess the impact of portfolio planning techniques on strategy and to understand situations such as the one at Norton, where portfolio planning affects some strategic issues but not others.

To arrive at a precise definition, it is useful to define three different levels of strategy that together form the overall strategy of the firm: *business strategy*, *corporate strategy*, and *institutional strategy*. Viewing strategy as having these three levels is consistent with Andrews' original concept of corporate strategy and reflects his most recent definition:

Corporate strategy is the pattern of decisions in a company that determines and reveals its objectives, purposes, or goals, produces the principal policies and plans for achieving those goals, and defines the range of business the company is to pursue, the kind of economic and human organization it is or intends to be, and the nature of the economic and noneconomic contribution it intends to make to its shareholders, employees, customers, and communities. In an organization of any size or diversity, "corporate strategy" usually applies to the whole enterprise, while "business strategy," less comprehensive, defines the choice of product or service and market of the individual business within the firm.

Recently, other researchers, including Ansoff and Hofer and Schendel, have begun to define strategy as consisting of multiple levels or aspects. Unique in the identification of three levels of strategy are the notions of institutional strategy and of all three levels comprising the total strategy of the firm.

Business Strategy

Business strategy is commonly defined as "the determination of how a company will compete in a given business and position itself among its competitors." Business strategy, then, refers to the competitive strategy of a particular business unit. A widely diversified company with numerous business units will have numerous business strategies.

Business strategy refers to a specific description of how a business unit is to compete in its markets. Although the description includes the goals and mission of a business, it also contains the support policies that will be adopted to achieve those goals. A goal to dominate a market does not constitute a business strategy; statement of the goal must be augmented by a specific statement of what products, technologies, distribution channels, manufacturing techniques, and service policies will be employed to achieve the goal.

The strategy wheel is a useful device for illustrating the degree of specificity and consistency that must be achieved in a business strategy. As shown in Figure 11.7, business strategy has at its core the goals of the business and the concepts of how the business will compete. Of equal importance are precise definitions of key functional policies and that these policies be consistent with each other and with the objective of the business.

FIGURE 11.7.   The wheel of business strategy.

Corporate Strategy

Corporate strategy is defined as the determination of the businesses in which a company will compete and the allocation of resources among the businesses. Corporate strategy decisions include divestitures, acquisitions, new business development projects, and the allocation of resources to each business. Obviously, a single business company will not have a corporate strategy except in the sense that its corporate strategy is to compete in one business, and that it will allocate all of its resources to that single business. For diversified companies, however, corporate strategy decisions are a key concern of top managers.

Institutional Strategy

Institutional strategy refers to the *basic character* and *vision of the company*. Though he did not label it as such, Andrews referred to institutional strategy in his definition when he stated that strategy determines "the kind of economic and human organization it is or intends to be, and the nature of the economic and noneconomic contribution it intends to make to its shareholders, employees, customers, and communities."

IBM is an example of a company that has a particularly well-defined institutional strategy. The strategy began with the vision of Thomas Watson, Sr., that the company would become a major worldwide enterprise. This vision long preceded the advent of the computer and was described in a 1940 *Fortune* article:

> "Ever onward," he told himself. "Aim high and think big figures; serve and sell; he who stops being better stops being good" . . . Mr. Watson caused the word **THINK** to be hung over the factory and offices. . . . Let him discourse on the manifest destiny of **IBM**, and you are ready to join the company for life.

IBM's institutional strategy has developed considerably since the days of Watson's exhortations. Today, company publications stress three basic concepts that define the character of the company and serve to guide the organization's choices and behavior:

1. *Respect for the individual*—respect for the dignity and the rights of each person in the organization
2. *Customer service*—to give the best customer service of any company in the world
3. *Excellence*—the conviction that an organization should pursue all tasks with the objective of accomplishing them in a superior way

As illustrated by IBM, a company's institutional strategy may pertain to its employees, to its customers, to its markets, or to how it competes. Some brief characterizations of each of these kinds of institutional strategy are listed in Table 11.1. In all of these examples, institutional strategy provides the *basic concepts* and *beliefs that guide the organization's choices and behavior*. Because institutional strategies embody what Donaldson and Lorsch referred to as the company's belief system, organization members tend to identify and agree with the institutional strategy or leave the company. The comment of an employee of the Lincoln Electric Company is typical, "It's like trying out for the high school football team. If

TABLE 11.1. Characterizations of institutional strategies.

Pertaining to	Company	Institutional Strategy
Employees	Lincoln Electric	Guaranteed employment and wages for all workers in proportion to their productivity
	Delta	A family feeling
	Hewlett-Packard	Innovative people at all levels
Customers	Caterpillar	Spare parts availability within 24 hours around the world
	IBM	Customer service
	McDonald's	Fast service, consistent product, low price
Manner of competing	Hewlett-Packard	High value, high margin, and innovation
	Texas Instruments	High volume, low margin, low costs
	McDonald's	High quality
	3M	Product innovation
Markets	Procter & Gamble	Packaged consumer products
	Dexter Corporation	Specialty industrial markets

you make it through the first few practices, you're usually going to stay through the whole season, especially after the games start."

However, institutional strategy is not the same thing as a corporate culture. In the sense that every organization has norms and accepted rules of behavior, all companies have a culture. Yet, all companies do not have institutional strategies, because the concept includes not only basic principles, but also a vision of where the company is headed and how it will operate. Vision is what has directed IBM's total attention to the opportunities created by the advent of data processing; it is a specific concept of what a company is trying to become. Writing in the *McKinsey Quarterly,* Fred Gluck has described the following characteristics of vision:

> the visions of the successful, excellent companies we have discussed were based not only on a clear notion of the markets in which they would compete, but also on specific concepts of how they would establish an economically attractive and sustainable role or position in that market. They were powerful visions grounded in deep understanding of industry and competitive dynamics, and company capabilities and potential. They were not mere wishful thinking as is the case with so many incomplete visions . . . the visions were generally directed at continually

strengthening the company's economic or market positions or both in some substantial way.

During the past two decades, the importance of institutional strategy has often been overlooked as attention has instead been focused on techniques of strategic analysis and issues of business and corporate strategy. Not surprisingly, in a paper delivered two years prior to publication of *In Search of Excellence*, Tom Peters reported that in a survey he conducted of 65 companies, only 13 (20 percent) had a strong set of beliefs that guided their actions. Interestingly, these 13 companies significantly outperformed the other companies in the sample.

Recently, several very popular books have pointed to the importance of corporate culture, superordinate goals, corporate values, and corporate belief systems. These books and concepts have served the important function of redirecting the attention of managers to these significant determinants of the success of their companies. However, the concepts, which only describe existing norms and practices, do not by themselves constitute an institutional strategy unless they are combined with a vision of the company's future purposes and objectives. In his fascinating description of Schlumberger and its CEO Jean Riboud, Ken Auletta has aptly described what we mean by institutional strategy. Auletta first described Schlumberger's strong norms of excellence and independent thought, and termed them "the Schlumberger Spirit." But he then added that CEO Riboud is concerned that the company will become complacent and therefore devotes his time to assuring that the Schlumberger Spirit is flexible enough to recognize and meet future challenges:

> One of Riboud's preoccupations is that Schlumberger will lose its drive as a company and grow complacent—a concern he had discussed on the plane to Houston. "Any business, any society has a built-in force to be conservative. The whole nature of human society is to be conservative. If you want to innovate, to change an enterprise or a society, it takes people willing to do what's not expected. The basic vision I have, and what I'm trying to do at Schlumberger, is no different from what I think should be done in French or American society." In other words, sow doubt. Rotate people. Don't measure just the profits in a given division—measure the man in charge, too, and his enthusiasm for change. . . .
>
> Summing up, Riboud said, "If we lose the drive, and fear searching for new technologies, or fear taking incredible gambles on new managers," or fear to heed the voices of "other countries and cultures, then we will become an establishment." If that happens, Schlumberger may remain powerful and profitable for the moment, but ultimately it will decline. "It's easy to

be the best," Riboud has said many times. "That's not enough. The goal is to strive for perfection."

Institutional strategy, like business and corporate strategy, can be managed and directed by strong corporate leadership. Just as top management is considered responsible for the quality of business and corporate strategies, it is similarly accountable for institutional strategy.

Implications

The three levels of strategy just described have their roots in the writings of many authors. They have been developed here to help explain the impact portfolio planning systems have on strategy. Simply put, the experiences of the companies studied suggested that portfolio planning had had or was having a substantial impact on some strategic issues and a negligible effect on others. In the Norton Company, for example, we saw that initially, portfolio planning had little impact on institutional strategy. Since institutional strategy was one of the main determinants of the objective to adopt for the Coated Abrasives Domestic business, portfolio analyses played a minor role in the final decision. Norton is only one company and one example. However, with additional data, the concept of three levels of strategy should enable us to state more precisely the level or levels of strategy on which portfolio planning has had its greatest impact.

Strategy Development and Implementation

The concept of three levels of strategy can help not only in assessing the impact of portfolio planning, but also in understanding the processes of strategy formulation and implementation. This assessment is especially significant in light of the importance of implementation and strategy development, and the slow progress in understanding them. Indeed, the academic literature on these topics has been bogged down in debates over whether formulation and implementation are separable, and which of the processes precedes the other.

One means to dismiss these arguments is simply to acknowledge that strategies are constantly changed and revised. Once a strategy is developed, managers begin to implement it. When problems or new opportunities are encountered, the strategy is often revised. Thus, the processes of strategy development and implementation are both continuous and symbiotic.

While the research undertaken for this book has confirmed the interrelationship of strategy formulation and implementation, it has also pointed to differences in how the three levels of strategy are formulated and implemented, and to important links between the processes. The notion that all three levels of strategy are being developed and implemented simultaneously and are constantly influencing each other is admittedly a complicated one. A clear understanding of what these processes entail at each strategic level can enable us to move from academic questioning of whether implementation takes place (a phenomenon to which any executive will readily attest) to understanding how the formulation and implementation of each level of strategy affect the other levels and are influenced by portfolio-planning techniques.

Strategy Development

Strategy development refers to the processes by which each of the three levels of strategy are formed. The terms strategy development and strategy formulation are used interchangeably here. Henry Mintzberg has suggested that strategies are developed in one of three ways: They are conceived as the entrepreneurial insight of one individual, they develop in an ad hoc manner as a result of the organization's reacting to current problems, or they develop as the result of systematic planning and analysis.

While this list could be expanded or modified, the point is still the same—there are a variety of approaches to development of strategy. In addition, the process can involve different people or levels in the organization, ranging from the chief executive to division managers. As shown in Figure 11.8, the combination of how strategy is developed and who develops it provides a more complete description of the strategy development process. A statement that a company uses formal planning, for example, is not a complete description of how it sets strategy, unless the statement also specifies who in the organization is involved in the planning effort. There is a great difference between the CEO and his or her staff's developing formal plans for a division and a division's preparing the plan itself.

Finally, it is important to recognize that, since there are three levels of strategy (institutional, corporate, and business), each must be developed, and often the processes are different. Figure 11.9 illustrates how these three factors—how, who, and at what level—combine to describe the entire strategy development process. For example, in one company, institutional strategy may be set by the CEO as a result of private insights, while business strategy is developed by planning teams in the divisions,

FIGURE 11.8. Strategy development.

What level develops strategy?

	Corporate management	Middle management	Division management
Entrepreneurial insight			
Ad hoc adaptation			
Systematic planning			

How is strategy developed?

FIGURE 11.9. Development of the three levels of strategy.

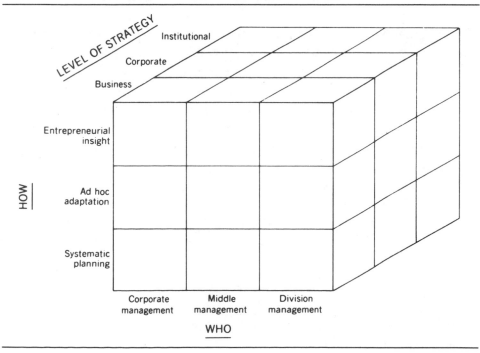

315

and corporate strategy emerges as the result of decisions at all levels of the organization. Such a company would be guided by the CEO's sense of overall purpose and would produce well-developed business plans, but it would still be keeping its options open as to acquisition, divestiture, and resource allocation choices. In another organization, both institutional and corporate strategy may be established at the corporate level as the result of detailed planning, while business strategy is developed in an ad hoc manner at the divisional level. This description probably is typical of those conglomerates that have thought in detail about acquisitions and divestitures, but have given less thought to the management of ongoing businesses.

Numerous ways to develop strategies are exemplified in the companies I've studied. This variety points to the need for adjustment of the use of portfolio planning techniques to conform to the ways a company develops its strategies.

Strategy Implementation

Strategy implementation is the process of ensuring that strategy is embodied in all that an organization does. The objective of implementation is to create fits between strategic objectives and the company's daily activities. For each level of strategy, important differences occur in the implementation task.

Implementation of business strategy requires the creation of *functional and administrative fits*. The creation of functional fits refers to the adoption and execution of policies in each of the functions—marketing, manufacturing, engineering, and finance—that reinforce the strategy. The following example illustrates how difficult this task can become:

> The manager in charge of a business that previously competed by producing unique products to order specifications, embarked on a new aggressive strategy. He believed he could increase the business's market share by selling the value of product availability rather than technology alone. The key to his approach was to release certain models to manufacturing before firm orders were in hand, thereby significantly shortening the delivery cycle.
>
> Months later, this manager began to have second thoughts about this idea. For one thing, the models built-in anticipation of demand required costly rework in order to match them to the orders ultimately received. Furthermore, customer complaints made it crystal clear that the publicized reduction in the delivery cycle had not been met. Missed schedules were also creating costly penalties.

An investigation proved the root of these problems to be the measurements used in district sales offices. For years, the bonuses of the sales engineers had been based on the dollar size of orders. Such a system prompted the engineers to give full rein to their customers' normal inclinations to demand tailored products rather than to worry about which model the customers ordered. Allusions to "king customer" were taken quite literally by field personnel. They did not recognize that their general manager's new strategy required a particular response from them.

This example illustrates many of the problems general managers encounter when trying to create the functional fits essential to the implementation of business strategy. Communicating strategy to the functional vice presidents (or even involving them in the strategy formulation process) is not always enough to ensure that functional policies reflect the strategy. This lack is because the basic character of the functions often leads to ingrained behaviors that are not easily changed simply because a general manager announces a new business strategy. Manufacturing's drive for standardization, marketing's for customer responsiveness, engineering's for innovation, and finance's for cost control are all natural functional postures that extend deep into each functional area. Yet, despite the difficulty of the task, these functional biases often just succumb before a business strategy can be achieved.

The other task of implementation of business strategies is the creation of administrative fits that assure that the business's systems and processes are consistent with and reinforce the strategy. These systems and processes include the organization structure, information systems, incentive and control systems, and decision processes. As with functional fits, the devising of each of these systems and processes so that it reflects business strategy is a difficult task requiring the involvement of the general manager, not only that of staff specialists.

Implementation of corporate strategy involves different tasks than does implementation of business strategy. To the extent that each corporate strategy concerns itself only with the acquisition and divestiture of businesses, implementation requires merely assembling the necessary staff resources to do the appropriate analyses and developing the contacts in the investment community to assure that acquisition candidates are brought to the attention of management. When the corporate strategy also concerns itself with the relative allocation of capital to the divisions and with the greater growth of some businesses than others, the task of implementing corporate strategy is more complex. Here, implementation requires creation of the appropriate organizational context—incentives, autonomy, level of responsibility—between the divisions and the corporate level, so that each division will indeed pursue the objectives that the corporate level has in mind for it.

Implementation of institutional strategy is an obscure process and has only recently attracted the attention of researchers. It involves the important tasks of choosing and educating (indoctrinating) employees as to the vision and values of the company and of managing the company over a long period consistent with those beliefs and objectives. Indeed, one of the distinguishing features of the companies cited in books such as *In Search of Excellence* and *Corporate Cultures* is the long time that they have adhered to their institutional strategies. Implementing institutional strategy seems to require consistency among many small actions and managerial practices over a long period. As Tom Peters has noted, "Repeatedly and conspicuously, the chief executive officers of these companies exhibited a common pattern of behavior: namely, obsessive attention to a myriad of small ways of shifting the organization's attention to the desired new theme . . . consistency in support of the theme, usually over a period of years."

Relationships Between Strategy Development and Implementation

In managing the development and implementation of the three levels of strategy, the CEO must keep all three of the strategies consistent with the demands of the external environment and with each other. One view of how CEOs manage this process is the sequential one shown in Figure 11.10, wherein each level of strategy is first formulated and then implemented. Implicit in this view are the assumptions that strategy is set in a top-down manner and that formulation and implementation are discrete, independent activities.

FIGURE 11.10.   A sequential view of the strategic process.

Institutional strategy formulation
↓
Institutional strategy implementation
↓
Corporate strategy formulation
↓
Corporate strategy implementation
↓
Business strategy formulation
↓
Business strategy implementation

While this sequential view is quite rational and is consistent with common prescriptions of how to use portfolio planning, it is not an accurate description of the strategic process. In most companies, strategy is set and achieved as the result of a continuous process of adjustment between the formulation and implementation of each level of strategy. This interactive view of the strategic process is illustrated in Figure 11.11. Admittedly, this view is more complicated than the sequential one, but it does describe common strategic processes unaccounted in the sequential view. The first of these is bottom-up strategy development, wherein a strategy is conceived at a low level of the organization, is gradually implemented, and eventually affects the entire strategy of the firm. The interactive view is also consistent with the notion that strategies emerge over time, rather than being conceived at one point by "one big brain" at the top of the organization. This notion is similar to Quinn's conclusion after studying strategic change in nine companies:

> Dramatic new sets of strategic goals rarely emerge full blown from individual bottom-up proposals or from comprehensive corporate strategic planning. Instead, a series of individual, logical, and perhaps somewhat disruptive decisions interact to create a new structure and cohesion for the company. Top managers create a new consensus through a continuous,

FIGURE 11.11.   Interactive view of the strategic process.

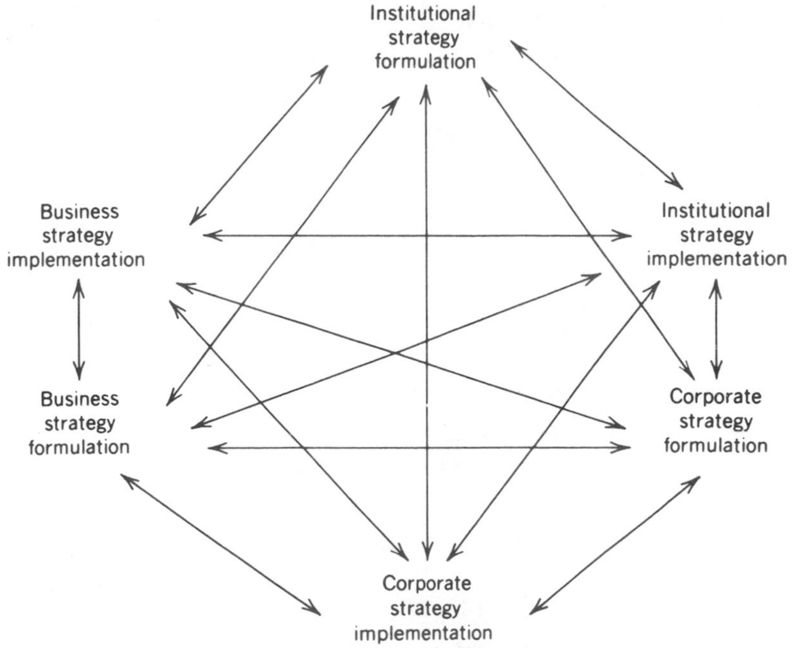

evolving incremental, and often highly political process that has no precise beginning or end.

The notion that the strategic process is interactive and continuous implies a need for top managers to adjust the way in which a technique such as portfolio planning is used. For, as a tool of rational analysis, portfolio planning conceives of strategies as being set at the top of the organization and cascading downward in a series of market share and cash flow objectives for each business unit. For those companies that instead make these decisions in a continuous process of discussions among many levels of the organization, the ways in which portfolio planning is used need considerable modification.

THE FORCES SHAPING STRATEGIC DECISION MAKING

In 1980, one of the companies I studied faced an interesting acquisition decision. This company, which was intensely serious about applying sophisticated strategic planning and resource allocation procedures, competed in five major business areas, each of which was headed by a group vice president. Of these five, the group in question competed in a slowly growing industry and had been given the status of a cash cow with a strategic mandate to hold market share and to produce cash. The group vice president was one of the most senior and respected executives in the company and over the years had done an excellent job of running the group in accordance with its strategic mandate.

The group proposed in 1980 to make a major acquisition that would give it entry to a growing segment of its industry. The group and its management strongly supported the acquisition even though, at a cost of $30 million, it would not be cheap and would be inconsistent with their mandate to produce a high cash flow.

The CEO of the company, who had held the position for only a few months and was several years younger than the group vice president, had serious reservations about the acquisition. First, the expenditure contradicted the strategic mandate of the business to produce cash and only to maintain market share. Second, the investment left the group dependent on the same customers to whom its already slowly growing products were sold. On the other hand, the new CEO wanted to foster risk taking within the company and knew that the company as a whole could afford the acquisition.

When the time came to decide the issue, the CEO told the group vice president that he would prefer that the acquisition not be made. But if the group vice president were able to raise the funds from within his group, the CEO would not object.

Within days, the group vice president was able to get the business units within his group to budget the necessary funds. Two months later, the acquisition was consummated.

This example is typical of many that I had observed. It shows a major strategic decision being influenced by more than portfolio analysis. Not to denigrate the importance of portfolio planning or other analytic tools, such as industry and competitive analysis or scenario planning. They have had a major impact on strategic decision making. In the company just described, for example, portfolio planning was one of the major forces that led to the divestiture of several weak businesses and to changes in the strategies of several others. Nonetheless, in making the acquisition decision, other factors, such as the seniority of the group vice president, the relatively new status of the CEO, and the CEO's interest in fostering risk taking, also influenced the decision.

While endless lists of factors that shape strategic decisions could be developed, the situations studied in this investigation repeatedly pointed to three forces in addition to portfolio and other forms of strategic analysis that played a role in shaping strategic decision making: administrative considerations, financial constraints, and the CEO's agenda and management approach (Figure 11.12). Interestingly, with the exception of the

FIGURE 11.12. Four forces shaping strategic decision making.

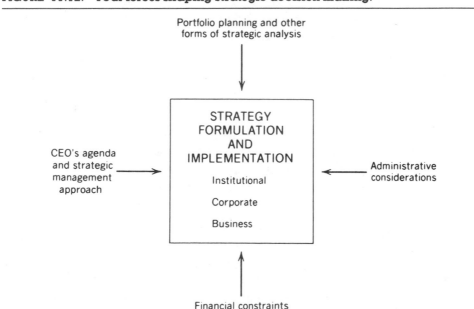

last factor, these forces correspond closely to what Donaldson and Lorsch's study of top management decision making in 12 companies called the three primary constituencies whose expectations top managers must meet. My delineation of the CEO as an additional major force in strategic decision making is not inconsistent with their findings, but it does place additional emphasis on the crucial role chief executives play in shaping strategy.

Administrative Considerations

Portfolio planning and other forms of strategic analysis attempt to provide an objective assessment of a company's competitive strengths and weaknesses in the markets within which it operates. Administrative considerations, financial constraints, and portfolio planning and other forms of strategic analysis correspond to what Donaldson and Lorsch termed the organizational constituency, the capital market constituency, and the product market constituency.

Such planning includes analyses of demand, industry structure, technological changes, raw materials supply, competition, and market segments. Portfolio planning is a useful device for helping to make these assessments and are thus one of the forces that shape strategic decisions. Portfolio analysis and most other planning techniques have the common characteristic of focusing on the link between a company and its product market environment, while they typically overlook the relationship between the firm and labor and government. This is a nontrivial oversight in light of the significant effect government policy and labor relations can have on a company's results. While this limitation is important, it was not studied explicitly in this research.

As was illustrated by the acquisition decision, however, strategic decisions are also determined by administrative considerations. These considerations are reflected in organizational structures, systems, and processes and in the individual managers who not only make strategic choices but who also must translate these decisions into reality.

In a large diversified company, usually three sets of administrative considerations shape strategy. The first is the opinion of members of the company's *dominant coalition*. The dominant coalition refers to that limited number of employees who determine the organization's basic policies. The members of the dominant coalition, in addition to the CEO, may include other senior executives such as vice chairpersons or executive vice presidents, influential board members, large shareholders, and some experienced division managers. Although the membership of the dominant coalition will change over time, the opinions of this group are a major determinant of how strategies are formulated and implemented. For example, in the acquisition decision previously discussed, the fact that the group vice president was a senior executive with a long track record of excellent performance made his support of the acquisition a force with which the CEO had to reckon.

The second set of administrative considerations that affects strategic decision making is the *opinion* and *commitment of the top managers of affected divisions.* For example, if the strategy of a division is being reappraised, the knowledge and opinions of the division managers will nearly always be solicited. Of course, the managers are not free to pursue any strategy they wish. However, if they are not committed to or doubt the wisdom of a particular strategy, rarely will a chief executive not factor this consideration into the decision making. Sometimes, this deliberation results in a slowdown in strategy formulation and implementation, while in other cases, division managers are replaced. The important point is that the affected managers' level of commitment to a course of action is an important administrative consideration that shapes how and what major decisions are made.

Finally, strategic processes are shaped by *an organization's ability and capacity to implement a particular strategy.* An otherwise brilliant strategy that cannot be implemented or that would undermine morale is often not worth pursuing. Andrews has made the following observation to explain the important role of an organization's ability to implement strategy:

> Since faulty implementation can make a sound decision ineffective and effective implementation can make a debatable choice successful, it is as important to examine the processes of implementation as to weigh the advantage of available strategic alternatives.

The significant impact that administrative considerations can have on the behavior of organizations has led some researchers to argue that large organizations cannot be purposefully directed and instead can make only incremental decisions that satisfy the needs of various organizational subgroups. However, while administrative considerations can play a significant role in shaping strategic decisions, purposeful top managers can recognize and deal directly with political and administrative aspects of their organizations. In this regard, Bower has been most explicit:

"Politics" is not pathology, it is a fact of large organization. Top management must manage its influence on "political" processes and then monitor the results of its performance.

Finally, it is important to recognize that, while administrative considerations are one of the major forces shaping strategic choices, they are not the only ones. Indeed one of the major conclusions that Quinn drew from his study of strategic change in nine major companies was that both political and strategic factors influence change:

> All my data suggest that strategic decisions do not come solely from political power interplays. Nor do they lend themselves to aggregation in a single massive matrix where all factors can be treated quantitatively or even relatively simultaneously to arrive at a holistic optimum.

Financial Constraints

The way in which the top management of a company approaches strategic decisions is also affected by the company's financial constraints. Not reaching financial goals can have the same effect on decision making as increasing financial constraints. In the companies studied here, however, the extent of financial constraints played a more significant role in shaping strategic decision making. All companies face financial constraints in the sense that none has an endless supply of capital available. But companies do differ in the degree to which they are dependent on the external capital markets and in how much of a cushion exists between their need for funds and their internally generated sources of cash. The more these internal sources of funds exceed a company's need for capital, the less financially constrained the company is. Not surprisingly, most managements try to reduce their dependence on external capital markets and work to make their companies financially self-sustaining.

When a company must rely heavily on external sources of capital, its overriding goal is to restore itself to a position of financial self-sufficiency, and this, in turn, can have a profound effect on strategic decision making. As Donaldson and Lorsch have noted, this effect is often reflected in a greater emphasis on return on investment:

> During times of heightened financial uncertainty or stress, these managers will also be particularly mindful of the rate of return on investment because of the importance accorded this figure by professional investors . . . .Therefore, the company's growth is secondary to its rate of return.

Most companies behave as if they were facing severe capital constraints long before a threat of bankruptcy, one again because most companies attempt to finance their growth from internally generated capital, profits, and depreciation. New equity is rarely issued, and debt is issued only within the limits of maintaining a targeted capital structure. When a company attempts to maintain a constant or slightly increasing dividend level and a stable capital structure, it is highly dependent on the profitability of current operations to fund its new investment. Consecutive decreases in either sales growth or profit margins will severely reduce the size of the capital budget and will necessitate difficult choices among investment projects competing for limited funds.

These points can be illustrated by projecting the income statement and the balance sheet of a hypothetical $500 million company. Table 11.2 shows the projected financial performance of such a company. The company is anticipating an annual sales growth of 15 percent and a 20 percent pretax return on sales for each of the next five years. The important numbers to note are the cash available for capital expenditures each year. These numbers total $104 million over the five-year period, meaning the division managers of this hypothetical company know that approximately $104 million is available for capital projects over the next five years.

Should sales growth or the return on sales decrease, the cash available for capital expenditures will fall dramatically. Figure 11.13 illustrates the implications of such declines. In Model 2, sales growth slows

TABLE 11.2. Projected performance with 15 percent sales growth and 20 percent profit margin ($ million).

Item	Performance ($ Million)				
	Year 1	Year 2	Year 3	Year 4	Year 5
Sales	500	575	661	760	874
Pretax profits (before interest)	100	115	132	152	174
Net earnings	48	56	64	73	84
Dividends	19	22	26	29	34
Total assets	386	448	521	604	701
Current liabilities and debt	186	215	249	288	333
Equity	200	233	272	316	366
Cash Flow Analysis					
Net cash flow	51	58	67	77	88
Less: Expenditures for asset replacement	35	40	46	53	61
Cash available for capital expenditures	16	18	20	23	27
Cumulative cash available for capital expenditures	16	34	54	77	104

FIGURE 11.13.   **Funds available for capital expenditure under three performance scenarios. Model 1 has a constant growth rate and constant margins, Model 2 has a moderating growth rate and falling margins, while Model 3 has a falling growth rate and deteriorating margins.**

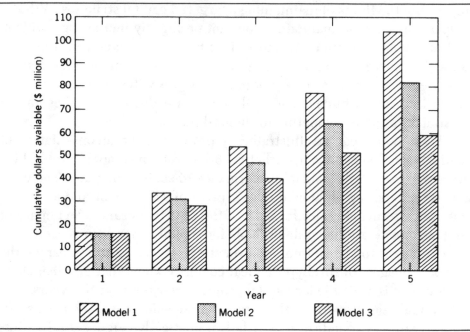

from 15 percent in the second year to 12 percent in the fifth year, while pretax return on sales falls from 20 percent to 16 percent. In Model 3, the declines are steeper, with sales growth slowing to 9 percent in year 5 and pretax returns falling to 12 percent. In these models, however, *the company is still profitable and growing;* the only changes are *slower-than-expected* sales growth and lower profit margins.

Given that this company attempts to maintain the same capital structure and fairly stable dividends, the impact on the capital budget is dramatic. As shown in Figure 11.13, by year 5, the cash available for capital expenditures has fallen to $82 million in Model 2 and to $59 million in Model 3. This decline in the capital budget, from an expected $104 million to either $82 or $59 million, would in turn put tremendous pressure on corporate management to limit the allocation of scarce capital to divisions demanding more funds than the corporation can supply.

Companies that are financially constrained, then, face different strategic and resource allocation problems than companies that are not. The top management of capital-short companies is in need of tools, systems, and procedures that will help it in the unpleasant tasks of rationing capital and encouraging strategies of consolidation and focus. Companies in a strong financial position must still be vigilant in the allocation of resources, but the problem facing their top managers is more one of encouraging their divisions to propose enough high-return projects and to pursue broad enough strategic objectives.

These diverse postures and needs do have an important effect on strategic decision making. For example, in the acquisition decision described earlier, the fact that the company had been producing cash surpluses in recent years and was in a very strong financial position had a positive effect on the decision to approve the $30 million expenditure. Had the opposite been true, a much different decision might have been made.

The CEO's Agenda and Management Approach

The last force that repeatedly plays a major role in the shaping of strategic decisions is the CEO. Simply put, business organizations do respond to the desires (and even the whims) of their chief executive. To understand how strategic decisions are made or how a tool such as portfolio planning is used, the goals and management approach of the CEO must be closely examined.

The CEO's Agenda

There is no dearth of theory about what the job of the CEO entails. There is also little consensus. For example, a large body of literature attests to the overwhelming impact of the CEO on corporate affairs and to the importance of appointing to the job someone with broad vision and leadership skills. According to this view, CEOs are in the center of decision making and have clear ideas about what business, corporate, and institutional strategies they want to achieve. Others, however, point to the limited power of CEOs and to the diversity of large companies, which make it virtually impossible for the CEO to understand all of the businesses and markets in which the firm competes. According to this view, the CEO cannot possibly formulate strategies, and this task is dispersed throughout the organization.

These views can be reconciled, however, by recognizing that most chief executives pick a few issues on which they focus their attention. As described by Wrapp:

The second skill of the good manager is that he knows how to save his energy and hours for those few particular issues, decisions, or problems to which he should give his personal attention . . . .Recognizing that he can bring his special talents to bear on only a limited number of matters, he chooses those issues which he believes will have the greatest long-term impact on the company, and on which his special abilities can be most productive. Under ordinary circumstances he will limit himself to three or four major objectives during any single period of sustained activity.

In other words, for three or four major issues, CEOs do become deeply involved in the outcome of strategic decisions. For other strategic questions, however, the substantive involvement of the CEO is more limited.

These few issues on which the CEO focuses his attention are what John Kotter calls the general manager's agenda. Kotter also found that CEOs tended to get deeply involved only with issues that were on their agenda:

The GMs [general managers] . . . did not waste time and energy intervening where it wasn't really necessary; they gave people who were capable of doing a good job the authority to do just that. They actively involved themselves in execution only when they felt something on their agenda would not be accomplished without their aid.

Management Approach

In addition to choosing an agenda, a CEO must determine the way in which she will attempt to affect the processes of strategy formulation and implementation. Although CEOs approach this task in countless ways, a few of the major dimensions that distinguish various approaches are identifiable.

One of these dimensions is whether the CEO chooses to *manage the outcome* of a strategic decision or to *manage the process* by which the decision is made. In the former case, the CEO knows the desired outcome and becomes directly involved to ensure that the outcome is both adopted and achieved. In the latter case, the CEO is less concerned with the outcome *per se,* and instead aims to ensure a thorough review of all options and to consult all affected parties.

Another difference in the way CEOs affect decision making is the extent to which they *pay attention to administrative constraints*. As noted earlier, these administrative constraints refer to the extent of agreement among the members of top management and the willingness and capability of subordinates to implement a strategy. In some instances, CEOs are reluctant to adopt or implement decisions not fully supported within their organization, while in others, they are willing to confront these obstacles.

The specific management approach that a CEO takes depends on many factors, not the least important of which is his personal management style. However, the approach also depends on whether the issue is on the chief executive's agenda. For issues that are high on the agenda, a CEO is more likely to manage outcomes and to not be dissuaded by administrative constraints.

Also, CEOs tend to adopt different management approaches, depending on the stage of their tenure. For example, early in their careers, CEOs are more concerned with establishing interpersonal relationships and their expectations with key subordinates than with managing major issues. This priority usually means that they manage processes and pay considerable attention to administrative constraints. For example, Kelly has reported that:

> New CEOs do not attack the large strategic issues as the first priority. They look to the structure of relationships and responsibilities—both formal and informal—in the organization as the first area for thought, concern, and change. They seek to change the infrastructure to gain control of the organization, and then they consider strategy.

After key relationships have been established and major responsibilities have been divided and assigned, CEOs do formulate their agendas. At this point, CEOs are likely to manage aggressively those issues that are highest on their agendas.

In the later years of a CEO's tenure, his attention increasingly shifts to the selection of a successor. As this shift occurs, strategic decisions tend to take on less significance than the task of structuring relationships and responsibilities so that key contenders can be equitably evaluated and compared.

Portfolio Planning—A Tool, Not a Solution

The chief executives of America's largest corporations face a bewildering range of problems. Responsible for the actions of thousands of employees, for the safety of numerous products, and for the impact of their factories on the environment, chief executives still face the vital economic problem of allocating resources within their companies. This task, never an easy one, is more difficult today because of the need to comprehend the rapidly changing competitive forces in numerous and diverse businesses, the tendency for all the levels in the management hierarchy to support investment proposals prepared by their divisions, and the insufficiency of most accounting information to clarify senior management's options.

In response to these problems, portfolio planning was developed in the mid and late 1960s. By focusing the attention of senior managers on the competitive performance and strategic plans of their divisions rather than on individual investment requests, portfolio planning offered significant advantages over traditional capital budgeting procedures. Indeed, for many companies, and particularly for those facing financial difficulties, portfolio planning has provided a solution to resource allocation problems.

However, resource allocation is only one of the strategic issues facing senior managers. By its very nature, portfolio planning deals mostly with issues of corporate strategy rather than either business or institutional strategy. Yet, the chief executive needs to ensure that the organization can develop appropriate business strategies and that a basic and enduring set of concepts and beliefs guide decision making within the organization. To the extent that portfolio planning keeps senior managers from addressing either of these tasks, its effects can be most harmful. More than an investment strategy is required to make a great company; basic purposes to guide the investments and involved operating managers to assure that the investments realize their full potential are also necessary.

Whether or not portfolio planning is used, it is the responsibility of the chief executive to take an active role in the establishment and embodiment of broad purposes and objectives for the organization. With a clear sense of purpose, chief executives are then best able to adapt a planning tool, such as the portfolio approach, to serve the objectives of the corporation. Without such a sense of purpose, chief executives too often allow portfolio planning to direct their attention to their role as banker rather than as institutional leader, and portfolio planning can even become a distraction from this more important task.

Portfolio planning, then, is not a solution to the many problems facing senior managers, nor is it a substitute for top management leadership. It is a useful tool that can help solve a number of strategic problems. Like any tool, its inappropriate use can have potentially disastrous repercussions. If used skillfully and with a sense of purpose, it can foster greater objectivity in resource allocation, more realistic and varied expectations for different businesses, more specific communication about objectives, greater attention to external rather than internal performance measures, and better understanding of the company's overall portfolio of businesses.

As useful as portfolio planning can be, however, it is insufficient as a prescribed approach for managing a diversified company. One chief executive, who was an enthusiastic user of the portfolio approach, described its deficiency this way:

> The missing ingredient from all portfolio analysis is any consideration of the quality of the management running your businesses. Ironically, that is probably the single most important determinant of the success of a business and its strategy.

In other words, portfolio planning is not a substitute for creativity, insight, or leadership. Companies are not merely strategic abstractions of assets for investment or disposal. Rather, they are composed of real businesses competing against very real competitors, staffed by fallible human beings who need leadership to give purpose to their efforts.

FOR FURTHER READING

Andrews, Kenneth, *The Concept of Corporate Strategy* (Homewood, IL: Richard D. Irwin, 1980).

Ansoff, Igor, *The New Corporate Strategy* (New York: John Wiley, 1988).

Hamermesh, Richard G., *Making Strategy Work: How Senior Managers Produce Results* (New York: John Wiley, 1986).

Harvard Business Review, *Strategic Management* (New York: John Wiley, 1983).

Porter, Michael, *Competitive Strategy* (New York: Free Press, 1980).

CONCLUSION

12 THE ROLE OF BUSINESS IN A DEMOCRATIC SOCIETY

Russell L. Ackoff

It has become commonplace to point out that we live in an age characterized by an increasing amount and rate of change. What is not so obvious is that not only are the world, societies, and their institutions changing, but our *concepts* of them are also changing. Not only are corporations changing, but our *concepts* of them are as well. Moreover, objective changes in corporations and subjective changes in our concepts of them interact: They affect each other. This interaction is revealed by tracing the evolution of our concept of business and how this conceptual evolution relates to changes in the "real world," in the nature of business and its environment.

Owners of business enterprises and society in general have considered these enterprises as instruments for *creating wealth*, but only recently have they come to be thought of as having the equally important social function of *distributing wealth*. They distribute wealth in many ways, the most important of which is through employment, by paying for work. All other ways of distributing wealth consume it and do not produce it, but employment alone can both produce and distribute wealth.

When corporations fail to create enough employment, wealth is inequitably distributed. This imbalance can seriously threaten the stability of a government and the political-economic system for which it stands. For this reason, governments often react strongly to severe unemployment by nationalizing companies and industries. They do so to preserve employment, even if it consumes more wealth than it creates.

To better understand how our concept of organizations has changed, let us examine how that view evolved—from business as a machine to an organism, to a social system.

BUSINESS AS A MACHINE

When the Industrial Revolution began in the Western world, the prevailing world view was Newtonian. Newton had conceptualized the universe as a clock-like mechanism that operated with a regularity dictated by its internal structure and the causal laws of nature. It was hermetically sealed, a self-contained closed system with no environment. In addition, Newton believed this machine had been created by God to do His work. Men of the time who accepted Newton's beliefs also believed they had been created in the image of God. Therefore, they tried to imitate Him by creating machines to do their work. The result was the Industrial Revolution.

Little wonder, then, that business enterprises were initially regarded as *machines* created by their gods, the owners, to do their work. Such enterprises were attributed with no purpose of their own, but with the function of serving their owners' purpose, to make a profit. Owners, who alone were entitled to that profit, were virtually omnipresent and omnipotent. They were unconstrained by laws and regulation, and could do much as they wanted within the miniworlds they had created. They treated their employees as replaceable machine parts. Since the work of most employees involved very little skill, and unskilled labor was plentiful, workers were easy to replace. The average worker had little education, hence low levels of personal aspiration. Furthermore, in the absence of any form of social security, unemployment often meant economic destitution. Therefore, workers were willing to work under almost any conditions for whatever they could earn. This circumstance enabled those owners who wanted to do so to subject their employees to terrible working conditions.

BUSINESS AS AN ORGANISM

The mechanistic view of the enterprise became less tenable as the nineteenth century came to an end. By the end of World War I, this view had been replaced largely by a biological view of the enterprise as an *organism* rather than a machine. There were a number of reasons for this transformation. Perhaps most important was the fact that many enterprises could not actualize all their growth potential even if all the profit they generated was reinvested in them. Therefore, owners either had to constrain their enterprises' growth while retaining complete control over them or relinquish some control in order to raise the money required to take full advantage of growth opportunities. Money was raised by selling stock, thereby sharing ownership. The survival rate was much higher among those enterprises that elected to maximize growth than among those that sought to maximize concentration of control.

When an enterprise went public, its "god" disappeared and became a diffuse abstract spirit, no longer a powerful concrete presence. Communication between the ordinary employee and this spirit was difficult, but there is a ready model for handling this difficulty. Nineteen hundred years earlier, the God now worshipped by much of the Western world disappeared and become an abstract spirit. An institution and a profession to manage it—the church and the clergy—were created to bridge the gap between ordinary people and God. Management and managers may be viewed as corresponding to the church and the clergy. They control in the name of their "gods," the stockholders, to communicate the will of the owners to the owned, and occasionally, the wishes of the owned to the owners. Managers came to "know" the will of their gods much as the clergymen came to know the will of their God, *by revelation.* However, as James Burnham pointed out in his book, *The Managerial Revolution,* despite managers' assertions to the contrary, enterprises came to be run by, and primarily for, the benefit of their managers, *not* their owners. Providing owners with an adequate return on their investment was like providing oxygen to a human being, necessary for survival of the enterprise, but not the reason for it. The reason for it was the satisfaction and reward that managers extracted from their enterprises' success, and success was defined biologically as *growth.*

Publicly owned businesses were called *corporations.* This word derives from *corpus,* Latin for "body," a biological concept. The chief executive came to be known as the corporation's *head,* also a biological concept. Such concepts infiltrated management literature, for example, the *health* of a corporation, *cancerous* growth or *organizational paralysis,* and the *brain* and *heart* of the firm.

Increasing access to publicly provided education and the compulsion to attend school combined to yield a better educated workforce. This suited the more sophisticated machinery used in the workplace. The cost of replacing skilled workers increased as their skills increased. As a result, they came to be treated more as difficult-to-replace organs of an organism than easily replaceable machine parts. The health and safety of workers were viewed as essential to the well-being (health) of the enterprise.

Under pressure from an increasingly articulate workforce and the unions it created to represent it, governments focused on working conditions and gradually eliminated the sweatshop and abusive employment practices. The enterprise was no longer viewed or treated as a closed autonomous system but as one that was affected by, and affected, its environment. Moreover, evolutionary concepts, then all the rage in the biological sciences, invaded business; competition was sanctified and survival of the fittest was proclaimed as a natural law of the marketplace.

The expansion of social security reduced the threat of economic destitution to the unemployed. Dissatisfied employees could protest against what they considered inhumane work and working conditions. Management (mind) and labor (muscle) came to be viewed as necessarily opposed.

BUSINESS AS A SOCIAL SYSTEM

The biological view of the enterprise began to erode during World War II. A major portion of the workforce was drafted into military service just when demands for production were maximized. Women, children, the infirm, and the elderly replaced the young men and women who went to war. These replacements were motivated more by patriotism than the need or desire for additional income. Managers who wanted productivity from such a workforce could not get it without treating its members as human beings with interests and purposes of their own that had to be served.

After the War, the skills required in the workplace, and therefore the educational level and aspirations of the workforce, continued to increase. More and more was invested in the education and training of employees at all levels. The effort to obtain a return on this investment intensified. This measure required using the maximum capabilities of employees, not the least, as had been the case when workers were treated as replaceable machine parts. At the end of World War II, discharged servicemen and women were not about to accept military-like authoritarianism and discipline in the workplace. (Recall that they became the permissive parents in the two decades that followed.)

Employees increasingly expected their interests to be served by their employing organizations. This reciprocity was reflected when after World War II many groups formed to protest the failure of societies and the institutions they contained to address effectively the interests of their members. For example, in the 1950s and 1960s, the womens' liberation movement, the civil rights movement, the generation gap, and the youthful protests based on it, and the emergence of the third world as a political force. Protests, demonstrations, riots, and alienation became commonplace. For example, according to *Work in America,* a report submitted to the Secretary of Health, Education, and Welfare in 1973:

> significant numbers of American workers are dissatisfied with the quality of their working lives. Dull, repetitive, seemingly meaningless tasks, offering little challenge or autonomy, are causing discontent among workers at all occupational levels. This is not so much because work itself has greatly changed; indeed, one of the main problems is that work has not changed fast enough to keep up with the rapid and widespread changes in worker attitudes, aspirations, and values. A general increase in their educational and economic status has placed many American workers in a position where having an interesting job is now as important as a job that pays well. Pay is still important: It must support an "adequate" standard of living and be perceived as equitable—but high pay alone will not lead to job (or life) satisfaction. (pp. xv–xvi)

Protest groups were formed outside as well as inside organizations. These groups consisted of people who, although not part of the target organization, felt that they were adversely affected by what that organization was doing. Examples were the movements that focused on consumerist and ecological issues. Their external pressure made it apparent that the public increasingly considered corporations to be responsible for their effects on society, its members, and their environment.

These internal and external pressures made corporate managers aware of the need to take into account two new types of purposes and interests: those of the systems that contained the one they managed, and those of the human parts of the system they managed, their employees. In addition, they had to be concerned with the purposes of the systems they managed. It became increasingly difficult for managers to fully conceptualize their organizations as either mechanical or biological systems. They began to think of their enterprises as *social* systems—systems that (1) had a purpose of their own, (2) were made up of parts that had specific purposes, and (3) were parts of systems that also had purposes of their own.

In this post-World War II period, the concept of "system" was emerging in both science and philosophy. It turned out to be focal in the development of contemporary managerial thought as well. To see why and how, we must first grasp the nature of systems.

THE NATURE OF SYSTEMS

A *system* is a set of elements (parts) that satisfies three conditions.

1. *The behavior of each element in the set can affect the behavior of the whole.* For example, in the human body, which is a biological system, each part—heart, lungs, stomach, brain, and so on—can affect the performance of the whole. The *appendix,* which appears to have no effect on the whole, is not a part of the system but is *added on* or *attached to,* as its names implies. If the appendix is ever discovered to have an effect on the body's performance, its name will have to be changed.

2. *The way the behavior of each element actually affects the behavior of the whole depends on the behavior of at least one other element.* Put another way: No element has an independent effect on the whole. For example, the way the heart affects the body depends on what the lungs are doing, and vice versa. The effect of manufacturing on corporate performance depends on what marketing is doing.

3. *No matter how the elements in the set are collected into subsets, these subsets also have the same two properties (1 and 2) as the elements.* Every subset of the elements of a system can affect its performance, but none can have an independent effect on it.

Phrased less technically, *a system is a whole that cannot be divided into parts which have independent effects on it.* For this reason, the performance of a system is not equal to the sum of the performances of its parts taken separately, but is a function of their interactions. This relationship has a significant implication to management: *When each part of a system taken separately is made to perform as well as possible, the system as a whole will not perform as well as possible.* In other words, the best parts do not the best system make. For example, suppose we determine which make and model of automobile has the best carburetor, which the best transmission, and so on for each part required to make an automobile. Suppose further that we remove these parts from their respective automobiles and try to assemble them into what we hope will be the best possible automobile, because it will be made up of the best parts available. We will not even get an automobile, because *the parts don't fit,* and if they did, they would not work well together.

Effective corporate management must be *synthetic* or *holistic,* that is, focus on the *interactions* of all the parts that make up the whole, rather than analytic, focusing on actions of the parts taken separately.

Nevertheless, most managers manage analytically because this is the way they were taught.

The essential properties of any system are properties of the whole that none of its parts have. For example, the essential property of an automobile is its ability to transport people from one place to another over land. No part of an automobile can accomplish this goal, not the engine, the wheels, the seats, or any other part taken separately. Therefore, *when a system is dissected, it loses its essential properties.* A disassembled automobile cannot take us anywhere.

Furthermore, *when a part of a system is separated from the system of which it is a part, that part loses its essential properties.* For example, when the engine is separated from the automobile, it cannot move itself, let alone anything else. A steering wheel removed from a car steers nothing.

When business executives manage analytically, seeing that each part of their businesses, taken separately, is optimally managed, they disassemble their business systems and do not deal with the essential properties of either the wholes or their parts.

Furthermore, the problematic situations with which managers must deal are themselves systems, systems having threats and opportunities. They are usually treated analytically—by taking them apart, identifying their components, prioritizing them, and addressing them separately in order of importance. Such treatment of the problematic situations misses their essential properties and those of their component threats and opportunities. Threats and opportunities, like the parts of an organization, ought to be dealt with interdependently, interactively, not separately.

THE SOCIETAL VIEW OF BUSINESS AS A SOCIAL SYSTEM

Up to this point, the focus has been on some of the principal effects of systems thinking on management's view of an enterprise and its method of managing it. Now, consider the systemic view of an enterprise from the perspective of its containing system, society. For reasons that will become apparent, this view has come to be called the *stakeholder view of the firm*.

Imagine a visitor from another planet who, although he does not know any of Earth's languages, has been sent to find out what a corporation is. He cannot talk or read about corporations; all he can do is observe what they do. In all likelihood his description would reflect the stakeholder view of the firm as shown schematically in Figure 12.1.

In this view, the firm is seen as a set of transactions, for example, an exchange of money for work with *employees*, an exchange of money for

FIGURE 12.1. A stakeholder view of the firm.

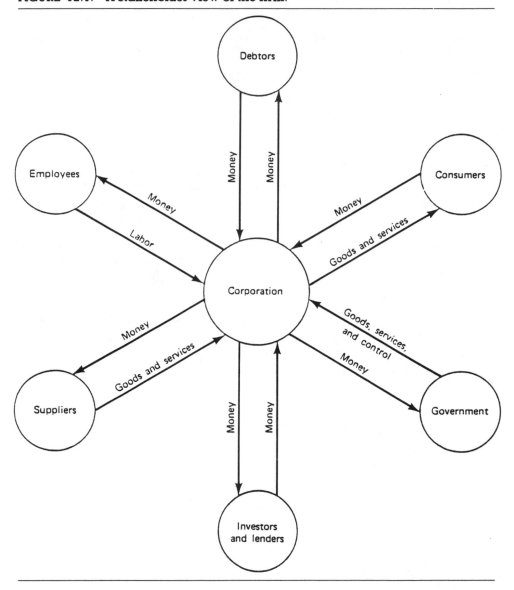

goods and services with *suppliers,* an exchange of goods or services for money with *customers,* an exchange for money received at an earlier time for money paid at a later time with *investors* and *lenders,* an exchange for money paid at an earlier time for money received at a later time with *debtors* (e.g., banks, and other companies in which the corporation has invested), and an exchange of money for the use of services and facilities from a source which exercises some control over the corporation, *government.*

The particular stakeholders identified are not the essential part of the stakeholder view of the firm; different observers will recognize different stakeholders for even the same firm. What is essential is the view of the firm as engaged in a set of transactions with various stakeholders, however they are identified.

One stakeholder group, larger than all the others combined, is almost always ignored: *future generations.* They may be the ones most seriously affected by what is done today. How can their interests be taken into account when we do not know what their interests will be?

We do know one thing about future generations: They will be interested in *making their own decisions,* not in having had us make their decisions for them. Future generations should be allowed to make their own decisions. This requires *keeping their options open.* Managers should not make decisions that reduce the range of choices available in the future, but they do so continually. In many of their decisions, they do not take into account even their own future interests.

In addition to its transactions with stakeholders, the corporation either adds value to the goods and services supplied to customers or makes them more accessible to customers without changing them (as is the case with a retail establishment). The flows in and out of a corporation are flows of resources. The flows constitute either *consumption* of resources by the corporation or *distribution* of the means to acquire products or services for consumption, or the products and services themselves.

The difference between the amount of resources consumed by a corporation and the amount of consumption it makes possible, is the amount of wealth *it creates.* Then, in society's systemic view of a corporation, its principal social functions are the *production and distribution of wealth.* Identification of the production of wealth as a corporate function is nothing new, but the focus on its distribution function is relatively new.

The principal means by which most businesses distribute wealth is compensation for work: employment. Furthermore, employment is the only way of distributing wealth which can also create it; all other means of distributing wealth consume it, rather than produce it. When private enterprises, taken collectively, fail to provide enough employment in a society to distribute wealth equitably and, therefore, to enable it to maintain political stability, governments frequently intervene and take over some enterprises, nationalizing them. Its purpose in doing so is to maintain or create employment rather than wealth. It is not surprising, then, that government-owned enterprises are seldom as productive as those that are privately owned and operated.

In an increasingly international and competitive environment, businesses must continually increase their productivity if they are to remain competitive. Increased productivity means less employment unless it is accompanied by increased demand. Therefore, the only way of assuring stable, much less increasing, employment in a competitive environment is through growth. Thus, growth becomes a means, not an end as it was in the organismic view of the firm. To what is it a means? *Development.*

THE ROLE OF SOCIAL SYSTEMS: DEVELOPMENT

Growth and development are not the same. In fact, neither is required for the other. A rubbish heap grows but does not develop, and a person can develop without physically getting larger. Growth is an increase in size or number. *Development is an increase in ability and desire to satisfy one's own needs and legitimate desires, and those of others.* A legitimate desire is one for which the satisfaction does not reduce or retard the development of another.

Purposeless objects and systems can grow but cannot develop; only purposeful individuals and systems develop.

Development is an increase in capacity and potential, not an increase in attainment. It is more a matter of learning than of earning. It has less to do with how much one has than with how much one can do with whatever one has. This connotation is why Robinson Crusoe and the Swiss Family Robinson are better models of development than John D. Rockefeller or J. Pierpont Morgan; and why *development implies more about quality of life than standard of living.* If we give wealth (resources) to an undeveloped people, they are not thereby developed. On the other hand, if we educate them, their development is facilitated even without our adding to their wealth.

Because development consists of both a desire and an ability, it cannot be given to or imposed on one person or organization by another. A government cannot develop the governed, and a corporation cannot develop its employees, even its managers. The only kind of development possible is self-development. However, one person or organization *can* encourage and facilitate the development of others.

Standards of living may increase at the cost of quality of life, and quality of life may increase without an increase in standard of living—in fact, with a decrease in it. This is not to say that wealth is irrelevant to development or quality of life; it is very relevant. How much people can actually improve their quality of life and that of others depends not only on their capabilities, but also on the resources available to them. One can build a better house with good tools and materials than with poor ones. On the other hand, a well-developed person can build a better house than a poorly developed person who has the same or even better and more tools and materials available. The quality of life that people can actually attain is the joint product of their development, and the quality and quantity of resources available to them.

Limited resources may limit growth but not development. The more developed an individual is, the less he or she is limited by available resources. Thus, the goal of successful organizations is omnicompetence. Unlike *omnipotence,* which connotes unlimited *power over, omnicompetence* connotes *power to.* Omnipotence implies control of others; omnicompetence implies self-control. When we discuss the effectiveness of self-directed workforces, omnicompetence is our objective. Development is therefore the key to productivity.

From Efficiency to Effectiveness: Adding Value

Science, technology, and economics focus on *efficiency,* not *effectiveness.* Both efficiency and effectiveness are determined relative to one or more ends (goals, objectives, or ideals). The *value* of these objectives is not relevant to the determination of efficiency, but is essential for the determination of effectiveness. The effectiveness of behavior is a function of both its efficiency for one or more outcomes and the values of those outcomes. The difference between efficiency and effectiveness is reflected in the difference between *growth* and *development.* Growth does not necessarily imply an increase in value; development does. A company can grow without increasing in value, but it cannot develop without increasing its value.

Hierarchical organizations where decisions are made without consulting those affected by the decisions provide limited developmental opportunities for employees. In the absence of developmental opportunities, the satisfaction one can derive from work is also limited.

In today's environment, we see more and more organizations that are driven by competitive pressures for increased productivity strive to create self-directed workforces within the confines of a traditional hierarchical organization. This pursuit rarely works. Managers must begin to rethink organizational design issues with an eye to creating democratic systems to support development and not just growth. The circular organization that is discussed next is designed to accomplish this purpose.

DEMOCRACY IN BUSINESS: THE CIRCULAR ORGANIZATION

From the preceding discussions, we can conclude that there is a need for participation of employees in making decisions that affect them directly. Providing opportunities for such participation may well be the most profound type of cultural change currently taking place in business. Perhaps more than any other, this change reflects the shift from thinking of businesses as organisms to thinking of them as social systems.

Participation implies democracy. Although most economically advanced countries are committed to democracy in the public sector, most of their organizations—corporations in particular, but even government agencies—are organized autocratically, not democratically. Explanations for this inconsistency usually center on the theory that hierarchy is required in organizations in which labor must be divided and managed efficiently, and hierarchy is believed to require centralized control, hence, autocracy. Decentralization does not reduce the authority concentrated at the top of an organization, however, it does increase the amount of authority located at lower levels. Keep in mind that this lower level authority can be overridden by the higher level authority.

The essence of democracy is the absence of an ultimate authority — what we call circularity of power. Democracy requires that anyone who has authority over others be subject to their collective authority. This requirement is met by a structure called a *circular organization*.

The Design of a Circular Organization

The design of a circular organization, as discussed here, should be treated as a theme around which each organization should write its own variation, one adapted to its unique characteristics and conditions.

The central idea in a circular organization is that every person in a position of authority—each manager and supervisor—is provided with a *management board*. We will first consider the composition of these boards, then their responsibilities, and finally, how they operate. (See Figure 12.2.)

Composition of Management Boards

The suggested *minimal* requirements for the composition of these boards at every level of the organization except at the top are:

1. The manager whose board it is
2. His/her immediate superior
3. His/her immediate subordinates

FIGURE 12.2. A circular organization.

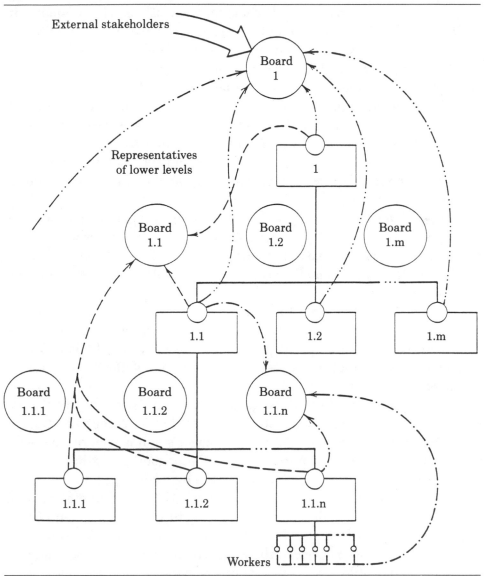

Therefore, in the board of any manager who has more than two subordinates, the subordinates constitute a majority.

Any board has the right to add members drawn either from the organization or outside. For example, it has been quite common for boards of functionally defined units—like marketing or finance—to invite other functional managers to participate on their boards as either voting or nonvoting members. Boards of units that have internal consumers of their products or services have frequently invited some of their customers to participate. In some cases, even external customers have been invited to be part of boards. In widely dispersed organizations—for example, in multinational corporations where different units are in different countries—representatives of various external stakeholder groups have been invited to participate. These have included representatives of relevant communities and consumer or environmental groups.

Chief executive officers (CEOs) of corporations already have boards on which only the shareholders and management are generally represented. The circular organization suggests adding to most of them all executives who report directly to the CEO, and representatives of other major stakeholder groups, for example, customers, suppliers, creditors, and the public at large.

Where an executive is supported by a staff, a separate staff board is usually established. If an executive has a chief of staff, then it will be that chief's board with the executive participating. If the executive acts as chief of staff, his/her immediate superior is generally not a member of the staff board.

In a unionized organization, union officials at each level of the organization are usually invited to participate on boards at the same level—shop stewards at lower levels, department representatives at higher levels, and union executives at the highest levels. (The role of unions in a circular organization is discussed next.)

Participation in boards is generally compulsory for managers/supervisors, but voluntary for others. Something is wrong with boards that fail to attract a majority of their manager's nonmanagerial subordinates. In such cases, the performance of the managers whose boards have this characteristic should be evaluated by their superiors.

Managers other than those at the top and bottom of an organization will interact directly with *five* levels of management through their participation on boards: two higher levels and their own level in their superiors' boards, and two lower levels in their subordinates' boards. Such interaction makes it possible to achieve a degree of coordination and integration of management that conventional organizations seldom attain.

Responsibilities of Management Boards

Boards normally have the following responsibilities:

1. *Planning* for the unit whose board it is
2. *Making policy* for the unit whose board it is
3. *Coordinating* the plans and policies of the next lower level

4. *Integrating* its own plans and policies and those of its immediately lower level with those made at higher levels
5. *Making decisions* that affect the quality of working life of those on the board

In addition, most, but not all, boards are given the power of:

6. *Evaluating the performance* of the manager whose board it is, and *removing* him from that position.

Now consider each of these functions in turn. Each board has responsibility for planning and making policy for the unit whose board it is. *A policy is a decision rule,* not a decision. For example, "Hire only college graduates for managerial positions" is a policy; hiring such a person is a decision. Boards do not make decisions other than those directly affecting the quality of working life of its members; except for these, managers make the decisions, not boards. In general, boards are analogous to the legislative branch of government, and managers to the executive branch. Note that Congress can make decisions regarding its own quality of worklife, but only policies with regard to the quality of life of others.

Managers may, of course, consult their boards on decisions to be made, but responsibility for decisions other than those directly involving the quality of the working life of the board's members belong with the manager alone, not his or her board. The use of boards in a consulting role is common, as is their use to facilitate communication up, down, and across. Because they are used as communication channels, the need for separate staff and other types of meetings is frequently reduced. The number of meetings a manger must attend is usually reduced in a circular organization.

Each board is responsible for coordinating and integrating the plans and policies made at the level below it. Since the managers at this level participate in the board and generally constitute a majority, coordination is self-coordination with participation of two higher levels of management. Integration involves preservation of hierarchy: No board can make a plan or policy incompatible with a higher level board's output. However, it can appeal for revision of such output since it contains members who participate in two higher level boards. Moreover, because its members have an extended vertical view of the organization, boards are not likely to make plans or policies that are either harmful to lower levels of the organization or incompatible with those made at higher levels.

No board is permitted to implement a plan or a policy that directly affects another unit of the organization at the same or a higher level without either agreement of that unit or, where such agreement cannot be obtained, approval of the lowest level board at which the affected units converge going up the hierarchy.

Quality-of-worklife decisions are those that directly affect the satisfaction employees derive from their work, and their perception of its meaningfulness. Responsibility for the amount of work done and its quality remains with the manager. However, when employees are given power over their quality of worklife, significant improvements in the quantity and quality of their work are usually attained, often with more dramatic improvements than have been obtained by programs explicitly directed at increasing productivity and quality.

The most controversial responsibility that boards can assume is for evaluating and improving the performance of the manager whose board it is. Where boards have this responsibility, managers cannot retain their positions without their board's approval, hence approval by a majority of their subordinates. Because this function is so controversial, only about half the corporations that have implemented the circular organization have initially given this responsibility to the boards. Some have added it after running without it for a year or more, and some have never adopted it. Without this provision, complete democracy in the workplace cannot be attained.

In few cases have boards removed their managers. Removal has not been necessary because the boards enable subordinates to obtain most of what they want from their manager through constructive criticism. Once each year, the subordinates on a board meet without their superiors to discuss what their manager could do to enable them to do their jobs more effectively. The subordinates are precluded from telling their boss what he or she should *not* do; they must confine their opinions to what might be done that would enhance their own, not their manager's, performance. When they have organized their suggestions, they meet with and present their proposals to their manager. In some cases, these evaluative groups use a facilitator who makes the presentation for them.

"Receiving managers" are expected to respond to the suggestions in one of three ways—accept, reject, or agree to consider further. In most cases, managers accept about 75 percent of the suggestions. These ideas usually involve aspects the manager had not thought of, the virtue of which he or she sees immediately. For example, one such group suggested that their manager use his full vacation allowance so they would not feel guilty if they used theirs. The manager was surprised to learn that his failure to use his vacation allowance was preventing his subordinates from using theirs. He accepted the suggestion and implemented it. Another suggestion involved more flexible budgets, particularly with respect to the purchase of minor equipment and external services. Again, the manager agreed, and appropriate changes in budget control were made.

Second, the manager can reject a suggestion but is required to explain fully. In most cases, refusal involves constraints imposed on the manager form above, of which subordinates are unaware. The subordinates do not have to agree with, but should understand, the reasons for rejection of their suggestion. However, in few cases did such explanations not produce the understanding required for gracious acceptance of the rejection.

Finally, the manager can ask for more time to consider a suggestion and commit to providing a response by a specific time.

These constructively oriented evaluations have generally brought manager and subordinates closer and have bound them into a more collaborative relationship. Such sessions emphasize the fundamental change in the concept of management that is implicit in the circular organization: *The principal responsibility of managers is to create an environment and conditions under which their subordinates can do their jobs as effectively as their capabilities allow.* It is not to supervise them. That is, the principal responsibility of a manger is to manage *over* and *up*, not down, to manage the *interactions* of their units with the rest of the organization and its environment, not to manage the actions of their subordinates. If subordinates require supervision beyond an initial break-in period, they should be replaced by persons who do not require it.

Managers who do not have the support of their subordinates have difficulty implementing their decisions. Such managers do not perform as well as they could. On the other hand, subordinates who approve of their manager try to make him or her look as good as they can.

Note that in a circular organization, a group of subordinates cannot fire their manager; they can only remove him or her from that position. A manager can fire a subordinate. This potential means that managers cannot hold their positions without the approval of both their managers and their subordinates.

Modes of Operation of Management Boards

Each board should prepare its own operating procedures, but most boards operate in similar ways. Most boards, for example, operate by *consensus* rather than majority rule. The advantage of consensus over split decisions is apparent. What is not apparent is how consensus can be obtained where there is a significant initial divergence of opinions. Before considering how to obtain consensus in such situations, consider the nature of consensus, in particular, how it differs from complete agreement.

In situations where a change from current practice is contemplated, different proposals are not unusual, nor is the lack of agreement as to which is best. In such cases, boards have been offered the following choice: They can either retain their current plan, policy, practice, or design—whichever is relevant—or permit one of the proposed changes to be selected at random. In most cases, they unanimously support a random choice. In other words, there is complete agreement that any of the alternatives is better than what is currently being done. In such cases, there is no agreement as to what is *best*, but complete agreement as to what is *better*. This procedure is consensus. Consensus, in this sense, can be reached relatively easily in at least 75 percent of the situations requiring a decision.

In the first "fall back" procedure, *a test of the alternatives* being considered is designed, one that *all* board members accept as adequate and fair. For example, in one company, agreement could not be reached as to whether plant maintenance in a multiplant operation should be placed under the plant manager or a corporate manager of engineering. A multiplant test was designed that all board members considered to be good and fair. The test was conducted and the findings were implemented across the system.

In most cases, such differences of opinion are based on different beliefs concerning a question of fact. The fact involved in the maintenance case involved the relative efficiency and responsiveness of maintenance personnel under two different organizational arrangements.

In some (but few) cases, either time is lacking that is required to design and conduct a test because a choice must be made quickly, or agreement on a test cannot be reached. Each board must decide how it wants to handle such cases. Most boards adopt a procedure much like the one described next.

When it is apparent that consensus cannot be reached through discussion, and a test is not practical, the chairperson goes around the room asking each person to state his or her position succinctly. Then, the chairperson states what decision he or she will make if consensus is not reached. Next, he or she goes around the room again for a restatement of positions. If consensus is reached among all but the chairperson, even if it is on a choice that differs from that the chairperson, that choice holds. If consensus is not reached, the chairperson's decision holds. Note that with this procedure, the lack of consensus on a decision other than the chairperson's constitutes consensus on the chairperson's decision.

Most boards are chaired by the manager whose board it is. In a few cases, boards use a rotating chairmanship. In no case that I know has a board selected as chairperson the superior of the manager whose board it is.

Each board either designates one of its members as recording secretary or engages an assistant or secretary to the manager whose board it is for this purpose. Minutes of each meeting are usually prepared and distributed shortly after that meeting. In most cases, every meeting begins with a review of tasks previously assigned. The "secretary" of the board is responsible for maintaining this list and distributing it to all board members.

Agendas for coming meetings are prepared by the secretary using input from any of the board members.

After the initial "break-in" period, most boards schedule monthly meetings which usually last about three hours. Additional meetings are called when required either by the manager whose board it is or by any of its other members.

Common Questions about Management Boards

Since managers may have as many as 10 or more boards to attend, when can they work? When one executive who had installed boards throughout his company was asked this question, his reply was essentially as follows: "The 10 boards in which I take part meet once per month for three to four hours each. Say four hours. That makes 40 hours per month. If I worked only 40 hours per week—like most managers, I work closer to sixty—this would be only 25 percent of my time. According to a number of studies of how managers spend their time, most managers spend no more than 20 percent of their time managing. Therefore, the question that should be asked is: What do I spend the other 55 percent of my time doing?"

He continued: "There is a better answer. In my boards, I plan, make policy, coordinate the plans and policies at the level reporting to me, integrate these with those made at my level, and evaluate and guide the performance of my subordinates two levels down. What should I be doing that is more important than this? Moreover," he concluded, "boards eliminate a number of other meetings, including staff meetings. I spend less time in meetings now that I did before boards were introduced."

Does it take any special skills to run board meetings? It does. For this reason most organizations that initiate boards provide managers at all levels with training in group skills. Such training usually takes only two or three days. In many cases, these sessions are made available to union and nonmanagerial personnel as well.

Does it help to have a skilled facilitator at board meetings? It often does, at least in the first few meetings. A facilitator can help establish the rules of procedure and keep the meetings flowing smoothly. Once the manager for the board gains confidence in her ability to run the meetings, she can take over. It often helps for the facilitator to remain as an observer for the first few meetings run by the manager. This transition time enables the facilitator to make constructive suggestions to the manager in charge.

At Metropolitan Life, a special training program was developed and conducted to provide the large number of facilitators that the company required. Most of those trained had previous experience facilitating various types of quality-improvement groups.

Have any of the organizations that started boards discontinued them? To the best of my knowledge, only two have, and both for the same reason. Shortly after their initiation, and before they were operating throughout the organization, the chief executive officers were replaced, and their replacements discontinued the boards along with many other innovations initiated by their predecessors.

What is the principal obstruction to the successful implementation of boards? Lack of commitment by middle managers. These managers seldom "buy in" unless they have been exposed to a presentation about boards and have had an opportunity to discuss them with someone experienced in their use. For this reason, appropriate education of managers, particularly those in middle ranks, is very important. Since there may be a large number of managers, and they may be geographically dispersed, video tapes of relevant presentations and discussions have often been used to inform and motivate managers. Availability of an experienced person to answer questions also helps.

What is usually done with managers who do not fully cooperate despite indoctrination? As previously noted, participation in boards is usually required of managers. Evaluation of their participation in boards is a significant part of their performance evaluation. Where boards have been introduced with unambiguous commitment of the senior executive, rarely do managers, once indoctrinated, fail to participate fully. In a few cases, uncooperative managers have been moved to nonmanagerial positions.

How do circular organizations affect the readiness, willingness, and ability of enterprises to change? Organizational resistance to change is a familiar phenomenon. Implementation of decisions involving significant organizational changes are often diluted or subverted during their establishment, because those who actually effect implementation do not "buy into" the decision. No matter how much authority decision makers in large organizations have, they seldom have the ability to oversee each step in the implementation of their decisions. Therefore, the larger the organization, the more difficult to obtain implementation as intended. *Power-over* and *power-to* differ significantly. For example, the last Shah of Iran, one of the most powerful rulers on Earth, in the sense of *power-over*, often complained of his inability to have his decisions implemented as he intended. The more democratic a culture and the more educated its members, the more negatively correlated are *power-over* and *power-to*. The circular organization does not reduce *power-over*, but it does increase *power-under* and, therefore, *power-to*.

What is done with boards where such groups as quality circles already exist? In some cases they run in parallel, but in most, the quality circles are incorporated into boards, thereby reducing the number of meetings required.

Where in an organization is the best place to introduce boards? Wherever you are. Boards have been initiated at every level of an organization and have subsequently spread throughout. In some organizations, Anheuser-Busch, for example, boards were initially established at the top. After the executives involved had experience with it, each started a board of his own. Then, they moved down layer by layer. This diffusion took more than a year to reach the lower levels.

At Kodak, the first boards were established in a unit where the manager was at the fifth level of the organization. Boards then spread up, down, and across. At Alcoa's Tennessee Operations, boards were simultaneously established at the top and bottom with the participation of the union at both levels. Boards subsequently moved up and down the organization until they met at the middle. In some smaller organizations, all managers have been indoctrinated at the same time, hence boards were initiated all over the organization at the same time.

In some cases, managers below the top of an organization initiated boards without the participation of their immediate superiors, who usually begged off, claiming to be too busy to be involved. However, as the boards manifested their value, most of these superiors began to participate.

Participating senior executives are not always able to attend all the board meetings of their immediate subordinates because of other demands on their time. In such cases, they keep informed through minutes of meetings, and they are notified when their attendance at an upcoming meeting is critical.

Is it easier or more difficult to introduce boards in a unionized company? Both. Where unions have collaborated, they make it easier to involve the workforce. Where they are opposed, it is difficult but possible to introduce boards. In a few such cases, unions have eventually come to support the idea and participate fully.

Are there certain types of organizational structures on which a circular organization cannot be superimposed, for example, a matrix organization? No. The concept has been used by organizations with just about every type of structure. This should not be surprising; democracy is associated with a wide variety of government structures.

Does the introduction of a circular organization involve a significant change in a corporation's culture? It does. In a circular organization, managers are no longer either commanders or supervisors, but are required to be leaders, facilitators, and educators. These are roles to which many managers are not accustomed. It takes time to make the conversions, but the rewards can be immense. For example, at the time boards were introduced in Alcoa's Tennessee Operations, in the early 1980s, these operations were scheduled to be shut down because of their low productivity and poor quality of product. In less than two years, their productivity and product quality improved so much that corporate headquarters reversed its decision and initiated a modernization program for the operations. At the end of 1987, the most advanced aluminum sheet rolling mill in the world opened at these operations.

Examples of Circular Organizations

During the 1980s, A&P closed all its supermarkets in the Delaware Valley, the metropolitan area of Philadelphia. The reason was lack of profitability. Subsequently, in a joint effort with Locals 27, 56, 1357, 1358, and 1360 of the United Food and Commercial Workers to which the A&P employees had belonged prior to losing their jobs, a new chain of supermarkets was designed. They used boards at all levels. The new chain, called *Super Fresh*, was initiated mostly in the old facilities. It is now the fastest growing chain in the area and is profitable. This chain is being extended, replacing traditional A&P stores.

In December 1985, the locals published a pamphlet called "Quality of Work Life" in which they describe the composition and content of boards at Super Fresh:

> There will be planning boards at all levels, including the corporation as a whole, support service units, marketing units, and stores.

In general, each board will consist of (1) the manger of the unit whose board it is, (2) his/her immediate superior (3) his/her immediate subordinates, and (4) representatives of the associates on higher level boards . . . .

The planning boards will be engaged in continuous interactive planning and research to redesign the system as needed.

The planning boards will be policy making bodies and not merely advisory committees, however, executive decisions will be left to the respective managers.

Organizational strategies, policies, and procedure will be formulated by the planning boards.

The planning boards will explicitly specify the objectives and consequences of the plans and policies designed by the board. These objectives and their attainment will be assessed on a regular basis by the management support system.

Decisions will be made by consensus of the board members. If consensus cannot be reached as to a course of action, the board will resolve the differences by research and experimentation done by special project committees.

Those holding management positions will be appointed by their immediate higher level manager, however, they will have to maintain the confidence of their respective planning boards.

The corporate planning board will make available through Human Resources, information and sources on internal and external training on the operation of the food retailing business and its environment. This information will be available to all associates.

At the corporate level the board will meet on a regular basis and will have the following members:

- The president of Super Fresh
- One store director and one associate selected on a rotating basis by each regional planning board
- The support service and the marketing unit directors
- The presidents of the unions and his/her representative
- External stakeholders, if the issue warrants it

When the number of stores increases, the corporate board will be divided into regional boards, meeting regionally. No more than fifteen stores will be included in a regional board. The regional boards will have the following members:

- The vice president of retail operations (representing the president) and his/her assistants (who may function as zone managers)
- The director of each store (maximum 15)

- An associate from each of the stores to be chosen on a rotating basis by each store planning board
- The support services and the marketing unit directors
- The representatives of the union's management

At the store level, the board will meet on a regular basis and will have the following members:

> The store director and his/her assistants
>
> The manager of each department and an associate to be chosen on a rotating basis by the department planning board

- Grocery
- Meat
- Produce
- Deli/Bakery
- Seafood

The front-end manager and an associate to be chosen on a rotating basis by the unit's planning board

- The union steward and committee person
- The representatives of the two unions
- A representative of the president of Super Fresh (zone manager)

At the department level, the board will meet on a regular basis and will include the department manager and all the associates of that department.

Planning board meetings at all levels are open for attendance by associates on a voluntary basis upon request.

Armco's Latin American Division (ALAD) was also reorganized around the use of boards and has experienced significant improvements in performance as well as morale. The same has been true of a number of other organizations including Metropolitan Life, Central Life Assurance, Clark Equipment, several new units of Alcoa, a variety of departments and divisions of Kodak, and Anheuser-Busch.

Democracy and efficiency are not inimicable.

SUMMARY

In this chapter, we have reviewed how the concept of a business enterprise evolved from one of a machine to one of a social system. So conceptualized, a corporation has responsibilities both to the society of which it is a part, and to its parts, its members. Its principal social function is the production and distribution of wealth. Its principal means of distributing wealth is through compensation for work—employment. The principal objective of a corporation conceptualized as a social system is its own development: To develop is to increase one's desire and ability to satisfy one's own needs and legitimate desires, and those of others. Business enterprises are also seen as having an obligation to encourage and facilitate the development of their members. Continuous development involves continuous progress in science and technology (the pursuit of truth), economics (the pursuit of plenty), ethics/morality (the pursuit of the good), and aesthetics (the pursuit of beauty). Science, technology, and economics focus on the *efficiency* with which ends are pursued. Ethics/morality and aesthetics focus on the *effectiveness* of such pursuits. Effectiveness takes into account the value of the needs pursued as well as the efficiency of their pursuit.

We have seen how the pursuit of corporate ethical/moral and aesthetic objectives requires providing employees at all levels with opportunities to participate in making decisions that affect them directly, and in exercising collective control over those who control them separately. Such opportunities for participation and exercise of control are best provided by a circular organization. In this type of organization, every employee has an opportunity to participate in his/her boss's board. These boards plan, make policy, coordinate horizontally and integrate vertically plans and policies, improve quality of work life, evaluate the performance of the manager whose board it is, and, with their manager's immediate superior, control occupancy of the position held by that manager. This type of organization makes it possible to convert corporate autocracies into industrial democracies without sacrificing any of the values of hierarchy.

Moreover, the boards of a circular organization facilitate the management of interactions. They make it possible to convert management from directing the actions of subordinates, to the creation of conditions under which subordinates can perform as effectively as possible. This feat is accomplished by managers coordinating the interactions of their subordinates, and the interactions of the units they manage, with other organizational units at the same and higher levels of the organization. Systemic management is the management of interactions. It is based on knowing that the performance of a system is not the sum of the performances of its parts but is the product of their interactions with each other and their environments.

Systemic management replaces supervision, direction, and command with leadership. Systemically managed corporations contribute to the development of all their stakeholders and to the society of which they are part. Therefore, they are increasingly in a position to lead society in its quest for an improved quality of life for all.

FOR FURTHER READING

Ackoff, Russell L., *Creating the Corporate Future* (New York: John Wiley, 1981).

——— and William B. Deane, "The Revitalization of ALCOA's Tennessee Operations," *National Productivity Review*, Summer 1984, 239–245.

Allport, G. W., and H. S. Odbert, "Trait Names: a Psycholexical Study," *Psychological Monographs*, No. 211, 1936.

Beer, Stafford, *The Heart of Enterprise* (New York: John Wiley, 1981).

Burnham, James, *The Managerial Revolution* (London: John Day, 1941).

Singer, Edgar A., Jr., *On the Contented Life* (New York: Henry Holt, 1923).

———, *In Search of a Way of Life* (New York: Columbia University Press, 1948).

Work in America: Report of a Special Task Force to the Secretary of Health, Education, and Welfare (Cambridge, MA:The MIT Press, 1973).

Chapter Notes

*Chapter 1: How to Think Like a Manager: The Art of
Managing for the Long Run*

Page

12   "Devices such as . . ."
      Porter, Michael, *Competitive Strategy*, (New York: Free Press, 1984).

Chapter 2: Managing People: The R Factor

24   "It is hard to develop . . ."
      Homans, George, *Social Behavior: Its Elementary Forms*, (New York:
      Harcourt, Brace & Jovanovich, 1961).
      A classic book on relationships, utilizing research on primitive soci-
      eties and companies. See also Homans' book, *The Human Group*, (New
      York: Harcourt, Brace, 1950) for wonderful material on small groups.

25   "In a classic study . . ."
      Roethlisberger, F. J., and W. Dickson, *Management and the Worker*,
      (Cambridge, MA: Harvard University Press, 1939).
      A classic study that helped focus attention on the power of relation-
      ships and sentiments at work.

26   "For example, when the oldest member . . ."
      Cohen, Allan R., S. Fink, S. Gadon, and R. Willits, *Effective Behavior in
      Organizations*, 4th ed., (Homewood, IL: Irwin, 1988).
      Many of the ideas in this chapter are developed in this textbook,
      used for introductory organizational behavior courses.

27   "As we head into the 1990s, . . ."
      Bradford, David L., and Allan R. Cohen, *Managing for Excellence: The
      Guide to Developing High Performance in Contemporary Organizations*
      (New York: John Wiley, 1984).

This presents a new model of leadership, emphasizing the need to go beyond heroic assumptions to create tangible vision, a shared responsibility team and continuous development of subordinates.

"The reader, like the sales manager . . ."
Healthco, Inc., (Cambridge, MA: Goodmeasure, Inc. 1984).

A simulation based on consulting work with a company in the health care industry.

Chapter 7: Marketing Management: Becoming a Market-Driven Company

180   "A thoughtful summary of . . ."
Adler, Lee, *Plotting Marketing Strategy*, (New York: Simon and Schuster, 1967).

187   "The Finnish economist . . ."
Mickwitz, Gosta, *Marketing and Competition*, (Helsingfors, Finland: Centraltryckeriet, 1959).

189   "They think strategic planning . . ."
Waterman, Robert, *The Renewal Factor*, (Toronto: Bantam, 1987).

217   "Figure 7.6, redrawn from . . ."
Henry, Porter, "Manage Your Sales Force as a System," *Harvard Business Review*, March-April, 1975.

Chapter 8: Human Resource Management: Competitive Advantage Through People

229   "In *The Transformational header* . . ."
Ticky, Noel, and Mary Anne Devanna, *The Transformational Leader*, (New York: John Wiley, 1986).

Chapter 9: The Strategic Use of Information Technology

238   "The popular press . . ."
BusinessWeek, 1985.

"Information power . . ."
BusinessWeek, October 14, 1986.

"Information business . . ."
BusinessWeek, August 25, 1986.

243   McKinsey & Co. published . . .
McKinsey & Co., *Unlocking the Computer's Profit Potential*. (New York: McKinsey & Co., 1986).

"William King proposed . . ."
King, William R., "Strategic Planning for Management Information Systems," *Management Information Systems Quarterly*, 2(1): 27–37, 1978.

For instance, Pyburn's study . . ."
Venkatraman, N., and T. S. Raghunathan, "Strategic Management of

Information Systems Function: Changing Roles and Planning Linkages."
Working Paper #1743-86, Sloan School of Management, MIT, 1986.

243   ". . . translating business strategy to IS strategy . . ."
International Business Machines Corporation, *Business System Planning*
(New York: IBM Corp, 1981).

244   "Accordingly, functions are . . ."
Fombrun, Charles, Noel Tichy, and Mary Anne Devanna, *Strategic
Human Resource Management* (New York: John Wiley, 1983).

"Similarly, several authors . . ."
Ives, Blake S., and G. P. Learmonth, "The Information System as a Competitive Weapon." *Communications of the ACM*, 27(12): 1193–1201
(1984); McFarlan, F. Warren, "Information Technology Changes the
Way You Compete." *Harvard Business Review*, 62(3): 98–103 (1984);
Wiseman, Charles, *Strategy and Computers: Information Systems as Competitive Weapons.* (Homewood, IL:; Dow Jones-Irwin, 1985).

"As William King noted in an . . ."
King, William R., "Information as a Strategic Resource," *Management
Information Systems Quarterly,* 7(3): iii–iv, 1983.

". . . production and manufacturing function . . ."
Wheelwright, Steven, "Manufacturing Strategy: Defining the Missing
Link," *Strategic Management Journal,* 5(1), 1986.

248   ". . . developed a framework . . ."
Barrett, Stephanie, and Benn Konsynski, "Inter-organization Information Sharing Systems," *MIS Quarterly*, Special Issue, 1982.

252   "McKesson Corp" (Table 9.2)
Clemons, Eric K., and Michael Row (1988), "McKesson Drug Company:
A Case Study of Economist—A Strategic Information System," *Journal
of Management Information Systems*, 5(1), 1988.

255   "Peter Keen, writing in 1981 . . ."
Keen, Peter G. W., "Communications in the 21st Century: Telecommunications and Business Policy," *Organizational Dynamics*, Autumn, 1981.

256   "Over the three decades . . ."
Benjamin, Robert I., John F. Rockart, Michael S. Scott Morton, and John
Wyman, "Information Technology: A Strategic Opportunity," *Sloan
Management Review*, 25(3), 3–10, 1984.

261   "Another perspective builds on . . ."
Porter, Michael E., *Competitive Strategy*, (New York: Free Press, 1980).

"For a fuller description . . ."
Porter, Michael E., *Competitive Advantage.*, (New York: Free Press,
1985).

"Warren McFarlan uses . . ."
McFarlan, F. Warren, and James L. McKenney, "The Information
Archipelago-Governing the New World," *Harvard Business Review*,
61(4): 91–99, 1983.

Chapter 10: Operations Management: Productivity and
Quality Performance

289   "Product structure improvement . . ."
Ritzman, C. P., B. E. King, and L. J. Krajewski, "Manufacturing
Performance—Pulling the Right Levers," *Harvard Business Review,*
March-April, 1984.

"This study also pointed . . ."
Hayes, Robert H., and Kim B. Clark, "Why Some Factories Are More
Productive Than Others," *Harvard Business Review,* September-October
1986.

Chapter 12: The Role of Business in a Democratic Society

337   "Burnham pointed out . . ."
Burnham, James, *The Managerial Revolution*, (London: John Day,
1941).

"Brain and heart of the firm . . ."
Beer, Stafford, *The Heart of Enterprise*, (Chichester: John Wiley,
1979); and Beer, Stafford, *Brain of the Firm,* 2nd ed., (Chichester: John
Wiley, 1981).

339   ". . . significant numbers of American workers . . ."
*Work in America: Report of a Special Task Force to the Secretary of
Health, Education, and Welfare* (Cambridge: The MIT Press, 1973).

350   "Increasing productivity and quality . . ."
Ackoff, Russell L., & William B. Deane, "The Revitalization of AL-
COA'S Tennessee Operations," *National Productivity Review,* Summer
1984, 239–245.

About the Authors

Russell L. Ackoff is Chairman of the Board and CEO of INTERACT: The Institute for Interactive Management, and Anheuser-Busch Professor Emeritus of Management Science at the Wharton School of the University of Pennsylvania. He served as president of the Operations Research Society of America and the Society for General Systems Research. His consulting has involved more than 300 corporations and 50 government agencies in the United States and abroad and is reflected in his 18 published books and more than 150 published articles. His books include: *Creating the Corporate Future*; *Management in Small Doses*; and *The Art of Problem Solving* all published by John Wiley & Sons.

Allan R. Cohen is the Walter H. Carpenter Professor of Management at Babson College. He is the author (with David Bradford) of the best selling *Managing For Excellence: The Guide To Developing High Performance in Contemporary Organizations* (John Wiley & Sons, 1984). *Managing For Excellence* has also been developed into a three-day training program through Wilson Learning Corporation. Dr. Cohen is also the co-author of a textbook, *Effective Behavior in Organizations* (Irwin, 4th ed., 1988). His book with Herman Gadon, *Alternative Work Schedules: Integrating Individual and Organizational Needs* (Addison Wesley, 1978) received the best book award by the American Society for Personnel Administration. His fourth book also co-authored with David Bradford is *Influence Without Authority* (John Wiley & Sons, 1990). Dr. Cohen holds an A.B. degree from Amherst College and MBA and DBA degrees from Harvard Business School.

Robert T. Davis is the Sebastian S. Kresge Professor of Marketing in the Graduate School of Business at Stanford University. He is the author of *Performance and Development of Field Sales Managers*, *The Changing Pattern of Europe's Grocery Trade*, and *Marketing in Emerging Companies*, and co-author of *Cases in Sales Management*, *Reading in Sales Management*, and *Marketing Management Casebook*.

After returning from a World War II assignment in Kunming, China with the OSS, he started his teaching career at the St. Lawrence University in New York. From there he taught at Dartmouth's Amos Tuck School of Business Administration and the Graduate School of Business Administration, Harvard University. During 1957–1958, he was a member of the first teaching faculty at IMEDE, Management Development Institute, Lausanne, Switzerland.

Dr. Davis directed the Stanford Sloan Program from 1970 to 1974. Twice he has been Director of the Stanford Executive Program. On leave from Stanford (1964 to 1966), he served as Vice President-Marketing for Varian Associates. Between 1983 and 1985, he was on a second leave from Stanford to join NIKE, Inc. as Vice President of Sales and Marketing. In 1968, Dr. Davis received the Salgo-Noren Distinguished Teaching Award.

Currently Dr. Davis is a member of the Board of Directors of Anthem Electronics, Armor All Products Corporation, and NIKE, Inc. In addition, he is a consultant to many other major corporations and a lecturer in management development programs at Stanford University and for various companies and associations.

Mary Anne Devanna is Associate Dean and Director of Executive Education at the Graduate School of Business, Columbia University. She is the co-author (with Noel Tichy) of *The Transformational Leader* (John Wiley & Sons, 1986) and co-editor (with Charles Fombrun and Noel Tichy) of *Strategic Human Resource Management* (John Wiley & Sons, 1984). Her articles have appeared in *The Journal of Applied Behavioral Science, Organizational Dynamics* and the *Sloan Management Review.* Dr. Devanna is editor of the Columbia Journal of World Business and she has done extensive research and writing on the role of women managers in American corporations. Dr. Devanna is a senior consultant for "Workout," a major change program at General Electric. Earlier in her career, Dr. Devanna was director of advertising at Longines. Her doctorate is from Columbia University.

Brian Forst teaches at George Washington University and is an experienced managerial consultant, with 20 years of experience in analyzing and improving the performance of businesses and public organizations. He is author of *Power in Numbers: How to Manage for Profit* (John Wiley & Sons, 1987) and numerous articles on performance measurement. He received his Bachelor of Science degree in statistics from the University of California, Los Angeles; his MBA degree from UCLA's Graduate School of Management; studied managerial economics in the Ph.D. program at Cornell University; was a fellow at the Massachusetts Institute of Technology. He has also lectured at the UCLA business school.

Richard G. Hamermesh is a founder and managing partner of The Center for Executive Development, (CED), the Cambridge, Massachusetts, executive education consulting firm. Prior to founding CED, he was a member of the faculty of the Harvard Business School from 1976 to 1988. A specialist in business policy, Dr. Hamermesh has taught extensively in Harvard's MBA and Executive Education Programs.

Dr. Hamermesh has provided management consulting services in the areas of strategic planning, organization design, and strategic change. He has also been an active consultant to the executive development programs of numerous corporations. Dr. Hamermesh was president of the Newton (Massachusetts) Schools Foundation and served on the Editorial Board of the *Harvard Business Review*. He is currently on the Board of Directors of four corporations including Synthes, Ltd. and Applied Extrusion Technologies.

Dr. Hamermesh's primary research has focused on the implementation of strategic planning systems. His book on this subject, *Making Strategy Work*, was published by John Wiley & Sons in 1986. Professor Hamermesh has also written five articles that have appeared in the *Harvard Business Review*, over twenty-five case studies, and one article for the *Academy of Management Review*. He is also a co-author of *Business Policy: Text and Cases* and the editor of *Strategic Management*.

Dr. Hamermesh received his **AB** degree from the University of California (1969), and his **MBA** (1971) and **DBA** (1976) from Harvard University.

Frank Lichtenberg is an Associate Professor at the Columbia University Graduate School of Business and a Research Associate at the National Bureau of Economic Research. He received a BA from the University of Chicago and an MA and PhD from the University of Pennsylvania. He has been a consultant to a number of private and government organizations and his work has appeared in numerous scholarly and popular publications.

John Leslie Livingstone is a Certified Public Accountant, and earned MBA and Ph.D. degrees at Stanford University. He is the Chairman of the Division of Accounting and Law at Babson College. Previously, he was a senior partner in the "Big 8" accounting firm of Coopers & Lybrand, and a principal in THE MAC GROUP (an international management consulting firm with offices in Boston, Chicago, San Francisco, London, Paris, Rome, Madrid, Buenos Aires, and Hong Kong). He has also held endowed professorial chairs at Ohio State University, Georgia Institute of Technology, and University of Southern California.

Leonard A. Schlesinger is an Associate Professor of Business Administration at the Harvard Business School, where he teaches the capstone MBA course on *Management Policy and Practice* and the MBA elective course on *Service Management* and currently conducts research on the Management of Service Organizations. He holds an AB from Brown University, an MBA in Corporate and Labor Relations from Columbia University, and a doctorate in Organizational Behavior from Harvard University.

From 1985 to 1988, Dr. Schlesinger served as Executive Vice President and Chief Operating Officer of Au Bon Pain Co., Inc., a rapidly growing chain of French bakery cafés which has pioneered the adoption of numerous human resource and service innovations which have fueled its profitability and growth.

Dr. Schlesinger has consulted on major organizational change efforts throughout North America and Mexico, with General Electric, Cummins Engine, Owens-Corning Fiberglass, General Motors, Citicorp and others; and has participated in the design and development of executive education activities for several Fortune 500 companies. The author of numerous articles and seven books (most recently *Chronicles of Corporate Change: Lessons for American Managers from AT&T and Its Offspring*, Lexington Books, 1986, and *The Management Game*, Viking Press, 1987). He serves on the editorial boards of the *Academy of Management Executive* and *Human Resource Management.*

Linda G. Sprague is Professor of Operations Management at the Whittemore School of Business and Economics, University of New Hampshire, and was Director of their Executive Programs from 1981–1986. In 1987, she was a Visiting Professor at the Amos Tuck School of Business, Dartmouth College. In 1984–1985 she was Professor of Operations Management at IMEDE, the international management development institute in Lausanne, Switzerland. In 1980, Dr. Sprague was a Founding Professor at the National Center for Industrial Science and Technology Management Development at Dalian, China.

Professor Sprague received her doctorate from the Harvard Business School; she also has a MBA from Boston University and an SB in Industrial Management from MIT Her consulting and research interests include capacity management and operations scheduling from manufacturing and service enterprises, production information systems and productivity improvement programs. She has published articles on material requirements planning, international manufacturing, inventory management, and production practices in China.

Mrs. Sprague is a past President of the Decision Sciences Institute and a vice president of the Operations Management Association. Dr. Sprague is a Certified Practitioner in Inventory Management and a member of the Production Activity Control Committee of the Certification Council of the American Production and Inventory Control Society. She is a Fellow of the Decision Sciences Institute.

Professor Sprague is Chairman of the Board of Directors of Protek, Inc., the U.S. subsidiary of Protek AG. The company, based in Switzerland, is dedicated to the design, development and distribution of precision joint replacement systems. Mrs. Sprague is the Management Advisor to SICOT, the Société Internationale de Chirurgie Orthopaedique et de traumatologie. She is a Trustee of the Advest Advantage Investment Trust.

N. Venkatraman, Assistant Professor of Management, Sloan School of Management, MIT, conducts research and teaches in the area of the formulation and implementation of business strategies, with particular emphasis on the emerging impact of information technology on the scope of business strategies. He has published extensively in several scholarly and managerial journals such as *Management Science, Strategic Management Journal*, and the *Sloan Management Review.* At MIT, he teaches an elective course on Strategic Management and Information Technology. Professor Venkatraman holds a PhD degree in business administration from the University of Pittsburgh (his dissertation was awarded the 1986 AT Kearney Award for Outstanding Research in General Management), an MBA degree from the Indian Institute of Management, and an undergraduate degree in mechanical engineering from the Indian Institute of Technology.

James E. Walter, before his untimely death in 1989, was Professor of Finance at the Wharton School of the University of Pennsylvania. He was the author of many books including *Financial Strategy: A Guide for the Corporate Manager* (John Wiley & Sons, 1989) and *Dividend Policy and Enterprise Valuation* (Wadsworth Publishing Company, 1967). Dr. Walter's many articles appeared in such publications as *Financial Management Journal, Journal of Finance*, and *Accounting Review*. He was also an Associate Editor of *The Journal of Finance*. Dr. Walter held a PhD from the University of California (Berkeley).

Akbar Zaheer is a doctoral candidate at the Sloan School of Management, MIT specializing in Strategic Management with an emphasis on information technology. His research focuses on how firms could leverage the capabilities of computers and communication technologies for obtaining competitive advantage. He holds an MBA degree from the Indian Institute of Management and has held managerial positions for over ten years.

Index